Elizabeth Cabot Cary, Louis Agassiz

A Journey in Brazil

Elizabeth Cabot Cary, Louis Agassiz

A Journey in Brazil

ISBN/EAN: 9783743312500

Manufactured in Europe, USA, Canada, Australia, Japa

Cover: Foto ©ninafisch / pixelio.de

Manufactured and distributed by brebook publishing software (www.brebook.com)

Elizabeth Cabot Cary, Louis Agassiz

A Journey in Brazil

A JOURNEY IN BRAZIL.

BY

PROFESSOR AND MRS. LOUIS AGASSIZ.

> And whenever the way seemed long,
> Or his heart began to fail,
> She would sing a more wonderful song,
> Or tell a more marvellous tale.
> LONGFELLOW.

BOSTON:
TICKNOR AND FIELDS.
1868.

Entered according to Act of Congress, in the year 1867, by
TICKNOR AND FIELDS,
in the Clerk's Office of the District Court of the District of Massachusetts.

FIFTH EDITION.

UNIVERSITY PRESS: WELCH, BIGELOW, & CO.,
CAMBRIDGE.

TO

MR. NATHANIEL THAYER,

THE FRIEND WHO MADE IT POSSIBLE TO GIVE THIS JOURNEY
THE CHARACTER OF A SCIENTIFIC EXPEDITION,

The Present Volume

IS GRATEFULLY INSCRIBED.

PREFACE.

In the winter of 1865 it became necessary for me, on account of some disturbance of my health, to seek a change of scene and climate, with rest from work. Europe was proposed; but though there is much enjoyment for a naturalist in contact with the active scientific life of the Old World, there is little intellectual rest. Toward Brazil I was drawn by a lifelong desire. After the death of Spix, when a student of twenty years of age, I had been employed by Martius to describe the fishes they had brought back with them from their celebrated Brazilian journey. From that time, the wish to study this fauna in the regions where it belongs had been an ever-recurring thought with me; a scheme deferred for want of opportunity, but never quite forgotten. The fact that the Emperor of Brazil was deeply interested in all scientific undertakings, and had expressed a warm sympathy with my efforts to establish a great zoölogical museum in this country, aiding me even by sending collections made expressly under his order for the purpose, was an additional incentive. I knew that the head of the government would give me every facility for my investigations. Nevertheless, tempting as was the prospect of a visit to Brazil, as a mere vacation it had little charm for me. Single-handed, I could make slight use of the opportunities I should have; and though the excursion might be a pleasant one for myself, it would have no important result for science. I could not forget that, had I only the necessary means, I might make collections on this journey which, whenever our building could be so enlarged as to give room for their exhibition, would place the Museum in Cambridge on a level with the first institutions of the kind. But for this a working force would be needed, and I saw no possibility of providing for such an undertaking. While I was brooding over these thoughts I chanced to meet Mr. Nathaniel Thayer, whom I have ever found a generous friend to science. The idea of appealing to him for a scheme of this magnitude had not, however, occurred to me; but he introduced the subject, and, after expressing his interest in my proposed journey, added, "You wish, of course, to give it a scientific character; take six assistants with you, and I will be responsible for all their expenses, personal and scientific." It was so simply said, and seemed to me so great a boon, that at first I hardly believed I had heard him rightly. In the end, I had cause to see in how large and liberal a sense he proffered his support to the expedition, which, as is usual in such cases, proved longer and more costly than was at first anticipated. Not only did he provide most liberally for assistants, but, until the last specimen was stored in the Museum, he continued to advance whatever sums were needed, always desiring me to inform him should any additional expenses occur on closing up the affairs of the expedition. It seems to me that the good arising from the knowledge of such facts justifies me in speaking here of these generous deeds, accomplished so unostentatiously that they might otherwise pass unnoticed.

All obstacles thus removed from my path, I made my preparations for departure as rapidly as possible. The assistants I selected to accompany me were Mr. James Burkhardt as artist, Mr. John G. Anthony as conchologist, Mr. Frederick C. Hartt and Mr. Orestes St. John as geologists, Mr. John A. Allen as ornithologist, and Mr. George Seeva as preparator. Beside these, my party was enlarged by several volunteers, to whom I was indebted for assistance as untiring and efficient as if they had been engaged for the purpose. These were Mr. Newton Dexter, Mr. William James, Mr. Edward Copeland, Mr. Thomas Ward, Mr. Walter Hunnewell, and Mr. S. V. R. Thayer. I should not omit to mention my brother-in-law, Mr. Thomas G. Cary, as one of my aids; for, though not nominally connected with the expedition, he made collections for me at Monte Video, Buenos Ayres, and other places. I was also joined by my friends Dr. and Mrs. Cotting. Dr. Cotting, like myself, was in need of a vacation, and it was his intention to remain with us for as long a time as he could spare from his professional practice. But the climate proved unfavorable to his health, and after passing a couple of months in Rio, and sharing with us all our excursions in that neighborhood, he sailed with Mrs. Cotting for Europe, where they passed the summer. His presence with us during that time was most fortunate, for it so happened that the only serious cases of illness we had among us occurred before he left, and his medical advice and care were of great service. I lost the assistance of Mr. Anthony, and Mr. Allen also, early in the expedition; their health, always delicate, obliging them to leave for home. With these exceptions, our working force remained intact, and I am happy to state that every member of the party returned in safety to the United States.*

No sooner was the Brazilian Expedition known to the public, than I received a letter from Mr. Allen McLane, President of the Pacific Mail Steamship Company, offering to me and my whole party the hospitality of their magnificent ship the Colorado, then just sailing from New York for the Pacific coast. She was going almost empty of passengers, being bound by the way of Cape Horn for San Francisco. We left New York on board this beautiful vessel, on the 1st of April, 1865. The record of our delightful voyage to Rio de Janeiro will

* There is but one sad record I have to make connected with this journey. My friend and companion of many years, Mr. Burkhardt, died about ten months after his return, of a disease which, though not contracted in Brazil, since it was of some years' standing, was no doubt aggravated by the hot climate. His great desire to accompany me led him, against my advice, to undertake a journey which, in his case, was a dangerous one. He suffered very much during our stay on the Amazons, but I could not persuade him to leave his work; and in the following pages it will be seen that his industry was unflagging.

be found in the narrative; but I wish here publicly to acknowledge my obligation to Mr. McLane for his generosity to the expedition. Besides the sympathy accorded me by private individuals, I have to thank the Hon. Gideon Welles, Secretary of the Navy, for a general order, received on the eve of my departure, desiring the officers of the United States Navy, wherever I should fall in with them, to afford me such assistance in my scientific researches as would not interfere with the regular service; and I learned at Rio that Mr. Seward had warmly recommended the expedition to General Webb, at that time United States Minister to Brazil. Finally, I would express my thanks also to Messrs. Garrison and Allen for the free passage offered to myself and my companions for our return, on board the line of steamers established between New York and Rio de Janeiro during our stay in Brazil.

It will be seen hereafter what facilities were granted me throughout this journey by the Brazilians themselves, and that the undertaking, so warmly speeded on its way, was welcomed no less cordially in the country to which it was bound.

One word as to the manner in which this volume has grown into its present shape, for it has been rather the natural growth of circumstances than the result of any preconceived design. Partly for the entertainment of her friends, partly with the idea that I might make some use of it in knitting together the scientific reports of my journey by a thread of narrative, Mrs. Agassiz began this diary. I soon fell into the habit of giving her daily the more general results of my scientific observations, knowing that she would allow nothing to be lost which was worth preserving. In consequence of this mode of working, our separate contributions have become so closely interwoven that we should hardly know how to disconnect them, and our common journal is therefore published, with the exception of a few unimportant changes, almost as it was originally written. In this volume I have attempted only to give such an account of my scientific work and its results as would explain to the public what were the aims of the expedition, and how far they have been accomplished. It is my hope to complete a work, already begun, on the Natural History, and especially on the Fishes of Brazil, in which will be recorded not only my investigations during the journey and those of my assistants in their independent excursions, but also the researches now regularly carried on in connection with the immense Brazilian collections stored in the Museum at Cambridge. This must, however, be the slow labor of many years, and can only be published very gradually. In the mean time I hope that this forerunner of the more special reports may serve to show that our year in Brazil, full as it was of enjoyment for all the party, was also rich in permanent results for science.

L. AGASSIZ.

TABLE OF CONTENTS.

CHAPTER I.

VOYAGE FROM NEW YORK TO RIO DE JANEIRO.

PAGE

First Sunday at Sea. — Gulf Stream. — Gulf-Weed. — Lectures proposed. — First Lecture: On the Gulf Stream in the Gulf Stream. — Aquarium established on board. — Second Lecture — Rough Sea. — Peculiar Tint of Water. — Third Lecture: Laying out Work of Expedition in Brazil; Distribution of Fishes in Brazilian Rivers; its Bearing on Origin of Species; Collecting of Eggs. — Tropical Sunset. — Fourth Lecture: Plan of Geological Investigations with special reference to Glacial Phenomena in South America. — Flying-Fish. — Fifth Lecture: Glacial Phenomena, continued. — Second Sunday at Sea. — Rough Water. — Sixth Lecture: Embryological Investigations as a Guide to sound Classification. — Seventh Lecture. — Moonlight Nights. — Trade-Winds. — Eighth Lecture: Importance of Precision in Localizing Specimens. — Southern Cross. — Ninth Lecture: Fresh-water Fishes of Brazil. — Easter Sunday. — First Sight of South American Shore. — Olinda. — Pernambuco. — Catamarans. — Tenth Lecture: Methods of Collecting. — Eleventh Lecture: Classification of Fishes as illustrated by Embryology. — Preparations for Arrival. — Twelfth Lecture: Practical Lesson in Embryology. — Closing Lecture: Transmutation Theory; Intellectual and Political Independence. — Resolutions and Speeches. — Singular Red Patches on the Surface of the Sea. . . 1–45

CHAPTER II.

RIO DE JANEIRO AND ITS ENVIRONS. — JUIZ DE FORA.

Arrival. — Aspect of Harbor and City. — Custom-House. — First Glimpse of Brazilian Life. — Negro Dance. — Effect of Emancipation in United States upon Slavery in Brazil. — First Aspect of Rio de Janeiro on Land. — Picturesque Street Groups. — Eclipse of the Sun. — At Home in Rio. — Larangeiras. — Passeio Publico. — Excursion on the Dom Pedro Railroad. — Visit of the Emperor to the Colorado. — Cordiality of the Government to the Expedition. — Laboratory. — Botanical Garden. — Alley of Palms. — Excursion to the Corcovado. — Juiz de Fora Road. — Petropolis. — Tropical Vegetation. — Ride from Petropolis to Juiz de Fora. — Visit to Senhor Lage. — Excursion to the Forest of the Empress. — Visit to Mr. Halfeld. — Return to Rio. — News of the Great Northern Victories, and of the President's Assassination. 46–79

CHAPTER III.

LIFE IN RIO CONTINUED. — FAZENDA LIFE.

Botafogo. — Insane Hospital. — Tijuca. — Erratic Drift. — Vegetation. — Birthday Dinner. — Arrangements for Parties to the Interior. — Public Lectures in Rio. — Procession of St. George. — Leave Rio on Excursion to the Fortaleza de Santa Anna. — Localities for Erratic Drift between Rio and Petropolis. — Departure from Juiz de Fora. — Arrival at the Fazenda. Ride in the Forest. — Eve of San Joaõ. — Cupim Nests. — Excursion to the Upper Fazenda. — Grand Hunt. — Picnic. — Coffee Plantation. — Return to Rio. — Mimic Snow-Fields. — Coffee Insect spinning its Nest. — Visit to the Fazenda of Commendador Breves. — Botanizing Excursion to Tijuca. — Preparations for leaving Rio. — Major Coutinho. — Collegio Dom Pedro Segundo. 80–125

CHAPTER IV.

VOYAGE UP THE COAST TO PARÁ.

On board the Cruzeiro do Sul. — Members of the Party. — Arrival at Bahia. — Day in the Country. — Return to the Steamer. — Conversation about Slavery in Brazil. — Negro Marriages. — Maceio. — Pernambuco. — Parahyba do Norte. — Ramble on Shore. — Ceará. — Difficult Landing. — Brazilian Baths. — Maranham. — Assai Palm. — Visit to Orphan Asylum. — Detained in Port. — Variety of Medusæ. — Arrival of American Gunboat. — More Medusæ. — Dinner on Shore. — Cordiality toward the Expedition. — Arrival at Pará. — Kind Reception. — Environs of Pará. — Luxuriant Growth. — Markets. — Indian Boats. — Agreeable Climate. — Excursion in the Harbor. — Curious Mushroom. — Success in collecting, with the assistance of our Host and other Friends. — Fishes of the Forests. — Public Expressions of Sympathy for the Expedition. — Generosity of the Amazonian Steamship Company. — Geological Character of the Shore from Rio to Pará. — Erratic Drift. — Letter to the Emperor. . 126–151

CHAPTER V.

FROM PARÁ TO MANAOS.

First Sunday on the Amazons. — Geographical Question. — Convenient Arrangements of Steamer. — Vast Dimensions of the River. — Aspect of Shores. — Village of Breves. — Letter about Collections. — Vegetation. — Variety of Palms. — Settlement of Tajapuru. — Enormous Size of Leaves of the Miriti Palm. — Walk on Shore. — Indian Houses. — Courtesy of Indians. — Row in the Forest. — Town of Gurupá. — River Xingu. — Color of Water. — Town of Porto do Moz. — Flat-topped Hills of Almeyrim. — Beautiful Sunset. — Monte Alégre. — Character of Scenery and Soil. — Santarem. — Send off Party on the River Tapajoz. — Continue up the Amazons. — Pastoral Scenes on the Banks. — Town of Villa Bella. — Canoe Journey at Night. — Esperança's Cottage. — Picturesque Scene at Night. — Success in Collecting. — Indian Life. — Making Farinha. — Dance in the Evening. — Howling Monkeys. — Religious Impressions of Indians. —

TABLE OF CONTENTS.

Cottage of Maia. — His Interest in Educating his Children. — Return to Steamer. — Scientific Results of the Excursion. 152–184

CHAPTER VI.

LIFE AT MANAOS. — VOYAGE FROM MANAOS TO TABATINGA.

Arrival at Manaos. — Meeting of the Solimoens with the Rio Negro. — Domesticated at Manaos. — Return of Party from the Tapajoz. — Generosity of Government. — Walks. — Water-Carriers. — Indian School. — Leave Manaos. — Life on board the Steamer. — Barreira das Cudajas. — Coari. — Wooding. — Appearance of Banks. — Geological Constitution. — Forest. — Sumaumeira-Tree. — Arrow-Grass. — Red Drift Cliffs. — Sand-Beaches. — Indian Huts. — Turtle-Hunting. — Drying Fish. — Teffé. — Doubts about the Journey. — Unexpected Adviser. — Fonte Bôa. — Geological Character of Banks. — Lakes. — Flocks of Water Birds. — Tonantins. — Picturesque Grouping of Indians. — San Paolo. — Land-Slides. — Character of Scenery. — Scanty Population. — Animal Life. — Tabatinga. — Aspect of the Settlement. — Mosquitoes. — Leave one of the Party to make Collections. — On our Way down the River. — Party to the Rivers Içá and Hyutahy. — Aground in the Amazons. — Arrival at Teffé. . . 185–211

CHAPTER VII.

LIFE IN TEFFÉ.

Aspect of Teffé. — Situation. — Description of Houses. — Fishing Excursion. — Astonishing Variety of Fishes. — Acará. — Scarcity of Laborers. Our Indoors Man. — Bruno. — Alexandrina. — Pleasant Walks. — Mandioca-shed in the Forest. — Indian Encampment on the Beach. — Excursion to Fishing Lodge on the Solimoens. — Amazonian Beaches. — Breeding-Places of Turtles. Fishes, etc. — Adroitness of Indians in finding them. — Description of a "Sitio." — Indian Clay-Eaters — Cuieira-Tree — Fish Hunt. — Forest Lake. — Water Birds — Success in Collecting. — Evening Scene in Sitio. — Alexandrina as Scientific Aid. — Fish Anecdote. — Relations between Fishes as shown by their Embryology. — Note upon the Marine Character of the Amazonian Faunæ. — Acará. — News from the Parties in the Interior. — Return of Party from the Içá. — Preparations for Departure. — Note on General Result of Scientific Work in Teffé. — Waiting for the Steamer. — Sketch of Alexandrina. — Mucuim. — Thunder-Storm. — Repiquete. — Geological Observations. . . 212–250

CHAPTER VIII.

RETURN TO MANAOS. — AMAZONIAN PICNIC.

Arrival at Manaos. — New Quarters. — The Ibicuhy. — News from Home. Visit to the Cascade. — Banheiras in the Forest. — Excursion to Lake Hyanuary. — Character and Prospects of the Amazonian Valley. — Reception at the Lake. — Description of Sitio. — Successful Fishing. — Indian Visitors. — Indian Ball. — Character of the Dancing. — Disturbed Night. —

Canoe Excursion. — Scenery. — Another Sitio. — Morals and Manners. — Talk with the Indian Women. — Life in the Forest. — Life in the Towns. Dinner-Party. — Toasts. — Evening Row on the Lake. — Night Scene. — Smoking among the Senhoras. — Return to Manaos. . . . 251 – 275

CHAPTER IX.

MANAOS AND ITS NEIGHBORHOOD.

Photographic Establishment. — Indian Portraits. — Excursion to the Great Cascade. — Its Geological Formation. — Bathing Pool. — Parasitic Plants. — Return by the Igarapé. — Public Ball. — Severity in Recruiting, and its Effects. — Collecting Parties. — Scenes of Indian Life. — Fête Champêtre at the Casa dos Educandos. — Prison at Manaos. — Prison Discipline on the Amazons. — Extracts from Presidential Reports on this Subject. — Prison at Teffé. — General Character of Brazilian Institutions. — Emperor's Birthday. — Illuminations and Public Festivities. — Return of Collecting Parties. — Remarks on the Races. — Leave Manaos for Mauhes. 276 – 300

CHAPTER X.

EXCURSION TO MAUHES AND ITS NEIGHBORHOOD.

Leave Manaos. — On board the Ibicuhy. — Navigation of the River Ramos. — Aspect of the Banks. — Arrival at Mauhes. — Situation of Mauhes. — Tupinambaranas. — Character of Population. — Appearance of the Villages of Mauhes. — Bolivian Indians. — Guaraná. — Excursion to Mucaja-Tuba. — Mundurucu Indians. — Aspect of Village. — Church. — Distribution of Presents. — Generosity of the Indians. — Their Indifference. — Visit to another Settlement. — Return to Mauhes. — Arrival of Mundurucus in the Village. — Description of Tattooing. — Collection. — Boto. — Indian Superstitions. — Palm Collection. — Walk in the Forest. — Leave Mauhes. — Mundurucu Indian and his Wife. — Their Manners and Appearance. — Indian Tradition. — Distinctions of Caste. . . . 301 – 321

CHAPTER XI.

RETURN TO MANAOS. — EXCURSION ON THE RIO NEGRO.

Christmas Eve at Manaos. — Ceremonies of the Indians. — Churches on the Amazons. — Leave Manaos for the Rio Negro. — Curious River Formation. — Aspect of the River. — Its Vegetation. — Scanty Population. — Village of Taua Péussu. — Padre of the Village. — Palms. — Village of Pedreira. — Indian Camp. — Making Palm-thatch. — Sickness and Want at Pedreira. — Row in the Forest. — Tropical Shower. — Geology of Pedreira. — Indian Recruits. — Collection of Palms. — Extracts from Mr. Agassiz's Notes on Vegetation. — Return to Manaos. — Desolation of the Rio Negro. — Its future Prospects. — Humboldt's Anticipations. — Wild Flowers. — Distribution of Fishes in the Amazonian Waters. — How far due to Migration. — Hydrographic System. — Alternation between the Rise and Fall of the Southern and Northern Tributaries. . . . . 322 – 350

CHAPTER XII.

DOWN THE RIVER TO PARÁ. — EXCURSIONS ON THE COAST.

Farewell Visit to the Great Cascade at Manaos. — Change in its Aspect. — Arrival at Villa Bella. — Return to the House of the Fisherman Main. — Excursion to the Lago Maximo. — Quantity of Game and Waterfowl. — Victoria regia. — Leave Villa Bella. — Arrive at Obydos. — Its Situation and Geology. — Santarem. — Visit to the Church. — Anecdote of Martius. — A Row overland. — Monte Alégre. — Picturesque Scenery. — Banheiras. — Excursion into the Country. — Leave Monte Alégre. — Anecdote of Indians. — Almeyrim. — New Geological Facts. — Porto do Moz. — Collections. — Gurupá. — Tajapurú. — Arrive at Pará. — Religious Procession. — Excursion to Marajo. — Sourés. — Jesuit Missions. — Geology of Marajo. — Buried Forest. — Vigia. — Igurapé. — Vegetation and Animal Life. — Geology. — Return to Pará. — Photographing Plants. — Notes on the Vegetation of the Amazons. — Prevalence of Leprosy. . . . 351-396

CHAPTER XIII.

PHYSICAL HISTORY OF THE AMAZONS.

Drift about Rio de Janeiro. — Decomposition of underlying Rock. — Different Aspect of Glacial Phenomena in different Continents. — Fertility of the Drift. — Geological Observations of Messrs. Hartt and St. John. — Correspondence of Deposits along the Coast with those of Rio and those of the Valley of the Amazons. — Primitive Formation of the Valley. — First known Chapter of its History. — Cretaceous Fossil Fishes. — Former Extent of the South-American Coast. — Cretaceous Fossils from the Rio Purus. — Comparison between North and South America. — Geological Formations along the Banks of the Amazons. — Fossil Leaves. — Clays and Sandstones. — Hills of Almeyrim. — Monte Alégre. — Situation and Scenery. — Serra of Ereré. — Comparison with Swiss Scenery. — Boulders of Ereré. — Ancient Thickness of Amazonian Deposits. — Difference between Drift of the Amazons and that of Rio. — Inferences drawn from the present Condition of the Deposits. — Immense Extent of Sandstone Formation. — Nature and Origin of these Deposits. — Referred to the Ice-Period. — Absence of Glacial Marks. — Glacial Evidence of another Kind. — Changes in the Outline of the South-American Coast. — Souré. — Igurapé Grande. — Vigia. — Bay of Braganza. — Anticipation. . 397-441

CHAPTER XIV.

CEARÁ.

Leaving Pará. — Farewell to the Amazons. — Ease of Travelling on the Amazons. — Rough Passage. — Arrival at Ceará. — Difficulty of Landing. — Aspect of the Town. — Rainy Season. — Consequent Sickliness. — Our Purpose in stopping at Ceará. — Report of Dr. Felice about Moraines. — Preparations for Journey into the Interior. — Difficulties and Delays in getting off. — On the Way. — Night at Arancho. — Bad Roads. — Carnauba Palm. — Arrival at Monguba. — Kind Reception by Senhor Franklin de Lima. — Geology of the Region. — Evening Games and Amusements. — Pacatuba. — Traces of ancient Glaciers. — Serra of Aratanha. — Climb up the Serra. — Hospitality of Senhor da Costa. — Picturesque Views. — The Sertaõ. — Drought and Rains. —Epidemics. — Return to Monguba. — Detained by extraordinary Rains. — Return to Ceará. — Overflowed Roads. — Difficulty of fording. — Arrival at Ceará. — Liberality of the President of the Province toward the Expedition. 442-465

CHAPTER XV.

PUBLIC INSTITUTIONS OF RIO. — ORGAN MOUNTAINS.

Voyage from Ceará. — Freshets at Pernambuco. — Arrival at Rio. — Collections. — Vegetation about Rio as compared with that on the Amazons. — Misericordia Hospital. — Charities connected with it. — Almsgiving in Brazil. — Insane Asylum. — Military School. — The Mint. — Academy of Fine Arts. — Heroism of a Negro. — Primary School for Girls. — Neglected Education of Women. — Blind Asylum. — Lectures. — Character of a Brazilian Audience. — Organ Mountains. — Walk up the Serra. —Theresopolis. — Visit to the St. Louis Fazenda. — Climate of Theresopolis. — Descent of the Serra. — Geology of the Organ Mountains. — The Last Word. 466-494

CHAPTER XVI.

GENERAL IMPRESSIONS OF BRAZIL.

Religion and Clergy. — Education. — Law, Medical, and Scientific Schools. — High and Common Schools. — Public Library and Museum in Rio de Janeiro. — Historical and Geographical Institute. — Social and Domestic Relations. — Public Functionaries. — Agriculture. — Zones of Vegetation. — Coffee. — Cotton. — Timber and other Products of the Amazons. — Cattle. — Territorial Subdivision of the Great Valley. — Emigration. — Foreigners. — Paraguayan War. 495-517

APPENDIX.

I. The Gulf Stream 519
II. Flying-Fishes 523
III. Resolutions passed on board the Colorado 525
IV. Dom Pedro Segundo Railroad 527
V. Permanence of Characteristics in different Human Species . . . 529
VI. Sketch of Separate Journeys undertaken by different Members of the Expedition 533

LIST OF WOODCUTS.

COCOEIRO PALM . . . . FRONTISPIECE

A species of Attalea common in the Serra d'Estrella. It bears two or three large bunches of olive-like berries, hanging immediately below the crown of leaves. The upper part of the stem is often overgrown with parasites, as in the specimen represented here.

From a photograph by G. Leuzinger.

                                                                                                                   Page

TREE ENTWINED BY SIPOS 54

There are a great many parasites, the stem and roots of which are attached to larger trees; this woodcut represents one of those strange "tree-killers," as they are called by the natives, belonging to the family of the Fig-trees, which, beginning their growth among the upper branches of trees, gradually descend to the ground, throw out branches around the stem they attack, and in the end kill it in their embrace. On the right are Lianas, from which hang parasitic flowers.

From a photograph by G. Leuzinger.

SIDE VIEW OF THE ALLEY OF PALMS 60

Part of the Botanical Garden in Rio de Janeiro. In the foreground a Pandanus covered with fruits. The Palms standing in pairs in the great alley are commonly called Palma Real. Their botanical name is Oreodoxa oleracea. The peak of Corcovado forms the background.

From a photograph by Messrs. Stahl & Wahnschaffe.

VISTA DOWN THE ALLEY OF PALMS 61

The objects are the same as in the preceding woodcut, only seen at right angles, to afford a view down the alley.

From a photograph by Messrs. Stahl & Wahnschaffe.

BOTAFOGO BAY 81

The great southeastern bay in the harbor of Rio de Janeiro. The highest peak in the centre is the Corcovado, at the foot of which stand the Insane Asylum and the Military School. On the left are the Gavia and the Sugar-Loaf; on the right, Tijuca. A beach runs all round the bay.

From a photograph by G. Leuzinger.

LIST OF WOODCUTS.

Mina Negress 83
 From a photograph by Messrs. Stahl & Wahnschaffe.

Mina Negress and Child 84
 From a photograph by Messrs. Stahl & Wahnschaffe.

Fallen Trunk overgrown by Parasites 91
 A comparison with the woodcut facing p. 54 will show how parasites growing upon living trees differ from those springing from dead trunks.
 From a photograph by G. Leuzinger.

Fazenda de Santa Anna, in Minas Geraes . . . 103
 The level grounds in front of the buildings are used for drying the coffee.
 From a photograph by Senhor Machado.

Esperança's Cottage 179
 From a water-colored painting by Mr. J. Burkhardt.

Veranda and Dining-Room at Teffé 214
 From a drawing by Mr. J. Burkhardt.

Head of Alexandrina 245
 Extraordinary as the head of hair of this girl may seem, it is in no way exaggerated; it stood six inches beyond the shoulders each way.
 From a sketch by Mr. Wm. James.

Dining-Room at Hyanuary 258
 The palm on the left is a Pupunha (Guilielma speciosa); the large-leaved trees back of the building are Bananas, and the Palm on the right a Javari (Astrocaryum Javari).
 From a water-colored painting by Mr. J. Burkhardt.

Maues River 304
 The Palm in the foreground is a Mucaja (Acrocomia lasiospatha); near the fence stand Banana-trees, and in the distance on the right a Tucuma Palm (Astrocaryum Tucuma).
 From a water-colored painting by Mr. J. Burkhardt.

Mundurucu Indian; male 313
 From a photograph by Dr. Gustavo, of Manaos.

Mundurucu Indian; female 314
 Also from a photograph by Dr. Gustavo, of Manaos.

LIST OF WOODCUTS.

FAN BACCÁBA 335
 This Palm, called Œnocarpus distychius by botanists, is remarkable for the arrangement of its leaves, which are placed opposite to each other on two sides of the trunk, and higher and higher alternately, so that, seen from one side, the two rows of leaves are equally visible, and have the appearance of a wide fan; seen in profile, they look like a narrow plume.
    From a drawing by Mr. J. Burkhardt.

SUMAUMEIRA 391
 This colossal tree is known to botanists under the name of Eriodendrum Sumauma, and may be seen everywhere in the basin of the Amazons.
    From a photograph presented by Senhor Pimenta Bueno.

GARAFOÁ, among the Organ Mountains 486
 This peak is called the Finger by the English residents of Rio. The Brazilians liken it to a bottle.
    From a photograph by G. Leuzinger.

ORGAN MOUNTAINS 490
 The loose boulder alluded to in the text stands on the fourth peak from the left.
    From a photograph by G. Leuzinger.

A JOURNEY IN BRAZIL.

CHAPTER I.

VOYAGE FROM NEW YORK TO RIO DE JANEIRO.

FIRST SUNDAY AT SEA. — GULF STREAM. — GULF-WEED. — LECTURES PROPOSED. — FIRST LECTURE: "ON THE GULF STREAM IN THE GULF STREAM." — AQUARIUM ESTABLISHED ON BOARD. — SECOND LECTURE. — ROUGH SEA. — PECULIAR TINT OF WATER. — THIRD LECTURE: LAYING OUT WORK OF EXPEDITION IN BRAZIL; DISTRIBUTION OF FISHES IN BRAZILIAN RIVERS; ITS BEARING ON ORIGIN OF SPECIES; COLLECTING OF EGGS. — TROPICAL SUNSET. — FOURTH LECTURE: PLAN OF GEOLOGICAL INVESTIGATIONS WITH SPECIAL REFERENCE TO GLACIAL PHENOMENA IN SOUTH AMERICA. — FLYING-FISH. — FIFTH LECTURE: GLACIAL PHENOMENA, CONTINUED. — SECOND SUNDAY AT SEA. — ROUGH WATER. — SIXTH LECTURE: EMBRYOLOGICAL INVESTIGATIONS AS A GUIDE TO SOUND CLASSIFICATION. — SEVENTH LECTURE. — MOONLIGHT NIGHTS. — TRADE-WINDS. — EIGHTH LECTURE: IMPORTANCE OF PRECISION IN LOCALIZING SPECIMENS. — SOUTHERN CROSS. — NINTH LECTURE: FRESH-WATER FISHES OF BRAZIL. — EASTER SUNDAY. — FIRST SIGHT OF SOUTH AMERICAN SHORE. — OLINDA — PERNAMBUCO. — CATAMARANS. — TENTH LECTURE: METHODS OF COLLECTING. — ELEVENTH LECTURE: CLASSIFICATION OF FISHES, AS ILLUSTRATED BY EMBRYOLOGY. — PREPARATIONS FOR ARRIVAL. — TWELFTH LECTURE: PRACTICAL LESSON IN EMBRYOLOGY — CLOSING LECTURE: TRANSMUTATION THEORY; INTELLECTUAL AND POLITICAL INDEPENDENCE. — RESOLUTIONS AND SPEECHES. — SINGULAR RED PATCHES ON THE SURFACE OF THE SEA.

April 2d, 1865. — Our first Sunday at sea. The weather is delicious, the ship as steady as anything on the water can be, and even the most forlorn of our party have little excuse for sea-sickness. We have had service from Bishop Potter this morning, and since then we have been on deck reading, walking, watching a singular cloud, which the captain says is a cloud of smoke, in the direction of Petersburg. We think it may be the smoke of a great decisive engagement going on while we sail peacefully along. What it means, or how the battle ends, if battle it be, we shall not know for two months perhaps.* Mr. Agassiz is busy to-day in taking notes, at regular intervals, of the temperature of the water, as we approach the Gulf Stream. To-night we cut it at right angles, and he will remain on deck to continue his observations.

April 3d. — The Professor sat up last night as he intended, and found his watch, which was shared by one or two of his young assistants, very interesting. We crossed the Gulf Stream opposite Cape Hatteras, at a latitude where it is comparatively narrow, some sixty miles only in breadth. Entering it at about six o'clock, we passed out of it a little after midnight. The western boundary of the warm waters stretching along the coast had a temperature of about 57°. Immediately after entering it, the temperature began to rise gradually, the maximum being about 74°, falling occasionally, however, when we passed through a cold streak, to 68°. These cold streaks in the Gulf Stream, which reach to a considerable depth, the warm and cold waters descending together in immediate contact for at least a hundred fathoms, are attributed by Dr. Bache to the fact that the Gulf Stream is not stationary. It sways as a whole sometimes a little toward the shore, sometimes a little away from it, and, in consequence of this, the colder water from the coast creeps in, forming these vertical layers in its midst. The eastern boundary is warmer

* On the 17th of May, nearly a month after our arrival in Rio, this cloud was interpreted to us. It was, indeed, charged with the issues of life and death, for it was on this day and the following that the final assaults on Petersburg were made, and the cloud which marred an otherwise stainless sky, as we were passing along the shores of Virginia, was, no doubt, the mass of smoke gathered above the opposing lines of the two armies.

than the western one, for the latter is chilled by the Arctic currents, which form a band of cold water all along the Atlantic shore. Their influence is felt nearly to the latitude of Florida. On coming out of the Gulf Stream the temperature of the water was 68°, and so it continued for an hour longer, after which Mr. Agassiz ceased his observations. To-day some of the gulf-weed was gathered by a sailor, and we found it crowded with life. Hydroids, in numbers, had their home upon it; the delicate branching plumularia and a pretty campanularia, very like some of our New England species; beside these, bryozoa, tiny compound mollusks, crusted its stem, and barnacles were abundant upon it. These are all the wonders that the deep has yielded us to-day, though the pretty Portuguese men-of-war go floating by the vessel, out of reach thus far. Such are the events of our life: we eat and drink and sleep, read, study Portuguese, and write up our journals.

April 4th. — It has occurred to Mr. Agassiz, as a means of preparing the young men who accompany him for the work before them, to give a course of lectures on shipboard. Some preparation of the kind is the more necessary, since much of the work must be done independently of him, as it will be impossible for so large a party to travel together; and the instructions needed will be more easily given in a daily lecture to all, than in separate conversations with each one singly. The idea finds general favor. The large saloon makes an excellent lecture-room; a couple of leaves from the dining-table with a black oil-cloth stretched across them serve as a blackboard. The audience consists, not only of our own company, but includes the few ladies who are on board, Mr. Bradbury, the captain of our steamer, Bishop Potter, some of the ship's officers, and a few additional passengers, all of whom seem to think the lecture a pleasant break in the monotony of a sea voyage. To-day the subject was naturally suggested by the seaweeds of the Gulf Stream, so recently caught and so crowded with life, — "A lecture on the Gulf Stream in the Gulf Stream," as one of the listeners suggests. It was opened, however, by a few words on the exceptional character of the position of this scientific commission on board the Colorado.

"Fifty years ago, when naturalists carried their investigations to distant lands, either government was obliged to provide an expensive outfit for them, or, if they had no such patronage, scanty opportunities grudgingly given might be granted them on ordinary conveyances. Even if such accommodation were allowed them, their presence was looked upon as a nuisance: no general interest was felt in their objects; it was much if they were permitted, on board some vessel, to have their bucket of specimens in a corner, which any sailor might kick over, unreproved, if it chanced to stand in his way. This ship, and the spirit prevailing in her command, opens to me a vista such as I never dreamed of till I stood upon her deck. Here, in place of the meagre chances I remember in old times, the facilities could hardly be greater if the ship had been built as a scientific laboratory. If any such occasion has ever been known before, if any naturalist has ever been treated with such consideration, and found such intelligent appreciation of his highest aims, on board a merchant-ship fitted up for purposes of trade, I am not aware of it. I hope the first trip of the Colorado will be remembered in the annals of science. I, at least, shall know whom to thank for an opportunity so unique. This voyage, and the circumstances connected with it, are, to me, the signs of a good time coming; when men of different interests will help each other; when naturalists will be more liberal and sailors more cultivated, and natural science and navigation will work hand in hand. And now for my lecture, — my first lecture on ship-board."

The lecture was given, of course, specimen in hand, the various inhabitants of the branch of sea-weed giving their evidence in succession of their own structure and way of life. To these living illustrations were added drawings on the blackboard to show the transformations of the animals, their embryological history, &c.* Since the lecture, Captain Bradbury has fitted up a large tank as an aquarium, where any specimens taken during the voyage may be preserved and examined. Mr. Agassiz is perfectly happy, enjoying every hour of the voyage, as well he may, surrounded as he is with such considerate kindness.

April 6th. — Though I took notes, as usual, of the lecture yesterday, I had not energy enough to enter them in my journal. The subject was the Gulf Stream, — the stream itself this time, not the animals it carries along with it. Mr. Agassiz's late observations, though deeply interesting to himself, inasmuch as personal confirmation of facts already known is always satisfactory, have nothing novel now-a-days; yet the history of the facts connected with the discovery of the Gulf Stream, and their gradual development, is always attractive, and especially so to Americans, on account of its direct connection with scientific investigations

---

* The species of Hydroids most numerous upon the gulf-weed have not yet been described, and would form a valuable addition to the Natural History of the Acalephs. For an account of the animals of this class inhabiting the Atlantic coast of North America, and especially the New England shores, I may refer to the third volume of my Contributions to the Natural History of the United States, and to the second number of the Illustrated Catalogue of the Museum of Comparative Zoölogy at Cambridge. — L. A.

carried on under our government. Mr. Agassiz gave a slight sketch of this in opening his lecture. "It was Franklin who first systematically observed these facts, though they had been noticed long before by navigators. He recorded the temperature of the water as he left the American continent for Europe, and found that it continued cold for a certain distance, then rose suddenly, and after a given time sank again to a lower temperature, though not so low as before. With the comprehensive grasp of mind characteristic of all his scientific results, he went at once beyond his facts. He inferred that the warm current, keeping its way so steadily through the broad Atlantic, and carrying tropical productions to the northern shores of Europe, must take its rise in tropical regions, must be heated by a tropical sun.* This was his inference: to work it out, to ascertain the origin and course of the Gulf Stream, has been, in a great degree, the task of the United States Coast Survey, under the direction of his descendant, Dr. Bache." †

* "This stream," he writes, "is probably generated by the great accumulation of water on the eastern coast of America, between the tropics, by the trade-winds which constantly blow there." These views, though vaguely hinted at by old Spanish navigators, were first distinctly set forth by Franklin, and, as is stated in a recent printed report of the Coast Survey Explorations, "they receive confirmation from every discovery which the advance of scientific research brings to aid in the solution of the great problem of oceanic circulation."

† No one can read the account of the explorations undertaken by the Coast Survey in the Gulf Stream, and continued during a number of successive years, and the instructions received by the officers thus employed from the Superintendent, Dr. A. D. Bache, without feeling how comprehensive, keen, and persevering was the intellect which has long presided over this department of our public works. The result is a very thorough survey of the stream, especially along the coast of our own continent, with sections giving the temperature to a great depth, the relations of the cold and warm streaks, the form of the ocean bottom, as well as various other details respecting the direction and

We are now fairly in the tropics. "The trades" blow heavily, and yesterday was a dreary day for those unused to the ocean; the beautiful blue water, of a peculiar metallic tint, as remarkable in color, it seemed to me, as the water of the Lake of Geneva, did not console us for the heavy moral and physical depression of sea-sick mortals. To-day the world looks brighter; there is a good deal of motion, but we are more accustomed to it. This morning the lecture had, for the first time, a direct bearing upon the work of the expedition. The subject was, "How to observe, and what are the objects of scientific explorations in modern times."

"My companions and myself have come together so suddenly and so unexpectedly on our present errand, that we have had little time to organize our work. The laying out of a general scheme of operations is, therefore, the first and one of the most important points to be discussed between us. The time for great discoveries is passed. No student of nature goes out now expecting to find a new world, or looks in the heavens for any new theory of the solar system. The work of the naturalist, in our day, is to explore worlds the existence of which is already known; to investigate, not to discover. The first explorers, in this modern sense, were Humboldt in the physical world, Cuvier in natural history, Lavoisier in chemistry, La Place in astronomy. They have been the pioneers in the kind of scientific work characteristic of our century. We who have chosen Brazil as our field must seek to make ourselves familiar with its physical features, its mountains and its rivers, its animals and plants. There is a change, however, to be introduced

force of the current, the density and color of the water, and the animal and vegetable productions contained in it. (See Appendix No. I.) — L. A.

in our mode of work, as compared with that of former investigators. When less was known of animals and plants the discovery of new species was the great object. This has been carried too far, and is now almost the lowest kind of scientific work. The discovery of a new species as such does not change a feature in the science of natural history, any more than the discovery of a new asteroid changes the character of the problems to be investigated by astronomers. It is merely adding to the enumeration of objects. We should look rather for the fundamental relations among animals; the number of species we may find is of importance only so far as they explain the distribution and limitation of different genera and families, their relations to each other and to the physical conditions under which they live. Out of such investigations there looms up a deeper question for scientific men, the solution of which is to be the most important result of their work in coming generations. The origin of life is the great question of the day. How did the organic world come to be as it is? It must be our aim to throw some light on this subject by our present journey. How did Brazil come to be inhabited by the animals and plants now living there? Who were its inhabitants in past times? What reason is there to believe that the present condition of things in this country is in any sense derived from the past? The first step in this investigation must be to ascertain the geographical distribution of the present animals and plants. Suppose we first examine the Rio San Francisco. The basin of this river is entirely isolated. Are its inhabitants, like its waters, completely distinct from those of other basins? Are its species peculiar to itself, and not repeated in any other river of the continent? Extraordinary as this result would seem,

I nevertheless expect to find it so. The next water-basin we shall have to examine will be that of the Amazons, which connects through the Rio Negro with the Orinoco. It has been frequently repeated that the same species of fish exist in the waters of the San Francisco and in those of Guiana and of the Amazons. At all events, our works on fishes constantly indicate Brazil and Guiana as the common home of many species; but this observation has never been made with sufficient accuracy to merit confidence. Fifty years ago the exact locality from which any animal came seemed an unimportant fact in its scientific history, for the bearing of this question on that of origin was not then perceived. To say that any specimen came from South America was quite enough; to specify that it came from Brazil, from the Amazons, the San Francisco, or the La Plata, seemed a marvellous accuracy in the observers. In the museum at Paris, for instance, there are many specimens entered as coming from New York or from Pará; but all that is absolutely known about them is that they were shipped from those sea-ports. Nobody knows exactly where they were collected. So there are specimens entered as coming from the Rio San Francisco, but it is by no means sure that they came exclusively from that water-basin. All this kind of investigation is far too loose for our present object. Our work must be done with much more precision; it must tell something positive of the geographical distribution of animals in Brazil. Therefore, my young friends who come with me on this expedition, let us be careful that every specimen has a label, recording locality and date, so secured that it shall reach Cambridge safely. It would be still better to attach two labels to each specimen, so that, if any mischance happens to one, our record may not be lost. We must try not to mix the fishes of different rivers, even though they flow into each other, but to keep our collections perfectly distinct. You will easily see the vast importance of thus ascertaining the limitation of species, and the bearing of the result on the great question of origin.

"Something is already known. It is ascertained that the South American rivers possess some fishes peculiar to them. Were these fishes then created in these separate water-systems as they now exist, or have they been transferred thither from some other water-bed? If not born there, how did they come there? Is there, or has there ever been, any possible connection between these water-systems? Are their characteristic species repeated elsewhere? Thus we narrow the boundaries of the investigation, and bring it, by successive approaches, nearer the ultimate question. But the first inquiry is, How far are species distinct all over the world, and what are their limits? Till this is ascertained, all theories about their origin, their derivation from one another, their successive transformation, their migration from given centres, and so on, are mere beating about the bush. I allude especially to the fresh-water fishes, in connection with this investigation, on account of the precision of their boundaries. Looking at the matter theoretically, without a positive investigation, I do not expect to find a single species of the Lower Amazons above Tabatinga.* I base this supposition upon my own ob-

* This anticipation was more than confirmed by the result of the journey. It is true that Mr. Agassiz did not go beyond the Peruvian frontier, and therefore could not verify his prophecy in that region. But he found the localization of species in the Amazons circumscribed within much narrower limits than he expected, the whole length of the great stream, as well as its tributaries, being broken up into numerous distinct faunæ. There can be no doubt that what is

servations respecting the distribution of species in the European rivers. I have found that, while some species occur simultaneously in the many upper water-courses which combine to form the Rhine, the Rhone, and the Danube, most of them are not found in the lower course of these rivers; that, again, certain species are found in two of these water-basins and do not occur in the third, or inhabit only one and are not to be met in the two others. The brook trout, for instance (*Salmo Fario*), is common to the upper course and the higher tributaries of all the three river-systems, but does not inhabit the main bed of their lower course. So it is, also, and in a more striking degree, with the Salmling (*Salmo Salvelinus*). The Huchen (*Salmo Hucho*) is only found in the Danube. But the distribution of the perch family in these rivers is, perhaps, the most remarkable. The Zingel (*Aspro Zingel*) and the Schraetzer (*Acerina Schraetzer*) are only found in the Danube; while *Acerina cernua* is found in the Danube as well as in the Rhine, but not in the Rhone; and *Aspro asper* in the Danube as well as in the Rhone, but not in the Rhine. The Sander (*Lucioperca Sandra*) is found in the Danube and the other large rivers of Eastern Europe, but occurs neither in the Rhine nor in the Rhone. The common perch (*Perca fluviatilis*), on the contrary, is found both in the Rhine and Rhone, but not in the Danube, which, however, nourishes another species of true Perca, already described by Schaeffer as *Perca vulgaris*. Again, the pickerel (*Esox Lucius*) is common to all these rivers, especially in their lower course, and so is also the cusk (*Lota vulgaris*). The special dis-

true for nearly three thousand miles of its course is true also for the head-waters of the Amazons; indeed, other investigators have already described some species from its higher tributaries differing entirely from those collected upon this expedition.

tribution of the carp family would afford many other striking examples, but they are too numerous and too little known to be used as an illustration here.

"This is among the most remarkable instances of what I would call the arbitrary character of geographical distribution. Such facts cannot be explained by any theory of accidental dispersion, for the upper mountain rivulets, in which these great rivers take their rise, have no connection with each other; nor can any local circumstance explain the presence of some species in all the three basins, while others appear only in one, or perhaps in two, and are absent from the third, or the fact that certain species inhabiting the head-waters of these streams are never found in their lower course when the descent would seem so natural and so easy. In the absence of any positive explanation, we are left to assume that the distribution of animal life has primary laws as definite and precise as those which govern anything else in the system of the universe.

"It is for the sake of investigations of this kind that I wish our party to divide, in order that we may cover as wide a ground as possible, and compare a greater number of the water-basins of Brazil. I wish the same to be done, as far as may be, for all the classes of Vertebrates, as well as for Mollusks, Articulates, and Radiates. As we have no special botanist in the party, we must be content to make a methodical collection of the most characteristic families of trees, such as the palms and tree ferns. A collection of the stems of these trees would be especially important as a guide to the identification of fossil woods. Much more is known of the geographical distribution of plants than of animals, however, and there is, therefore, less to be done that is new in that direction.

"Our next aim, and with the same object, namely, its bearing upon the question of origin, will be the study of the young, the collecting of eggs and embryos. This is the more important, since museums generally show only adult specimens. As far as I know, the Zoölogical Museum at Cambridge is the only one containing large collections of embryological specimens from all the classes of the animal kingdom. One significant fact, however, is already known. In their earliest stages of growth all animals of the same class are much more alike than in their adult condition, and sometimes so nearly alike as hardly to be distinguished. Indeed, there is an early period when the resemblances greatly outweigh the differences. How far the representatives of different classes resemble one another remains to be ascertained with precision. There are two possible interpretations of these facts. One is that animals so nearly identical in the beginning must have been originally derived from one germ, and are but modifications or transmutations, under various physical conditions, of this primitive unit. The other interpretation, founded on the same facts, is, that since, notwithstanding this material identity in the beginning, no germ ever grows to be different from its parent, or diverges from the pattern imposed upon it at its birth, therefore some other cause besides a material one must control its development; and if this be so, we have to seek an explanation of the differences between animals outside of physical influences. Thus far both these views rest chiefly upon personal convictions and opinions. The true solution of the problem must be sought in the study of the development of the animals themselves, and embryology is still in its infancy; for, though a very complete study of the embryology of a few animals has been made, yet these investigations include so small a number of representatives from the different classes of the animal kingdom that they do not yet give a basis for broad generalizations. Very little is known of the earlier stages in the formation of hosts of insects whose later metamorphoses, including the change of the already advanced larva, first to the condition of a chrysalis and then to that of a perfect insect, have been carefully traced. It remains to be ascertained to what extent the caterpillars of different kinds of butterflies, for instance, resemble one another during the time of their formation in the egg. An immense field of observation is open in this order alone.

"I have, myself, examined over one hundred species of bird embryos, now put up in the museum of Cambridge, and found that, at a certain age, they all have bills, wings, legs, feet, &c., &c. exactly alike. The young robin and the young crow are web-footed, as well as the duck. It is only later that the fingers of the foot become distinct. How very interesting it will be to continue this investigation among the tropical birds! — to see whether, for instance, the toucan, with its gigantic bill, has, at a certain age, a bill like that of all other birds; whether the spoonbill ibis has, at the same age, nothing characteristic in the shape of its bill. No living naturalist could now tell you one word about all this; neither could he give you any information about corresponding facts in the growth of the fishes, reptiles, or quadrupeds of Brazil, not one of the young of these animals having ever been compared with the adult. In these lectures I only aim at showing you what an extensive and interesting field of investigation opens before us; if we succeed in cultivating even a few corners of it we shall be fortunate."

In the evening, which is always the most enjoyable part of our day, we sat on the guards and watched the first tropical sunset we had yet seen. The sun went down in purple and gold, and, after its departure, sent back a glow that crimsoned the clouds almost to the zenith, dying off to paler rose tints on the edges, while heavy masses of gray vapor, just beginning to be silvered by the moon, swept up from the south.

April 7th. — To-day the lecture was upon the physical features of South America, something with reference to the geological and geographical work in which Mr. Agassiz hopes to have efficient aid from his younger assistants. So much of the lecture consisted of explanations given upon geological maps that it is difficult to record it. Its principal object, however, was to show in what direction they should work in order to give greater precision to the general information already secured respecting the formation of the continent. "The basin of the Amazons, for instance, is a level plain. The whole of it is covered with loose materials. We must watch carefully the character of these loose materials, and try to track them to their origin. As there are very characteristic rocks in various parts of this plain, we shall have a clew to the nature of at least some portion of these materials. My own previous studies have given me a special interest in certain questions connected with these facts. What power has ground up these loose materials? Are they the result of disintegration of the rock by ordinary atmospheric agents, or are they caused by the action of water, or by that of glaciers? Was there ever a time when large masses of ice descended far lower than the present snow line of the Andes, and, moving over the low lands, ground these materials to powder? We know that such an agency has been at work on the northern half of this hemisphere. We have now to look for its traces on the southern half, where no such investigations have ever been made within its warm latitudes; though to Darwin science is already indebted for much valuable information concerning the glacial phenomena of the temperate and colder portions of the South American continent. We should examine the loose materials in every river we ascend, and see what relation they bear to the dry land above. The color of the water in connection with the nature of the banks will tell us something. The waters of the Rio Branco, for instance, are said to be milky white; those of the Rio Negro, black. In the latter case the color is probably owing to the decomposition of vegetation. I would advise each one of our parties to pass a large amount of water from any river or stream along which they travel through a filter, and to examine the deposit microscopically. They will thus ascertain the character of the detritus, whether from sand, or lime, or granite, or mere river mud formed by the decomposition of organic matter. Even the smaller streams and rivulets will have their peculiar character. The Brazilian table-land rises to a broad ridge running from west to east, and determining the direction of the rivers. It is usually represented as a mountain range, but is in fact nothing but a high flat ridge serving as a water-shed, and cut transversely by deep fissures in which the rivers flow. These fissures are broad in their lower parts, but little is known of their upper range; and whoever will examine their banks carefully will do an important work for science. Indeed, very little is known accurately of the geology of Brazil. On the geological maps almost the whole country is represented as consisting of granite.

If this be correct, it is very inconsistent with what we know of the geological structure of other continents, where the stratified rocks are in much larger proportions."

Upon this followed some account of the different kinds of valley formation and of terraces. "Do the old terraces above the rivers of South America correspond to the river terraces on any of our rivers, — those of the Connecticut, for instance, — showing that their waters had formerly a much greater depth and covered a much wider bottom? There must of course have been a cause for this great accumulation of water in ancient periods. I account for it in the northern half of the hemisphere by the melting of vast masses of ice in the glacial period, causing immense freshets. There is no trustworthy account of the river terraces in Brazil. Bates, however, describes flat-topped hills between Santarem and Pará in the narrow part of the valley, near Almeyrim, rising 800 feet above the present level of the Amazons. If this part of the valley were flooded in old times, banks might have been formed of which these hills are a remnant. But because such a theory might account for the facts it does not follow that the theory is true. Our work must be to study the facts, to see, among other things, of what these hills are built, whether of rock or of loose materials. No one has told us anything as yet of their geological constitution." *

To-day we have seen numbers of flying-fish from the deck, and were astonished at the grace and beauty of their motion, which we had supposed to be rather a leap than actual flight. And flight indeed it is not, their pectoral

---

* Mr. Agassiz afterward visited these hills himself, and an account of their structure and probable origin will be found in the chapter on the physical history of the Amazons.

fins acting as sails rather than wings, and carrying them along on the wind. They skim over the water in this way to a great distance. Captain Bradbury told us he had followed one with his glass and lost sight of it at a considerable distance, without seeing it dip into the water again. Mr. Agassiz has great delight in watching them.* Having never before sailed in tropical seas, he enjoys every day some new pleasure.

April 9th. — Yesterday Mr. Agassiz lectured upon the traces of glaciers as they exist in the northern hemisphere, and the signs of the same kind to be sought for in Brazil. After a sketch of what has been done in glacial investigation in Europe and the United States, showing the great extension of ice over these regions in ancient times, he continued as follows: " When the polar half of both hemispheres was covered by such an ice shroud, the climate of the whole earth must have been different from what it is now. The limits of the ancient glaciers give us some estimate of this difference, though of course only an approximate one. A degree of temperature in the annual average of any given locality corresponds to a degree of latitude; that is, a degree of temperature is lost for every degree of latitude as we travel northward, or gained for every degree of latitude as we travel southward. In our times, the line at which the average annual temperature is 32°, that is, at which glaciers may be formed, is in latitude 60° or thereabouts, the latitude of Greenland; while the height at which they may originate in latitude 45° is about 6,000 feet. If it appear that the ancient southern limit of glaciers is in latitude 36°, we must admit that in those days the present climate of Greenland extended to that line. Such a change of climate with

* See Appendix No. II.

reference to latitude must have been attended by a corresponding change of climate with reference to altitude. Three degrees of temperature correspond to about one thousand feet of altitude. If, therefore, it is found that the ancient limit of glacier action descends on the Andes, for instance, to 7,000 feet above the level of the sea under the equator, the present line of perpetual snow being at 15,000, it is safe to infer that in those days the climate was some 24° or thereabouts below its present temperature. That is, the temperature of the present snow line then prevailed at a height of 7,000 feet above the sea level, as the present average temperature of Greenland then prevailed in latitude 36°. I am as confident that we shall find these indications at about the limit I have pointed out as if I had already seen them. I would even venture to prophesy that the first moraines in the valley of the Marañon should be found where it bends eastward above Jaen."*

Although the weather is fine, the motion of the ship continues to be so great that those of us who have not what are popularly called "sea-legs," have much ado to keep our balance. For my own part, I am beginning to feel a personal animosity to "the trades." I had imagined them to be soft, genial breezes wafting us gently southward; instead of which they blow dead ahead all the time, and give us no rest night or day. And yet we are very unreasonable to grumble; for never were greater comforts and conveniences

* It proved in the sequel unnecessary to seek the glacial phenomena of tropical South America in its highest mountains. In Brazil the moraines are as distinct and as well preserved in some of the coast ranges on the Atlantic side, not more than twelve or fifteen hundred feet high, as in any glaciated localities known to geologists in more northern parts of the world. The snow line, even in those latitudes, then descended so low that masses of ice formed above its level actually forced their way down to the sea-coast. — L A.

provided for voyagers on the great deep than are to be found on this magnificent ship. The state-rooms large and commodious, parlor and dining-hall well ventilated, cool, and cheerful, the decks long and broad enough to give a chance for extensive "constitutionals" to everybody who can stand upright for two minutes together, the attendance punctual and admirable in every respect; in short, nothing is left to be desired except a little more stable footing.

April 10th. — A rough sea to-day, notwithstanding which we had our lecture as usual, though I must say, that, owing to the lurching of the ship, the lecturer pitched about more than was consistent with the dignity of science. Mr. Agassiz returned to the subject of embryology, urging upon his assistants the importance of collecting materials for this object as a means of obtaining an insight into the deeper relations between animals.

"Heretofore classification has been arbitrary, inasmuch as it has rested mainly upon the interpretation given to structural differences by various observers, who did not measure the character and value of these differences by any natural standard. I believe that we have a more certain guide in these matters than opinion or the individual estimate of any observer, however keen his insight into structural differences. The true principle of classification exists in Nature herself, and we have only to decipher it. If this conviction be correct, the next question is, How can we make this principle a practical one in our laboratories, an active stimulus in our investigations? Is it susceptible of positive demonstration in material facts? Is there any method to be adopted as a correct guide, if we set aside the idea of originating systems of classification of our own, and seek only to read that already written in nature? I answer, Yes. The standard is to be found in the changes animals undergo from their first formation in the egg to their adult condition.

"It would be impossible for me here and now to give you the details of this method of investigation, but I can tell you enough to illustrate my statement. Take a homely and very familiar example, that of the branch of Articulates. Naturalists divide this branch into three classes.—Insects, Crustacea, and Worms; and most of them tell you that Worms are lowest, Crustacea next in rank, and that Insects stand highest, while others have placed the Crustacea at the head of the group. We may well ask why. Why does an insect stand above a crustacean, or, *vice versa*, why is a grasshopper or a butterfly structurally superior to a lobster or a shrimp? And indeed there must be a difference in opinion as to the respective standing of these groups so long as their classification is allowed to remain a purely arbitrary one, based only upon interpretation of anatomical details. One man thinks the structural features of Insects superior, and places them highest; another thinks the structural features of the Crustacea highest, and places them at the head. In either case it is only a question of individual appreciation of the facts. But when we study the gradual development of the insect, and find that in its earliest stages it is worm-like, in its second, or chrysalis stage, it is crustacean-like, and only in its final completion it assumes the character of a perfect insect, we have a simple natural scale by which to estimate the comparative rank of these animals. Since we cannot suppose that there is a retrograde movement in the development of any animal, we must believe that the insect stands highest, and our classification in this instance is dictated by Nature herself. This is one of the most striking examples, but there are others quite as much so, though not as familiar. The frog, for instance, in its successive stages of development, illustrates the comparative standing of the orders composing the class to which it belongs. These orders are differently classified by various naturalists, according to their individual estimate of their structural features. But the growth of the frog, like that of the insects, gives us the true grade of the type.* There are not many groups in which this comparison has been carried out so fully as in the insects and frogs; but wherever it has been tried it is found to be a perfectly sure test. Occasional glimpses of these facts, seen disconnectedly, have done much to confirm the development theory, so greatly in vogue at present, though under a somewhat new form. Those who sustain these views have seen that there was a gradation between animals, and have inferred that it was a material connection. But when we follow it in the growth of the animals themselves, and find that, close as it is, no animal ever misses its true development, or grows to be anything but what it was meant to be, we are forced to

* In copying the journal from which these notes are taken, I have hesitated to burden the narrative with anatomical details. But for those who take an interest in such investigations it may be well to add here that the frog, when first hatched, is simply an oblong body, without any appendages, and tapering slightly towards its posterior end. In that condition it resembles the Cecilia. In its next stage, that of the tadpole, when the extremity has elongated into a tail, the gills are fairly developed, and it has one pair of imperfect legs, it resembles the Siren, with its rudimentary limbs. In its succeeding stages, when the same animal has two pairs of legs and a fin around the tail, it recalls the Proteus and Menobranchus. Finally the gills are suppressed, the animal breathes through lungs, but the tail still remains; it then recalls Menopoma and the Salamanders. At last the tail shrinks and disappears, and the frog is complete. This gives us a standard by which the relative position of the leading groups of the class may safely be determined. — L. A.

admit that the gradation which unquestionably unites all animals is an intellectual, not a material one. It exists in the Mind which made them. As the works of a human intellect are bound together by mental kinship, so are the thoughts of the Creator spiritually united. I think that considerations like these should be an inducement for us all to collect the young of as many animals as possible on this journey. In so doing we may change the fundamental principles of classification, and confer a lasting benefit on science.

"It is very important to select the right animals for such investigations. I can conceive that a lifetime should be passed in embryological studies, and yet little be learned of the principles of classification. The embryology of the worm, for instance, would not give us the natural classification of the Articulates, because we should see only the first step of the series; we should not reach the sequence of the development. It would be like reading over and over again the first chapter of a story. The embryology of the Insects, on the contrary, would give us the whole succession of a scale on the lowest level of which the Worms remain forever. So the embryology of the frog will give us the classification of the group to which it belongs, but the embryology of the Cecilia, the lowest order in the group, will give us only the initiatory steps. In the same way the naturalist who, in studying the embryology of the reptiles, should begin with their lowest representatives, the serpents, would make a great mistake. But take the alligator, so abundant in the regions to which we are going. An alligator's egg in the earliest condition of growth has never been opened by a naturalist. The young have been occasionally taken from the egg just before hatching, but absolutely nothing is known of their first phases of development. A complete emoryology of the alligator would give us not only the natural classification of reptiles as they exist now, but might teach us something of their history from the time of their introduction upon earth to the present day. For embryology shows us not only the relations of existing animals to each other, but their relations to extinct types also. One prominent result of embryological studies has been to show that animals in the earlier stages of their growth resemble ancient representatives of the same type belonging to past geological ages The first reptiles were introduced in the carboniferous epoch, and they were very different from those now existing. They were not numerous at that period; but later in the world's history there was a time, justly called the 'age of reptiles,' when the gigantic Saurians, Plesiosaurians, and Ichthyosaurians abounded. I believe, and my conviction is drawn from my previous embryological studies, that the changes of the alligator in the egg will give us the clew to the structural relations of the Reptiles from their first creation to the present day, — will give us, in other words, their sequence in time as well as their sequence in growth. In the class of Reptiles, then, the most instructive group we can select with reference to the structural relations of the type as it now exists, and their history in past times, will be the alligator. We must therefore neglect no opportunity of collecting their eggs in as large numbers as possible.

"There are other animals in Brazil, low in their class to be sure, but yet very important to study embryologically, on account of their relation to extinct types. These are the sloths and armadillos, — animals of insignificant size in our days, but anciently represented in gigantic proportions. The Megatherium, the Mylodon, the Megalonyx, were some of these immense Mammalia. I believe that the embryonic changes of the sloths and armadillos will explain the structural relations of those huge Edentata and their connection with the present ones. South America teems with the fossil bones of these animals, which indeed penetrated into the northern half of the hemisphere as high up as Georgia and Kentucky, where their remains have been found. The living representatives of the family are also numerous in South America, and we should make it one of our chief objects to get specimens of all ages and examine them from their earliest phases upward. We must, above all, try not to be led away from the more important aims of our study by the diversity of objects. I have known many young naturalists to miss the highest success by trying to cover too much ground, — by becoming collectors rather than investigators. Bitten by the mania for amassing a great number and variety of species, such a man never returns to the general consideration of more comprehensive features. We must try to set before ourselves certain important questions, and give ourselves resolutely to the investigation of these points, even though we should sacrifice less important things more readily reached.

"Another type full of interest, from an embryological point of view, will be the Monkeys. Since some of our scientific colleagues look upon them as our ancestors, it is important that we should collect as many facts as possible concerning their growth. Of course it would be better if we could make the investigation in the land of the Orangs, Gorillas, and Chimpanzees, — the highest monkeys and the nearest to man in their development. Still even the process of growth in the South American monkey will be very instructive. Give a mathematician the initial elements of a series, and he will work out the whole; and so I believe when the laws of embryological development are better understood, naturalists will have a key to the limits of these cycles of growth, and be able to appoint them their natural boundaries even from partial data.

"Next in importance I would place the Tapirs. This is one of a family whose geological antecedents are very important and interesting. The Mastodons, the Palæotherium, the Dinotherium, and other large Mammalia of the Tertiaries, are closely related to the Tapir. The elephant, rhinoceros, and the like, are of the same family. From its structural standing next to the elephant, which is placed highest in the group, the embryology of the Tapir would give us a very complete series of changes. It would seem from some of the fossil remains of this family that the Pachyderms were formerly more nearly related to the Ruminants and Rodents than they now are. Therefore it would be well to study the embryology of the Capivari, the Paca, and the Peccary, in connection with that of the Tapir. Lastly, it will be important to learn something of the embryology of the Manatee or Sea-Cow of the Amazons. It is something like a porpoise in outline, and seems to be the modern representative of the ancient Dinotherium."

April 12th. — The lecture to-day was addressed especially to the ornithologists of the party, its object being to show how the same method of study, — that of testing the classification by the phases of growth in the different groups, — might be applied to the birds as profitably as to other types.

We have made good progress in the last forty-eight hours, and are fast leaving our friends "the trades" behind. The captain promises us smooth waters in a day or two. With the dying away of the wind will come greater heat, but as yet we have had no intensely warm weather. The sun, however, keeps us within doors a great part of the day, but in the evening we sit on the guards, watch the sunset over the waters, and then the moonlight, and so while away the time till nine or ten o'clock, when one by one the party disperses. The sea has been so rough that we have not been able to capture anything, but when we get into smoother waters, our naturalists will be on the look out for jelly-fish, argonautas, and the like.

April 13th. — In to-day's lecture Mr. Agassiz returned again to the subject of geographical distribution and the importance of localizing the collections with great precision.

"As Rio de Janeiro is our starting-point, the water-system in its immediate neighborhood will be as it were a school-room for us during the first week of our Brazilian life. We shall not find it so easy a matter as it seems to keep our collections distinct in this region. The head-waters of some of the rivers near Rio, flowing in opposite directions, are in such close proximity that it will be difficult sometimes to distinguish them. Outside of the coast range, to which the Organ Mountains belong, are a number of short streams, little rills, so to speak, emptying directly into the ocean. It will be important to ascertain whether the same animals occur in all these short water-courses. I think this will be found to be the case, because it is so with corresponding small rivers on our northern coast. There are little rivers along the whole coast from Maine to New Jersey; all these disconnected rivers contain a similar fauna. There is another extensive range inland of the coast ridge, the Serra de Mantiquera, sloping gently down to the ocean south of the Rio Belmonte or Jequitinhonha. Rivers arising in this range are more complex; they have large tributaries.

Their upper part is usually broken by waterfalls, their lower course being more level; probably in the lower courses of these rivers we shall find fishes similar to those of the short coast streams, while in the higher broken waters we shall find distinct faunæ." The lecture closed with some account of the excursions likely to be undertaken in the neighborhood of Rio de Janeiro on arriving, and with some practical instructions about collecting, based upon Mr. Agassiz's personal experience.*

* On account of the many exploring expeditions for which the Bay of Rio de Janeiro has been a favorite port, it has acquired a special interest for the naturalist. It may seem at first sight as if the fact that French, English, German, Russian, and American expeditions have followed each other in this locality, during the last century, each bringing away its rich harvest of specimens, by diminishing its novelty would rather lessen than increase its interest as a collecting ground. On the contrary, for the very reason that the specimens from which the greater part of the descriptions and figures contained in the published accounts of these voyages were obtained from Rio de Janeiro and its neighborhood, it becomes indispensable that every zoölogical museum aiming at scientific accuracy and completeness should have original specimens from that very locality for the identification of species already described. Otherwise doubts respecting the strict identity or specific difference of specimens obtained on other parts of the Atlantic shore, not only in South America but in Central and North America, may at any time invalidate important generalizations concerning the distribution of animals in these seas. From this point of view, the Bay of Rio de Janeiro forms a most important centre of comparison, and it was for this reason that we made so prolonged a stay there. Although the prospect of discovering any novelties was diminished by the extensive investigations of our predecessors, I well knew that whatever we collected there would greatly increase the value of our collections elsewhere. One of my special aims was to ascertain how far the marine animals inhabiting the coast of Brazil to the south of Cape Frio differed from those to the north of it, and furthermore, how the animals found along the coast between Cape Frio and Cape St. Roque differed from or agreed with those inhabiting the more northern shore of the continent and the West Indian Islands. In the course of the following chapters I shall have occasion to return, more in detail, to this subject. — L. A.

April 14*th.* — Last evening was the most beautiful we have had since we left home; perfectly clear with the exception of soft white masses of cloud on the horizon, all their edges silvered by the moonlight. We looked our last for many months to come on the north star, and saw the southern cross for the first time. With the visible image I lost a far more wonderful constellation which had lived in my imagination; it has vanished with all its golden glory, a celestial vision as amazing as that which converted Constantine, and in its place stands the veritable constellation with its four little points of light.

The lecture to-day was upon the fishes of South America. "I will give you this morning a slight sketch of the characteristic fishes in South America, as compared with those of the Old World and North America. Though I do not know how the fishes are distributed in the regions to which we are going, and it is just upon the investigation of this point that I want your help, I know their character as distinguished from those of other continents. We must remember that the most important aim of all our studies in this direction will be the solution of the question whether any given fauna is distinct and has originated where it now exists. To this end I shall make you acquainted with the Brazilian animals so far as I can in the short time we have before beginning our active operations, in order that you may be prepared to detect the law of their geographical distribution. I shall speak to-day more especially of the fresh-water fishes.

"In the northern hemisphere there is a remarkable group of fishes known as the Sturgeons. They are chiefly found in the waters flowing into the Polar seas, as the Mackenzie River on our own continent, the Lena and Yenissei in the

Old World, and in all the rivers and lakes of the temperate zone, communicating with the Atlantic Ocean. They occur in smaller numbers in most tributaries of the Mediterranean, but are common in the Volga and Danube, as well as in the Mississippi, in some of the rivers on our northern Atlantic and Pacific coasts, and in China. This family has no representatives in Africa, Southern Asia, Australia, or South America, but there is a group corresponding in a certain way to it in South America, — that of the Goniodonts. Though some ichthyologists place them widely apart in their classifications, there is, on the whole, a striking resemblance between the Sturgeons and Goniodonts. Groups of this kind, reproducing certain features common to both, but differing by special structural modifications, are called 'representative types.' This name applies more especially to such groups when they are distributed over different parts of the world. To naturalists the comparison of one of these types with another is very interesting, as touching upon the question of origin of species. To those who believe that animals are derived from one another the alternative here presented is very clear: either one of these groups grew out of the other, or else they both had common ancestors which were neither Sturgeons nor Goniodonts, but combined the features of both and gave birth to each.

"There is a third family of fishes, the Hornpouts or Bullheads, called Siluroids by naturalists, which seem by their structural character to occupy an intermediate position between the Sturgeons and Goniodonts. There would seem to be, then, in these three groups, so similar in certain features, so distinct in others, the elements of a series. But while their structural relations suggest a common origin, their geographical distribution seems to exclude it. Take, for instance, the Hornpouts; they are very few in the northern hemisphere, hardly ever occurring in those rivers where the Sturgeons abound, and they are very numerous in the southern hemisphere, in southern Asia, Australia, Africa, and South America, where the Sturgeons are altogether wanting. In South America the Siluroids everywhere exist with the Goniodonts, in all other parts of the world without them; the Goniodonts being only found in South America. If these were the ancestors of the Siluroids in South America, they were certainly not their ancestors anywhere else. If the Sturgeons were the ancestors of the Siluroids and of the Goniodonts, it is strange that their progeny should consist of these two families in South America, and in the Old World of the Siluroids only. But if all three had some other common ancestry, it would be still more extraordinary that its progeny should exhibit so specific a distribution upon the surface of our globe. The Siluroids lay very large eggs, and as they are very abundant in South America we shall no doubt have opportunities of collecting them. Of the reproduction of the Goniodonts absolutely nothing is known. Of course the embryology of both these groups would have a direct bearing on the problem of their origin.

"Another family very abundant in various parts of the world is that of the Perches. They are found all over North America, Europe, and Northern Asia; but there is not one to be found in the fresh waters of the southern hemisphere. In South America and in Africa they are represented however by a very similar group, that of the Chromids. These two groups are so much akin that from their structure it would seem natural to suppose that the Chromids were transformed Perches; the more so, since in the western hemisphere the latter extend from the high north to Texas, south of which they are represented by the Chromids. Here the geographical as well as the structural transition would seem an easy one. But look at the eastern hemisphere. Perches abound in Asia, Europe, and Australia, but there are no Chromids there. How is it that the Perches of this continent have been so fertile in producing Chromids, and the Perches of all other continents, except Africa, absolutely sterile in this respect? Or if we reverse the proposition, and suppose the Perches to have grown out of the Chromids, why have their ancestry disappeared so completely on the Asiatic side of the world, while they do not seem to have diminished on this? And if Perches and Chromids should be represented as descending from an older common type, I would answer that Palæontology knows nothing of such a pedigree.

"Next come the Chubs, or in scientific nomenclature the Cyprinoids. These fishes, variously called Chubs, Suckers, or Carps, abound in all the fresh waters of the northern hemisphere. They are also numerous in the eastern part of the southern hemisphere, but have not a single representative in South America. As the Goniodonts are characteristic of the southern hemisphere in its western half, so this group seems to be characteristic of it in its eastern half. But while the Cyprinoids have no representative in South America, there is another group there, structurally akin to them, called the Cyprinodonts. They are all small sized; our Minnows belong to this group. From Maine to Texas they are found in all the short rivers or creeks all along the coast. It is for this reason that I expect to find the short coast rivers of South America abounding in Minnows. I remember to have found in the neighborhood of

Mobile no less than six new species in the course of an afternoon's ramble. These fishes are almost all viviparous, or at least lay their eggs in a very advanced state of development of the young. The sexes differ so greatly in appearance that they have sometimes been described as distinct species, nay, even as distinct genera.* We must be on our guard against a similar mistake. Here again we have two groups, the Cyprinoids and Cyprinodonts, so similar in their structural features that the development of one out of the other naturally suggests itself. But in South America there are no Cyprinoids at all, while the Cyprinodonts abound; in Europe, Asia, and North America on the contrary, the Cyprinoids are very numerous and the Cyprinodonts comparatively few." The Characines were next considered with reference to their affinities as well as their geographical distribution; and a few remarks were added upon the smaller families known to have representatives in the fresh waters of South America, such as the Erythrinoids, the Gymnotines, &c. "I am often asked what is my chief aim in this expedition to South America? No doubt in a general way it is to collect materials for future study. But the conviction which draws me irresistibly, is that the combination of animals on this continent, where the faunæ are so characteristic and so distinct from all others, will give me the means of showing that the transmutation theory is wholly without foundation in facts." The lecture closed with some account of the Salmonidæ, found all over the northern hemisphere, but represented in South America by the Characines, distinct species of which may be looked for in the separate water-basins of Brazil; and also of several other important families of South American fishes, espe-

* Molinesia and Pœcilia.

cially the Osteoglossum, the Sudis, &c., interesting on account of their relation to an extinct fossil type, that of the Cœlacanths.*

April 17th. — Yesterday was Easter Sunday, and the day was beautiful. The services from Bishop Potter in the morning were very interesting; the more so for us on account of the God speed he gave us. Wind and weather permitting, it is the last Sunday we shall pass on board ship together. The Bishop spoke with much earnestness and sympathy of the objects of the expedition, addressing himself especially to the young men, not only with reference to their duties as connected with a scientific undertaking, but as American citizens in a foreign country at this time of war and misapprehension.

This morning we were quite entertained at meeting a number of the so-called "Catamarans," the crazy crafts of the fishermen, who appear to be amphibious animals on this coast. Their boats consist of a few logs lashed together, over which the water breaks at every moment without apparently disturbing the occupants in the least. They fish, walk about, sit, lie down or stand, eat, drink, and sleep, to all appearance as contented and comfortable as we are in our princely steamer. Usually they go into port at nightfall, but are occasionally driven out to sea by the wind, and may sometimes be met with two hundred miles and more from the shore. To-day we have fairly come upon the South American coast. Yesterday we could catch sight occasion

* This lecture was accompanied by careful descriptions and drawings on the blackboard, showing the structural differences between these groups. These are omitted, as they would have little interest for the general reader. The chief object in reporting these lectures is to show the aims which Mr. Agassiz placed before himself and his companions in laying out the work of the expedition, and these are made sufficiently clear without further scientific details.

ally of low sand banks; but this morning we have sailed past the pretty little town of Olinda, with its convent on the hill, and the larger city of Pernambuco, whose white houses come quite down to the sea-shore. Immediately in front of the town lies the reef, which runs southward along the coast for a hundred miles and more, enclosing between itself and the shore a strip of quiet waters, forming admirable anchorage for small shipping. Before Pernambuco this channel is quite deep, and directly in front of the town there is a break in the reef forming a natural gateway through which large vessels can enter. We have now left the town behind, but the shore is still in sight; a flat coast rising into low hills behind, and here and there dotted with villages and fishing-huts.

The lecture on Saturday was rather practical than scientific, on the best modes of collecting and preserving specimens, the instruments to be used, &c. To-day it was upon the classification of fishes as illustrated by embryology; the same method of study as that explained the other day and now applied to the class of fishes. "All fishes at the time when the germ becomes distinct above the yolk have a continuous fin over the whole back, around the tail, and under the abdomen. The naked reptiles, those which have no scales, such as frogs, toads, salamanders, and the like, share in this embryological feature of the fishes. From this identity of development I believe the naked reptiles to be structurally nearer to the true fishes than to the scaly reptiles. All fishes, and indeed all Vertebrates, even the highest, have, at this early period, fissures in the side of the neck. These are the first indications of gills, an organ the basis for which exists in all Vertebrates at a certain period of their life, but is fully developed and functionally active only in the lower ones, in which it acquires a special final structure; giving place to lungs in the higher ones before they reach their adult condition. From this time forward not only the class characters, but those of the family, begin to be distinguished. I will show you to-day how we may improve the classification of fishes by studying their embryology. Take, for instance, the family of Cods in its widest acceptation. It consists of several genera, among which are the Cod proper, the Cusk, and the Brotula. Naturalists may differ in their estimation of the relative rank of these genera, and even with reference to their affinity, but the embryology of the Cod seems to me to give the natural scale. In its early condition the Cod has the continuous fin of the Brotula, next the dorsal and caudal fins become distinct, as in the Cusk, and lastly the final individualization of the fins takes place, and they break up into the three dorsals and two anals of the Cod. Thus the Brotula represents the infantile condition of the Cod, and of course stands lowest, while the Cusk has its natural position between the two. There are other genera belonging to this family, as, for instance, the Lota or fresh-water Cusk and the Hake, the relative position of which may be determined by further embryological studies. I had an opportunity of observing something in the development of the Hake which throws some light on the relation of the Ophidini to the Cod family, though thus far they have been associated with the Eel. The little embryonic Hake on which I made my investigation was about an inch and a half in length; it was much more slender and elongated in proportion to its thickness than any of the family of Cods in their adult condition, and had a continuous fin all around the body. Although the structural relations of the Eels are not fully understood, some of them, at least, now united as a distinct family under the name of Ophidini, are known to be closely connected with the Cods, and this character of the Hake in its early condition would seem to show that this type of Eel is a sort of embryonic form of the Cod family.

"Another well-known family of fishes is that of the Lophioides. To this group belongs the Lophius or Goose-fish, with which the Cottoids or Sculpins, and the Blennioids, with Zoarces and Anarrhichas, the so-called Sea-cat, ought to be associated. It was my good fortune to have an opportunity of studying the development of the Lophius, and to my surprise I found that its embryonic phases included the whole series here alluded to, thus presenting another of those natural scales on which I hope all our scientific classifications will be remodelled when we obtain a better knowledge of embryology. The Lophius in its youngest stage recalls the Tænioids, being long and compressed; next it resembles the Blennioids, and growing stouter passes through a stage like Cottus, before it assumes the depressed form of Lophius. In the family of Cyprinodonts I have observed the young of Fundulus. They are destitute of ventrals, thus showing that the genus Orestias stands lowest in its family. I would allude to one other fact of this kind observed by Professor Wyman. There has been a doubt among naturalists as to the relative standing of the Skates and Sharks. On geological evidence I had placed the Skates highest, because the Sharks precede them in time; but this fact had not been established on embryological evidence. Professor Wyman has followed the embryology of the Skate through all its phases, and has found that in its earlier condition it is slender in outline, with the appearance of a diminutive shark, and that only later it assumes the broad shield-like form and long tapering tail of the skate. Were it only that they enable us to set aside all arbitrary decisions and base our classifications on the teachings of nature, these investigations would be invaluable; but their importance is increased by the consideration that we are thus gradually led to recognize the true affinities which bind all organized beings into one great system."

April 20*th*. — The day after to-morrow we shall enter the Bay of Rio de Janeiro. One begins to see already that little disturbance in the regularity of sea life which precedes arrival. People are making up their letters, and rearranging their luggage; there is a slight stir pervading our small party of passengers and breaking up the even tenor of the uniform life we have been leading together for the last three weeks. It has been a delightful voyage, and yet, under the most charming circumstances, life at sea is a poor exchange for life on land, and we are all glad to be near our haven.

On Tuesday the lecture was upon the formation and growth of the egg; a sort of practical lesson in the study of embryology; yesterday, upon the importance of ascertaining, at the outset, the spawning season of the animals in Brazil, and the means to that end. "It will often be impossible for us to learn the breeding season of animals, a matter in which country people are generally very ignorant. But when we cannot obtain it from persons about us, there are some indications in the animals themselves which may serve as a guide. During my own investigations upon the development of the turtles, when I opened many thousands of eggs, I found that in these animals, at least, the appearance of the ovaries is a pretty good guide. They always contain several sets of eggs. Those which will be laid this year are the largest; those of the following year are next in size; those of two years hence still smaller, until we come to eggs so small that it is impossible to perceive any difference between their various phases of development. But we can readily tell whether there are any eggs so advanced as to be near laying, and distinguish between the brood of the year and those which are to be hatched later. When the eggs are about to be laid the whole surface is covered with ramifying bloodvessels, and the yolk is of a very clear bright yellow. Before the egg drops from the ovary this network bursts; it shrivels up and forms a little scar on the side of the ovary. Should we, therefore, on examining the ovary of a turtle, find that these scars are fresh, we may infer that the season for laying is not over; or if we find some of the eggs much larger than the rest and nearly mature, we shall know that it is about to begin. How far this will hold good with respect to alligators and other animals I do not know. I have learned to recognize these signs in the turtles from my long study of their embryology. With fishes it could hardly be possible to distinguish the different sets of eggs because they lay such numbers, and they are all so small. But if we cannot distinguish the eggs of the different years, it will be something to learn the size of their broods, which differs very greatly in different families."

The lecture concluded with some advice as to observing and recording the metamorphoses of insects. "Though much has been written on the societies of ants and other like communities in Brazil, the accounts of different naturalists do not agree. It would be well to collect the larvæ of a great many insects, and try to raise them; but as this will be difficult and often impossible in travelling, we must at least get the nests of ants, bees, wasps, and the like, in order to ascertain all we can respecting their communities. When these are not too large it is easy to secure them by slipping a bag over them, thus taking the whole settlement captive. It may then be preserved by dipping into alcohol, and examined at leisure, so as to ascertain the number and nature of the individuals contained in it, and learn something at least of their habits. Nor let us neglect the domestic establishments of spiders. There is an immense variety of spiders in South America, and a great difference in their webs. It would be well to preserve these on sheets of paper, to make drawings of them, and examine their threads microscopically."

April 21st. — Yesterday Mr. Agassiz gave his closing lecture, knowing that to-day all would be occupied with preparations for landing. He gave a little history of Steenstrup and Sars, and showed the influence their embryological investigations have had in reforming classification, and also their direct bearing upon the question of the origin of species. To these investigators science owes the discovery of the so-called "alternate generations," in which the Hydroid, either by budding or by the breaking up of its own body, gives rise to numerous jelly-fishes; these lay eggs which produce Hydroids again, and the Hydroids renew the process as before.*

"'These results are but recently added to the annals of sci-

* As these investigations have been published with so much detail (Steenstrup, Alternate Generation, Sars's Fauna Norwegica; L. Agassiz, Contr. to Nat. Hist. of U. S.), it has not been thought necessary to reproduce this part of the lecture here. Any one who cares to read a less technical account of these investigations than those originally published, will find it in "Methods of Study," by L. Agassiz.

ence, and are not yet very extensively known in the community; but when the facts are more fully understood, they cannot fail to affect the fundamental principles of zoölogy. I have been astonished to see how little weight Darwin himself gives to this series of transformations; he hardly alludes to it, and yet it has a very direct bearing on his theory, since it shows that, however great the divergence from the starting-point in any process of development, it ever returns to the road of its normal destiny; the cycle may be wide, but the boundaries are as impassable as if it were narrower. However these processes of development may approach, or even cross each other, they never end in making any living being different from the one which gave it birth, though in reaching that point it may pass through phases resembling other animals.

"In considering these questions we should remember how slight are most of those specific differences, the origin of which gives rise to so much controversy, in comparison with the cycle of changes undergone by every individual in the course of its development. There are numerous genera, including many very closely allied species, distinguished by differences which, were it not for the fact that they have remained unchanged and invariable through ages, might be termed insignificant. Such, for instance, are the various species of corals found in the everglades of Florida, where they lived and died ages ago, and had the identical specific differences by which we distinguish their successors in the present Florida reefs. The whole science of zoölogy in its present condition is based upon the fact that these slight differences are maintained generation after generation. And yet every individual on such a coral stock,— and the same is true of any individual in any class whatsoever of the whole animal kingdom, whether Radiate, Mollusk, Articulate, or Vertebrate, — before reaching its adult condition and assuming the permanent characters which distinguish it from other species, and have never been known to vary, passes in a comparatively short period through an extraordinary transformation, the successive phases of which differ far more from each other than do the adult species. In other words, the same individual differs more from himself in successive stages of his growth than he does in his adult condition from kindred species of the same genus. The conclusion seems inevitable, that, if the slight differences which distinguish species were not inherent, and if the phases through which every individual has to pass were not the appointed means to reach that end, themselves invariable, there would be ever-recurring deviations from the normal types. Every naturalist knows that this is not the case. All the deviations known to us are monstrosities, and the occurrence of these, under disturbing influences, are to my mind only additional evidence of the fixity of species. The extreme deviations obtained in domesticity are secured, as is well known, at the expense of the typical characters, and end usually in the production of sterile individuals. All such facts seem to show that so-called varieties or breeds, far from indicating the beginning of new types, or the initiating of incipient species, only point out the range of flexibility in types which in their essence are invariable.

"In the discussion of the development theory in its present form, a great deal is said of the imperfection of the geological record. But it seems to me that, however fragmentary our knowledge of geology, its incompleteness does not invalidate certain important points in the evidence. It is well known that the crust of our earth is divided into a number of layers, all of which contain the remains of distinct populations. These different sets of inhabitants who have possessed the earth at successive periods have each a character of their own. The transmutation theory insists that they owe their origin to gradual transformations, and are not, therefore, the result of distinct creative acts. All agree, however, that we arrive at a lower stratum where no trace of life is to be found. Place it where we will: suppose that we are mistaken in thinking that we have reached the beginning of life with the lowest Cambrian deposit; suppose that the first animals preceded this epoch, and that there was an earlier epoch, to be called the Laurentian system, beside many others older still; it is nevertheless true that geology brings us down to a level at which the character of the earth's crust made organic life impossible. At this point, wherever we place it, the origin of animals by development was impossible, because they had no ancestors. This is the true starting-point, and until we have some facts to prove that the power, whatever it was, which originated the first animals has ceased to act, I see no reason for referring the origin of life to any other cause. I grant that we have no such evidence of an active creative power as Science requires for positive demonstration of her laws, and that we cannot explain the processes which lie at the origin of life. But if the facts are insufficient on our side, they are absolutely wanting on the other. We cannot certainly consider the development theory proved, because a few naturalists think it plausible: it seems plausible only to the few, and it is demonstrated by none. I bring this subject before you now, not to urge upon you this or that theory, strong as my own convictions are. I wish only to warn you, not against the development theory itself, but against the looseness in the methods of study upon which it is based. Whatever be your ultimate opinions on this subject, let them rest on facts and not on arguments, however plausible. This is not a question to be argued, it is one to be investigated.

"As I have advanced in these talks with you, I have become more and more dissatisfied, feeling the difficulty of laying out our work without a practical familiarity with the objects themselves. But this is the inevitable position of one who is seeking the truth: till we have found it, we are more or less feeling our way. I am aware that in my lectures I have covered a far wider range of subjects than we can handle, even if every man do his very best; if we accomplish one tenth of the work I have suggested, I shall be more than satisfied with the result of the expedition. In closing, I can hardly add anything to the impressive admonitions of Bishop Potter in his parting words to us last Sunday, for which I thank him in your name and my own. But I would remind you, that, while America has recovered her political independence, while we all have that confidence in our institutions which makes us secure, that so far as we are true to them, doing what we do conscientiously and in full view of our responsibilities we shall be in the right path, we have not yet achieved our intellectual independence. There is a disposition in this country to refer all literary and scientific matters to European tribunals; to accept a man because he has obtained the award of societies abroad. An American author is often better satisfied if he publish his book in England than at home. In my opinion, every man who publishes his work on the other side of the water deprives his country of so much intellectual capital to which she has a right. Publish your results at home, and let Europe discover whether they are worth reading. Not until you are faithful to your citizenship in your intellectual as well as your political life, will you be truly upright and worthy students of nature."

At the conclusion of these remarks a set of resolutions was read by Bishop Potter.* They were followed by a few little friendly speeches, all made in the most informal and cordial spirit ; and so ended our course of lectures on board the Colorado. Later in the day we observed singular bright red patches in the sea. Some were not less than seven or eight feet in length, rather oblong, and the whole mass looked as red as blood. Sometimes they seemed to lie on the very top of the water, sometimes to be a little below it, so as only to tinge the rippling surface. One of the sailors succeeded in catching a portion of it in a bucket, when it was found to consist of a solid mass of little crustaceans, bright red in color. They were all very lively, keeping up a constant rapid motion. Mr. Agassiz examined them under the microscope and found them to be the young of a crab. He has no doubt that every such patch is a single brood, floating thus compactly together like spawn.

* See Appendix No. III.

CHAPTER II.

RIO DE JANEIRO AND ITS ENVIRONS. — JUIZ DE FORA.

ARRIVAL. — ASPECT OF HARBOR AND CITY. — CUSTOM-HOUSE. — FIRST GLIMPSE OF BRAZILIAN LIFE. — NEGRO DANCE. — EFFECT OF EMANCIPATION IN UNITED STATES UPON SLAVERY IN BRAZIL. — FIRST ASPECT OF RIO DE JANEIRO ON LAND. — PICTURESQUE STREET GROUPS. — ECLIPSE OF THE SUN. — AT HOME IN RIO. — LARANGEIRAS. — PASSEIO PUBLICO. — EXCURSION ON THE DOM PEDRO RAILROAD. — VISIT OF THE EMPEROR TO THE COLORADO. — CORDIALITY OF GOVERNMENT TO THE EXPEDITION. — LABORATORY. — BOTANICAL GARDEN. — ALLEY OF PALMS. — EXCURSION TO THE CORCOVADO. — JUIZ DE FORA ROAD. — PETROPOLIS. — TROPICAL VEGETATION. — RIDE FROM PETROPOLIS TO JUIZ DE FORA. — VISIT TO SENHOR LAGE. — EXCURSION TO THE "FOREST OF THE EMPRESS." — VISIT TO MR. HALFELD. — RETURN TO RIO. — NEWS OF THE GREAT NORTHERN VICTORIES, AND OF THE PRESIDENT'S ASSASSINATION.

April 23d. — Yesterday at early dawn we made Cape Frio light, and at seven o'clock were aroused by the welcome information that the Organ Mountains were in sight. The coast range here, though not very lofty, (its highest summits ranging only from two to three thousand feet,) is bold and precipitous. The peaks are very conical, and the sides slope steeply to the water's edge, where, in many places, a wide beach runs along their base. The scenery grew more picturesque as we approached the entrance of the bay, which is guarded by heights rising sentinel-like on either side. Once within this narrow rocky portal, the immense harbor, stretching northward for more than twenty miles, seems rather like a vast lake enclosed by mountains than like a bay. On one side extends the ridge which shuts it from the sea, broken by the sharp peaks of the Corcovado, the Tijuca, and the flat-topped Gavia; on the other side, and more inland, the Organ

Mountains lift their singular needle-like points, while within the entrance rises the bare bleak rock so well known as the Sugar Loaf (*Paō de Assucar*). Were it not for the gateway behind us, through which we still have a glimpse of the open ocean, and for the shipping lying here at anchor, leaving the port or entering it, we might easily believe that we were floating on some great quiet sheet of inland water.

We reached our anchorage at eleven o'clock, but were in no haste to leave the ocean home where we have been so happy and so comfortable for three weeks past ; and as the captain had kindly invited us to stay on board till our permanent arrangements were made, we remained on deck, greatly entertained by all the stir and confusion attending our arrival. Some of our young people took one of the many boats which crowded at once around our steamer, and went directly to the city ; but we were satisfied with the impressions of the day, and not sorry to leave them undisturbed. As night came on, sunset lit up the mountains and the harbor. In this latitude, however, the glory of the twilight is soon over, and as darkness fell upon the city it began to glitter with innumerable lights along the shore and on the hillsides. The city of Rio de Janeiro spreads in a kind of crescent shape around the western side of the bay, its environs stretching out to a considerable distance along the beaches, and running up on to the hills behind also. On account of this disposition of the houses, covering a wide area and scattered upon the water's edge, instead of being compact and concentrated, the appearance of the city at night is exceedingly pretty. It has a kind of scenic effect. The lights run up on the hill-slopes, a little cluster crowning their summits here and there, and they glimmer all along the shore for two or three miles on either side of the central, business part of the town.

Soon after our arrival Mr. Agassiz received an official visit from a custom-house agent, saying that he had orders to land all our baggage without examination, and that a boat would be sent at any day and hour convenient to him to bring his effects on shore. This was a great relief, as the scientific apparatus, added to the personal luggage of so large a party, makes a fearful array of boxes, cases, &c. It would be a long business to pass it all through the cumbrous ceremonies of a custom-house. This afternoon, while Mr. Agassiz had gone to San Christovão* to acknowledge this courtesy and to pay his respects to the Emperor, we were wandering over a little island (*Ilha das Enxadas*) near which our ship lies, and from which she takes in coal for her farther voyage. The proprietor, besides his coal-wharf, has a very pretty house and garden, with a small chapel adjoining. It was my first glimpse of tropical vegetation and of Brazilian life, and had all the charm of novelty. As we landed, a group of slaves, black as ebony, were singing and dancing a fandango. So far as we could understand, there was a leader who opened the game with a sort of chant, apparently addressed to each in turn as he passed around the circle, the others joining in chorus at regular intervals. Presently he broke into a dance which rose in wildness and excitement, accompanied by cries and ejaculations. The movements of the body were a singular combination of negro and Spanish dances. The legs and feet had the short, jerking, loose-jointed motion of our negroes in

---

* The winter palace of the Emperor.

dancing, while the upper part of the body and the arms had that swaying, rhythmical movement from side to side so characteristic of all the Spanish dances. After looking on for a while we went into the garden, where there were cocoanut and banana trees in fruit, passion-vines climbing over the house, with here and there a dark crimson flower gleaming between the leaves. The effect was pretty, and the whole scene had, to my eye, an aspect half Southern, half Oriental. It was nearly dark when we returned to the boat, but the negroes were continuing their dance under the glow of a bonfire. From time to time, as the dance reached its culminating point, they stirred their fire, and lighted up the wild group with its vivid blaze. The dance and the song had, like the amusements of the negroes in all lands, an endless monotonous repetition. Looking at their half-naked figures and unintelligent faces, the question arose, so constantly suggested when we come in contact with this race, "What will they do with this great gift of freedom?" The only corrective for the half doubt is to consider the whites side by side with them: whatever one may think of the condition of slavery for the blacks, there can be no question as to its evil effects on their masters. Captain Bradbury asked the proprietor of the island whether he hired or owned his slaves. "Own them,—a hundred and more; but it will finish soon," he answered in his broken English. "Finish soon! how do you mean?" "It finish with you; and when it finish with you, it finish here, it finish everywhere." He said it not in any tone of regret or complaint, but as an inevitable fact. The death-note of slavery in the United States was its death-note everywhere. We thought this significant and cheering.

4

April 24th. — To-day we ladies went on shore for a few hours, engaged our rooms, and drove about the city a little. The want of cleanliness and thrift, in the general aspect of Rio de Janeiro is very striking as compared with the order, neatness, and regularity of our large towns. The narrow streets, with the inevitable gutter running down the middle, — a sink for all kinds of impurities, — the absence of a proper sewerage, the general aspect of decay (partly due, no doubt, to the dampness of the climate), the indolent expression of the people generally, make a singular impression on one who comes from the midst of our stirring, energetic population. And yet it has a picturesqueness that, to the traveller at least, compensates for its defects. All who have seen one of these old Portuguese or Spanish tropical towns, with their odd narrow streets and many-colored houses with balconied windows and stuccoed or painted walls, only the more variegated from the fact that here and there the stucco has peeled off, know the fascination and the charm which make themselves felt, spite of the dirt and discomfort. Then the groups in the street, — the half-naked black carriers, many of them straight and firm as bronze statues under the heavy loads which rest so securely on their heads, the padres in their long coats and square hats, the mules laden with baskets of fruit or vegetables, — all this makes a motley scene, entertaining enough to the new-comer. I have never seen such effective-looking negroes, from an artistic point of view, as here. To-day a black woman passed us in the street, dressed in white, with bare neck and arms, the sleeves caught up with some kind of armlet, a large white turban of soft muslin on her head, and a long bright-colored shawl passed crosswise under one arm and thrown over the other shoulder, hanging almost to the feet behind. She no doubt was of the colored gentry. Just beyond her sat a black woman on the curbstone, almost without clothing, her glossy skin shining in the sun, and her naked child asleep across her knees. Or take this as another picture : an old wall several feet wide, covered with vines, overhung with thick foliage, the top of which seems to be a stand for the venders of fruits, vegetables, &c. Here lies at full length a powerful negro looking over into the street, his jetty arms crossed on a huge basket of crimson flowers, oranges and bananas, against which he half rests, seemingly too indolent to lift a finger even to attract a purchaser.

April 25th. — Nature seems to welcome our arrival, not only by her most genial, but also by her exceptional moods. There has been to-day an eclipse of the sun, total at Cape Frio, sixty miles from here, almost total here. We saw it from the deck of the ship, not having yet taken up our quarters in town. The effect was as strange as it was beautiful. There was a something weird, uncanny in the pallor and chill which came over the landscape; it was not in the least like a common twilight, but had a ghastly, phantom-like element in it. Mr. Agassiz passed the morning at the palace where the Emperor had invited him to witness the eclipse from his observatory. The clouds are poor courtiers, however, and unfortunately a mist hung over San Christovão, obscuring the phenomenon at the moment of its greatest interest. Our post of observation was better for this special occasion than the Imperial observatory, and yet, though the general scene was perhaps more effective in the harbor than on the shore, Mr. Agassiz had an opportunity of making some interesting observations on the action of animals under these novel circumstances. The following extract is from his notes. "The effect of the waning light on animals was very striking. The bay of Rio is daily frequented by large numbers of frigate-birds and gannets, which at night fly to the outer islands to roost, while the carrion-crows (*urubús*) swarming in the suburbs, and especially about the slaughter-houses of the city, retire to the mountains in the neighborhood of Tijuca, their line of travel passing over San Christovão. As soon as the light began to diminish, these birds became uneasy; evidently conscious that their day was strangely encroached upon, they were uncertain for a moment how to act. Presently, however, as the darkness increased, they started for their usual night quarters, the water-birds flying southward, the vultures in a northwesterly direction, and they had all left their feeding-grounds before the moment of greatest obscurity arrived. They seemed to fly in all haste, but were not half-way to their night home when the light began to return with rapidly increasing brightness. Their confusion was now at its height. Some continued their flight towards the mountains or the harbor, others hurried back to the city, while others whirled about wholly uncertain what to do next. The re-establishment of the full light of noon seemed to decide them, however, upon making another day of it, and the whole crowd once more moved steadily toward the city."

The cordial interest shown by the Emperor in all the objects of the present expedition is very encouraging to Mr. Agassiz. So liberal a spirit in the head of the government will make his own task comparatively easy. He has also seen several official persons on business appertaining to his scientific schemes. Everywhere he receives the warmest expressions of sympathy, and is assured that the administration will give him every facility in its power to carry out his plans. To-night finds us established in our rooms, and our Brazilian life begins; with what success remains to be seen. While still on board the "Colorado" we seemed to have one foot on our own soil.

April 26th. — This morning Mrs. C—— and myself devoted to the arranging of our little domestic matters, getting out our books, desks, and other knickknacks, and making ourselves at home in our new quarters, where we suppose we are likely to be for some weeks to come. This afternoon we drove out on the Larangeiras road (literally, the "orangery"). Our first drive in Rio left upon my mind an impression of picturesque decay; things seemed falling to pieces, it is true, but mindful of artistic effect even in their last moments. This impression was quite effaced to-day. Every city has its least becoming aspect, and it seems we had chosen an unfavorable direction for our first tour of observation. The Larangeiras road is lined on either side by a succession of country houses; low and spreading, often with wide verandas, surrounded by beautiful gardens, glowing at this season with the scarlet leaves of the Poinsettia, or "Estrella do Norte" as they call it here, with blue and yellow Bignonias, and many other shrubs and vines, the names of which we have hardly learned as yet. Often, as we drove along, a wide gateway, opening into an avenue of palms, would give us a glimpse of Brazilian life. Here and there a group of people were sitting in the garden, or children were playing in the grounds under the care of their black nurses. Farther out of town the country houses were less numerous, but the scenery was more picturesque. The road winds in mediately under the mountains to the foot of the Corcovado, where it becomes too steep for carriages, the farther ascent being made on mules or horses. But it was too late for us, — the peak of the Corcovado was already bathed in the setting sun. We wandered a little way up the romantic path, gathered a few flowers, and then drove back to the city, stopping on our return to ramble for half an hour in the " Passeio Publico." This is a pretty public garden on the bay, not large but tastefully laid out, its great charm being a broad promenade built up from the water's edge with very solid masonry, against which the waves break with a refreshing coolness. To-morrow we are invited by Major Ellison, chief engineer of the Dom Pedro Railroad, to go out to the terminus of the road, some hundred miles through the heart of the Serra do Mar.

April 27th. — Perhaps in all our journeyings through Brazil we shall not have a day more impressive to us all than this one; we shall, no doubt, see wilder scenery, but the first time that one looks upon nature, under an entirely new aspect, has a charm that can hardly be repeated. The first view of high mountains, the first glimpse of the broad ocean, the first sight of a tropical vegetation in all its fulness, are epochs in one's life. This wonderful South American forest is so matted together and intertwined with gigantic parasites that it seems more like a solid, compact mass of green than like the leafy screen, vibrating with every breeze and transparent to the sun, which represents the forest in the temperate zone. Many of the trees in the region we passed through to-day seemed in the embrace of immense serpents, so large were the stems of the parasites winding about them; orchids of various kinds and large size grew upon their trunks; and

Tree entwined by Sipos.

vines climbed to their summits and threw themselves down in garlands to the ground. On the embankments also between which we passed, vines of many varieties were creeping down, as if they would fain clothe in green garments the ugly gaps the railroad had made. Yet it must be confessed that, in this instance, the railroad has not destroyed, but rather heightened, the picturesque scenery, cutting, as it does, through passes which give beautiful vistas into the heart of the mountain range. Once, as we issued from a tunnel, where the darkness seemed tangible, upon an exquisite landscape all gleaming in the sunshine, a general shout from the whole party testified their astonishment and admiration. We were riding on an open car in front of the engine, so that nothing impeded our view, and we had no inconvenience from smoke or cinders. During the latter part of the ride we came into the region of the most valuable coffee-plantations; and indeed the road is chiefly supported by the transportation of the immense quantities of coffee raised along its track or beyond it. Near its terminus is an extensive fazenda, from which we were told that five or six hundred tons of coffee are sent out in a good year. These fazendas are singular-looking establishments, low (usually only one story) and very spreading, the largest of them covering quite an extensive area. As they are rather isolated in situation, they must include within their own borders all that is needed to keep them up. There is something very primitive in the way of life of these great country proprietors. Major Ellison told me that some time ago a wealthy Marqueza living at some distance beyond him in the interior, and going to town for a stay of a few weeks, stopped at his house to rest.

She had a troop of thirty-one pack-mules, laden with all conceivable baggage, besides provisions of every sort, fowls, hams, &c., and a train of twenty-five servants. Their hospitality is said to be unbounded; you have only to present yourself at their gates at the end of a day's journey, and if you have the air of a respectable traveller, you are sure of a hearty welcome, shelter and food. The card of a friend or a note of introduction insures you all the house can afford for as long as you like to stay.

The last three miles of our journey was over what is called the "temporary road," the use of which will be discontinued as soon as the great tunnel is completed. I must say, that to the inexperienced this road looks exceedingly perilous, especially that part of it which is carried over a wooden bridge 65 feet high, with a very strong curvature and a gradient of 4 per cent (211 feet per mile). As you feel the engine laboring up the steep ascent, and, looking out, find yourself on the edge of a precipitous bank, and almost face to face with the hindmost car, while the train bends around the curve, it is difficult to resist the sense of insecurity. It is certainly greatly to the credit of the management of the line that no accident has occurred under circumstances where the least carelessness would be fatal.*

It gives one an idea of the labor expended on this railroad, to learn that for the great tunnel alone, now almost completed (one of fourteen), a corps of some three

---

* Some weeks after this I chanced to ask a beautiful young Brazilian woman, recently married, whether she had ever been over this temporary road for the sake of seeing the picturesque scenery. "No," she answered with perfect seriousness, "I am young and very happy, and I do not wish to die yet." It was an amusing comment on the Brazilian estimate of the dangers attending the journey.

hundred men, relieving each other alternately, have been at work day and night, excepting Sundays, for seven years. The sound of hammer and pick during that time has hardly ever been still, and so hard is the rock through which the tunnel is pierced, that often the heaviest blows of the sledge yield only a little dust, — no more in bulk than a pinch of snuff.*

On our return we were detained for half an hour at a station on the bank of the river Parahyba. This first visit to one of the considerable rivers of Brazil was not without its memorable incident. One of our friends of the Colorado, who parts from us here on his way to San Francisco, said he was determined not to leave the expe-

* This road, which is but the beginning of railroad travel in Brazil, opens a rich prospect for scientific study. From this time forward the difficulty of transporting collections from the interior to the seaboard will be diminishing. Instead of the few small specimens of tropical vegetation now preserved in our museums, I hope that hereafter, in every school where geology and palæontology are taught, we shall have large stems and portions of trunks to show the structure of palms, tree-ferns, and the like, — trees which represent in modern times the ancient geological forests. The time is coming when our text-books of botany and zoölogy will lose their local, limited character, and present comprehensive pictures of Nature in all her phases. Then only will it be possible to make true and pertinent comparisons between the condition of the earth in former times and its present aspect under different zones and climates. To this day the fundamental principle guiding our identification of geological formations in different ages rests upon the assumption that each period has had one character throughout; whereas the progress of geology is daily pressing upon us the evidence that at each period different latitudes and different continents have always had their characteristic animals and plants, if not as diversified as now, at least varied enough to exclude the idea of uniformity. Not only do I look for a vast improvement in our collections with improved methods of travel and transportation in Brazil, but I hope that scientific journeys in the tropics will cease to be occasional events in the progress and civilization of nations, and will be as much within the reach of every student as journeys in the temperate zone have hitherto been. For further details respecting the building of this road, see Appendix No. IV. — L A.

dition without contributing something to its results. He improvised a fishing apparatus, with a stick, a string, and a crooked pin, and caught two fishes, our first harvest from the fresh waters of Brazil, one of which was entirely new to Mr. Agassiz, while the other he had never seen, and only knew from descriptions.

April 28th. — This morning we went over to the Colorado, which still lies in the harbor, and where the visit of the Emperor was expected. We all felt an interest in the occasion, for we have a kind of personal pride in the fine ship whose first voyage has been the source of so much enjoyment to us. The Imperial yacht arrived punctually at twelve o'clock, and was received by the captain with a full salute from his Parrott guns, fired with a promptness and accuracy which the Emperor did not fail to notice. His Majesty went over the whole steamer; and really an exploring expedition over such a world in little, with its provision-shops, its cattle stalls, its pantries and sculleries, its endless accommodations for passengers and freight, its variety of decks and its great central fires, deep below all, is no contemptible journey for a tropical morning. The arrangements of the vessel seemed to excite the interest and admiration both of the Emperor and his suite. Captain Bradbury invited his Majesty to lunch on board; he very cordially accepted, and remained some time afterward, conversing chiefly about scientific subjects, and especially on matters connected with the expedition. The Emperor is still a young man; but though only forty, he has been the reigning sovereign of Brazil for more than half that time, and he looks careworn and somewhat older than his years. He has a dignified, manly presence, a face rather stern in repose, but animated and genial in conversation; his manner is courteous and friendly to all.

May 1*st*. — We celebrated May-day in a strange land, where May ushers in the winter, by driving to the Botanical Garden. When I say *we*, I mean usually the unprofessional members of the party. The scientific corps are too busily engaged to be with us on many of our little pleasure excursions. Mr. Agassiz himself is chiefly occupied in seeing numerous persons in official positions, whose influence is important in matters relative to the expedition. He is very anxious to complete these necessary preliminaries, to despatch his various parties into the interior, and to begin his personal investigations. He is commended to be patient, however, and not to fret at delays; for, with the best will in the world, the dilatory national habits cannot be changed. Meanwhile he has improvised a laboratory in a large empty room over a warehouse in the Rua Direita, the principal business street of the city. Here in one corner the ornithologists, Mr. Dexter and Mr. Allen, have their bench, — a rough board propped on two casks, the seat an empty keg; in another, Mr. Anthony, with an apparatus of much the same kind, pores over his shells; a dissecting-table of like carpentry occupies a conspicuous position; and in the midst the Professor may generally be seen sitting on a barrel, for chairs there are none, assorting or examining specimens, or going from bench to bench to see how the work progresses. In the midst of the confusion Mr. Burkhardt has his little table, where he is making colored drawings of the fish as they are brought in fresh from the fishing-boats. In a small adjoining room Mr. Seeva is preparing skeletons for mounting. Every one, in short, has his special task and is busily at work. A very questionable perfume, an "ancient and fish-like smell," strongly tinged with alcohol, guides one to this abode of

Science, where, notwithstanding its unattractive aspect, Mr. Agassiz receives many visitors, curious to see the actual working process of a laboratory of Natural History, and full of interest in the expedition. Here also pour in specimens from all quarters and of every kind; voluntary contributions, which daily swell the collections.* Those of the party who are not engaged here have their work elsewhere. Mr. Hartt and Mr. St. John are at various stations along the railroad line, making geological sections of the road ; several of the volunteers are collecting in the country, and Mr. Hunnewell is studying at a photographic establishment, fitting himself to assist Mr. Agassiz in this way when we are beyond the reach of professional artists.

Our excursion of to-day took us to another of those exquisite drives in the neighborhood of the city, always along the harbor or some inlet of it, always in sight of the mountains, always bordered by pretty country houses and gardens. The Botanical-Garden is about eight miles from the centre of the town. It is beautiful, because the situation is admirably well chosen, and because anything

* Among the frequent visitors at the laboratory, and one to whom Mr. Agassiz was indebted for most efficient aid in making his collection of fishes from the harbor of Rio, was our friend Dr. Pacheco de Silva, who never lost an opportunity of paying us all sorts of friendly attentions. He added quite a number of luxuries to the working-room described above. Another friend who was often at the laboratory was Dr. Nägeli. Notwithstanding his large practice, he found time to assist Mr. Agassiz not only with collections but with drawings of various specimens. Being himself an able naturalist, his co-operation was very valuable. The collections were indeed enriched by contributions from so many sources that it would be impossible to enumerate them all here. In the more technical reports of the expedition all such gifts are recorded, with the names of those persons from whom the specimens were received.

Side View of the Alley on Palms.

Vista down the Alley of Palms

that calls itself a garden can hardly fail to be beautiful in a climate where growth is so luxuriant. But it is not kept with great care. Indeed, the very readiness with which plants respond to the least culture bestowed upon them here makes it very difficult to keep grounds in that trim order which we think so essential. This garden boasts, however, one feature as unique as it is beautiful, in its long avenue of palms, some eighty feet in height. I wish it were possible to give in words the faintest idea of the architectural beauty of this colonnade of palms, with their green crowns meeting to form the roof. Straight, firm, and smooth as stone columns, a dim vision of colonnades in some ancient Egyptian temple rises to the imagination as one looks down the long vista.*

May 6th. — Yesterday, at the invitation of our friend Mr. B――, we ascended the famous Corcovado peak. Leaving the carriages at the terminus of the Larangeiras road, we made the farther ascent on horseback by a winding narrow path, which, though a very fair road for mountain travelling in ordinary weather, had been made exceedingly slippery by the late rains. The ride was lovely through the fragrant forest, with enchanting glimpses of view here and there, giving promise of what was before us. Occasionally a brook or a little cascade made pleasant music by the roadside, and when we stopped to rest our horses we heard the wind rustle softly in the stiff palms overhead. The beauty of vegetation is enhanced here by the singular character of the soil. The color of the earth is peculiar all about Rio; of a rich warm red, it seems to glow beneath the mass of vines and large-leaved plants above it, and every now and then crops out in vivid, striking

---

* The palm is the beautiful *Oreodoxa oleracea.*

contrast to the surrounding verdure. Frequently our path followed the base of such a bank, its deep ochre and vermilion tints looking all the softer for their framework of green. Among the larger growth, the Candelabra-tree (*Cecropia*) was conspicuous. The strangely regular structure of the branches and its silvery-tinted foliage make it stand out in bold relief from the darker background. It is a striking feature of the forest in this neighborhood.

A wide panoramic prospect always eludes description, but certainly few can combine such rare elements of beauty as the one from the summit of the Corcovado. The immense landlocked harbor, with its gateway open to the sea, the broad ocean beyond, the many islands, the circle of mountains with soft fleecy clouds floating about the nearer peaks, — all these features make a wonderful picture. One great charm of this landscape consists in the fact, that, though very extensive, it is not so distant as to deprive objects of their individuality. After all, a very distant view is something like an inventory : so many dark, green patches, forests ; so many lighter green patches, fields ; so many white spots, lakes ; so many silver threads, rivers, &c. But here special effects are not lost in the grandeur of the whole. On the extreme peak of the height a wall has been built around the edge, the descent on one side being so vertical that a false step might hurl one to instant destruction. At this wall we dismounted and lingered long, unwilling to leave the beautiful view before sunset. We were, however, anxious to return by daylight, and, to confess the truth, being a timorous and inexperienced rider at best, I was not without some anxiety as to the descent, for the latter part of the slippery road had been a sheer scramble. Putting a bold face on the matter, however, I resumed my seat, trying to look as if it were my habit to mount horses on the tops of high mountains and slide down to the bottom. This is really no inaccurate description of our descent for the first ten minutes, after which we regained the more level path at the little station called "the Païneiras." We are told to-day that parties usually leave their horses at this station and ascend the rest of the way on foot, the road beyond that being so steep that it is considered unsafe for riding. However, we reached the plain without accident, and I look back upon yesterday's ride with some complacency as a first lesson in mountain travelling.*

May 20th. — On Friday, the 12th of May, we left Rio on our first excursion of any length. A day or two after our arrival Mr. Agassiz had received an invitation from the President of the Union and Industry Company to go with some of his party over their road from Petropolis to Juiz de Fora, in the Province of Minas Geräes, a road celebrated not only for the beauty of its scenery, but also for its own excellence. A word as to the circumstances under which it has been built may not be amiss here; and it must be confessed, that, if the Brazilians are, as they are said to be, slow in their progress, the improvements they do undertake are carried out with great thoroughness. It is true that the construction of the road has been intrusted to French engineers, but the leading man in its projection and ultimate completion has been a Brazilian, Senhor

---

* Lenzinger's admirable photographs of the scenery about the Corcovado, as well as from Petropolis, the Organ Mountains, and the neighborhood of Rio generally, may now be had in the print-shops of Boston and New York. I am the more desirous to make this fact known as I am indebted to Mr. Lenzinger for very generous assistance in the illustration of scientific objects. — L. A.

Mariano Procopio Ferreira Lage, a native of the province of Minas Geräes. This province is said to be remarkable for the great energy and intelligence of its inhabitants, as compared with those of the adjoining provinces. Perhaps this may be owing to its cooler climate, most of its towns lying among the highlands of the Serras, and enjoying a fresher, more stimulating air than those nearer the sea-coast. Before undertaking the building of this road, Senhor Lage travelled both in Europe and America with the purpose of learning all the modern improvements in works of a similar character. The result bears testimony to the energy and patience with which he has carried out his project.* Twelve years ago the only means of going into the interior from Petropolis was through narrow, dangerous, broken mule-tracks, and a journey of a hundred miles involved a difficult ride of three or four days. Now one travels from Petropolis to Juiz de Fora between sunrise and sunset over a post-road equal to any in the world, changing mules every ten or twelve miles at pretty little stations, built somewhat in the style of Swiss châlets, each one of which is a settlement for the German colonists who have been induced to come out as workmen on the road. This emigration in itself is a great advantage to the country; wherever these little German villages occur, nestled down among the hills, there are the neat vegetable and flower gardens, the tidy houses, the general aspect of thrift and comfort, so characteristic of the better classes of the German peasantry. Nominally no slaves are

---

* A commemorative tablet, set in the rocks on the dividing line between the provinces of Rio de Janeiro and Minas Geräes, recording the speech of the Emperor on the occasion of the opening of the road, testifies the appreciation in which this undertaking was held by the government of Brazil.

allowed on the service of the road, Portuguese and German workmen being chiefly employed. This is a regulation which applies not only here, but on other public works about Rio. The contracts granted by the government expressly exclude the employment of slaves, though unfortunately this rule is not adhered to strictly, because for the performance of certain kinds of work no substitute for slave labor has yet been found. In the direct care of the road, however, in the repairs, for instance, requiring gangs of men who are constantly at work blasting rock and cracking the fragments into small pieces for the fresh macadamizing of any imperfect spot, mending any defects in the embankments or walls, &c., none but free labor is employed.

This attempt to exclude slaves from the public works is an emancipation movement, undertaken with the idea of gradually limiting slave labor to agricultural processes, and ridding the large cities and their neighborhood of the presence of slavery. The subject of emancipation is no such political bugbear here as it has been with us. It is very liberally and calmly discussed by all classes; the general feeling is against the institution, and it seems to be taken for granted that it will disappear before many years are over. During this very session of the Assembly one or two bills for emancipation have been brought forward. Even now any enterprising negro may obtain his freedom, and, once obtained, there is no obstacle to his rising in social or political station. But while from this point of view slavery is less absolute than it was with us, it has some appalling aspects. The slaves, at least in the cities, are literally beasts of burden. One sees the most cumbersome furniture, — pianos and the like,

5

and the heaviest trunks or barrels, piled one on top of the other, or bales of sugar and coffee weighing hundreds of pounds, — moving about the streets on the heads of the negroes. The result of this is that their limbs often become crippled, and it is common to see negroes in the prime of life who are quite crooked and maimed, and can hardly walk without a stick to lean upon. In justice I must add, however, that this practice, though it shocks a stranger even now, is gradually disappearing. We are told that a few years ago there were hardly any baggage-wagons except these living ones, and that the habit of using the blacks in this way is going out of vogue. In this as in other matters the Emperor's opinions are those of an enlightened and humane man, and were his power equal to his will, slavery would vanish from his dominions at once. He is, however, too wise not to know that all great social changes must be gradual; but he openly declares his abhorrence of the system.*

But to return from this digression to the road of the Union and Industry Company. It is now completed as far as Juiz de Fora, affording every convenience for the transport of the rich harvest of coffee constantly travelling over it from all the fazendas in the region. As the whole district is very rich in coffee-plantations, the improvement in the means of transportation is of course very important to the commercial interests of the country, and

---

* Since this was written the Emperor, at a large pecuniary sacrifice, has liberated all the slaves belonging to the property of the crown, and a general scheme of emancipation has been announced by the Brazilian government, the wisdom, foresight, and benevolence of which can hardly be too highly praised. If this be adopted, slavery in Brazil will disappear within the century by a gradual process, involving no violent convulsion, and perilling neither the safety of the slave nor the welfare of his master.

Senhor Lage is making practicable roads to the smallest settlements in his neighborhood. He has not, however, been free from the difficulties which men encounter whose schemes are in advance of their surroundings. No doubt a great part of the dissatisfaction is owing to the fact that the road is not so remunerative as was anticipated, the advance of the Dom Pedro Railroad having impaired its success. Still it must be considered as a monument to the public spirit and energy of the men who undertook it. Not wishing to interrupt the course of the narrative, I have thought it best to preface the story of our journey by some account of this road, the building of which is a significant fact in the present history of Brazil. I will now take up again the thread of our personal adventures.

Leaving the city at two o'clock in the ferry-boat, we kept up the harbor some fifteen miles. There was a cool breeze, and the day, though warm, was not oppressive. Passing the large Ilha do Governador, the smaller but exceedingly pretty island of Paqueta, and many others, with their palms, banana and acacia trees, dotting the harbor of Rio and adding another grace to its beauty, we landed in about an hour and a quarter at the little town of Mauá.* Here we took the cars, and an hour's ride through low and marshy grounds brought us to the foot of the Serra (*Raiz da Serra*), where we left the railroad for the post-coach, which runs regularly from this station. The drive was delightful, in an open diligence drawn by four mules on the full gallop over a road as smooth as a floor. It wound zigzag up the mountains,

---

* To the Baron de Mauá, a leader in the great improvements now going on in Brazil, the citizens of Rio de Janeiro owe their present convenient road to Petropolis, their favorite summer residence.

through the wildest scenery, while below us lay the valley broken into a billowy sea of green hills, and the harbor with the coast range beyond, growing soft and mellow in the afternoon sunshine. To complete the picture, one must clothe it in palms and acacias and tree-ferns, and drape it in a tangle of parasitic growth, with abundant bloom of the purple Quaresma (Flower of Lent),* the Thunbergia vine, with its little straw-colored blossoms creeping over every wall and shrub, and the blue and yellow Bignonias. We are constantly astonished at the variety of palms. A palm is such a rarity in our hot-houses, that we easily forget how numerous and varied they are in their native forests. We have the scarlet-oak, the white-oak, the scrub-oak, the chestnut-oak, the swamp-oak, and many others. And so in the tropical forest there is the cocoanut-palm, with its swollen, bulb-like stem when young, its tall, straight trunk when full grown, its cluster of heavy fruit, and its long, plume-like, drooping flower; † the Coccoeiro, with its slighter trunk and pendant branches of small berry-like fruit; the Palmetto, with its tender succulent bud on the summit of the stem, which is used as a vegetable here, and makes an excellent substitute for cabbage; the thorny Icaree or Cari, a variety of fan-palms, with their leaves cut like ribbons; and very many others, each with its characteristic foliage and appearance.‡

* A species of Melastoma, with very large, conspicuous flowers. — L. A.
† This is not, however, native to Brazil.
‡ Indeed, their diversity is much greater even than that of our Oaks, and it would require a comprehensive comparison with a majority of our forest-trees to match the differences they exhibit among themselves; and their native names, far more euphonic than the systematic names under which they are entered in our scientific works, are as familiar to the Indians as those of our beeches, birches, hazels, chestnuts, poplars, or willows to our farmers. There

The mountains along the road, as indeed throughout the neighborhood of Rio, are of very peculiar forms, steep and conical, suggesting at first sight a volcanic origin. It is this abruptness of outline which gives so much grandeur to mountain ranges here, the average height of which does not exceed two or three thousand feet. A closer examination of their structure shows that their wild, fantastic forms are the result of the slow processes of disintegration, not of sudden convulsions. Indeed, the rocks here differ so much in external character from those of the Northern Hemisphere, that the European geologist stands at first bewildered before them, and feels that the work of his life is to be done over again. It is some time before he obtains a clew to the facts and brings them into harmony with his previous knowledge. Thus far Mr. Agassiz finds himself painfully perplexed by this new aspect of phenomena so familiar to him in other regions, but so baffling here.

are four essentially different forms among the palms : the tall ones, with a slender and erect stem, terminating with a crown of long feathery leaves, or with broad fan-shaped leaves ; the bushy ones, the leaves of which rise as it were in tufts from the ground, the stem remaining hidden under the foliage ; the brush-like ones, with a small stem, and a few rather large leaves ; and the winding, creeping, slender species. Their flowers and fruits are as varied as their stock. Some of these fruits may be compared to large woody nuts, with a fleshy mass inside ; others have a scaly covering ; others resemble peaches or apricots, while others still are like plums or grapes. Most of them are eatable and rather pleasant to the taste. It is a thousand pities that so many of these majestic trees should have been deprived of their sonorous native names, to bear henceforth, in the annals of science, the names of some unknown princes, whom flattery alone could rescue from oblivion. The Inaja has become a Maximiliana, the Jara a Leopoldinia, the Pupunha a Guilielma, the Pachiuba an Iriartea, the Carana a Mauritia. The changes from Indian to Greek names have not been more felicitous. I would certainly have preferred Jacitara to Desmonchus, Mucaja to Acrocomia, Baccaba to Œnocarpus, Tucuma to Astrocaryum. Even Euterpe for Assai is hardly an improvement. — L. A.

He comes upon a rock, for instance, or a rounded elevation which by its outline he would suppose to be a "roche moutonnée," but approaching it more nearly he finds a decomposed crust instead of a glaciated surface. It is the same with the loose materials corresponding to the drift of the Northern hemisphere, and with all boulders or detached masses of rock; on account of their disintegration wherever they are exposed to the atmosphere, nothing is to be learned from their external appearance. There is not a natural surface of rock, unless recently broken, to be found anywhere.

The sun had set before we drove into the pretty town of Petropolis, the summer paradise of all Rio Janeirans whose circumstances enable them to leave the heat and dirt and vile smells of the city, for the pure air and enchanting views of the Serra. In a central position stands the summer palace of the Emperor, a far gayer and more cheerful-looking edifice than the palace at San Christovão. Here he passes six months of the year. Through the midst of the town runs the pretty river Piabanha, a shallow stream, now rippling along in the bottom of its bed between high green banks; but we were told that a night of rain in the hot season is enough to swell its waters till they overflow and flood the road. I could not but think how easy it would be for any one who cares to see tropical scenery to come here, when the direct line of steamers from New York is established, and, instead of going to Newport or Nahant, to take a house in Petropolis for the summer. It commands all the most beautiful scenery about Rio, and the horseback rides are without end. During our summer the weather is delightful here, just admitting a semblance of wood-fire morning and evening, while the orange orchards are golden with fruit, and flowers are everywhere. We had little time to become acquainted with the beauty of the place, which we hope to explore more at our leisure on some future visit, for sunrise the next morning saw us on our road again. The soft clouds hanging over the tops of the mountains were just tinged with the first rays of the sun when we drove out of the town on the top of the diligence, the mules at full gallop, the guard sounding a gay reveille as we rattled over the little bridge and past the pretty houses where closed windows and doors showed that the inhabitants were hardly yet astir.

The first part of our road lay through the lovely valley of the Piabanha, the river whose acquaintance we had already made in Petropolis, and which accompanied us for the first forty or fifty miles of our journey, sometimes a restless stream broken into rapids and cascades, sometimes spreading into a broad, placid river, but always enclosed between mountains rising occasionally to the height of a few thousand feet, lifting here and there a bare rocky face seamed with a thousand scars of time and studded with Bromelias and Orchids, but more often clothed with all the glory of the Southern forest, or covered from base to summit with coffee shrubs. A thriving coffee plantation is a very pretty sight; the rounded, regular outline of the shrubs gives a tufted look to the hillside on which they grow, and their glittering foliage contrasts strikingly at this season with their bright red berries. One often passes coffee plantations, however, which look ragged and thin; in this case the trees are either suffering from the peculiar insect so injurious to them, (a kind of Tinea,) or have run out and become exhausted. As we drove along, the scenes upon the road were often as amusing as they were picturesque. Now we came upon a troop of pack mules with a *tropeiro* (driver) at their head; if a large troop, they were divided into companies of eight, with a man to guide each company. The guard wound his horn to give warning of our coming, and a general struggle, garnished with kicks, oaths, and many lashes, ensued, to induce the mules to make way for the coach. These troops of mules are beginning to disappear from the seaboard since the modern improvements in railroads and stage lines, making transportation so much easier; but until lately it was the only way of bringing down the produce from the interior. Or again we fell in with a line of country wagons made of plaited bamboo, a kind of fabric which is put to a variety of uses here, such as the building of fences and lining of ceilings or roofs, as well as the construction of carts. Here and there the laborers were sitting in groups at the roadside, their work suspended while they cooked their midday meal, their kettles hanging over the fire, their coffee-pot simmering over the coals, and they themselves lying about in gypsy-like freedom of attitude.

At Posse, the third stage of our road, after having gone some thirty miles, we also stopped to breakfast, a meal which was by no means unacceptable after our three hours' ride. It is an almost universal custom with the Brazilians, especially when travelling, to take their cup of black coffee on rising, and defer their more solid breakfast till ten or eleven o'clock. I do not know whether my readers will sympathize with me, but I am always disappointed myself if any book of travels, having led me along the weary road, does not tell me what the hungry wanderers had to eat. It seems hardly fair, having shared their fatigues, that I should not also share their refreshment and be invited to sit down at table with them. Doing, therefore, as I would be done by, I shall give our bill of fare, and take an opportunity of saying a word at the same time of the characteristic Brazilian dishes. In the first place we had black beans stewed with *carne secca* (dried meat), the invariable accompaniment of every meal in Brazil. There is no house so poor that it does not have its *feijões*, no house so rich as to exclude this homely but most excellent dish, a favorite alike with high and low. Then there was chicken stewed with potatoes and rice, almost as marked a feature of the Brazilian cuisine as the black beans. Beside these, there were eggs served in various ways, cold meat, wine, coffee, and bread. Vegetables seem to be rare, though one would expect a plentiful variety in this climate.* At Posse Mr. Agassiz found a cordial co-operator in Mr. Charles Taylor, who expressed a warm interest in his scientific researches, and kept one of the collecting cans that he might fill it with fishes from the neighboring rivers and streams.†

Our kind friend Senhor João Baptista da Fonseca, who was our guide and our host on this journey, had neglected nothing which could contribute to the success

---

* This observation was confirmed by our year's travel. The Brazilians care little for a variety of vegetables, and do not give much attention to their cultivation. Those they do use are chiefly imported in cans from Europe.

† On our return from the Amazons a year later we heard with great regret of the death of Mr. Taylor For many months he took an active part in the objects of the Expedition, being himself a good naturalist, and not only made valuable collections for Mr. Agassiz, but also some admirable colored drawings of fishes and insects, which it is hoped may be published at a future time with the other scientific results of this journey.

4

and pleasure of the party, and had so prepared the way for the scientific objects of the excursion that at several points of the road we found collections of fishes and other animals awaiting us by the roadside. Once or twice, as we passed a fazenda, a negro carrying a basket came out to stop the diligence, and, lifting the cool green leaves which covered them, showed freshly caught fishes of all hues and sizes. It was rather aggravating, especially as we approached the end of our long drive, and the idea of dinner readily suggested itself, to see them disappear in the alcohol cans.*

At about midday we bade good by to the pretty river we had followed thus far, and at the Estaçaõ d'Entre Rios (between the rivers) crossed the fine bridge which spans the Parahyba at this point. The Parahyba is the large river which flows for a great part of its course between the Serra do Mar and the Serra da Mantiqueira, emptying into the Atlantic at San Joaõ da Barra considerably to the northeast of Rio de Janeiro. One is a little bewildered at first by the variety of Serras in Brazil, because the

* My experience of this day might well awaken the envy of any naturalist, and I was myself no less astonished than grateful for its scientific results. Not only had Senhor Lage provided us with the most comfortable private conveyance, but he had sent messengers in advance to all the planters residing near our line of travel, requesting them to provide all the fishes that were to be had in the adjoining rivers and brooks. The agents of the stations situated near water-courses had also received instructions to have similar collections in readiness, and in two places I found large tanks filled with living specimens of all the species in the neighborhood. The small number of species subsequently added, upon repeated excursions to different parts of the basin of the Parahyba, convinced me that in this one day, thanks to the kindness of our host and his friends, I had an opportunity of examining nearly its whole ichthyological fauna, and of making probably as complete a collection from it as may be found from any of the considerable rivers of Europe in the larger museums of the Old World. — L. A.

word is used to express not only important chains of mountains, but all their spurs. Any mountainous elevation is a Serra; but though there is an endless number of them between the Serra do Mar and the Serra da Mantiqueira, these are the two most important chains, running parallel with the sea-coast. Between them flows the Parahyba with its many branches. It is important to make collections here, as the peculiar character of this water basin, the many tributaries of which drain the southern watershed of the Serra da Mantiqueira, and the northern watershed of the Serra do Mar, make it of especial interest for the naturalist. On account of its neighborhood to the sea, it is also desirable to compare its inhabitants with those of the many short, disconnected rivers which empty into the Atlantic on the other side of the coast range. In short, it gives a good opportunity for testing those questions of the geographical distribution of living beings, as connected with their origin, which Mr. Agassiz so strongly urged upon his assistants during our voyage.

Soon after crossing the Parahyba, the road strikes the Parahybuna, a tributary which enters the main river on its northern side, nearly opposite the Piabanha. The latter part of the journey is less wild than the first half; the mountains fall away in somewhat gentler slopes, and do not shut in the road with the steep rugged precipices so striking in the valley of the Piabanha. But though perhaps less picturesque on approaching Luiz de Fora,* the scenery is beautiful enough throughout the whole ride to satisfy the most fastidious and keep the attention constantly awake. We arrived at the end of our journey at about six o'clock, and found most comfortable accommodations prepared for

---

* In some maps this place is inscribed under the name of Parahybuna.

us at a little cottage, built somewhat in the style of a Swiss chalet, and kept by the company for the use of their guests or for the directors of the road. An excellent dinner awaited us at the little hotel just opposite, the door of which is shaded by two stately palms; and with a ramble in the neighboring grounds of Senhor Lage, and a concert by a band of German musicians, consisting of employees on the road, our day closed, — a day full of pleasure.

The following morning we were indebted to Senhor Lage for a walk, as instructive as it was charming, through his gardens and orange orchards. Not only has he arranged his grounds with exquisite taste, but has endeavored to bring together the shrubs and trees most characteristic of the country, so that a stroll through his place is a valuable lesson to the botanist, the more so if he is fortunate enough to have the proprietor as a companion, for he may then learn the name and history of every tree and flower he passes. Such a guide is invaluable here, for the Brazilians seem to remain in blissful ignorance of systematic nomenclature; to most of them all flowers are "flores," all animals, from a fly up to a mule or an elephant, "bixos." One of the most beautiful features of Senhor Lage's grounds is a plantation of parasites, — an extensive walk, bordered on either side by a rustic fence, over which are trained some of the most exquisite parasitic plants of the Brazilian forests. In the midst of this walk is the Grotto of the Princesses, so called after the daughters of the Emperor who, on occasion of a visit made by the Imperial family to Juiz de Fora, at the opening of the road, were exceedingly pleased with this pretty spot, where a spring all overhung with parasitic vines, Orchids, &c. flows out from the rock. The spring, however, is artificial, and is a part of the admirable system of irrigation introduced over the whole estate. So rapid is the growth of everything here that one can hardly believe this beautiful country place to have been under cultivation only five or six years; a few years more under the same direction will make it a tropical paradise.

A variety of plans combining pleasure and science had been arranged for the next day. First on the list was a drive to the "Forest of the Empress." Everything of any interest in the neighborhood recalls the visit of the Imperial family at the opening of the road. From this event all loyal Juiz de Forans date, and the virgin forest we were to visit is consecrated by the fact that on this great occasion the Emperor with his family and suite breakfasted here in presence of a numerous assemblage of their loving subjects. Surely a more stately banqueting-hall could scarcely be found. The throne was cut in the broad buttressed trunk of a huge figueira; the rustic table, built of rough stems, stood under the shadow of great palm-trees; and around was the tropical forest, tapestried with vines, and embroidered with Orchids. These were royal accompaniments, even though the whole entertainment was conducted with a simplicity in harmony with the scene. Neither gold nor silver nor glass was brought to vie with the beauties of nature; the drinking-cups were made from the hollow stems of the wild bamboo-tree, and all the service was of the same rustic description. The tables, seats, &c. stand, undisturbed, as they were on that day, and of course this spot remains a favorite resort for humbler picnics than the one by which it was inaugurated. We wandered about for some time in the cool shade of the wood, lunched under the rustling palms, and then drove homeward, stopping for a while by the side of the river, where a pretty cascade rushes over the stones, and a rustic house built for the same memorable occurrence makes a pleasant resting-place. In the afternoon a heavy rain kept us within doors, but we were not sorry, for we were in danger of having a surfeit of pleasure, and quiet was very grateful.

A great part of our last day at Juiz de Fora was spent at the hospitable house of Mr. Halfeld, the German engineer who has gained an honorable distinction by his explorations in the interior. His work on the Rio San Francisco was well known to Mr. Agassiz, so that they found themselves at once on familiar ground, and Mr. Halfeld was able to give him a great deal of valuable information respecting the prospects of the present expedition, especially that department of it which will go to the Amazons by way of the Rio San Francisco and the Tocantins. He has also an interesting collection of objects of natural history, and cordially offered his assistance in obtaining the fishes of the neighborhood. As for the collections, they had been going on famously during our whole visit. We had hardly been in Juiz de Fora twenty-four hours before a dozen collectors were actively at work. All the urchins of the neighborhood and many of the Germans employed on the road lent a helping hand. Even the ladies did their full share, and Mr. Agassiz was indebted to our friend Mrs. K—— for some of the most interesting specimens from this locality. No doubt such as were left of the "bixos" of Juiz de Fora must have congratulated themselves on our departure the following morning.

We enjoyed our return over the same road scarcely less than our first introduction to it; but the latter part of

the day was full of an interest which touched us more
nearly. At Posse, where we had breakfasted on our way
up, Mr. Taylor welcomed us with a Portuguese paper
containing a bulletin announcing the great victories of
the North. Petersburg and Richmond taken, — Lee in
full retreat. — the war virtually over. This was the substance
of the news received with delight and acclamation,
not without tears of gratitude also, and we went on our
way rejoicing. As we drove up to the Hotel Inglez after
dark that evening, hoping to get a glimpse of an American
paper, or at least to have the good news confirmed through
the American Minister, General Webb, whose residence is
at Petropolis, we were greeted by the announcement of the
assassination of Lincoln and Seward, both believed at
this time to be dead. At first it seemed absolutely incredible,
and the more sanguine among us persisted in
regarding it as a gigantic street rumor, invented perhaps
by Secession sympathizers, till on our return to town the
next morning our worst fears were confirmed by the French
steamer just arrived. The days seemed very long till the
next mail, which reassured us somewhat, as it brought
the news of Mr. Seward's probable recovery and strengthened
our faith in the stability of the national character.
All the accounts, public and private, assure us that, though
there is mourning throughout the land, there is no disturbance
of the general regularity and order.

CHAPTER III.

LIFE IN RIO CONTINUED. — FAZENDA LIFE.

BOTAFOGO. — INSANE HOSPITAL. — TIJUCA. — ERRATIC DRIFT. — VEGETATION. — BIRTHDAY DINNER. — ARRANGEMENTS FOR PARTIES TO THE INTERIOR. — PUBLIC LECTURES IN RIO. — PROCESSION OF ST. GEORGE. — LEAVE RIO ON EXCURSION TO THE FORTALEZA DE SANTA ANNA. — LOCALITIES FOR ERRATIC DRIFT BETWEEN RIO AND PETROPOLIS. — DEPARTURE FROM JUIZ DE FORA. — ARRIVAL AT THE FAZENDA. — RIDE IN THE FOREST. — EVE OF SAN JOAÕ. — CUPIM NESTS. — EXCURSION TO THE UPPER FAZENDA — GRAND HUNT. — PICNIC. — COFFEE PLANTATION. — RETURN TO RIO. — MIMIC SNOW-FIELDS. — COFFEE INSECT SPINNING ITS NEST. — VISIT TO THE FAZENDA OF COMMENDADOR BREVES. — BOTANIZING EXCURSION TO TIJUCA. — PREPARATIONS FOR LEAVING RIO. — MAJOR COUTINHO. — COLLEGIO DOM PEDRO SEGUNDO.

May 22d. — This afternoon Dr. and Mrs. C―― and myself went out for a country ramble, somewhat at a venture, it is true, but feeling sure that in the beautiful scenery about Rio we could hardly go amiss. We took one of the many ferry-boats in the neighborhood of our hotel, and presently found ourselves on the way to Botafogo. Almost all the environs of the city are built along beaches; there is the beach or Praia of Botafogo, the Praia of San Christovão, the Praia of San Domingo, and half a dozen others, all of which mean some suburb of the town situated on the shore with a beach in front of it. As it is rather the fashion for the better class of people to live out of town, the houses and gardens in these suburbs are often delightful. We enjoyed the sail exceedingly. For a part of the way the boat keeps close under the mountains, and no description can give an idea of their picturesque outlines, or of the wonderful coloring which softens all their asperities and mellows the whole landscape. We landed at a jetty

Botafogo Bay.

thrown out from a romantic-looking road, and as we found no carriage on the wharf, and ascertained that the boat did not return for two hours, we wandered up this road to see where chance would lead us. The afternoon would have been full of interest had it ended in the walk along the crescent-shaped bay, with the water rippling on the sands, and the mountains opposite all purple in the afternoon sunshine. The road brought us, however, to a magnificent hospital for the insane, the hospital of Dom Pedro Segundo, which we had seen and admired from the deck of the steamer on the day of our arrival. We entered the grounds, and as the great door of the building was open and the official on guard looked by no means forbidding, we ascended the steps and went in. It is difficult to imagine an edifice more appropriate for the purpose to which it is devoted. It is true we saw only the public rooms and corridors, as a permit was required to enter the wards; but a plan hanging near the entrance gave us an idea of the arrangement of the building, and its general aspect bore testimony to the cleanliness, cheerfulness, and order of the establishment. Some of the public rooms were very handsome, — especially one, at the end of which stands a statue of the boy Emperor, taken, no doubt, at the time of his coronation. In the man of forty you still recognize the frank, intelligent, manly face of the lad on whom such great responsibility was thrown at the age of fifteen. As we went up the spacious staircase, the sound of music brought us to the door of the chapel, where the evening service was going on. Patients and nurses were kneeling together; a choir of female voices was singing sweetly a calm, peaceful kind of music; that somewhat monotonous chanting, so passionless in its regular movement, which one hears in the Catholic Church; the candles were burning before the altar, but the great window just outside the door was open to the setting sun, and, as I stood in the balcony looking out on the mountains and listening to the music, I thought that a mind which had gone astray might find its way back again in such scenes and under such influences. Certainly, if nature has any healing power, it must be felt here. We lingered and listened as long as we dared, and stole away as the services were closing, just in time to take the evening boat.

May 25th. — The fish-market is, in all seaport towns, a favorite haunt with Mr. Agassiz, and here it has an especial interest for him on account of the variety and beauty of the fishes brought in every morning. I sometimes accompany him in these rambles for the pleasure of seeing the fresh loads of oranges, flowers, and vegetables, and of watching the picturesque negro groups selling their wares or sitting about in knots to gossip. We have already learned that the fine-looking athletic negroes of a nobler type, at least physically, than any we see in the States, are the so-called Mina negroes, from the province of Mina, in Western Africa. They are a very powerful-looking race, and the women especially are finely made and have quite a dignified presence. I am never tired of watching them in the street and market, where they are to be seen in numbers, being more commonly employed as venders of fruit and vegetables than as house-servants. It is said that a certain wild and independent element in their character makes them unfit for domestic service. The women always wear a high muslin turban, and a long, bright-colored shawl, either crossed on the breast and thrown carelessly over the

Minn Negress.

shoulder, or, if the day be chilly, drawn closely around them, their arms hidden in its folds. The amount of expression they throw into the use of this shawl is quite amazing. I watched a tall, superbly made woman in the street to-day who was in a great passion. Gesticulating violently, she flung her shawl wide, throwing out both arms, then, drawing it suddenly in, folded it about her, and stretched herself to her full height; presently opening it once more, she shook her fist in the face of her opponent,

Mina Negress and Child.

and then, casting one end of her long drapery over her shoulder, stalked away with the air of a tragedy queen. It serves as a cradle also, for, tying it loosely round their hips, they slip the baby into the folds behind, and there it hangs, rocked to sleep by the mother's movement as she walks on with her long, swinging tread. The Mina negress is almost invariably remarkable for her beautiful hand and arm. She seems to be conscious of this, and usually wears close-fitting bracelets at the wrist, made of some bright-colored beads, which set off the form of the hand and are exceedingly becoming on her dark, shining skin. These negroes are Mohammedans, and are said to remain faithful to their prophet, though surrounded by the observances of the Catholic Church. They do not seem to me so affable and responsive as the Congo negroes, but are, on the contrary, rather haughty. One morning I came upon a cluster of them in the market breakfasting after their work was done, and I stopped to talk with them, asking what they had for breakfast, and trying various subjects on which to open an acquaintance. But they looked at me coldly and suspiciously, barely answering my questions, and were evidently relieved when I walked away.

May 26*th*. — Tijuca. In the pleasant environs of Rio there is no resort more frequented than the establishment of Mr. Bennett at Tijuca, and we were not sorry the day before yesterday to leave the hot, dusty city, with a pleasant party of friends, for this cluster of mountains, some eighteen hundred feet above the sea level and about eight miles from Rio. It takes its name from the peak of Tijuca, so conspicuous an object in the coast range. On our arrival we were very cordially welcomed by our host himself, who was not quite a stranger to us, for Mr. Agassiz has been already indebted to him for valuable collections. Mr. Bennett has an Englishman's love of nature, and is very familiar with the botany and zoölogy of the beautiful region which has been his home for many years. Under his guidance, we have taken a number of pleasant rambles and rides, regretting only that we cannot avail ourselves for a longer time of his intimate knowledge of the locality and its productions.

I have alluded before to the perplexing character of the

geology, and the almost universal decomposition of the rock surfaces, making it difficult to decipher them. The presence of the drift phenomena, so universal in the Northern hemisphere, has been denied here; but, in his long walk to-day, Mr. Agassiz has had an opportunity of observing a great number of erratic boulders, having no connection with the rocks in place, and also a sheet of drift studded with boulders and resting above the partially stratified metamorphic rock in immediate contact with it. I introduce here a letter written by him to his friend, Professor Peirce of Harvard University, under the first impression of the day's experience, which will best explain his view of the subject.

"May 27th, 1865, Tijuca.

"My dear Peirce: —

"Yesterday was one of the happiest days of my life, and I want to share it with you. Here I am at Tijuca, a cluster of hills, about eighteen hundred feet high and some seven or eight miles from Rio, in a charming cottage-like hotel, from the terrace of which you see a drift hill with innumerable erratic boulders, as characteristic as any I have ever seen in New England. I had before seen sundry unmistakable traces of drift, but there was everywhere connected with the drift itself such an amount of decomposed rocks of various kinds, that, though I could see the drift and distinguish it from the decomposed primary rocks in place, on account of my familiarity with that kind of deposits, yet I could probably never have satisfied anybody else that there is here an equivalent of the Northern drift, had I not found yesterday, near Bennett's hotel at Tijuca, the most palpable superposition of drift and decomposed rocks, with a distinct line of demarcation between the two, of which I shall secure a good photograph. This locality afforded me at once an opportunity of contrasting the decomposed rocks which form a characteristic feature of the whole country (as far as I have yet seen it) with the superincumbent drift, and of making myself familiar with the peculiarities of both deposits; so that I trust I shall be able hereafter to distinguish both, whether they are in contact with one another or found separately. These decomposed rocks are quite a new feature to me in the structure of the country. Imagine granite, gneiss, mica slate, clay slate, and in fact all the various kinds of rocks usually found in old metamorphic formations, reduced to the condition of a soft paste, exhibiting all the mineralogical elements of the rocks, as they may have been before they were decomposed, but now completely disintegrated and resting side by side, as if they had been accumulated artificially in the manner you have seen glass cylinders filled with variously colored sands or clays to imitate the appearance of the beds of Gay-Head. And through this loose mass there run, here and there, larger or smaller dikes of quartz-rock or of granite or other rocks equally disintegrated; but they retain the arrangement of their materials, showing them to be disintegrated dikes in large disintegrated masses of rock; the whole passing unmistakably to rocks of the same kind in which the decomposition or disintegration is only partial, or no trace of it visible, and the whole mass exhibiting then the appearance of an ordinary metamorphic set of rocks.

"That such masses forming everywhere the surface of the country should be a great obstacle to the study of the erratic phenomena is at once plain, and I do not therefore wonder that those who seem familiar with the country should now entertain the idea that the surface rocks are everywhere decomposed, and that there is no erratic formation or drift here. But upon close examination it is easy to perceive that, while the decomposed rocks consist of small particles of the primitive rocks which they represent, with their dikes and all other characteristic features, there is not a trace of larger or smaller boulders in them; while the superincumbent drift, consisting of a similar paste, does not show the slightest sign of the indistinct stratification characteristic of the decomposed metamorphic rocks below it, nor any of the decomposed dikes, but is full of various kinds of boulders of various dimensions. I have not yet traced the boulders to their origin; but the majority consist of a kind of greenstone composed of equal amounts of a greenish black hornblende and feldspar. In Entre Rios on the Parahyba, I was told by an engineer on the road that in Minas Geräes iron mines are worked in a rock like these boulders. This week I propose to explore the Serra da Mantiqueira,* which separates the province of Rio from Minas, and may advance the question further. But you see that I need not go to the Andes to find erratics, though it may yet be necessary for me to go, in order to trace the evidence of glacier action in the accumulation of this drift; for you will notice that I have only given you the evidence of extensive accumulations of drift similar in its characteristics to Northern drift. But I have not yet seen a trace of glacial action properly speaking, if polished surfaces and scratches and furrows are especially to be considered as such.

"The decomposition of the surface rocks to the extent to which it takes place here is very remarkable, and points

* Mr. Agassiz was prevented from making this excursion.

to a new geological agency, thus far not discussed in our geological theories. It is obvious here (and to-day with the pouring rain which keeps me in doors I have satisfactory evidence of it) that the warm rains falling upon the heated soil must have a very powerful action in accelerating the decomposition of rocks. It is like torrents of hot water falling for ages in succession upon hot stones. Think of the effect, and, instead of wondering at the large amount of decomposed rocks which you meet everywhere, you will be surprised that there are any rocks left in their primitive condition. It is, however, the fact, that all the rocks you see are encased, as it were, in a lining of the decomposed part of their surface; they are actually covered with a rotten crust of their own substance.

" Ever truly yours,
" L. Agassiz."

Among the objects of special interest which we have seen here for the first time are the colossal fruits of the Sapucaia-tree, a species of Lecythis, belonging to the same family as the Brazilian nuts. These fruits, of which there are a number of species, vary from the size of an apple to that of an ordinary melon; they resemble an urn closed with a lid, and contain about fifty seeds as large as almonds. The woods all over these Tijuca hills are beautiful and wonderfully luxuriant; but I lack names for the various trees. We are not yet familiar enough with the aspect of the forest to distinguish readily its different forms of vegetation; and it is besides exceedingly difficult here to ascertain the common names of plants. The Brazilians do not seem to me observant of nature in its details; at all events, I never get a satisfactory answer to the question I am constantly putting, "What do you call this tree or flower?" And if you ask a botanist, he invariably gives you the scientific, not the popular name, nor does he seem to be aware that any such exists. I have a due respect for nomenclature, but when I inquire the name of some very graceful tree or some exquisite flower, I like to receive a manageable answer, something that may fitly be introduced into the privacy of domestic life, rather than the ponderous official Latin appellation. We are struck with the variety of Melastomas in full flower now, and very conspicuous, from their large purple blossoms, and have remarked also several species of the Bombaceæ, easily distinguished by their peculiar foliage and large cotton fruits. The Candelabra-tree (Cecropia) is abundant here, as throughout the neighborhood of Rio, and is covered at this season with fruit resembling somewhat the fruit of the bread-tree, but more slender and cylindrical in form. Large Euphorbias, of the size of forest-trees, also attract our attention, for it is the first time we have seen them except as shrubs, such as the "Estrella do Norte" (Poinsettia). But there is before Mr. Bennett's house a very large nut-tree, "Nogueira," of this family. The palms are numerous; among them the Astrocaryum Cari, whose spiny stems and leaves make it difficult to approach, is very common. Its bunches of bright chestnut-brown fruit hang from between the leaves which form its crown, each bunch about a foot in length, massive and compact, like a large cluster of black Hamburg grapes. The Syagrus palm is also frequent; it has a greenish fruit not unlike the olive in appearance, also hanging in large pendent bunches just below the leaves. The mass of foliage is everywhere knit together by parasitic vines without number, and every dead branch or fallen trunk is overgrown by parasites. Foreign tropical trees are cultivated about the houses everywhere, — bread-fruit

Fallen Trunk overgrown by Parasites.

trees and Ameixas, a kind of plum of the hawthorn family, bananas, etc. The bamboo of the East Indies also is used to form avenues in Rio de Janeiro and its environs. The alleys of bamboo in the grounds of the palace at San Christovão are among its most beautiful ornaments.

Mr. Agassiz has been surprised to find that shrimps of considerable size are common in all the brooks and even in the highest pools of Tijuca. It seems strange to meet with Crustacea of marine forms in mountain streams.

To-day we are kept in the house by a violent rain, but there is enough to do in looking over specimens, working up journals, writing letters, &c., to prevent the time from hanging heavy on our hands. To-morrow we return to town.

May 28th, Rio. — To-day is Mr. Agassiz's birthday, and it has been so affectionately remembered here that it is difficult to believe ourselves in a foreign country. The Swiss citizens gave him a dinner yesterday on the eve of the anniversary, where everything recalled the land of his birth, without excluding the land of his adoption. The room was draped with the flags of all the Cantons, while the ceiling was covered by two Swiss national flags, united in the centre just above his own seat by the American flag, thus recognizing at once his Swiss nationality and his American citizenship.* The Brazilian flag which gave them all hospitality and protection had also an honored place. The fête is reported to have been most genial and gay, closing with a number of student songs in which all bore their share, and succeeded by a serenade under our windows. To-day our room is festive with flowers and other decorations, and friendly greetings on every side remind us that, though in a foreign land, we are not among strangers.

June 14th. — Since our return from Tijuca we have been almost constantly in town, Mr. Agassiz being engaged, often from early morning till deep into the night, in taking care of the specimens which come in from every quarter, and making the final preparations for the parties which he intends sending into the interior. The most important of these, or rather the one for which it is most difficult to procure the necessary facilities, is bound for the upper course of the San Francisco. At this point one or more of their number will strike across the country to

---

* Though a resident of the United States for nearly twenty years, Mr. Agassiz was only naturalized in 1863. At the moment when a general distrust of our institutions prevailed in Europe, it was a satisfaction to him to testify by some personal and public act his confidence in them.

the Tocantins, and descend that river to the Amazons, while the others will follow the valley of the Piauhy to the coast. This is a long, difficult, but, as we are assured, not a dangerous journey for young and vigorous men. But wishing to anticipate every trouble that may befall them, Mr. Agassiz has made it his business to ascertain, as far as possible, the nature of the route, and to obtain letters to the most influential people for every step of the road. This has been no light task; in a country where there are no established means of internal communication, where mules, guides, camaradas, and even an armed escort may be necessary, and must be provided for in advance, the preparation for a journey through the interior requires a vast deal of forethought. Add to this the national habit of procrastination, the profound conviction of the Brazilian that to-morrow is better than to-day, and one may understand how it happens that, although it has been a primary object since our arrival to expedite the party to the Tocantins, their departure has been delayed till now. And yet it would be the height of ingratitude to give the impression that there has been any backwardness on the part of the Brazilians themselves, or of their government, to facilitate the objects of the expedition. On the contrary, they not only show a warm interest, but the utmost generosity, and readiness to give all the practical aid in their power. Several leading members of the Cabinet, the Senate, and the House of Representatives have found time now, when they have a war upon their hands, and when one ministry has been going out and another coming in, not only to prepare the necessary introductions for these parties from Rio to the Amazons, but also to write out the routes, giving the most important directions and information for the separate journeys.* Yet with the best will in the world the Brazilians know comparatively little of the interior of their own country. It is necessary to collect all that is known from a variety of sources, and then to combine it as well as may be, so as to form an organized plan. Even then a great deal must be left to be decided in accordance with circumstances which no one can foresee. No pains have been spared to anticipate all the probable difficulties, and to provide for them as far as it is humanly possible to do so; and we feel that this journey, a part of which has been made by very few persons before, has never been undertaken under better auspices. This party will explore the upper course of the Rio Doce, the Rio das Velhas, and the San Francisco, with the lower course of the Tocantins and its tributaries, as far as they can; making also collections of fossils in certain regions upon the route. Another party, starting at about the same time, is to keep nearer the coast, exploring the lower course of the Rio Doce and the San Francisco. Mr. Agassiz thus hopes to make at least a partial survey of this great water system, while he himself undertakes the Amazons and its tributaries.† In the mean time, the result of the weeks he has been obliged to spend in Rio, while organizing the work of these parties and making the practical arrangements for its prosecution, has been very satisfactory. The collections are large, and will give a tolerably complete idea of the fauna of this province, as well as a part of

* A short account of these explorations may be found at the end of the volume — L. A.

† I am particularly indebted to Senator Th. Ottoni, Baron de Prados, Senator Pompeo, Senator Paranagua, Senhor Paula Souza, and Senhor J. B. da Fonseca, for information, maps, and other documents relative to the regions intended to be explored by my young friends and myself. — L. A.

that of Minas Geräes. A survey of the Dom Pedro Railroad, made under his direction by his two young friends, Messrs. Hart and St. John, is also an excellent beginning of the work in this department, and his own observations on the drift phenomena have an important bearing on the great questions on which he hoped to throw new light in coming here. The closing words of a lecture delivered by him last evening at the Collegio Dom Pedro Segundo will best express his own estimation of the facts he has collected in their bearing on the drift phenomena in other parts of the world. After giving some account of the erratic blocks and drift observed by him at Tijuca and already described in his letter to Mr. Peirce, he added: "I wish here to make a nice distinction that I may not be misunderstood. I *affirm* that the erratic phenomena, viz. erratic drift, in immediate superposition with partially decomposed stratified rock, exist here in your immediate neighborhood: I *believe* that these phenomena are connected, here as elsewhere, with the action of ice. It is nevertheless possible that a more intimate study of these subjects in tropical regions may reveal some phase of the phenomena not hitherto observed, just as the investigation of the glacial action in the United States has shown that immense masses of ice may move over a plain, as well as over a mountain slope. Let me now urge a special study of these facts upon the young geologists of Rio, as they have never been investigated and their presence is usually denied. If you ask me, 'To what end?—of what use is such a discovery?'—I answer, It is given to no mortal man to predict what may be the result of any discovery in the realms of nature. When the electric current was discovered, what was it?

A curiosity. When the first electric machine was invented, to what use was it put? To make puppets dance for the amusement of children. To-day it is the most powerful engine of civilization. But should our work have no other result than this, — to know that certain facts in nature are thus and not otherwise, that their causes were such and no others, — this result in itself is good enough, and great enough, since the end of man, his aim, his glory, is the knowledge of the truth."

One word upon these lectures, since we are told by the Brazilians themselves that the introduction of public lectures among them is a novelty and in a certain sense an era in their educational history. If any subject of science or letters is to be presented to the public here, it is done under special conditions before a selected audience, where the paper is read in presence of the Emperor with all due solemnity. Popular instruction, with admittance for all who care to listen or to learn, has been hitherto a thing unknown. The suggestion was made by Dr. Pacheco, the Director of the Collegio Dom Pedro II., a man of liberal culture and great intelligence, who has already done much for the progress of education in Rio de Janeiro; it found favor with the Emperor, who is keenly alive to anything which can stimulate the love of knowledge among his people, and at his request Mr. Agassiz has given a course of lectures in French on a variety of scientific subjects. He was indeed very glad to have an opportunity of introducing here a means of popular education which he believes to have been very salutary in its influence among us. At first the presence of ladies was objected to, as too great an innovation on national habits; but even that was overcome, and the doors were opened to all comers, the lectures being given after the true New England fashion. I must say that, if the absolutely uninterrupted attention of an audience is any test of its intelligence, no man could ask a better one than that which Mr. Agassiz has had the pleasure of addressing in Rio de Janeiro. It has also been a great pleasure to him, after teaching for nearly twenty years in English, to throw off the fetters of a foreign tongue and speak again in French. After all, with a few exceptions, a man's native language remains for him the best; it is the element in which he always moves most at ease.

The Emperor, with his family, has been present at all these lectures, and it is worthy of note, as showing the simplicity of his character, that, instead of occupying the raised platform intended for them, he caused the chairs to be placed on a level with the others, as if to show that in science at least there is no distinction of rank.*

June 11*th*. — To-day has been a festa, but one the significance of which it is somewhat difficult to understand, so singularly is the religious element mingled with the grotesque and quaint. In the Church it is the feast of Corpus Christi, but it happens to fall on the same date as another festival in honor of St. George, which is kept with all sorts of antique ceremonies. I went in the morning with our young friend, Mr. T——, to the Imperial chapel, where high mass was celebrated, and at the close of the services we had some difficulty in finding our way back to the hotel, before which the procession was to pass, for the street was already draped with all sorts of gay colors

---

* Since it was reported in the newspapers that the proceeds of these lectures were devoted to the expedition, it may be well to mention here that they were free, given simply at the request of the Emperor, and open to all without charge.

and crowded with spectators. First in order came the religious part of the procession; a long array of priests and church officials carrying lighted candles, pyramids of flowers, banners, &c. Then came the host, under a canopy of white satin and gold, supported by massive staffs; the bearers were the highest dignitaries of the land, first among them being the Emperor himself and his son-in-law, the Duke of Saxe. In strange contrast with these solemnities was the stuffed equestrian figure of St. George, a huge, unwieldy shape on horseback, preceded and followed by riders almost as grotesque as himself. With him came a number of orders resembling, if not the same as, the Free-Masons, the Odd Fellows, and like societies. The better educated Brazilians speak of this procession as an old legacy from Portugal, which has lost its significance for them, and which they would gladly see pass out of use, as it is already out of date.

This evening Mr. Agassiz gave the closing lecture of his course. It is to be followed next week by a lecture from Dr. Capanema, the Brazilian geologist, and there will be an attempt made to organize courses of public lectures on the same plan hereafter. Our numbers are gradually diminishing. Last week the party for the interior, consisting of Messrs. St. John, Allen, Ward, and Sceva, started, and Messrs. Hartt and Copeland leave in a day or two to undertake an exploration of the coast between the Parahyba do Sul and Bahia.

June 30*th*. — On the 21st we left Rio on our way to the province of Minas Geräes, where we were to pass a week at the coffee fazenda of Senhor Lage, who received us so courteously on our former visit to Juiz de Fora, and who was so influential in projecting and carrying out the Union and Industry road. The journey to Juiz de Fora, though we had made it once before, had lost nothing of its beauty by familiarity, and had gained in interest of another kind; for his examination of the erratic drift at Tijuca has given Mr. Agassiz the key to the geological constitution of the soil, and what seemed to him quite inexplicable on our first excursion over this road is now perfectly legible. It is interesting to watch the progress of an investigation of this character, and to see how the mental process gradually clears away the obscurity. The perception becomes sharpened by dwelling upon the subject, and the mind adapts itself to a difficult problem as the eye adapts itself to darkness. That which was confused at first presently becomes clear to the mental vision of the observer, who watches and waits for the light to enter. There is one effect of the atmospheric influence here, already alluded to in the previous pages, which at first sight is very deceptive. Wherever there is any cut through drift, unless recently opened, it becomes baked at the surface so as to simulate stone in such a way as hardly to be distinguished from the decomposed rock surfaces in place, unless by a careful examination. This, together with the partial obliteration of the stratification in many places, makes it, at first glance, difficult to recognize the point of contact between the stratified rock and the drift resting above it. A little familiarity with these deceptive appearances, however, makes it as easy to read the broken leaves of the book of nature here as elsewhere, and Mr. Agassiz has now no more difficulty in following the erratic phenomena in these Southern regions than in the Northern hemisphere. All that is wanting to complete the evidence of the actual presence of ice here, in former times, is the glacial writing, the striæ and furrows and polish which mark its track in the temperate zone. These one can hardly hope to find where the rock is of so perishable a character and its disintegration so rapid. But this much is certain,— a sheet of drift covers the country, composed of a homogeneous paste without trace of stratification, containing loose materials of all sorts and sizes, imbedded in it without reference to weight, large boulders, smaller stones, pebbles, and the like. This drift is very unevenly distributed; sometimes rising into high hills, owing to the surrounding denudations; sometimes covering the surface merely as a thin layer; sometimes, and especially on steep slopes, washed completely away, leaving the bare face of the rock; sometimes deeply gullied, so as to produce a succession of depressions and elevations alternating with each other. To this latter cause is due, in great degree, the billowy, undulating character of the valleys. Another cause of difficulty in tracing the erratic phenomena consists in the number of detached fragments which have fallen from the neighboring heights. It is not always easy to distinguish these from the erratic boulders. But a number of localities exist, nevertheless, where the drift rests immediately above stratified rock, with the boulders protruding from it, the line of contact being perfectly distinct. It is a curious fact, that one may follow the drift everywhere in this region by the prosperous coffee plantations. Here as elsewhere ice has been the great fertilizer,— a gigantic plough grinding the rocks to powder and making a homogeneous soil in which the greatest variety of chemical elements are brought together from distant localities. So far as we have followed these phenomena in the provinces of Rio and Minas Geraës, the thriving coffee plantations are upon erratic drift, the poorer growth upon decomposed rock in place. Upon remarking this, we were told that the farmers who are familiar with the soil select that in which they find loose rocks imbedded, because it is the most fertile. They unconsciously seek the erratic drift. It may not be amiss to point out some of the localities in which these geological phenomena may be most readily studied, since they lie along the public road, and are easy of access. The drift is very evident in the swamp between Mauá and Raiz da Serra on the way to Petropolis. In ascending the Serra at the half-way house there is an excellent locality for observing drift and boulders; and beyond one may follow the drift up to the very top of the road. The whole tract between Villa Theresa and Petropolis is full of drift. Just outside of Petropolis, the Piabanha has excavated its bed in drift, while the banks have been ravined by the rains. At the station of Correio, in front of the building, is also an admirable opportunity for observing all the erratic phenomena, for here the drift, with large boulders interspersed throughout the mass, overlies the rock in place. A few steps to the north of the station Pedro do Rio there is another great accumulation of large boulders in drift. These are but a few of the localities where such facts may be observed.

On the evening of the 22d we arrived at Juiz de Fora, and started at sunrise the next morning for the fazenda of Senhor Lage, some thirty miles beyond. We had a gay party, consisting of the family of Senhor Lage and that of his brother-in-law, Senhor Machado, with one or two other friends and ourselves. The children were as merry as possible, for a visit to the fazenda was a rarity, and looked upon by them as a great festivity. To transport us all with our luggage, two large coaches were provided, several mules, and a small carriage, while a travelling photographic machine, belonging to Senhor Machado, who is an admirable photographist, brought up the rear.* The day was beautiful and our road lay along the side of the Serra, commanding fine views of the inland country and the coffee plantations which covered the hillsides wherever the primeval forest had been cut down. The road is another evidence of the intelligence and energy of the proprietor. The old roads are mere mule tracks up one side of the Serra and down the other, gullied of course by all the heavy rains and rendered at times almost impassable. Senhor Lage has shown his neighbors what may be done for their comfort in a country life by abandoning the old method, and, instead of carrying the road across the mountain, cutting it in the side with so gradual an ascent as to make the ride a very easy one. It is but a four hours' drive now from Juiz de Fora to the fazenda, whereas, until the last year, it was a day's, or even in bad weather a two days' journey on horseback. It is much to be desired that his example should be followed, for the absence of any tolerable roads in the country makes travelling in the interior almost an impossibility, and is the most serious obstacle to the general progress and prosperity. It seems strange that the governments of the different provinces, at least of the more populous ones, such as Minas Geräes and Rio, should not organize a system of good highways for the greater facility of commerce. The present mode of transportation on mule back is slow and cumbrous

---

* Mr. Agassiz was indebted to Senhor Machado for a valuable series of photographs and stereoscopic views of this region, begun on this excursion and completed during our absence in the North of Brazil.

Fazenda de Santa Anna in Minas Geraes

in the highest degree; it would seem as if, where the produce of the interior is so valuable, good roads would pay for themselves very soon.

At about eleven o'clock we arrived at the "Fazenda," the long, low, white buildings of which enclosed an oblong, open space divided into large squares, where the coffee was drying. Only a part of this extensive building is occupied as the living rooms of the family; the rest is devoted to all sorts of objects connected with the care of the coffee, provision for the negroes, and the like.

When we reached the plantation the guests had not all arrived. The special occasion of this excursion to the fazenda was the festival of San João, kept always with great ceremonies in the country; the whole week was to be devoted to hunting, and Senhor Lage had invited all the best sportsmen in the neighborhood to join in the chase. It will be seen in the end that these hunters formed themselves into a most valuable corps of collectors for Mr. Agassiz. After an excellent breakfast we started on horseback for the forest with such of the company as had already assembled. The ride through the dense, deep, quiet wood was beautiful; and the dead pause when some one thought the game was near, the hushed voices, the breathless waiting for the shot which announced success or failure, only added a charm to the scene. They have a strange way of hunting here; as the forest is perfectly impenetrable, they scatter food in a cleared space for the animals, and build green screens, leaving holes to look through; behind such a screen the hunter waits and watches for hours perhaps, till the paca, or peccary, or capivara steals out to feed. The ladies dismounted and found a cool seat in one of these forest lodges, where they waited for the hunt. No great success, after all, this afternoon, but some birds which were valuable as specimens. We rode home in the evening to a late dinner, after which an enormous bonfire, built by the negroes in honor of the Eve of St. João, was lighted in front of the house. The scene was exceedingly picturesque, the whole establishment, the neighboring negro huts, and the distant forest being illuminated by the blaze, around which the blacks were dancing, accompanying their wild gestures with song and drum. Every now and then a burst of fireworks added new brightness to the picture.

The next day, the 24th, began with a long ride on horseback before breakfast, after which I accompanied Mr. Agassiz on a sort of exploration among the Cupim nests (the nests of the Termites). These are mounds sometimes three or four or even six feet high, and from two to three or four feet in diameter, of an extraordinary solidity, almost as hard as rock. Senhor Lage sent with us several negroes carrying axes to split them open, which, with all their strength, proved no easy task. These nests appear usually to have been built around some old trunk or root as a foundation; the interior, with its endless serpentine passages, looked not unlike the convolutions of a meandrina or brain coral; the walls of the passages seemed to be built of earth that had been chewed or kneaded in some way, giving them somewhat the consistency of paper. The interior was quite soft and brittle, so that as soon as the negroes could break through the outer envelope, about six inches in thickness, the whole structure readily fell to pieces. It had no opening outside, but we found, on uprooting one of these edifices from the bottom, that the whole base was perforated with holes leading into the ground beneath. The interior of all of them swarmed with the different kinds of inhabitants; the little white ones, the larger black ones with brown heads and powerful forceps, and in each were found one or two very large swollen white ones, quite different in dimensions and appearance from the rest, probably the queens. With the assistance of the negroes, Mr. Agassiz made, for future examination, a large collection of all the different kinds of individuals thus living together in various numeric proportions, and he would gladly have carried away one of the nests, but they are too cumbersome for transportation. The Cupim nests are very different from the dwellings of the Sauba ants, which have large external openings. The latter make houses by excavating, and sometimes undermine a hill so extensively, with their long galleries, that when a fire is lighted at one of the entrances to exterminate them, the smoke issues at numerous openings, distant perhaps a quarter of a mile from each other, showing in how many directions they have tunnelled out the hill, and that their winding passages communicate with each other throughout. So many travellers have given accounts of these ant-houses, and of the activity of their inhabitants in stripping and carrying off the leaves of trees to deposit them in their habitations, that it hardly seems worth while to repeat the story. Yet no one can see without astonishment one of these ant-armies travelling along the road they have worn so neatly for themselves, those who are coming from the trees looking like a green procession, almost hidden by the fragments of leaves they carry on their backs, while the returning troops, who have already deposited their burden, are hurrying back for more. There seems to be another set of individuals running to and fro,

5 *

whose office is not quite so clear, unless it be to marshal the whole swarm and act as a kind of police. This view is confirmed by an anecdote related by an American resident here, who told us that he once saw an ant, returning without his load to the house, stopped by one of these anomalous individuals, severely chastised and sent back to the tree apparently to do his appointed task. The Sauba ants are very injurious to the coffee shrubs, and difficult to exterminate.*

In the afternoon, the hunters of the neighborhood began to come in and the party was considerably enlarged. (This fazenda life, at least on an informal jovial occasion like this, has a fascinating touch of the Middle Ages in it.) I am always reminded of this when we assemble for dinner in the large dimly lighted hall, where a long table, laden with game and with large haunches of meat, stands ready for the miscellaneous company, daily growing in numbers. At the upper end sit the family with their immediate guests; below, with his family, is the "Administrador," whose office I suppose corresponds to that of overseer on a Southern plantation. In this instance he is a large picturesque-looking man, generally equipped in a kind of gray blouse strapped around the waist by a broad black belt, in which are powder-flask and knife, with a bugle slung over his shoulder, a slouched hat, and high top-boots. During dinner a number of chance cavaliers drop in, entirely without ceremony, in hunter's costume, as they return from the chase. Then at night, or rather early in the morning, (for the Brazilian habit is "early to bed and early to rise," in order to avoid the heat,) what jollity and song, sounding

---

* The most complete account of these curious animals is to be found in Bates's "Naturalist on the Amazons."

the bugles long before the dawn, twanging the guitar and whistling on the peculiar instrument used here to call the game. Altogether it is the most novel and interesting collection of social elements, mingling after a kind of picnic fashion without the least formality, and we feel every day how much we owe to our kind hosts for admitting us to an occasion where one sees so much of what is national and characteristic. The next day we went to breakfast at a smaller fazenda belonging also to Senhor Lage, higher up on the Serra da Babylonia. Again, starting before sunrise, we went slowly up the mountain, the summit of which is over 3,000 feet above the sea level. We were preceded by the "liteira," a queer kind of car slung between two mules, in which rode the grandmamma and the baby; as carriages are impossible on these mountain roads, some such conveyance is necessary for those who are too old or too young for horseback travelling. The view was lovely, the morning cool and beautiful, and after a two hours' ride we arrived at the upper fazenda. Here we left our horses and went on foot into the forest, where the ladies and children wandered about, gathering flowers and exploring the wood walks, while the gentlemen occupied themselves with fishing and hunting till midday, when we returned to the house to breakfast. The result of the chase was a monkey, two caititú (wild pigs), and a great variety of birds, all of which went to swell the scientific collections.* We returned to dine at

* I was especially interested in examining the vegetable productions of a little lake, hardly larger than a mill-pond, near this fazenda. It was strange to see Potamogeton and Myriophyllum, plants which we associate exclusively with the fresh waters of the temperate zone, growing in the shadow of tropical forests where monkeys have their home. Such combinations are very puzzling to the student of the laws of geographical distribution. — L. A.

the lower fazenda, and all retired soon after, for the next day the great hunt of the week would take place, and we were to be early astir.

At dawn the horses were at the door, and we were mounting the Serra before sunrise. We were bound to a fazenda on the Serra da Babylonia, some two leagues from the one at which we were staying, and on higher ground, too high indeed for the culture of coffee, and devoted to pasture land. It is here that Senhor Lage has his horses and cattle. The ride along the zigzag road winding up the Serra was delightful in the early morning. The clouds were flushed with the dawn; the distant hills and the forest, spreading endlessly beneath us, glowed in the sunrise. The latter part of the road lay mostly through the woods, and brought us out, after some two hours' ride, on the brow of a hill overlooking a small lake, sunk in a cup-like depression of the mountain, just beyond which was the fazenda. The scenic effect was very pretty, for the border of the lake was ornamented with flags, and on its waters floated a little miniature steamer with the American flag at one end and the Brazilian at the other. Our host invited us to ride in at the gate of the fazenda, in advance of the rest of our cavalcade, a request which we understood when, as we passed the entrance, the little steamer put into shore, and, firing a salute in our honor, showed its name, AGASSIZ, in full. It was a pleasant surprise very successfully managed. After the little excitement of this incident was over, we went to the house to tie up our riding-habits and prepare for the woods. We then embarked in the newly-christened boat and crossed the lake to a forest on the other side. Here were rustic tables and seats arranged under a tent where we were to breakfast;

but while the meal was making ready and a fire building for the boiling of coffee, the stewing of chicken, rice, and other creature comforts, we wandered at will in the wood. This was the most beautiful, because the wildest and most primitive, specimen of tropical forest we have yet seen. I think no description prepares one for the difference between this forest and our own, even though the latter be the " forest primeval." It is not merely the difference of the vegetation, but the impenetrability of the mass here that makes the density, darkness, and solemnity of the woods so impressive. It seems as if the mode of growth — many of the trees shooting up to an immense height, but branching only toward the top — were meant to give room to the legion of parasites, sipos, lianas, and climbing plants of all kinds which fill the intervening spaces. There is one fact which makes the study of the tropical forest as interesting to the geologist as to the botanist, namely, its relation to the vegetable world of past ages hidden in the rocks. The tree-ferns, the Chamærops, the Pandanus, the Araucarias, are all modern representatives of past types, and this walk in the forest was an important one to Mr. Agassiz, because he made out one of those laws of growth which unite the past and the present. The Chamærops is a palm belonging to the ancient vegetable world, but having its representatives in our days. The modern Chamærops, with its fan-like leaves spreading on one level, stands structurally lower than the Palms with pinnate leaves, which belong almost exclusively to our geological age, and have numerous leaflets arranged along either side of a central axis. The young Palms were exceedingly numerous, springing up at every step upon our path, some of them not more than two inches high, while their elders towered fifty feet above them. Mr. Agassiz gathered and examined great numbers of them, and found that the young Palms, to whatever genus they may belong, invariably resemble the Chamærops, having their leaves extending fan-like on one plane, instead of being scattered along a central axis, as in the adult tree. The infant Palm is in fact the mature Chamærops in miniature, showing that among plants as among animals, at least in some instances, there is a correspondence between the youngest stages of growth in the higher species of a given type and the earliest introduction of that type on earth.*

At the close of our ramble, from which the Professor returned looking not unlike an ambulatory representative of tropical vegetation, being loaded down with palm-branches, tree-ferns, and the like, we found breakfast awaiting us. Some of our party were missing, however, the hunters having already taken their stations at some distance near the water. The game was an Anta (Tapir), a curious animal, abounding in the woods of this region. It has a special interest for the naturalist, because it resembles certain ancient mammalia now found only among the fossils, just as the tree-fern, Chamærops, &c. resemble past vegetable types. Although Mr. Agassiz had seen it in confinement, he had a great desire to observe it in action under its natural condition, and in the midst of a tropical forest as characteristic of old geological times as the creature itself. It was, in fact, to gratify this desire that Mr. Lage had planned the hunt. "L'homme propose et Dieu dispose," however, and, as the sequel will show,

* In the same way, it may be said that in its incipient growth the Dicotyledonous Plant exhibits, in the structure of its germinative leaves, the characteristic features of Monocotyledonous Plants. — L. A.

we were not destined to see an Anta this day. The forest being, as I have said, impenetrable to the hunter, except where paths have been cut, the game is roused by sending the dogs into the wood, the sportsmen stationing themselves at certain distances on the outskirts. The Anta has his haunts near lakes or rivers, and when wearied and heated with the chase he generally makes for the water, and, springing in, is shot as he swims across. As we were lingering over the breakfast-table we heard the shout of Anta! Anta! In an instant every man sprang to his gun and ran down to the water-side, while we all stood waiting, listening to the cries of the dogs, now frantic with excitement, and expecting every moment the rush of the hunted animal and his spring into the lake. But it was a false alarm; the cries of the dogs died away in the distance: the day was colder than usual, the Anta turned back from the water, and, leading his pursuers a weary chase, was lost in the forest. After a time the dogs returned, looking tired and dispirited. But though we missed the Tapir, we saw enough of the sport to understand what makes the charm to the hunter of watching for hours in the woods, and perhaps returning, after all, empty-handed. If he does not get the game, he has the emotion; every now and then he thinks the creature is at hand, and he has a momentary agitation, heightened by the cries of the dogs and the answering cry of the sportsmen, who strive to arouse them to the utmost by their own shouts, and then if the animal turns back into the thicket all sound dies away, and to a very pandemonium of voices succeed the silence and solitude of the forest. All these things have their fascination, and explain to the uninitiated, to whom it seems at first incomprehensible, why these men will wait motionless for hours, and think themselves repaid (as I heard one of them declare) if they only hear the cry of the dogs and know they have roused the game, even if there be no other result. However, in this instance, we had plenty of other booty. The Anta lost, the hunters, who had carefully avoided firing hitherto, lest the sounds of their guns should give him warning, now turned their attention to lesser game, and we rode home in the afternoon rich in spoils, though without a Tapir.

The next day was that of our departure. Before leaving, we rode with Mr. Lage through his plantation, that we might understand something of the process of coffee culture in this country. I am not sure that, in giving an account of this model fazenda, we give a just idea of fazendas in general. Its owner carries the same large and comprehensive spirit, the same energy and force of will, into all his undertakings, and has introduced extensive reforms on his plantations. The Fazenda da Fortaleza de Santa Anna lies at the foot of the Serra da Babylonia. The house itself, as I have already said, makes a part of a succession of low white buildings, enclosing an oblong square divided into neat lots, destined for the drying of coffee. This drying of the coffee in the immediate vicinity of the house, though it seems a very general custom, must be an uncomfortable one ; for the drying-lots are laid down in a dazzling white cement, from the glare of which, in this hot climate, the eye turns wearily away, longing for a green spot on which to rest. Just behind the house on the slope of the hill is the orangery. I am never tired of these golden orchards, and this was one of especial beauty. The small, deep-colored tangerines, sometimes twenty or thirty in one cluster, the large, choice orange, " Laranja selecta," as it is called, often ten or twelve together in a single bunch, and bearing the branches to the ground with their weight; the paler "Limão dôce," or sweet lemon, rather insipid, but greatly esteemed here for its cool, refreshing properties,— all these, with many others, — for the variety of oranges is far greater than we of the temperate zone conceive it to be,— make a mass of color in which gold, deep orange, and pale yellow are blended wonderfully with the background of green. Beyond the house enclosure, on the opposite side of the road, are the gardens, with aviary, and fish-ponds in the centre. With these exceptions, all of the property which is not forest is devoted to coffee, covering all the hillsides for miles around. The seed is planted in nurseries especially prepared, where it undergoes its first year's growth. It is then transplanted to its permanent home, and begins to bear in about three years, the first crop being of course a very light one. From that time forward, under good care and with favorable soil, it will continue to bear and even to yield two crops or more annually, for thirty years in succession. At that time the shrubs and the soil are alike exhausted, and, according to the custom of the country, the fazendeiro cuts down a new forest and begins a new plantation, completely abandoning his old one, without a thought of redeeming or fertilizing the exhausted land. One of the long-sighted reforms undertaken by our host is the manuring of all the old, deserted plantations on his estate; he has already a number of vigorous young plantations, which promise to be as good as if a virgin forest had been sacrificed to produce them. He wishes not only to preserve the wood on his own estate, and to show that agriculture need not be cultivated at the expense of taste and beauty, but to remind his country people also, that, extensive as are the forests, they will not last forever, and that it will be necessary to emigrate before long to find new coffee grounds, if the old ones are to be considered worthless. Another of his reforms is that of the roads, already alluded to. The ordinary roads in the coffee plantations, like the mule-tracks all over the country, are carried straight up the sides of the hills between the lines of shrubs, gullied by every rain, and offering, besides, so steep an ascent that even with eight or ten oxen it is often impossible to drive the clumsy, old-fashioned carts up the slope, and the negroes are obliged to bring a great part of the harvest down on their heads. An American, who has been a great deal on the coffee fazendas in this region, told me that he had seen negroes bringing enormous burdens of this kind on their heads down almost vertical slopes. On Senhor Lage's estate all these old roads are abandoned, except where they are planted here and there with alleys of orange-trees for the use of the negroes, and he has substituted for them winding roads in the side of the hill with a very gradual ascent, so that light carts dragged by a single mule can transport all the harvest from the summit of the plantation to the drying-ground. It was the harvesting season, and the spectacle was a pretty one. The negroes, men and women, were scattered about the plantations with broad, shallow trays, made of plaited grass or bamboo, strapped over their shoulders and supported at their waists; into these they were gathering the coffee, some of the berries being brilliantly red, some already beginning to dry and turn brown, while here and there was a green one not yet quite ripe, but soon to ripen in the scorching sun. Little black children were sitting on the ground and gathering what fell under the bushes, singing at their work a monotonous but rather pretty snatch of song in which some took the first and others the second, making a not inharmonious music. As their baskets were filled they came to the Administrador to receive a little metal ticket on which the amount of their work was marked. A task is allotted to each one, — so much to a full-grown man, so much to a woman with young children, so much to a child, — and each one is paid for whatever he may do over and above it. The requisition is a very moderate one, so that the industrious have an opportunity of making a little money independently. At night they all present their tickets and are paid on the spot for any extra work. From the harvesting-ground we followed the carts down to the place where their burden is deposited. On their return from the plantation the negroes divide the day's harvest, and dispose it in little mounds on the drying-ground. When pretty equally dried, the coffee is spread out in thin even layers over the whole enclosure, where it is baked for the last time. It is then hulled by a very simple machine in use on almost all the fazendas, and the process is complete. At noon we bade good by to our kind hosts, and started for Juiz de Fora. Our stage was not a bad imitation of Noah's ark, for we carried with us the beasts of the field and the birds of the air and the fishes from the waters,* to say nothing of the trees from the forest. The party with whom we had passed such pleasant days collected to bid us farewell, and followed

---

* Senhor Lage had caused an extensive collection of fishes to be gathered from the waters of the Rio Novo, so that this excursion greatly extended the range of my survey of the basin of the Parahyba. — L. A.

us, as we passed out from the gate, with vivas and waving hats and handkerchiefs.

The following day we were fortunate in having cool weather with a somewhat cloudy sky, so that our ride of ten hours from Juiz de Fora to Petropolis, on the top of the stage, was delightful. The next morning in driving down the Serra to Mauá we witnessed a singular phenomenon, common enough, I suppose, to those who live in high regions. As we turned the corner of the road which first brings us in sight of the magnificent view below the Serra, there was a general exclamation of surprise and admiration. The valley and harbor, quite out to the sea, were changed to a field of snow, white, soft, and fleecy, as if fallen that night. The illusion was perfect, and though recognized at once as simply an effect of the heavy morning fog, we could hardly believe that it would disperse at our approach and not prove to be the thing it seemed. Here and there the summit of a hill pierced through it like an island, making the deception more complete. The incident was especially interesting to us as connecting itself with our late discussions as to the possible former existence of glaciers in this region. In his lecture a few nights before, describing the greater extension of the ice in former geological ages, when the whole plain of Switzerland between the Alps and Jura must have been filled with glaciers, Mr. Agassiz had said "there is a phenomenon not uncommon in the autumn in Switzerland which may help us to reconstruct this wonderful picture. Sometimes in a September morning the whole plain of Switzerland is filled with vapor which, when its pure white, undulating surface is seen from the higher summits of the Jura, looks like a snowy 'mer de glace,' appearing to descend from the peaks of the Alps and extending toward the Jura, while from all the tributary valleys similar masses pour down to meet it." It was as if the valley and harbor of Rio had meant to offer us a similar picture of past times, with the image of which our minds had been filled for the last few days in consequence of the glacial phenomena constantly presented to us on our journey.

July 6th. — To-morrow was to have been the day of our departure for the Amazons, but private interests must yield to public good, and it seems that the steamer which was to have left for Pará to-morrow has been taken by the government to transport troops to the seat of war. The aspect of the war grows daily more serious, and the Emperor goes himself the day after to-morrow to Rio Grande do Sul, accompanied by his son-in-law, the Duke of Saxe, soon to be followed by the Comte d'Eu, who is expected by the French steamer of the 18th of this month. Under these circumstances, not only are we prevented from going at the appointed date, but it seems not improbable that the exigencies of war may cause a still further delay, should other steamers be needed. A very pleasant public dinner, intended to be on the eve of his departure, was given to Mr. Agassiz yesterday by Messrs. Fleiuss and Linde. Germans, Swiss, French, Americans, and Brazilians made up the company, a mingling of nationalities which resulted in a very general harmony.

July 9th. — For some time Mr. Agassiz has been trying to get living specimens of the insect so injurious to the coffee-tree; the larva of a little moth akin to those which destroy the vineyards in Europe. Yesterday he succeeded in obtaining some, and among them one just spinning his cocoon on the leaf. We watched him for a long time with the lens as he wove his filmy tent. He had arched the threads upwards in the centre, so as to leave a little hollow space into which he could withdraw; this tiny vault seemed to be completed at the moment we saw him, and he was drawing threads forward and fastening them at a short distance beyond, thus lashing his house to the leaf as it were. The exquisite accuracy of the work was amazing. He was spinning the thread with his mouth, and with every new stitch he turned his body backward, attached his thread to the same spot, then drew it forward and fastened it exactly on a line with the last, with a precision and rapidity that machinery could hardly imitate. It is a curious question how far this perfection of workmanship in many of the lower animals is simply identical with their organization, and therefore to be considered a function, as inevitable in its action as digestion or respiration, rather than an instinct. In this case the body of the little animal was his measure: it was amazing to see him lay down his threads with such accuracy, till one remembered that he could not make them longer or shorter; for, starting from the centre of his house, and stretching his body its full length, they must always reach the same point. The same is true of the so-called mathematics of the bee. The bees stand as close as they can together in their hive for economy of space, and each one deposits his wax around him, his own form and size being the mould for the cells, the regularity of which when completed excites so much wonder and admiration. The mathematical secret of the bee is to be found in his structure, not in his instinct. But in the industrial work of some of the lower animals, the ant for instance, there is a power of adaptation which is not susceptible of the same explanation. Their social organization, too intelligent, it seems, to be the work of any reasoning powers of their own, yet does not appear to be directly connected with their structure. While we were watching our little insect, a breath stirred the leaf and he instantly contracted himself and drew back under his roof; but presently came out again and returned to his work.

July 14*th.*—I have passed two or three days of this week very pleasantly with a party of friends who invited me to join them on a visit to one of the largest fazendas in this neighborhood, belonging to the Commendador Breves. A journey of some four hours on the Dom Pedro Railroad brought us to the " Barra do Pirahy," and thence we proceeded on mule-back, riding slowly along the banks of the Parahyba through very pleasant, quiet scenery, though much less picturesque than that in the immediate vicinity of Rio. At about sunset we reached the fazenda, standing on a terrace just above the river, and commanding a lovely view of water and woodland. We were received with a hospitality hardly to be equalled, I think, out of Brazil, for it asks neither who you are nor whence you come, but opens its doors to every wayfarer. On this occasion we were expected; but it is nevertheless true that at such a fazenda, where the dining-room accommodates a hundred persons if necessary, all travellers passing through the country are free to stop for rest and refreshment. At the time of our visit there were several such transient guests; among others a couple quite unknown to our hosts, who had stopped for the night, but had been taken ill and detained there several days. They seemed entirely at home. On this estate there are about two thousand slaves, thirty of whom are house-servants; it includes within its own borders all that would be required by such a population in the way of supplies: it has its drug-shop and its hospital; its kitchens for the service of the guests and for that of the numerous indoor servants, its church, its priest, and its doctor. Here the church was made by throwing open a small oratory, very handsomely fitted up with gold and silver service, purple altar-cloth, &c., at the end of a very long room, which, though used for other purposes, serves on such an occasion to collect the large household together. The next morning our hostess showed us the different working-rooms. One of the most interesting was that where the children were taught to sew. I have wondered, on our Southern plantations, that more pains was not taken to make clever seamstresses of the women. Here plain sewing is taught to all the little girls, and many of them are quite expert in embroidery and lace-making. Beyond this room was a store-room for clothing, looking not unlike one of our sanitary rooms, with heaps of woollen and cotton stuffs which the black women were cutting out and making up for the field hands. The kitchens, with the working and lodging rooms of the house negroes, enclosed a court planted with trees and shrubs, around which extended covered brick walks where blacks, young and old, seemed to swarm, from the withered woman who boasted herself a hundred, but was still proud to display her fine lace-work, and ran like a girl, to show us how sprightly she was, to the naked baby creeping at her feet. The old woman had received her liberty some time ago, but seemed to be very much attached to the family and never to have thought of leaving them. (These are the things which make one hopeful about slavery in Brazil;

emancipation is considered there a subject to be discussed, legislated upon, adopted ultimately, and it seems no uncommon act to present a slave with his liberty.) In the evening, while taking coffee on the terrace after dinner, we had very good music from a brass-band composed of slaves belonging to the estate. The love of the negroes for music is always remarkable, and here they take pains to cultivate it. Senhor Breves keeps a teacher for them, and they are really very well trained. At a later hour we had the band in the house and a dance by the black children which was comical in the extreme. Like little imps of darkness they looked, dancing with a rapidity of movement and gleeful enjoyment with which one could not but sympathize. While the music was going on, every door and window was filled with a cloud of dusky faces, now and then a fair one among them; for here, as elsewhere, slavery brings its inevitable and heaviest curse, and white slaves are by no means uncommon. The next morning we left the fazenda, not on mule-back, however, but in one of the flat-bottomed coffee-boats, an agreeable exchange for the long, hot ride. We were accompanied to the landing by our kind hosts, and followed by quite a train of blacks, some of them bringing the baggage, others coming only for the amusement of seeing us off. Among them was the old black woman who gave us the heartiest cheers of all, as we put off from the shore. The sail down the river was very pleasant; the coffee-bags served as cushions, and, with all our umbrellas raised to make an awning, we contrived to shelter ourselves from the sun. Neither was the journey without excitement, the river being so broken by rocks in many places that there are strong rapids, requiring a skilful navigation.

July 15*th.* — A long botanizing excursion to-day among the Tijuca hills with Mr. Glaziou, director of the Passeio Publico, as guide. It has been a piece of the good fortune attending Mr. Agassiz thus far on this expedition to find in Mr. Glaziou a botanist whose practical familiarity with tropical plants is as thorough as his theoretical knowledge. He has undertaken to enrich our scientific stores with a large collection of such palms and other trees as illustrate the relation between the present tropical vegetation and the ancient geological forests. Such a collection will be invaluable as a basis for palæontological studies at the Museum of Comparative Zoölogy in Cambridge.

July 23*d.* — At last our plans for the Amazons seem definitely settled. We sail the day after to-morrow by the Cruzeiro do Sul. The conduct of the government toward the expedition is very generous ; free passages are granted to the whole party, and yesterday Mr. Agassiz received an official document enjoining all persons connected with the administration to give him every facility for his scientific objects. We have another piece of good fortune in the addition to our party of Major Coutinho, a member of the government corps of engineers, who has been engaged for several years in explorations on the Amazonian rivers. Happily for us, he returned to Rio a few weeks ago, and a chance meeting at the palace, where he had gone to report the results of the journey just completed, and Mr. Agassiz to discuss the plans for that about to begin, brought them together. This young officer's investigations had made his name familiar to Mr. Agassiz, and when the Emperor asked the latter how he could best assist him, he answered that there was nothing he so much desired or which would so materially aid him as the companionship of Major Coutinho. The Emperor cordially consented, Major Coutinho signified his readiness, and the matter was concluded. Since then there have been frequent conferences between Mr. Agassiz and his new colleague, intent study of maps and endless talk about the most desirable mode of laying out and dividing the work. He feels that Major Coutinho's familiarity with the scenes to which we are going will lighten his task of half its difficulties, while his scientific zeal will make him a most sympathetic companion.* We found to-day some large leaves of the Terminalia Catappa of the most brilliant colors; red and gold as bright as any of our autumnal leaves. This would seem to confirm the opinion that the turning of the foliage with us is not an effect of frost, but simply the ripening of the leaf; since here, where there is no frost, the same phenomenon takes place as in our northern latitudes.

July 24th. — Our last preparations for the journey are completed; the collections made since our arrival, amounting to upwards of fifty barrels and cases, are packed, in readiness for the first opportunity which occurs for the United States, and to-morrow morning we shall be on our way to the great river. We went this morning to the Collegio Dom Pedro Segundo to bid farewell to our excellent friend Dr. Pacheco, to whose kindness we owe much of our enjoyment during our stay here. The College building was once a "seminario," a charitable institution where boys were taken to be educated as priests.

* Never were pleasant anticipations more delightfully fulfilled. During eleven months of the most intimate companionship I had daily cause to be grateful for the chance which had thrown us together. I found in Major Coutinho an able collaborator, untiring in his activity and devotion to scientific aims, an admirable guide, and a friend whose regard I trust I shall ever retain. — L. A.

The rules of the establishment were strict; no servants were kept, the pupils were obliged to do their own work, cooking, &c., and even to go out into the streets to beg after the fashion of the mendicant orders. One condition only was attached to the entrance of the children, namely, that they should be of pure race; no mulattoes or negroes were admitted. I do not know on what ground this institution was broken up by the government and the building taken as a school-house. It has still a slightly monastic aspect, though it has been greatly modified; but the cloisters running around closed courts remind one of its origin. The recitations were going on at the moment of our visit, and as we had seen nothing as yet of the schools, Dr. Pacheco took us through the establishment. A college here does not signify a university as with us, but rather a high school, the age of the pupils being from twelve to eighteen. It is difficult to judge of methods of education in a foreign language with which one is not very familiar. But the scholars appeared bright and interested, their answers came promptly, their discipline was evidently good. One thing was very striking to a stranger in seeing so many young people collected together; namely, the absence of pure type and the feeble physique. I do not know whether it is in consequence of the climate, but a healthy, vigorous child is a rare sight in Rio de Janeiro. The scholars were of all colors, from black through intermediate shades to white, and even one of the teachers having the direction of a higher class in Latin was a negro. It is an evidence of the absence of any prejudice against the blacks, that, on the occasion of a recent vacancy among the Latin professors, this man, having passed the best examination, was unanimously chosen in preference to several Brazilians, of European descent, who presented themselves as candidates at the same time. After hearing several of the classes we went over the rest of the building. The order and exquisite neatness of the whole establishment, not forgetting the kitchen, where the shining brasses and bright tins might awaken the envy of many a housekeeper, bear testimony to the excellence of the general direction. Since the institution passed into Dr. Pacheco's hands he has done a great deal to raise its character. He has improved the library, purchased instruments for the laboratory, and made many judicious changes in the general arrangement.

CHAPTER IV.

VOYAGE UP THE COAST TO PARÁ.

On board the "Cruzeiro do Sul." — Members of the Party. — Arrival at Bahia. — Day in the Country. — Return to the Steamer. — Conversation about Slavery in Brazil. — Negro Marriages. — Maceio. — Pernambuco. — Parahyba do Norte. — Ramble on Shore. — Ceará. — Difficult Landing. — Brazilian Baths. — Maranham. — Assai Palm. — Visit to Orphan Asylum. — Detained in Port. — Variety of Medusæ — Arrival of American Gunboat. — More Medusæ. — Dinner on Shore. — Cordiality toward the Expedition. — Arrival at Pará. — Kind Reception. — Environs of Pará. — Luxuriant Growth. — Markets. — Indian Boats. — Agreeable Climate. — Excursion in the Harbor. — Curious Mushroom. — Success in collecting, with the assistance of our Host and other Friends. — Fishes of the Forests. — Public Expressions of Sympathy for the Expedition. — Generosity of the Amazonian Steamship Company. — Geological Character of the Shore from Rio to Pará. — Erratic Drift. — Letter to the Emperor.

July 25th. — On board the "Cruzeiro do Sul." We sailed to-day at 11 o'clock, bidding good by with regret, though not without hope of return, to the beautiful bay and mountains on which we have been looking for three months. Our party consists of Major Coutinho, Mr. Burkhardt, Monsieur Bourget, who accompanies Mr. Agassiz to the Amazons as collector and preparator, our two young friends Mr. Hunnewell and Mr. James, and ourselves. At Bahia we shall be joined by Mr. Dexter and Mr. Thayer, two of our party who have preceded us up the coast, and have been collecting in the neighborhood of Bahia for two or three weeks. The aspect of the steamer is not very inviting, for it has been used of late for the transportation of troops to the south, in consequence of which it is very dirty; it is also overcrowded on account of the number of persons bound northward, who have been detained in Rio by the interruption of the regular trips on this line. We are promised better accommodations after a few days, however, as many of the passengers will drop off at Bahia and Pernambuco.

July 28th. — Bahia. Half the enjoyment of life borrows intensity from contrast, and to this principle we certainly owe a part of our pleasure to-day. After three half seasick days on a dirty, crowded steamer, the change is delightful to a breezy country house, where we are received with that most gracious hospitality which relieves both host and guests of the sense of entertaining or being entertained. Here I have been sitting under the deep shade of a huge mango-tree, with a number of the " Revue des Deux Mondes " on my knee, either reading or listening lazily to the rustle of the leaves or the cooing of the pigeons as they patter up and down on the tiled floor of the porch near by, or watching the negroes as they come and go with trays of vegetables or baskets of fruit and flowers on their heads, for the service of the house. In the mean time, Mr. Agassiz is engaged in examining the collections made by Mr. Dexter and Mr. Thayer during their visit here. They have been aided most cordially by our friend Mr. Antonio de Lacerda, at whose hospitable house we are staying, and where we found our travelling companions quite domesticated. He received them on their arrival, and has given them every facility during their stay here for the objects they had in view, his own love of natural history, to which he devotes every spare hour from his active business life, rendering him an efficient ally. He has a large and very valuable collection of insects, admirably arranged and in excellent preservation. They are also greatly indebted to Mr. Nicolai, the resident English clergyman here, who has accompanied them on some of their excursions, and put them in the way of seeing whatever was most interesting in the neighborhood.

On arriving in South America one should land first in Bahia, for in its aspect it is the most national and characteristic of the cities. As we passed directly through the town this morning, we can give but little account of it, and yet we saw enough to confirm all that has been said of its quaint and picturesque character. On first disembarking, you find yourself at the foot of an almost perpendicular hill, and negro-bearers appear at your side to carry you up the steep ascent, almost impassable for carriages, in a "cadeira," or curtained chair. This is in itself an odd experience for one to whom it is new, and the rest of the city, with its precipitous streets, its queer houses, its old churches, is as quaint and antique as these original carriages.

July 29th. — To-day we have the "revers de la médaille"; we have returned to our prison, and a violent rain drives us all to take refuge in the hot, close dining-room, our only resort when the weather is bad.

July 30th. — Off Macció. Last evening, when the rain was over and the moonlight tempted every one on deck, we had a long conversation with our pleasant travelling companion, Mr. Sinimbu, senator from the province of Alagôas, on the aspect of slavery in Brazil. It seems to me that we may have something to learn here in our own perplexities respecting the position of the black race among us, for the Brazilians are trying gradually and by installments some of the experiments which are forced upon us without previous preparation. The absence of all restraint upon the free blacks, the fact that they are eligible to office, and that all professional careers are open to them, without prejudice on the ground of color, enables one to form some opinion as to their ability and capacity for development. Mr. Sinimbu tells us that here the result is on the whole in their favor; he says that the free blacks compare well in intelligence and activity with the Brazilians and Portuguese. But it must be remembered, in making the comparison with reference to our own country, that here they are brought into contact with a less energetic and powerful race than the Anglo-Saxon. Mr. Sinimbu believes that emancipation is to be accomplished in Brazil by a gradual process which has already begun. A large number of slaves are freed every year by the wills of their masters; a still larger number buy their own freedom annually; and as there is no longer any importation of blacks, the inevitable result of this must be the natural death of slavery. Unhappily, the process is a slow one, and in the mean while slavery is doing its evil work, debasing and enfeebling alike whites and blacks. The Brazilians themselves do not deny this, and one constantly hears them lament the necessity of sending their children away to be educated, on account of the injurious association with the house-servants. In fact, although politically slavery has a more hopeful aspect here than elsewhere, the institution from a moral point of view has some of its most revolting characters in this country, and looks, if possible, more odious than it did in the States. The other day, in the neighborhood of Rio, I had an opportunity of seeing a marriage between two negroes, whose owner made the religious, or, as it appeared to me on this occasion, irreligious ceremony, obligatory. The bride, who was as black as jet, was dressed in white muslin, with a veil of coarse white lace, such as the negro women make themselves, and the husband was in a white linen suit. She looked, and I think she really felt, diffident, for there were a good many strangers present, and her position was embarrassing. The Portuguese priest, a bold, insolent-looking man, called them up and rattled over the marriage service with most irreverent speed, stopping now and then to scold them both, but especially the woman, because she did not speak loud enough and did not take the whole thing in the same coarse, rough way that he did. When he ordered them to come up and kneel at the altar, his tone was more suggestive of cursing than praying, and having uttered his blessing he hurled an amen at them, slammed the prayer-book down on the altar, whiffed out the candles, and turned the bride and bridegroom out of the chapel with as little ceremony as one would have kicked out a dog. As the bride came out, half crying, half smiling, her mother met her and showered her with rose-leaves, and so this act of consecration, in which the mother's benediction seemed the only grace, was over. I thought what a strange confusion there must be in these poor creature's minds, if they thought about it at all. They are told that the relation between man and wife is a sin, unless confirmed by the sacred rite of marriage; they come to hear a bad man gabble over them words which they cannot understand, mingled with taunts and abuse which they understand only too well, and side by side with their own children grow up the little fair-skinned slaves to tell them practically that the white man does not keep himself the law he imposes on them. What a monstrous lie the whole system must seem to them if they are ever led to think about it at all. I am far from supposing that the instance I have given should be taken as representing the state of religious instruction on plantations generally. No doubt there are good priests who improve and instruct their black parishioners; but it does not follow because religious services are provided on a plantation, the ceremony of marriage observed, &c., that there is anything which deserves the name of religious instruction. It would be unjust not to add the better side of the question in this particular instance. The man was free, and I was told that the woman received her liberty and a piece of land from her master as her marriage dower.

We arrived at Macció this morning, and went on shore with Mr. Sinimbu, who leaves us here, and with whose family we passed a delightful day, welcomed with that hearty cordiality so characteristic of Brazilians in their own homes. Although our stay was so short, a considerable addition was made here to the collections. On arriving at any port the party disperses at once, the young men going in different directions to collect, Mr. Bourget hurrying to the fish-market to see what may be found there of interest, and Mr. Agassiz and Mr. Coutinho generally making a geological excursion. In this way, though the steamer remains but a few hours at each station, the time is not lost.

July 31*st*. — Pernambuco. Arrived to-day off Pernambuco, and were too happy, after a stormy night, to find ourselves behind the famous reef which makes such a quiet harbor at this port. Our countryman, Mr. Hitch, met us on landing, and drove us at once out to his "chacara," (country place,) where it was delightful to be welcomed, like old friends, to an American home.* Pernambuco is by no means so picturesque as Bahia or Rio de Janeiro. It has a more modern air than either of these, but looks also more cleanly and more prosperous. Many of the streets are wide, and the river running through the business part of the city, crossed by broad, handsome bridges, is itself suggestive of freshness. The country is more open and flat than farther south. In our afternoon drive some of the views across wide, level meadows, if we could have put elms here and there in the place of palms, would have reminded us of scenery at home.

August 2d. — Yesterday we left Pernambuco, and this morning found ourselves at the mouth of the Parahyba do Norte, a broad, beautiful river, up which we steamed to within a few miles of the little town bearing the same name. Here we took a boat and rowed to the city, where we spent some hours in rambling about, collecting specimens, examining drift formations, &c. In the course of our excursion we fell in with some friends of Major Coutinho's, who took us home with them to an excellent breakfast of fresh fish, with bread, coffee, and wine. The bread is to be noticed here, for it is said to be the best in Brazil. The flour is the same as elsewhere, and the people generally attribute the superiority of their bread to some quality of the water. Whatever be the cause, there is no bread in all Brazil so sweet, so light, and so white as that of Parahyba do Norte.

August 5th. — We arrived yesterday at Ceará, where we were warmly welcomed and most hospitably entertained

---

* Mr. Agassiz was indebted to Mr. Hitch for valuable additions to his collections, and for many acts of kindness in behalf of the expedition.

at the house of Dr. Mendes, an old acquaintance of Major Coutinho. It was blowing hard and raining when we left the steamer; our boat put into the beach in a heavy surf, and I was wondering how I should reach the shore, when two of our negro rowers jumped into the water, and, standing at the side of the boat behind me, motioned me to come, crossing their arms basket-fashion, as we do sometimes to carry children. They looked as if it were the ordinary mode of conveyance, so I seated myself, and with one arm around the neck of each of my black bearers, they laughing as heartily as I did, I was landed triumphantly on the sands. After the first greetings at the house of Dr. Mendes were over, we were offered the luxury of a bath before breakfast. The bath is a very important feature in a Brazilian household. This one was of the size of a small room, the water (about two feet deep and of a delicious, soft, velvety character) constantly flowing through over the smooth sand floor. They are often larger than this, from four to five feet deep, and sometimes lined with blue and white tiles, which make a very clean and pretty floor. It is a great luxury in this warm climate, and many persons bathe several times a day. The bathhouse is usually in the garden, at a convenient distance from the house, but not immediately adjoining it. The bath was followed by an excellent breakfast, after which we drove through the city. Ceará is a wonderfully progressive town for Brazil. Five years ago it had not a paved street; now all the streets are well paved, with good sidewalks, and the city is very carefully laid out, with a view to its future growth.* To-day we are again

---

* Here, as elsewhere, I found ready and willing coadjutors among amateur collectors. On my return from the Amazons, many months later, I found

coasting along within sight of land, with a quiet sea and a delicious breeze. The ocean is covered with white caps, and of a very peculiar greenish, aquamarine tint, the same which I observed as soon as we reached these latitudes in coming out. This singular color is said to be owing to the nature of the sea bottom and the shallowness of the water, combined, farther north, with the admixture of fresh water along the coast.

August 6th. — Arrived early this morning before Maranham, and went on shore to breakfast at the hotel; for, wonderful to relate, Maranham possesses a hotel, a great rarity in many Brazilian towns. We passed the greater part of the day in driving about the city with Dr. Braga, who kindly undertook to show us everything of interest.* The town and harbor are very pretty, the city itself standing on an island, formed by two bays running up on either side and enclosing it. The surrounding country is flat and very thickly wooded, though the woods are rather low. Here, at the house of Dr. Braga's brother-in-law, we saw, for the first time, the slender, graceful Assai palm, from which the drink is made so much appreciated in Pará and on the Lower Amazons. It is curious to see the negroes go up the tree to gather

collections made in my absence by Dr. Mendes and Senhor Barroso, who had been our companions on board the steamer. At Parahyba do Norte I was indebted in the same way to Dr. Justa. These collections will afford invaluable materials for the comparison of the Coast Faunæ. — L. A.

* At a later period I owed to Dr. Braga far more than the ordinary courtesy extended to a stranger. I had informed him that Mr. St. John, then following the course of the Rio San Francisco, on his way to the province of Piauhy, would arrive in Maranham at the close of his journey. When he reached that city he was very seriously ill with fever. Dr Braga took him into his house, where he was attended by him and his family as if he had been one of their kindred. I have, indeed, little doubt that my young friend owed his recovery to the considerate care with which he was treated under their kindly roof. — L. A.

the fruit. The trunk is perfectly smooth, the fruit growing in a heavy cluster of berries, just below the crown of leaves on its summit. The negro fastens a cord or a strip of palm-leaf around his insteps, thus binding his feet together that they may not slide apart on the smooth stem, and by means of this kind of stirrup he contrives to cling to the slippery trunk and scramble up.

We were much interested in seeing here an admirably well conducted institution for the education of poor orphans. Its chief aim is to educate them, not as scholars, though they receive elementary instruction in reading, writing, and ciphering, but to teach them a variety of occupations by which they can earn an honest livelihood. They are trained in several trades, are taught to play on a number of instruments, and there is also a school of design connected with the establishment. A faultless order and scrupulous neatness prevailed through the whole building, which was not the result of an exceptional preparation, since our visit was wholly unexpected. This surprised us the more, because, notwithstanding their fondness for bathing, order and neatness in their houses are not a virtue among the Brazilians. This may be owing to slave labor, — rarely anything better than eye-service. The large dormitories looked fresh and airy, with the hammocks rolled up and laid on a shelf, each one above the peg to which it belonged; the shoes were hung on nails along the walls, and the little trunks, holding the clothing of each scholar, were neatly arranged beneath them. On the upper story was the hospital, a large, well-ventilated room, with numerous windows commanding beautiful views, and a cool breeze blowing through it. Here were cots instead of hammocks, but I thought the sick boys might prefer the swinging, cradle-like beds to which they were accustomed, and which they evidently find very comfortable. When Mr. Agassiz remarked, as we passed through the dormitory, that sleeping in a hammock was an experience he had yet to make, one of the boys took his down from the shelf, and, hanging it up, laughingly threw himself into it, with a lazy ease which looked quite enviable. The kitchen and grocery rooms were as neat as the rest of the house, and the simplicity of the whole establishment, while it admitted everything necessary for comfort and health, was well adapted for its objects. A pretty little chapel adjoined the house, and the house itself was built around an open square planted with trees, — a pleasant playground for the boys, who have their music there in the evening. On our return to town we heard that, owing to the breakage of some part of the machinery, the steamer would be detained in this port for a couple of days. We have, however, returned to our quarters on board, preferring to spend the night on the water rather than in the hot, close town.

August 7th. — To-day we have all been interested in watching the beautiful Medusæ swept along by the tide, so close to the side of the steamer that they could easily be reached from the stairway. We have now quite a number disposed about the deck in buckets and basins, and Mr. Burkhardt is making colored sketches of them. They are very beautiful, and quite new to Mr. Agassiz. In some the disk has a brown tracery like seaweed over it, while its edge is deeply lobed, every lobe being tinged with an intensely brilliant dark blue; the lobes are divided into eight sets of four each, making thirty-two in all, and an eye is placed on the margin between each set; the tubes running to the eyes are much larger than those in the intervals between, and the network of vessels on the margin is wonderfully fine and delicate; the curtains hanging from the mouth are white and closely fringed with full flounces, somewhat like our Aurelia. The movement is quick, the margin of the disk beating with short, rapid pants. Another is altogether brown and white, the seaweed-like pattern being carried down to the edge of the lobes, and the lobes themselves being more delicate than those of the blue-edged one, the disk thinning out greatly towards the periphery. The brown marks are, however, darker, more distinct, and cover a larger space in some specimens than in others. This is also true of those with the blue margin, the brown pattern covering the whole disk in some, confined to a simple zone around the disk in others, and even entirely absent occasionally. Mr. Agassiz inclines to think, from the similarity of their other features, however, that, notwithstanding their difference of color, they all belong to the same species, the variety in coloration being probably connected with difference of sex. He has, at any rate, ascertained that all the wholly brown specimens caught to-day are males.

We were rejoiced this morning by the sight of our own flag coming into harbor. We presently found that the ship was the gunboat Nipsic. She had sailed from Boston on the 4th of July, and brought papers of a later date than any we have seen. The officers were kind enough to send us a large bundle of papers, which we have been eagerly devouring.

August 8th. — Another quite new and beautiful Medusa to-day. As we were waiting for breakfast this morning a number floated past, so dark in color that in the water they appeared almost black. Two of our party took a boat and went in search of them, but the tide was so swift that they swept past like lightning, and one had hardly time to point them out before they were gone again. However, after many efforts, we succeeded in getting one, whose portrait Mr. Burkhardt is now taking. The disk is of a chocolate-brown, shading into a darker, more velvety hue toward the edge, which is slightly scalloped, but not cut up into deep lobes like those of yesterday. The eyes, eight in number, are distinctly visible as lighter-colored specks on the margin. The appendages hanging from the mouth are more solid and not so thickly fringed as in those of yesterday. It moves rather slowly in its glass prison, the broad margin shading from lighter brown to a soft chocolate color almost verging on black, as it flaps up and down somewhat languidly, but still with a regular, steady pulsation.*

August 9th. — We passed yesterday afternoon with the Braga family in town. The weather was charming, a cool breeze blowing through the veranda where we dined. There were a number of guests to meet us, and we had again cause to acknowledge how completely the stranger is made to feel himself at home among these hospitable people. We sailed this morning, Mr. Agassiz taking with him a valuable collection, though our time was so short. The fact is, that, not only here, but at every town where we have stopped in coming up the coast, the ready, cordial desire of the people to help in the work has enabled him to get together collections which it would otherwise have been impossible to make in so short a time. If he is

---

* These two Medusæ belong to the Rhizostomidæ, and I shall take an early opportunity to publish a description of them, with the drawings of Mr. Burkhardt. — L. A.

VOYAGE UP THE COAST TO PARÁ.

unexpectedly successful in this expedition, it is as much owing to the active sympathy of the Brazilians themselves, and to their interest in the objects he has so much at heart, as to the efforts of himself and his companions.

August 11*th.* — Pará. Early yesterday morning, a few yellowish patches staining the ocean here and there gave us our first glimpse of the water of the Amazons. Presently the patches became broad streaks, the fresh waters encroaching gradually upon the sea, until, at about ten o'clock, we fairly entered the mouth of the river, though, as the shores are some hundred and fifty miles apart, we might have believed ourselves on the broad ocean. As we neared the city, the numerous islands closing up about Pará and sheltering its harbor limited the view and broke the enormous expanse of the fresh-water basin. We anchored off the city at about three o'clock, but a heavy thundershower, with violent rain, prevented us from going on shore till the next morning. None of the party landed except Major Coutinho. He went to announce our arrival to his friend, Mr. Pimenta Bueno, who has kindly invited us to make his house our home while we stay in Pará. The next morning was beautiful after the rain, and at seven o'clock two boats were sent to take us and our effects on shore. On landing we went at once to Mr. Pimenta's large business establishment near the wharves. Here he has provided several excellent working-rooms to serve as laboratories and storage-places for the specimens, and besides these a number of airy, cool chambers on the floor above, for the accommodation of our companions, who have already slung their hammocks, arranged their effects, and are keeping a kind of bachelor's hall. Having disposed of the scientific apparatus, we drove out to Mr

Pimenta's "chacara," some two miles out of town, on the Rua de Nazareth, where we were received with the utmost kindness. Mr. Agassiz and Major Coutinho soon returned to town, where no time is to be lost in beginning work at the laboratory. I remained at home and passed a pleasant morning with the ladies of the family, who made me acquainted with the peculiar beverage so famous in these regions, prepared from the berries of the Assai palm. They are about the size of cranberries, and of a dark-brown color. Being boiled and crushed they yield a quantity of juice, which when strained has about the consistency of chocolate, and is of a dark purplish tint like blackberry juice. It has a sweetish taste, and is very nice eaten with sugar and the crisp "farinha d'agua," a kind of coarse flour made from the mandioca root. People of all classes throughout the province of Pará are exceedingly fond of this beverage, and in the city they have a proverb which runs thus : —

"Who visits Pará is glad to stay,
Who drinks Assai goes never away.'

August 12th. — This morning we rose early and walked into town. Great pains have been taken with the environs of Pará, and the Rua de Nazareth is one of the broad streets leading into the country, and planted with large trees (chiefly mangueiras) for two or three miles out of town. On our way we saw a lofty palm-tree completely overpowered and stifled in the embrace of an enormous parasite. So luxuriant is the growth of the latter that you do not perceive, till it is pointed out to you, that its spreading branches and thick foliage completely hide the tree from which it derives its life ; only from the extreme summit a few fan-like palm-leaves shoot upwards as if trying to escape into the air and light. The palm cannot long survive, however, and with its death it seals the doom of its murderer also. There is another evidence, and a more pleasing one, of the luxuriance of nature on this same road. The skeleton of a house stands by the wayside; whether a ruin or unfinished, I am unable to say, but at all events only the walls are standing, with the openings for doors and windows. Nature has completed this imperfect dwelling; — she has covered it over with a green roof, she has planted the empty enclosure with a garden of her own choosing, she has trained vines around the open doors and windows; and the deserted house, if it has no other inmates, is at least a home for the birds. It makes a very pretty picture. I never pass it without wishing for a sketch of it. On our arrival in town we went at once to the market. It is very near the water, and we were much amused in watching the Indian canoes at the landing. The "montaria," as the Indian calls his canoe, is a long, narrow boat, covered at one end with a thatched roof, under which is the living-room of the family. Here the Indian has his home; wife and children, hammock, cooking utensils. — all his household goods, in fact. In some of the boats the women were preparing breakfast, cooking the coffee or the tapioca over a pan of coals. In others they were selling the coarse pottery, which they make into all kinds of utensils, sometimes of quite graceful, pretty forms. We afterwards went through the market. It is quite large and neatly kept; but the Brazilian markets are only good as compared with each other. The meats are generally poor; there is little game to be seen; they have no variety of vegetables, which might be so easily cultivated here, and even the display of fruit in the market is by no means what one would expect it to be. To-night Mr. Agassiz goes off with a party of gentlemen on an excursion to some of the islands in the harbor. This first expedition in the neighborhood of Pará, from which the Professor promises himself much pleasure, is planned by Dr. Couto de Magalhaēs, President of the Province.*

August 14*th*. — We are very agreeably surprised in the climate here. I had expected from the moment of our arrival in the region of the Amazons to be gasping in a fierce, unintermitting, intolerable heat. On the contrary, the mornings are fresh; a walk or ride between six and eight o'clock is always delightful; and though during the middle of the day the heat is certainly very great, it cools off again towards four o'clock; the evenings are delightful, and the nights always comfortable. Even in the hottest part of the day the heat is not dead; there is always a breeze stirring. Mr. Agassiz returned this afternoon from his excursion in the harbor, more deeply impressed than ever with the grandeur of this entrance to the Amazons and the beauty of its many islands, "An archipelago of islands," as he says, "in an ocean of fresh water." He describes the mode of fishing of the Indians as curious. They row very softly up the

---

* To Dr. Couto de Magalhaēs Mr. Agassiz was indebted for unremitting attentions during our stay in the region of the Amazons. He never failed to facilitate the success of the expedition by every means in his power, and the large collections made under his directions during our sojourn upon the Upper Amazons were among the most valuable contributions to its scientific results. When he heard that Mr. Ward, one of our young companions, was coming down the Tocantins, he sent a boat and boatmen to meet him, and on his arrival in Pará received him in his own house, where he remained his guest during his stay in the city.

creek, having first fastened the seine across from shore to shore at a lower point, and when they have gained a certain distance above it, they spring into the water with a great plash and rush down the creek in a line, driving the fish before them into the net. One draught alone filled the boat half full of fish. Mr. Agassiz was especially interested in seeing alive for the first time the curious fish called "Tralhote" by the Indians, and known to naturalists as the Anableps tetrophthalmus. This name, signifying "four-eyed," is derived from the singular structure of the eye. A membranous fold enclosing the bulb of the eye stretches across the pupil, dividing the visual apparatus into an upper and lower half. No doubt this formation is intended to suit the peculiar habits of the Anableps. These fishes gather in shoals on the surface of the water, their heads resting partly above, partly below the surface, and they move by a leaping motion somewhat like that of frogs on land. Thus, half in air, half in water, they require eyes adapted for seeing in both elements, and the arrangement described above just meets this want.

August 19*th*. — To-night at ten o'clock we go on board the steamer, and before dawn shall be on our way up the river. This has been a delicious week of rest and refreshment to me. The quiet country life, with morning walks in the fresh, fragrant lanes and roads immediately about us, has been very soothing after four months of travel or of noisy hotel life. The other day as we were going into town we found in the wet grass by the roadside one of the most beautiful mushrooms I have ever seen. The stem was pure white, three or four inches in height, and about half an inch in diameter, surmounted by a club-shaped head, brown in color, with a blunt point.

and from the base of this head was suspended an open white net of exquisitely delicate texture, falling to within about an inch of the ground; a fairy web that looked fit for Queen Mab herself.* The week, so peaceful for me, has been one, if not of rest, at least of intense interest for Mr. Agassiz. The very day of his arrival, by the kindness of our host, his working-rooms were so arranged as to make an admirable laboratory, and, from the hour he entered them, specimens have poured in upon him from all quarters. His own party make but a small part of the scientific corps who have worked for and with him here. In Pará alone he has already more than fifty new species of fresh-water fishes; enough to reveal unexpected and novel relations in the finny world, and to give the basis of an improved classification. He is far from attributing this great success wholly to his own efforts. Ready as he is to work, he could not accomplish half that he does, except for the active good-will of those about him. Among the most valuable of these contributions is a collection made by Mr. Pimenta Bueno, of the so-called fishes of the forest. When the waters overflow after the rainy season and fill the forest for a considerable distance on either side, these fish hover over the depressions and hollows, and as the waters subside are left in the pools and channels. They do not occur in the open river, but are always found in

---

* This mushroom belongs to the genus Phallus, and seems to be an undescribed species. I preserved it in alcohol, but was unable to have any drawing made from it before its beauty and freshness were quite gone. In the early morning, while the grass was still damp, we often found a peculiar snail, a species of Bulimus, creeping by the roadside. The form of the anterior part of the foot was unlike that of any species known thus far from this group. Such facts show the desirableness of making drawings from the soft parts of these animals as well as from their solid envelopes. — L. A.

these forest retreats, and go by the name of the "Peixe do Mato."

Mr. Agassiz has not only to acknowledge the untiring kindness of individuals here, but also the cordial expression of sympathy from public bodies in the objects of the expedition. A committee from the municipality of the city has waited upon him to express the general satisfaction in the undertaking, and he has received a public demonstration of the same kind from the college. The bishop of the province and his coadjutor have also been most cordial in offers of assistance. Nor does the interest thus expressed evaporate in empty words. Mr. Pimenta Bueno is director of the Brazilian line of steamers from Pará to Tabatinga.* The trip to Manaos, at the mouth of the Rio Negro, is generally made in five days, allowing only for stoppages of an hour or two at different stations, to take or leave passengers and to deposit or receive merchandise. In order that we may be perfectly independent, however, and stop wherever it seems desirable to make collections, the company places at our disposition a steamer for one month between Pará and Manaos. There are to be no passengers but ourselves, and the steamer is provided with everything necessary for the whole company during that period, — food, service, &c. I think it may fairly be said that in no part of the world could a private scientific undertaking be greeted with more cordiality or receive a more liberal hospitality than has been accorded to the present

---

* The President of this line is the Baron de Mazá, esteemed by his countrymen as a financier of great ability and a man of rare energy, perseverance, and patriotism. As he was in Europe during the year of my visit to Brazil, I had not the pleasure of a personal acquaintance with him, and I therefore welcome this opportunity of thanking him for the liberality shown in all their dealings with me by the company of which he is the moving spirit. — L. A.

expedition. I dwell upon these things and recur to them often, not in any spirit of egotism, but because it is due to the character of the people from whom they come to make the fullest acknowledgment of their generosity.

While Mr. Agassiz has been busy with the zoölogical collections, Major Coutinho has been no less so in making geological, meteorological, and hydrographic investigations. His regular co-operation is invaluable, and Mr. Agassiz blesses the day when their chance meeting at the Palace suggested the idea of his joining the expedition. Not only his scientific attainments, but his knowledge of the Indian language (*lingua geral*), and his familiarity with the people, make him a most important coadjutor. With his aid Mr. Agassiz has already opened a sort of scientific log-book, in which, by the side of the scientific name of every specimen entered by the Professor, Major Coutinho records its popular local name, obtained from the Indians, with all they can tell of its haunts and habits.

I have said nothing of Mr. Agassiz's observations on the character of the soil since we left Rio, thinking it best to give them as a whole. Along the entire length of the coast he has followed the drift, examining it carefully at every station. At Bahia it contained fewer large boulders than in Rio, but was full of small pebbles, and rested upon undecomposed stratified rock. At Macció, the capital of the province of Alagôas, it was the same, but resting upon decomposed rock, as at Tijuca. Below this was a bed of stratified clay, containing small pebbles. In Pernambuco, on our drive to the great aqueduct, we followed it for the whole way; the same red clayey homogeneous paste, resting there on decomposed rock. The line of contact at Monteiro, the aqueduct station, was very clearly marked, however, by an intervening bed of pebbles. At Parahyba do Norte the same sheet of drift, but containing more and larger pebbles, rests above a decomposed sandstone somewhat resembling the decomposed rock of Pernambuco. In the undecomposed rock below, Mr. Agassiz found some fossil shells. In the neighborhood of Cape St. Roque we came upon sand-dunes resembling those of Cape Cod, and wherever we sailed near enough to the shore to see the banks distinctly, as was frequently the case, the bed of drift below the shifting superficial sands above was distinctly noticeable. The difference in color between the white sand and the reddish soil beneath made it easy to perceive their relations. At Ceará, where we landed, Mr. Agassiz had an opportunity of satisfying himself of this by closer examination. At Maranham the drift is everywhere conspicuous, and at Pará equally so. This sheet of drift which he has thus followed from Rio de Janeiro to the mouth of the Amazons is everywhere of the same geological constitution. It is always a homogeneous clayey paste of a reddish color, containing quartz pebbles; and, whatever be the character of the rock in place, whether granite, sandstone, gneiss, or lime, the character of the drift never changes or partakes of that of the rocks with which it is in contact. This certainly proves that, whatever be its origin, it cannot be referred to the localities where it is now found, but must have been brought from a distance. Whoever shall track it back to the place where this peculiar red soil with its constituent elements forms the primitive rock, will have solved the problem. I introduce here a letter written by Mr. Agassiz, a few days later, to the Emperor, which will better give his views on the subject.

A BORD DE L'ICAMIABA, SUR L'AMAZONE,
le 20 Aout, 1865.

SIRE : — Permettez moi de rendre un compte rapide à Votre Majesté, de ce que j'ai observé de plus intéressant depuis mon départ de Rio. La première chose qui m'a frappé en arrivant à Bahia, ce fut d'y trouver le terrain erratique, comme à la Tijuca et comme dans la partie méridionale de Minas, que j'ai visitée. Ici comme là, ce terrain, d'une constitution identique, repose sur les roches en place les plus diversifiées. Je l'ai retrouvé de même à Maceio, à Pernambuco, à Parahyba do Norte, à Ceará, à Maranham, et au Pará. Voilà donc un fait établi sur la plus grande échelle ! Cela démontre que les matériaux superficiels, que l'on pourrait désigner du nom de drift, ici comme dans le Nord de l'Europe et de l'Amérique, ne sauraient être le résultat de la décomposition des roches sous-jacentes, puisque celles-ci sont tantôt du granit, tantôt du gneiss, tantôt du schiste micacé ou talqueux, tantôt du grès, tandis que le drift offre partout la même composition. Je n'en suis pas moins aussi éloigné que jamais de pouvoir signaler l'origine de ces materiaux et la direction de leur transport. Aujourd'hui que le Major Coutinho a appris à distinguer le drift des roches décomposées, il m'assure que nous le retrouverons dans toute la vallée de l'Amazône. L'imagination la plus hardie recule devant toute espèce de généralisation à ce sujet. Et pourtant, il faudra bien en venir à se familiariser avec l'idée que la cause qui a dispersé ces matériaux, quelle qu'elle soit, a agi sur la plus grande échelle, puisqu'on les retrouvera probablement sur tout le continent. Déjà j'apprends que mes jeunes compagnons de voyage ont observé le drift dans les environs de Barbacena et d'Ouro-Preto et dans la vallée du Rio das

Velhas. Mes résultats zoologiques ne sont pas moins satisfaisants ; et pour ne parler que des poissons, j'ai trouvé à Pará seulement, pendant une semaine, plus d'espèces qu'on n'en a décrit jusqu'à présent de tout le bassin de l'Amazône ; c. à. d. en tout soixante-trois. Cette étude sera, je crois, utile à l'ichthyologie, car j'ai déjà pu distinguer cinq familles nouvelles et dix-huit genres nouveaux et les espèces inédites ne s'élèvent pas à moins de quarante-neuf. C'est une garantie que je ferai encore une riche moisson, lorsque j'entrerai dans le domaine de l'Amazône proprement dit ; car je n'ai encore vu qu'un dixième des espèces fluviatiles que l'on connait de ce bassin et les quelques espèces marines qui remontent jusqu'au Pará. Malheureusement M. Burkhardt est malade et je n'ai encore pu faire peindre que quatre des espèces nouvelles que je me suis procurées, et puis près de la moitié n'ont été prises qu'en exemplaires uniques. Il faut absolument qu'à mon retour je fasse un plus long séjour au Pará pour remplir ces lacunes. Je suis dans le ravissement de la nature grandiose que j'ai sous les yeux. Votre Majesté règne sans contredit sur le plus bel empire du monde et toutes personelles que soient les attentions que je reçois partout où je m'arrête, je ne puis m'empêcher de croire que n'était le caractère généreux et hospitalier des Brésiliens et l'intérêt des classes supérieures pour le progrès des sciences et de la civilisation, je n'aurais point rencontré les facilités qui se pressent sous mes pas. C'est ainsi que pour me faciliter l'exploration du fleuve, du Pará à Manaos, M. Pimenta Bueno, au lieu de m'acheminer par le steamer régulier, a mis à ma disposition, pour un mois ou six semaines, un des plus beaux bateaux de la compagnie, où je suis instalé aussi commodément que dans mon Musée à Cambridge. M. Coutinho est plein d'attention et me rend mon travail doublement facile en le préparant à l'avance par tous les renseignements possibles.

Mais je ne veux pas abuser des loisirs de Votre Majesté et je la prie de croire toujours au dévouement le plus complet et à l'affection la plus respectueuse

De son très humble et très obéissant serviteur,

L. AGASSIZ.*

* ON BOARD THE ICAMIABA, ON THE AMAZONS,
August 20, 1865.

SIRE: — Allow me to give your Majesty a rapid sketch of the most interesting facts observed by me since leaving Rio. The first thing which struck me on arriving at Bahia was the presence of the erratic soil, corresponding to that of Tijuca and the southern part of Minas-Geräes, which I have visited. Here, as there, this soil, identical in its constitution, rests upon rocks in place, of the most diversified character. I have found it also at Maccíó, at Pernambuco, at Parahyba do Norte, at Ceará, at Maranham, and at Pará. This is a fact, then, established on the largest scale. It shows that the superficial materials which, here as in the North of Europe and America, may be designated as drift, cannot be the result of the decomposition of underlying rocks, since the latter are sometimes granite, sometimes gneiss, sometimes mica or talcose slate, sometimes sandstone, while the drift presents the same composition everywhere. I am as far as ever from being able to point out the origin of these materials and the direction of their transportation. Now that Major Coutinho has learned to distinguish the drift from the decomposed rocks, he assures me that we shall find it throughout the valley of the Amazons. The boldest imagination shrinks from any generalization on this subject, and yet we must gradually familiarize ourselves with the idea that the cause which has dispersed these materials, whatever it be, has acted on the largest scale, since they are probably to be found all over the continent. Already I learn that my young travelling companions have observed the drift in the environs of Barbacena and Ouro-Preto, and in the valley of the Rio das Velhas. My zoölogical results are not less satisfactory; and to speak of the fishes alone, I have found at Pará during one week more species than have as yet been described from the whole basin of the Amazons, — sixty-three in all. This study will be useful, I hope, to ichthyology, for I have already succeeded in distinguishing five new families and eighteen new genera, while the unpublished species do not number less than forty-nine. It is a guaranty of the rich harvest I shall make when I enter upon the domain of the Amazons properly so called; for I have seen as yet but a tenth part of the fluviatile species known from this basin, and some of the marine species which come up to Pará. Unhappily, Mr. Burkhardt is ill, and has been able to paint but four of the new species we have procured; and of nearly half the number, only single specimens have been secured. On my return I must make a longer stay in Pará in order to fill these deficiencies. I am enchanted with the grandeur of nature here. Your Majesty certainly reigns over the most beautiful empire of the world; and, personal as are the attentions which I receive wherever I stop, I cannot but believe that, were it not for the generous and hospitable character of the Brazilians and the interest of the higher classes in the progress of science and civilization, I should not have met with the facilities which crowd my path. Thus, in order to render the exploration of the river from Pará to Manaos more easy, Mr. Pimenta Bueno, instead of allowing me to take the regular steamer, has put at my disposition, for a month or six weeks, one of the finest boats of the company, where I am installed as conveniently as in my Museum at Cambridge. Mr. Coutinho is full of attention, and renders my work doubly light by procuring, in advance, all the information possible. But I will not further abuse your Majesty's leisure, only begging you to believe in the complete devotion and respectful affection of

Your humble and obedient servant,

L. AGASSIZ.

CHAPTER V.

FROM PARÁ TO MANAOS.

First Sunday on the Amazons. — Geographical Question. — Convenient Arrangements of Steamer. — Vast Dimensions of the River. — Aspect of Shores. — Village of Breves. — Letter about Collections. — Vegetation. — Variety of Palms. — Settlement of Tajapurú. — Enormous Size of Leaves of the Miriti Palm. — Walk on Shore. — Indian Houses. — Courtesy of Indians. — Row in the Forest. — Town of Gurupá. — River Xingu. — Color of Water. — Town of Porto do Moz. — Flat-topped Hills of Almeyrim. — Beautiful Sunset. — Monte Alégre. — Character of Scenery and Soil. — Santarem. — Send off Party on the River Tapajos. — Continue up the Amazons. — Pastoral Scenes on the Banks. — Town of Villa Bella. — Canoe Journey at Night to the Lake of José Assú. — Esperança's Cottage. — Picturesque Scene at Night. — Success in Collecting. — Indian Life. — Making Farinha. — Dance in the Evening. — Howling Monkeys. — Religious Impressions of Indians. — Cottage of Maia the Fisherman. — His Interest in Educating his Children. — Return to Steamer. — Scientific Results of the Excursion.

August 20th. — On board the "Icamiaba." Our first Sunday on the Amazons; for, notwithstanding the warm dispute as to whether both the rivers enclosing the island of Marajó must be considered as parts of the great river, it is impossible not to feel from the moment you leave Pará that you have entered upon the Amazons. Geology must settle this knotty question. If it should be seen that the continent once presented an unbroken line, as Mr. Agassiz believes, from Cape St. Roque to Cayenne, the sea having encroached upon it so as to give it its present limits, the Amazons must originally have entered the ocean far to the east of its present mouth, at a time when the Island of Marajó divided the river in two channels flowing on either side of it and uniting again beyond it.

We came on board last night, accompanied to the boat by a number of the friends who have made our sojourn in Pará so agreeable, and who came off to bid us farewell. Thus far the hardships of this South American journey seem to retreat at our approach. It is impossible to travel with greater comfort than surrounds us here. My own suite of rooms consists of a good-sized state-room, with dressing-room and bath-room adjoining, and, if the others are not quite so luxuriously accommodated, they have space enough. The state-rooms are hardly used at night, for a hammock on deck is far more comfortable in this climate. Our deck, roofed in for its whole length, and with an awning to let down on the sides, if needed, looks like a comfortable, unceremonious sitting-room. A table down the middle serving as a dinner-table, but which is at this moment strewn with maps, journals, books, and papers of all sorts, two or three lounging-chairs, a number of camp-stools, and half a dozen hammocks, in one or two of which some of the party are taking their ease, furnish our drawing-room, and supply all that is needed for work and rest. At one end is also a drawing-table for Mr. Burkhardt, beside a number of kegs and glass jars for specimens. This first day, however, it is almost impossible to do more than look and wonder. Mr. Agassiz says: "This river is not like a river; the general current in such a sea of fresh water is hardly perceptible to the sight, and seems more like the flow of an ocean than like that of an inland stream." It is true we are constantly between shores, but they are shores, not of the river itself, but of the countless islands scattered throughout its enormous breadth. As we coast along their banks, it is delightful to watch the exquisite vegetation with which we have yet to become familiar. The

7 *

tree which most immediately strikes the eye, and stands out from the mass of green with wonderful grace and majesty, is the lofty, slender Assai palm, with its crown of light plume-like leaves, and its bunches of berry-like fruit, hanging from a branch that shoots out almost horizontally, just below the leaves. Houses on the shore break the solitude here and there. From this distance they look picturesque, with thatched, overhanging roofs, covering a kind of open porch. Just now we passed a cleared nook at the water-side, where a wooden cross marked a single mound. What a lonely grave it seemed! We are now coasting along the Isle of Marajó, keeping up the so-called Pará river ; we shall not enter the undisputed waters of the Amazons till the day after to-morrow. This part of the river goes also by the name of the Bay of Marajó.

August 21*st.* — Last evening we stopped at our first station, — the little town of Breves. Its population, like that of all these small settlements on the Lower Amazons, is made up of an amalgamation of races. You see the regular features and fair skin of the white man combined with the black, coarse, straight hair of the Indian, or the mulatto with partly negro, partly Indian features, but the crisp taken out of the hair ; and with these combinations comes in the pure Indian type, with its low brow, square build of face, and straight line of the shoulders. In the women especially the shoulders are rather high. In the first house we entered there was only an old half-breed Indianwoman, standing in the broad open porch of her thatched home, where she seemed to be surrounded with live stock, — parrots and parroquets of all sorts and sizes, which she kept for sale. After looking in at several of the houses, buying one or two monkeys, some parroquets, and some articles of the village pottery, as ugly, I must say, as they were curious, we wandered up into the forest to gather plants for drying. The palms are more abundant, larger, and in greater variety than we have seen them hitherto. At dusk we returned to the steamer, where we found a crowd of little boys and some older members of the village population, with snakes, fishes, insects, monkeys, &c. The news had spread that the collecting of "bixos" was the object of this visit to their settlement, and all were thronging in with their live wares of different kinds. Mr. Agassiz was very much pleased with this first harvest. He added a considerable number of new species to his collection of Amazonian fishes made in Pará, already so full and rare. We remained at the Breves landing all night, and this morning we are steaming along between islands, in a channel which bears the name of the river Aturiá. It gives an idea of the grandeur of the Amazons, that many of the channels dividing the islands by which its immense breadth is broken are themselves like ample rivers, and among the people here are known by distinct local names. The banks are flat; we have seen no cliffs as yet, and the beauty of the scenery is wholly in the forest. I speak more of the palms than of other trees, because they are not to be mistaken, and from their peculiar port they stand out in bold relief from the mass of foliage, often rising above it and sharply defined against the sky. There are, however, a host of other trees, the names of which are unknown to us as yet, many of which I suppose have no place even in botanical nomenclature, forming a dense wall of verdure along the banks of the river. We have sometimes heard it said that the voyage up the Amazons is monotonous; but to me it seems delightful to coast along by these woods, of a character so new to us, to get glimpses into their dark depths or into a cleared spot with a single stately palm here and there, or to catch even the merest glance at the life of the people who live in the isolated settlements, consisting only of one or two Indian houses by the river-side. We are keeping so near to the banks to-day, that we can almost count the leaves on the trees, and have an excellent opportunity of studying the various kinds of palms. At first the Assai was most conspicuous, but now come in a number of others. The Mirití (Mauritia) is one of the most beautiful, with its pendant clusters of reddish fruit and its enormous, spreading, fan-like leaves cut into ribbons, one of which Wallace says is a load for a man. The Jupatí (Rhaphia), with its plume-like leaves, sometimes from forty to fifty feet in length, seems, in consequence of its short stem, to start almost from the ground. Its vase-like form is peculiarly graceful and symmetrical. Then there is the Bussù (Manicaria), with stiff, entire leaves, some thirty feet in length, more upright and close in their mode of growth, and serrated along their edges. The stem of this palm also is comparatively short. The banks in this part of the river are very generally bordered by two plants forming sometimes a sort of hedge along the shore; namely, the Aninga (Arum), with large, heart-shaped leaves on the summit of tall stems, and the Murici, a lower growth, just on the water's edge. We are passing out of the so-called river Aturia into another channel of like character, the river Tajapurú. In the course of the day we shall arrive at a little settlement bearing the same name, where is to be our second station.

August 22d. — Yesterday we passed the day at the settlement mentioned above. It consists only of the house of a Brazilian merchant,* who lives here with his family, having no neighbors except the inhabitants of a few Indian houses in the forest immediately about. One wonders at first what should induce a man to isolate himself in this solitude. But the India-rubber trade is very productive here. The Indians tap the trees as we tap our sugar-maples, and give the produce in exchange for various articles of their own domestic consumption. Our day at Tajapurú was a very successful one in a scientific point of view, and the collections were again increased by a number of new species. Much as has been said of the number and variety of fishes in the Amazons, the fauna seems far richer than it has been reported. For those of my readers who care to follow the scientific progress of the expedition as well as the thread of personal adventure, I add here a letter on the subject, written a day or two later by Mr. Agassiz to Mr. Pimenta Bueno, in Pará, the generous friend to whom he owes in a great degree the facilities he enjoys in this voyage.

22 Aout, au matin: entre Tajapurú et Gurupá.

MON CHER AMI: — La journée d'hier a été des plus instructives, surtout pour les poissons "do Mato." Nous avons obtenu quinze espèces en tout. Sur ce nombre il y en a dix nouvelles, quatre qui se trouvent aussi au Pará et une déjà décrite par moi dans le voyage de Spix et Martius ; mais ce qu'il y a de plus intéressant, c'est la preuve que fournissent ces espèces, à les prendre dans leur totalité, que l'ensemble des poissons qui habitent les eaux à l'ouest

---

* Senhor Sepeda, a most hospitable and courteous gentleman, to whom we were indebted then and afterwards for much kindness, and also for valuable collections put up during our journey to the Upper Amazons.

du groupe d'iles qu'on appelle Marajó, diffère de ceux des eaux du Rio do Pará. La liste des noms que nous avons demandée aux Indiens prouve encore que le nombre des espèces qui se trouvent dans ces localités est beaucoup plus considérable que celui des espèces que nous avons pu nous procurer ; aussi avons nous laissé des bocaux à Breves et à Tajapurú pour compléter la collection.

Voici quelques remarques qui vous feront mieux apprécier ces differences, si vous voulez les comparer avec le catalogue des espèces du Pará que je vous ai laissé. A tout prendre, il me parait évident dès à présent que notre voyage fera une révolution dans l'Ichthyologie. Et d'abord, le Jacundá de Tajapurú est différent des espèces du Pará ; de même l'Acará ; puis nous avons une espèce nouvelle de Sarapó et une espèce nouvelle de Jeju ; une espèce nouvelle de Rabeca, une espèce nouvelle d'Anojá, un genre nouveau de Candiru, un genre nouveau de Bagre, un genre nouveau d'Acary et une espèce nouvelle d'Acary du même genre que celui du Pará ; plus une espèce nouvelle de Matupirim. Ajoutez à ceci une espèce d'Aracu déjà décrite, mais qui ne se trouve pas au Pará et vous aurez à Tajapurú onze espèces qui n'existent pas au Pará, auxquelles il faut ajouter encore quatre espèces qui se trouvent à Tajapurú aussi bien qu'au Pará, et une qui se trouve au Pará, à Breves, et à Tajapurú. En tout vingt espèces, dont quinze nouvelles, en deux jours. Malheureusement les Indiens ont mal compris nos directions, et ne nous ont rapporté qu'un seul exemplaire de chacune de ces espèces. Il reste donc beaucoup à faire dans ces localités, surtout à en juger d'après le catalogue des noms recueillis par le Major Coutinho qui renferme vingt-six espèces " do Mato" et quarante-six " do Rio." Il nous en manque donc au moins cinquante-deux de Tajapurú, même à supposer que cette localité renferme aussi les cinq espèces de Breves. Vous voyez que nous laisserons encore énormément à faire à nos successeurs.

Adieu pour aujourd'hui, votre bien affectioné

L. AGASSIZ.*

* August 22d, morning : between Tajapurú and Gurupá.

MY DEAR FRIEND: — Yesterday was a most instructive day, — above all, in the "forest fishes." We have obtained fifteen species in all. Out of this number ten are new, four are found also in Pará, and one has been already described by me in the voyage of Spix and Martins; but what is most interesting is the proof furnished by these species, taken in their totality, that the fishes inhabiting the waters west of the group of islands called Marajó, when considered as a whole, differ from those of the Pará river. The list of names which we have asked from the Indians shows, further, that the number of species found in these localities exceeds greatly that which we have been able to procure; for this reason we have left caus at Breves and at Tajapurú in order to complete the collection. I add some remarks which will help you to appreciate these differences, if you wish to compare them with the catalogue of the Pará species which I left with you. Considering all, it seems to me already apparent that our voyage will make a revolution in Ichthyology. In the first place, the Jacundá of Tajapurú is different from those of Pará; so is the Acará; then we have a new species of Sarapó, and also one of Jeju; a new species of Rabeca, a new species of Anojá, a new genus of Candiru, a new genus of Bagre, a new genus of Acary, and a new species of Acary belonging to the same genus as that of Pará; also a new species of Matupirin. Add to this a species of Aracú, already described, but which is not found at Pará, and you will have at Tajapurú eleven species which do not exist at Pará, to which must be added four species which are found at Tajapurú as well as at Pará, and one which occurs at Pará, Breves, and Tajapurú. In all twenty species, of which fifteen are new, in two days. Unhappily, the Indians have misunderstood our directions, and have brought us but one specimen of each species. There remains, then, much to do in these localities, judging from the catalogue of names collected by Major Coutinho, which includes twenty-six species from the forest and forty-six from the river. We are still lacking at least fifty-two species from Tajapurú, even supposing that this locality contains also the five species from Breves. You see that we shall yet leave a large share of the work to our successors.

Adieu for to-day, your affectionate

L. AGASSIZ.

160   A JOURNEY IN BRAZIL.

The Indians here are very skilful in fishing, and instead of going to collect, Mr. Agassiz, immediately on arriving at any station, sends off several fishermen of the place, remaining himself on board to superintend the drawing and putting up of the specimens as they arrive.* He

* The opportunity of watching these fishes in their natural element, and keeping many of them alive for hours or days in our glass tanks, was very instructive, and suggested comparisons not dreamed of before. Our arrangements were very convenient; and as the commander of the steamer allowed me to encumber the deck with all sorts of scientific apparatus, I had a number of large glass dishes and wooden tubs in which I kept such specimens as I wished to investigate with special care and to have drawn from life. One of the most striking changes made by J. Müller, in the classification of the spiny fishes, was the separation into a distinct order, under the name of Pharyngognathi, of all those in which the pharyngeal bones are soldered together. With these the illustrious German anatomist has associated a number of soft-rayed types, formerly united with the Pickerels and Herrings, and characterized by the same structure. It would thus seem that there is here a definite anatomical character easily traceable, by the aid of which a vast number of fishes might be correctly classified. But the question at once arises, Are these fishes truly related to one another, and so combined in this new order of Pharyngognathi as to include all which properly belong with them, and none others? I think not. I believe that Müller has always placed too much value upon isolated anatomical characters; and, while he was undoubtedly one of the greatest anatomists and physiologists of our age, he lacked zoölogical tact. This is especially evident with reference to the order of Pharyngognathi, for though the Scomberesoces have fixed pharyngeals like Chromides, Pomacentrides, Labroids, Holconotes, and Gerrides, they have no real affinities with these families. Again, the character assigned to this order is not constant even in the typical Pharyngognathi. I have found Chromides and Gerrides with movable pharyngeals ; in the genus Cychla they are normally so. It is therefore not out of place to state here that the Chromides of South America are in reality closely related to a group of fishes very generally found in the United States, known as Pomotis, Bryttus, Centrarchus, etc., and usually referred to the family of Perches, from which they have, however, been separated by Dr. Holbrook under the name of Helichthyoids. They not only resemble the Chromides in their form, but even in their habits, mode of reproduction, peculiar movements, and even in their coloration. Cuvier has already shown that Enoplosus is not a member of the family made at Tajapurú a collection of the leaves and fruit of palms, of which there were several very beautiful ones near the shore. I sat for a long time on the deck watching an Indian cutting a leaf from a Mirití palm. He was sitting in the crotch of a single leaf, as safe and as perfectly supported as if he had been on the branch of an oak-tree, and it took many blows of his heavy axe to separate the leaf at his side which he was trying to bring down. The heat during the day was intense, but at about five o'clock it became quite cool and R—— and I strolled on shore. Walking here is a peculiar process, and seems rather alarming till you become accustomed to it. A great part of the land, even far up into the forest, is overflowed, and single logs are thrown across the streams and pools, over which the inhabitants walk with as much security as on a broad road, but which seem anything but safe to the new-comer. After we had gone a little way we came to an Indian house on the border of the wood. Here we were very cordially invited to enter, and had again cause to comment on the tidy aspect of the porch, which is their general reception-room. A description of one of these dwellings will do for all. Their materials are drawn from the forest about them. The frames are made

---

of Chætodonts, and I may now add that it is a near relative of the Chromides, and should stand by the side of Pterophyllum in a natural system. Monocirrus of Heckel, which I consider as the type of a small family under the name of Folhidæ, is also closely allied to these, though provided with a barbel, and should be placed with Polycentrus side by side with the Chromides and Helichthyoids. The manner in which Pterophyllum moves is quite peculiar. The profile of the head and the extended anterior margin of the high dorsal are brought on a level, parallel to the surface of the water, when the long ventrals and high anal hang down vertically, and the fish progresses slowly by the lateral beating of the tail. — L. A.

of tall, slender tree-trunks, crossing each other at right angles. Between these are woven long palm-leaves, making an admirable thatch, or sometimes the walls are filled in with mud. The roof overhangs, covering the wide, open porch, which extends the length of one side of the house, and is as deep as a good-sized room; it is usually left open on the sides as well as in front. Within, the rest of the house is divided off into one or more chambers, according to its size. I have not penetrated into these, but can bear testimony to the usual cleanliness and order of the outer room. The hard mud-floor is neatly swept, there is no litter about, and, except for the mosquitoes, I should think it no hardship to sling my hammock for the night under the thatched roof of one of these primitive veranda-like apartments. There is one element of dirt common in the houses of our own poor which is absent here. Instead of the mass of old musty bedding, a nest for vermin, the Indians have their cool hammocks, slung from side to side of the room. One feature in their mode of building deserves to be mentioned. Owing to the submerged state of the ground on which they live, the Indians often raise their houses on piles sunk in the water. Here we have the old lacustrine buildings, so much discussed of late years, reproduced for us. One even sees sometimes a little garden lifted in this way above the water.

But to return to our walk. One of the Indians invited us to continue our ramble to his house, which he said was not far beyond, in the forest. We readily complied, for the path he pointed out to us looked tempting in the extreme, leading into the depth of the wood. Under his guidance we continued for some distance, every now and then crossing one of the forest creeks on the logs. Seeing that I was rather timid, he cut for me a long pole, with the aid of which I felt quite brave. But at last we came to a place where the water was so deep that I could not touch bottom with my pole, and as the round log on which I was to cross was rather rocking and unsteady, I did not dare to advance. I told him, in my imperfect Portuguese, that I was afraid. "Naõ, mia branca" (No, my white) he said, reassuringly; "naõ tem medo" (don't be afraid). Then, as if a thought struck him, he motioned me to wait, and, going a few steps up the creek, he unloosed his boat, brought it down to the spot where we stood, and put us across to the opposite shore. Just beyond was his pretty, picturesque home, where he showed me his children, telling me their ages, and introduced me to his wife. There is a natural courtesy about these people which is very attractive, and which Major Coutinho, who has lived among them a great deal, tells me is a general characteristic of the Amazonian Indians. When we took leave of them and returned to the canoe, I supposed our guide would simply put us across to the other shore, a distance of a few feet only, as he had done in coming. Instead of that he headed the canoe up the creek into the wood. I shall never forget that row, the more enchanting that it was so unexpected, through the narrow water-path, overarched by a solid roof of verdure, and black with shadows; and yet it was not gloomy, for outside, the sun was setting in crimson and gold, and its last beams struck in under the boughs and lit the interior of the forest with a warm glow. Nor shall I easily forget the face of our Indian friend, who had welcomed us so warmly to his home, and who evidently enjoyed our exclamations of delight and the effect of the surprise he had given us. The creek led by a détour back into the river, a few rods above the landing where our steamer lay. Our friendly boatman left us at the stairway with a cordial good-by, and many thanks from us at parting.

We left our landing early this morning, and at about half past ten turned into the main Amazons. Thus far we have been in what is called the Pará river, and the branches connecting it with the Amazons proper. The proportions of everything in nature amaze one here, however much one may have heard or read about them. For two days and nights we have been following the isle of Marajo, which, though but an island in the mouth of the Amazons, is half as large as Ireland. I add here a second letter from Mr. Agassiz to Mr. Pimenta Bueno, giving a short summary of his scientific progress.

MON CHER AMI : — Je suis exténué de fatigue, mais je ne veux pas aller me reposer avant de vous avoir écrit un mot. Hier soir nous avons obtenu vingt-sept espèces de poissons à Gurupá et ce matin, cinquante-sept à Porto do Moz, en tout quatre-vingt-quatre espèces en moins de douze heures et, sur ce nombre, il y en a cinquante et une nouvelles. C'est merveilleux. Je ne puis plus mettre en ordre ce qu'on m'apporte au fur et à mesure que cela arrive ; et quant à obtenir des dessins coloriés du tout, il n'en est plus question, à moins qu'à notre retour nous ne passions une semaine entière ici.

Tout à vous,
L. AGASSIZ.*

* ON THE XINGU, August 23d, 1865.

MY DEAR FRIEND : — I am worn out with fatigue, but I will not go to rest before writing you a word. Yesterday evening we obtained twenty-seven

August 23*d.* — Yesterday morning, before reaching the little town of Gurupá, we passed a forest of Miriti palms; it is the first time we have seen a palm wood exclusive of other trees. In the afternoon we stopped at Gurupá and went on shore; but just as we landed, a violent thunder-storm burst upon us with sheets of rain, and we saw little of the town except the inside of the house where we took shelter. Mr. Agassiz obtained a most valuable collection of "forest fishes," containing a number of new species; the Indians enumerate, however, some seventy distinct species of forest fishes in this vicinity, so that, notwithstanding his success, he leaves much to be done by those who shall come after him. We left during the night, and this morning we entered the river Xingu, stopping at Porto do Moz. The water is very blue and dark as compared with the muddy waters of the main river. Here Mr. Agassiz found two collections, one of forest fishes, the other of river fishes, awaiting him. Mr. Pimenta Bueno having sent messengers by the last steamer to a number of ports, desiring that collections should be in readiness for him. The harvest of this morning, however, was such an one as makes an era in the life of a naturalist, for it contained forty-eight new species, — more, Mr. Agassiz said, than it had ever fallen to his lot to find in the course of a single day. Ever since we entered the Amazons the forest seems to me, though more luxuriant, less sombre than it did about Rio. It is more transparent and more smiling; one sees into it,

species of fish at Gurupá and this morning fifty-seven at Porto do Moz, — eighty-four species in all, in less than twelve hours, and of this number fifty-one are new. It is wonderful. I can no longer put in order what is brought to me as fast as it arrives, and as to obtaining colored drawings of all, it is no longer possible, unless we pass a whole week here on our return.

Wholly yours,
L. Agassiz.

and sees the sunshine glimmering through it and lighting up its depths. The steamer has just left behind the first open land we have passed, — wide, extensive flats, with scarcely a tree, and covered with thick, coarse grass.

August 24*th*. — Yesterday afternoon we saw, on the north side of the river, the first elevations of any consequence one meets on the Amazons, the singular flat-topped hills of Almeirim. They are cut off as squarely on the top as if levelled with a plane, and divided from each other by wide openings, the sides being shaved down with the same evenness as the summits. Much has been said about the geology of these singular hills, but no one has fairly investigated it. Von Martius landed, and ascertained their height to be about eight hundred feet above the level of the river, but beyond this, no one seems to know anything of their real nature. They are generally represented as spurs of the higher table-land of Guiana.* Last evening was the most beautiful we have seen on the Amazons. We sat on the front upper deck as the crimson sun went down, his broad red pathway across the water followed presently by the pale trembling line of light from the crescent moon above. After the sun had vanished, broad rays of rose-color, shooting almost to the zenith, still attested his power, lending something of their glow also to a great mass of white clouds in the east, the reflection of which turned the yellow waters of the river to silver, while between glory and glory the deep blue sky of night gathered over the hills of Almeirim. This morning at dawn we stopped at the little settlement of Prainha, but did not land, and we are now on our way to Monte Alégre, where we shall pass a day and a half.

* Representations of these hills may be found in the Atlas of Martius and in Bates's "Naturalist on the Amazons."

August 25th. — Monte Alégre. We arrived before this town, situated on the north side of the Amazons, at the mouth of the river Gurupatuba, yesterday at about midday, but the heat was so great that I did not go on shore till towards evening. The town is situated on the summit of a hill sloping rather steeply upward from the shore, and it takes its name from a mountain some four leagues to the northwest of it. But though the ground is more broken and various than we have seen it hitherto, the place does not seem to me to deserve its name of Monte Alégre (the gay mountain). To me the aspect of the country here is, on the contrary, rather sombre; the soil consists everywhere of sand, the forest is low, while here and there intervene wide, swampy flats, covered with coarse grass. The sand rests above the same reddish drift, filled with smooth rounded quartz pebbles, that we have followed along our whole road. Here and there the pebbles are disposed in undulating lines, as if a partial stratification had taken place; and in some localities we saw indications of the drift having been worked over by water, though not absolutely stratified. Both at sunset and sunrise I took a walk to the village churchyard, which commands the prettiest view in the neighborhood. It is enclosed in a picket fence, a large wooden cross stands in the centre, and there are a few other small crosses marking graves; but the place looked uncared for, grown over, wherever the sand was not bare, by the same coarse, rank shrubs which spring up everywhere in this ungenial soil.* At a little distance from the churchyard, the hill

---

* Afterwards I made a longer stay at Monte Alégre, and learned to know its picturesque nooks and dells, where a luxuriant vegetation is watered by delicious springs. I feel that the above description is superficial; but I let it remain, as perfectly true to my first impressions.

slopes abruptly down, and from its brow one looks across a wide plain covered with low forest, to the mountain on the other side, from which the town takes its name. Looking southward, the foreground is filled with lakes divided from each other by low alluvial lands, forming the level flats alluded to above. Though one of the earliest settlements on the Amazons, this town is, by all accounts, rather decreasing than increasing in population. In the midst of its public square stands what seems at first to be the ruin of a large stone church, but which is, in fact, the framework of a cathedral begun forty years ago, and standing unfinished to this day. Cows were pastured in its grass-grown aisles, and it seemed a rather sad memorial, bespeaking a want of prosperity in the place. We were most kindly entertained in the house of Senhor Manuel, who, finding that the mosquitoes were likely to be very thick on board the steamer, invited us to pass the night under his roof. This morning we are sailing about in the neighborhood, partly for the sake of getting fish, but passing also a couple of hours at a cattle-farm near by, in order to bring on board a number of cows and oxen for the Manaos market. It seems that one of the chief occupations here is the raising of cattle. This, with the sale of fish, cacáo, and India-rubber, constitutes the commerce of the place.

August 26th. — This morning found us again on the southern side of the river, off Santarem, at the mouth of one of the great branches of the Amazons, the Tapajoz. Here we leave a number of our party. Mr. Dexter, Mr. James, and Mr. Talisman, a young Brazilian who joined our party at Pará, go on a collecting expedition up the Tapajoz. Mr. Bourget and Mr. Hunnewell remain at Santarem, the former to make collections, the latter to attend to the repairs of his photographing apparatus, which has met with some disasters. We are all to meet again at Manaos for our farther voyage up to Tabatinga.* We remained at Santarem only long enough to see the party fitted out with a canoe and the necessary supplies, and as they put off from the steamer we weighed anchor and proceeded on our way, reserving our visit to Santarem for our return. As we left the port the black waters of the Tapajoz met the yellow stream of the Amazons, and the two ran together for a while, like the waters of the Arve and Rhone in Switzerland, meeting but not mingling. Instead of returning at once to the main river, the Captain, who omits nothing which can add to the pleasure or the profit of our voyage, put the steamer through a narrow channel, which, on the Mississippi, would be called a "bayou," but goes here by the name of an "Igarapé." Nothing could be prettier than this "Igarapé Assú," hardly more than wide enough to admit the steamer, and bordered on either side by a thick wood, in which are conspicuous the Munguba,

---

* I soon became convinced after leaving Pará that the faunæ of our different stations were not repetitions of each other. On the contrary, at Breves, Tajapurú, Gurupá, — in short, at each stopping-place, as has been seen, — we found another set of inhabitants in the river, if not wholly different from the last, at least presenting so many new species that the combination was no longer the same. It became at once very important to ascertain whether these differences were permanent and stationary, or were, in part at least, an effect of migration. I therefore determined to distribute our forces in such a way as to keep collecting parties at distant points, and to repeat collections from the same localities at different seasons. I pursued this method of investigation during our whole stay in the Amazons, dividing the party for the first time at Santarem, where Messrs. Dexter, James, and Talisman separated from us to ascend the Tapajoz, while Mr. Bourget remained at Santarem, and I, with the rest of my companions, kept on to Obydos and Villa Bella. — L. A.

8

with its oval, red fruit, the Imbauba-tree, neither so lofty nor so regular in form as about Rio, and the Taxi, with its masses of white flowers and brown buds. For two days past we have lost the palms in a great degree; about Monte Alégre they were comparatively few, and here we see scarcely any.

The shore between Santarem and Obydos, where we shall arrive this evening, seems more populous than the regions we have been passing through. As we coast along, keeping close to the land, the scenes revive all our early visions of an ancient pastoral life. Groups of Indians — men, women, and children — greet us from the shore, standing under the overarching trees, usually trained or purposely chosen to form a kind of arbor over the landing-place, — the invariable foreground of the picture, with the "montaria" moored in front. One or two hammocks are often slung in the trees, and between the branches one gets a glimpse of the thatched roof and walls of the little straw cottage behind. Perhaps if we were to look a little closer at these pictures of pastoral life, we should find they have a coarse and prosaic side. But let them stand. Arcadia itself would not bear a too minute scrutiny, nor could it present a fairer aspect than do these Indian homes on the banks of the Amazons. The primitive forest about the houses is usually cleared, and they stand in the midst of little plantations of the cacáo-tree, mingled with the mandioca shrub, from the roots of which the Indians make their flour, and occasionally also with the India-rubber-tree, though, as the latter grows plentifully in the forest, it is not often cultivated. The cacáo and the India-rubber they send to Pará, in exchange for such domestic goods as they require. We have passed so close to the shore to-day that it has been easy to make geological observations from the deck. For a considerable distance above Santarem we have followed drift cliffs, resting upon sandstone; the drift of the same reddish color, and pasty, clayey consistence, and the sandstone seemingly the same in character, as that of Monte Alégre.

August 27th. — Villa Bella. Last evening we stopped to wood at the town of Obydos, but without landing; keeping straight on to this port, on the southern side of the river, at the mouth of the river Tupinambaranas. Here we were very cordially received by Dr. Marcus, an old correspondent of Mr. Agassiz, who has several times sent specimens from the Amazons to the Cambridge Museum. Tonight we are to start in canoes on an excursion to some of the lakes in the neighborhood of this port.

August 28th. — In the porch of an Indian house on the lake José Assú. We passed a pleasant day yesterday at the house of Dr. Marcus, keeping the Sabbath rather after the Jewish than the Christian rule, as a veritable day of rest, lounging in hammocks, and the gentlemen smoking. We returned to the steamer at five o'clock, intending to start at six, in order to have the benefit of the night fishing, said to be always the most successful. But a violent thunder-storm, with heavy rain, lasting almost till midnight, delayed our departure. We loaded the boats, however, before night, that we might be ready to start whenever the weather should clear. We have two canoes, in one of which Mr. Agassiz, myself, and Mr. Burkhardt have our quarters, while Major Coutinho, Dr. Marcus, who accompanies us, and Mr. Thayer occupy the other. The former, which is rather the larger of the two, has a tiny cabin at one end, some three feet high and six feet long, roofed in with wood; the other has also one end covered in, but with thatch instead of wood. In the larger boat we have our luggage, compressed to the utmost, the live stock, — a small sheep, a turkey, and several fowls, — besides a number of barrels and kegs, containing alcohol, for specimens. The Captain has supplied us not only with all the necessaries, but, so far as is possible, with every luxury, for a week's voyage. All our preparations being made, and no prospect of clear weather, at nine o'clock we betook ourselves to our hammocks, — or those of us who had stowed their hammocks out of reach, — to chairs and benches, and had a broken sleep till three o'clock. The stars were then shining, and everything looked fair for our voyage. The wind had gone down, the river was smooth as glass when we paddled away from the side of the steamer, and, though we had no moon, one or two planets threw a bright reflection across the water to cheer our way. After keeping for some time down the river, we turned, just at dawn, into a very narrow channel leading through the forest. It was hardly day, but perhaps the scene was none the less impressive for the dim half-light in which we saw it. From the verdant walls, which rose on either side and shut us in, lofty trees, clothed from base to summit in vines, stood out here and there like huge green columns, in bold relief against the morning sky; hidden flowers filled the air with fragrance, great roots stretched out into the water, and now and then a floating log narrowed the passage so as just to leave room for the canoe to pass. After a while a broader, fuller light shone under the boughs, and we issued from this narrow pathway into an extensive lake. Here it was found that the large net, which was to have made a part of the outfit of the canoe, had been left behind, and, after calling at two or three Indian houses to see if we could supply the deficiency, we were obliged to send back to Villa Bella for it. In the mean time we moored our boats at the foot of a little hill, on which stands an Indian house, where we stopped to breakfast, and where we are still waiting for the return of our messengers. I must say, that a near view of Arcadia tends to dispel illusions; but it should be added, that this specimen is by no means a favorable one. The houses at Tajapurú were far more attractive, and the appearance of their inhabitants much neater and more respectable, than those of our friends here. Yet at this moment the scene is not altogether uninviting. Some of the party are lounging in the hammocks, which we have slung under the great porch, as we are to pass several hours here; an improvised rustic table, consisting of a board resting on forked sticks, stands at one side; the boatmen are clearing away the remains of our late repast; the Indian women, dirty, half clad, with their hair hanging uncombed around their faces, are tending their naked children, or kneading the mandioca in a huge trough. The men of the house have just returned from fishing, the morning having been more successful in that respect than was expected, and are now fitting up a rough forge, in which they are repairing some of their iron instruments. In the mean time Science has its sacred corner, where Mr. Agassiz is investigating new species, the result of the morning's fishing, while Mr. Burkhardt is drawing them.

August 29*th*. — Finding yesterday that our shelter grew more uncomfortable as the day wore on, and being obliged to wait for the night fishing, we determined to cross the lake to a " Sitio " (as the inhabitants call their plantations) on the other side of the lake. Here we found one of the better specimens of Indian houses. On one side of the house is the open porch, quite gay at this moment with our brightly colored hammocks; adjoining this is a large chamber, opening into the porch by a wide straw, or rather palm-leaf door; which does not swing on hinges, however, but is taken down and put up like a mat. On the other side of the room is an unglazed window, closed at will in the same way by a palm-leaf mat. For the present this chamber is given up to my use. On the other side of the porch is another veranda-like room, also open at the sides, and apparently the working-room of the family; for here is the great round oven, built of mud, where the farinha is dried, and the baskets of mandioca-root are standing ready to be picked and grated, and here also is the rough log table where we take our meals. Everything has an air of decency and cleanliness; the mud-floors are swept, the ground about the house is tidy and free from rubbish, the little plantation around it of cacáo and mandioca, with here and there a coffee-shrub, is in nice order. The house stands on a slightly rising ground, sloping gently upward from the lake, and just below, under some trees on the shore, are moored the Indian's "Montaria" and our two canoes. We were received with the most cordial friendliness, the Indian women gathering about me and examining, though not in a rough or rude way, my dress, the net on my hair, touching my rings and watch-chain, and evidently discussing the "branca" between themselves. In the evening, after dinner, I walked up and down outside the house, enjoying the picturesqueness of the scene. The husband had just come in from the lake, and the fire on the ground, over which the fresh fish was broiling for the supper of the family, shone on the figures of the women and children as they moved about, and shed its glow under the thatched roof of the working-room, making its interior warm and ruddy; a lantern in the corner of the porch threw a dim, uncertain light over hammocks and half-recumbent figures, and without, the moon shone over lake and forest. The mosquitoes, however, presently began to disturb the romance of the scene, and, as we were all rather tired from our broken rest the night before, we retired early. My own sleep, under an excellent mosquito-net, was very quiet and refreshing, but there were some of the party who had not provided themselves with this indispensable accompaniment of a hammock, and they passed the night in misery, affording a repast to the voracious hordes buzzing about them. I was awakened shortly after daylight by the Indian women, bringing me a bouquet of roses and jessamine from the vines which grew about the cottage, and wishing me good morning. After such a kindly greeting, I could not refuse them the pleasure of assisting at my toilet, of watching the opening of my valise, and handling every article as it came out.

The night fishing was unfavorable, but this morning the fishermen have brought in new species enough to keep Mr. Agassiz and his artist busy for many hours, so that we are likely to pass another night among these hospitable people. I must say that the primitive life of the better class of Indians on the Amazons is much more attractive than the so-called civilized life in the white settlements. Anything more bald, dreary, and uninviting than life in the Amazonian towns, with an attempt at the conventionalisms of civilization, but without one of its graces, I can hardly conceive. This morning my Indian friends have been showing me the various processes to which the Mandioca is subjected. This plant is invaluable to these people. It gives them their farinha,—a coarse kind of flour, their only substitute for bread,—their tapioca, and also a kind of fermented juice called tucupí,—a more questionable blessing, perhaps, since it affords them the means of getting intoxicated. After being peeled, the roots of the mandioca are scraped on a very coarse grater; in this condition they make a moist kind of paste, which is then packed in elastic straw tubes, made of the fibres of the Jacitará Palm (Desmonchus). When her tube, which has always a loop at either end, is full, the Indian woman hangs it on the branch of a tree; she then passes a pole through the lower loop and into a hole in the trunk of the tree, and, sitting down on the other end of the pole, she thus transforms it into a primitive kind of lever, drawing out the tube to its utmost length by the pressure of her own weight. The juice is thus expressed, flowing into a bowl placed under the tube. This juice is poisonous at first, but after being fermented becomes quite harmless, and is then used for the tucupí. The tapioca is made by mixing the grated mandioca with water. It is then pressed on a sieve, and the fluid which flows out is left to stand. It soon makes a deposit like starch, and when hardened they make it into a kind of porridge. It is a favorite article of food with them.

August 30th. — As time goes on, we grow more at home with our rustic friends here, and begin to understand their relations to each other. The name of our host is Laudigári (I spell the name as it sounds), and that of his wife Esperança. He, like all the Indians living upon the Amazons, is a fisherman, and, with the exception of such little care as his small plantation requires, this is his only occupation. An Indian is never seen to do any of the work of the house, not even to bring wood or water or lift the heavy burdens, and as the fishing is done chiefly at certain seasons, he is a very idle fellow for a great part of the time. The women are said, on the contrary, to be very industrious; and certainly those whom we have an opportunity of seeing here justify this reputation. Esperança is always busy at some household work or other, — grating mandioca, drying farinha, packing tobacco, cooking or sweeping. Her children are active and obedient, the older ones making themselves useful in bringing water from the lake, in washing the mandioca, or in taking care of the younger ones. Esperança can hardly be called pretty, but she has a pleasant smile and a remarkably sweet voice, with a kind of child-like intonation, which is very winning; and when sometimes, after her work is over, she puts on her white chemise, falling loose from her brown shoulders, her dark skirt, and a rose or a sprig of white jessamine in her jetty hair, she is by no means unattractive in her personal appearance, though I must confess that the pipe which she is apt to smoke in the evening injures the general effect. Her husband looks somewhat sombre; but his hearty laugh occasionally, and his enjoyment of the glass of cachaça which rewards him when he brings in a new lot of specimens, shows that he has his bright side. He is greatly amused at the value Mr. Agassiz attaches to the fishes, especially the little ones, which appear to him only fit to throw away. It seems that the other family who have been about here since our arrival are neighbors, who have come in to help in the making of mandioca. They come in the morning with all their children and remain through the day. The names of the father and mother are Pedro Manuel and Michelina. He is a tall, handsome fellow, whose chief occupation seems to be that of standing about in picturesque attitudes, and watching his rather pretty wife, as she bustles round in her various work of grating or pressing or straining the mandioca, generally with her baby astride on her hip, — the Indian woman's favorite way of carrying her child. Occasionally, however, Pedro Manuel is aroused to bear some part in the collecting; and the other day, when he brought in some specimens which seemed to him quite valueless, Mr. Agassiz rewarded him with a chicken. His surprise and delight were great, perhaps a little mingled with contempt for the man who would barter a chicken for a few worthless fishes, fit only to throw into the river.

Last evening, with some difficulty, we induced Laudigári to play for us on a rough kind of lute or guitar, — a favorite instrument with the country people, and used by them as an accompaniment for dancing. When we had him fairly *en train* with the music, we persuaded Esperança and Michelina to show us some of their dances; not without reluctance, and with an embarrassment which savored somewhat of the self-consciousness of civilized life, they stood up with two of our boatmen. The dance is very peculiar; so languid that it hardly deserves the name. There is almost no movement of the body; they lift the arms, but in an angular position with no freedom of motion, snapping the fingers like castanets in time to the music, and they seem rather like statues gliding from place to place than like dancers. This is especially true of the women, who are still more quiet than the men. One of the boatmen was a Bolivian, a finely formed, picturesque-looking man, whose singular dress heightened the effect of his peculiar movements. The Bolivian Indians wear a kind of toga; at least I do not know how otherwise to designate their long straight robe of heavy twilled cotton cloth. It consists of two pieces, hanging before and behind, fastened on the shoulder; leaving only ar

Esperança's Cottage.

aperture for the head to pass through. It is belted around the waist, leaving the sides open so that the legs and arms are perfectly free. The straight folds of his heavy white drapery gave a sort of statuesque look to our Bolivian as he moved slowly about in the dance. After it was over, Esperança and the others urged me to show them the dance "of my country," as they said, and my young friend R—— and I waltzed for them, to their great delight. It seemed to me like a strange dream. The bright fire danced with us, flickering in under the porch, fitfully lighting its picturesque interior and the group of wondering Indians around us, who encouraged us every now and then with a "Mûito bonito, mia branca, mûito bonito" (Very pretty, my white, very pretty). Our ball kept up very late, and after I had gone to my hammock I still heard, between waking and sleeping, the plaintive chords of the guitar, mingling with the melancholy note of a kind of whippoorwill, who sings in the woods all night. This morning the forest is noisy with the howling monkeys. They sound very near and very numerous; but we are told that they are deep in the forest, and would disappear at the slightest approach.

September 1st. — Yesterday morning we bade our friendly hosts good-by, leaving their pretty picturesque home with real regret. The night before we left, they got together some of their neighbors in our honor, and renewed the ball of the previous evening. Like things of the same kind in other classes, the second occasion, got up with a little more preparation than the first, which was wholly impromptu, was neither so gay nor so pretty. Frequent potations of cachaça made the guests rather noisy, and their dancing, under this influence, became far more animated, and by no means so serious and dignified as the evening before. One thing which occurred early in the entertainment, however, was interesting, as showing something of their religious observances. In the morning Esperança's mother, a hideous old Indian woman, had come into my room to make me a visit. Before leaving, I was rather surprised to see her kneel down by a little trunk in the corner, and, opening the lid slightly, throw in repeated kisses, touching her lips to her fingers and making gestures as if she dropped the kisses into the trunk, crossing herself at intervals as she did so. In the evening she was again at the dance, and, with the other two women, went through with a sort of religious dance, chanting the while, and carrying in their hands a carved arch of wood which they waved to and fro in time to the chant. When I asked Esperança the meaning of this, she told me that, though they went to the neighboring town of Villa Bella for the great fête of our Lady of Nazareth, they kept it also at home on their return, and this was a part of their ceremonies. And then she asked me to come in with her, and, leading the way to my room, introduced me to the contents of the precious trunk: there was our Lady of Nazareth, a common coarse print, framed in wood, one or two other smaller colored prints and a few candles; over the whole was thrown a blue gauze. It was the family chapel, and she showed me all the things, taking them up one by one with a kind of tender, joyful reverence, only made the more touching by their want of any material value.

We are now at another Indian house on the bank of an arm of the river Ramos, connecting the Amazons, through the Mauhes, with the Madeira. Our two hours' canoe-journey yesterday, in the middle of the day, was somewhat hot and wearisome, though part of it lay through one of the shady narrow channels I have described before. The Indians have a pretty name for these channels in the forest; they call them Igarapés, that is, boat-paths, and they literally are in many places just wide enough for the canoe. At about four o'clock we arrived at our present lodging, which is by no means so pretty as the one we have left, though it stands, like that, on the slope of a hill just above the shore, with the forest about it. But it lacks the wide porch and the open working-room which made the other house so picturesque. Mosquitoes are plentiful, and at nightfall the house is closed and a pan of turf burned before the door to drive them away. Our host and hostess, by name José Antonio Maia and Maria Joanna Maia, do what they can, however, to make us comfortable, and the children as well as the parents show that natural courtesy which has struck us so much among these Indians. The children are constantly bringing me flowers and such little gifts as they have it in their power to bestow, especially the painted cups which the Indians make from the fruit of the Crescentia, and use as drinking-cups, basins, and the like. One sees numbers of them in all the Indian houses along the Amazons. My books and writing seem to interest them very much, and while I was reading at the window of my room this morning, the father and mother came up, and, after watching me a few minutes in silence, the father asked me, if I had any leaves out of some old book which was useless to me, or even a part of any old newspaper, to leave it with him when I went away. Once, he said, he had known how to read a little, and he seemed to think if he had something to practise upon, he might recover the lost art. His face fell when I told him all my books were English: it was a bucket of cold water to his literary ambition. Then he added, that one of his little boys was very bright, and he was sure he could learn, if he had the means of sending him to school. When I told him that I lived in a country where a good education was freely given to the child of every poor man, he said if the "branca" did not live so far away, he would ask her to take his daughter with her, and for her services to have her taught to read and write. The man has a bright, intelligent face, and speaks with genuine feeling of his desire to give an education to his children.

September 3d. — Yesterday we started on our return, and after a warm and wearisome row of four hours reached our steamer at five o'clock in the afternoon. The scientific results of this expedition have been most satisfactory. The collections, differing greatly from each other in character, are very large from both our stations, and Mr. Burkhardt has been indefatigable in making colored drawings of the specimens while their tints were yet fresh. This is no easy task, for the mosquitoes buzz about him and sometimes make work almost intolerable. This morning Maia brought in a superb Pirarara (fish parrot). This fish is already well known to science; it is a heavy, broad-headed hornpout, with a bony shield over the whole head; its general color is jet black, but it has bright yellow sides, deepening into orange here and there. Its systematic name is Phractocephalus bicolor. The yellow fat of this fish has a curious property; the Indians tell us that when parrots are fed upon it they become tinged with yellow, and they often use it to render their " papagaios" more variegated.*

---

* I was especially interested in seeing living Gymnotini. I do not here allude to the electric Gymnotus, already so fully described by Humboldt that nothing remains to be said about it; but to the smaller representatives of that curious family, known as Carapus, Sternopygus, Sternarchus and Rhamphichthys. The Carapus, called Sarapos throughout Brazil, are very numerous, and the most lively of the whole group. Their motions are winding and rapid like those of the Eel, but yet different, inasmuch as they do not glide quickly forward, but, like Cobitis and Petromyzon, turn frequent somersets and change their direction constantly. This is also the case with the Sternopygus and Sternarchus, and even the larger and more slender Rhamphichthys have a kind of rolling motion. Though I had expected to find many Cyprinodonts,

During our absence the commander of our steamer, Captain Anacleto, and one or two gentlemen of the town, among others Senhor Augustinho, and also Father Torquato, whose name occurs often in Bates's work on the Amazons, have been making a collection of river fishes, in which Mr. Agassiz finds some fifty new species. Thus the harvest of the week has been a rich one. To-day we are on our way to Manaos, where we expect to arrive in the course of to-morrow.

yet their great variety astonished me, and still more was I struck by their resemblance to Melanura, Umbra, and the Erythrinoids. The presence of Belone and allied forms also surprised me. Our stay on the shores of José Assú and Lago Maximo was particularly instructive on account of the numerous specimens of each species daily brought in by Laudigári and Maia. It afforded me a welcome opportunity for studying the differences exhibited by these fishes at different periods of life. No type passes, in that respect, through greater changes than the Chromides, and among them the genus Cychla is perhaps the most variable. I am sure that no ichthyologist could at first sight believe that their young are really the early stage of the forms known in our ichthyological works as Cychla monoculus, Cychla temensis, and Cychla saxatilis. The males and females also vary greatly during the spawning season, and the hump on the top of the head described as a specific character in Cychla nigro-maculata is a protuberance only found in the male, swelling during the period of spawning and soon disappearing. Once familiar with the young brood of some species of Chromides, it became easy for me to distinguish a great variety of small types, no doubt hitherto overlooked by naturalists travelling in this region, simply under the impression that they must be the young of larger species. A similar investigation of the young of Serrasalmo, Myletes, Tetragonopterus, Cynodon, Anodus, &c. led me to the discovery of an equally large number of diminutive types of Characines, many of which, when full grown, do not exceed one inch in length; among them are some of the most beautiful fishes I have ever seen, so far as the brilliancy and variety of their colors are concerned. Thus everything contributed to swell the collections, — the localities selected as well as the mode of investigating. I should add here, that, several years before my own journey on the Amazons, I had been indebted to the Rev. Mr. Fletcher for a valuable collection of fishes from this and other Amazonian localities. The familiarity thus obtained with them was very useful to me in pursuing my studies on the spot. — L. A.

CHAPTER VI.

LIFE AT MANAOS. — VOYAGE FROM MANAOS TO TABATINGA.

Arrival at Manaos. — Meeting of the Solimoens with the Rio Negro. — Domesticated at Manaos. — Return of Party from the Tapajoz. — Generosity of Government. — Walks. — Water-Carriers. — Indian School. — Leave Manaos. — Life on board the Steamer. — Barreira das Cudajas. — Coari. — Wooding. — Appearance of Banks. — Geological Constitution. — Forest. — Sumaumeira-Tree. — Arrow-Grass. — Red Drift Cliffs. — Sand-Beaches. — Indian Huts. — Turtle-Hunting. — Drying Fish. — Teffé. — Doubts about the Journey. — Unexpected Adviser. — Fonte Bôa. — Geological Character of Banks. — Lakes. — Flocks of Water Birds. — Tonantins. — Picturesque Grouping of Indians. — San Paolo. — Land-Slides. — Character of Scenery. — Scanty Population. — Animal Life. — Tabatinga. — Aspect of the Settlement. — Mosquitoes. — Leave one of the Party to make Collections. — On our Way down the River. — Party to the Rivers Içá and Hyutahy. — Aground in the Amazons. — Arrival at Teffé.

September 5th. — Manaos. Yesterday morning we entered the Rio Negro and saw the meeting of its calm, black waters with the rushing yellow current of the Amazons, or the Solimoens, as the Upper Amazon is called. They are well named by the Indians the "living and the dead river," for the Solimoens pours itself down upon the dark stream of the Rio Negro with such a vital, resistless force, that the latter does indeed seem like a lifeless thing by its side. It is true, that at this season, when the water in both the rivers is beginning to subside, the Rio Negro seems to offer some slight resistance to the stronger river; it struggles for a moment with the impetuous flood which overmasters it, and, though crowded up against the shore, continues its course for a little distance side by side with the Solimoens. But at the season when the waters are highest, the latter closes the mouth of the Rio Negro so completely that not a drop of its inky stream is seen to mingle with the yellow waters outside. It is supposed that at this season the Rio Negro sinks at once under the Solimoens; at all events, the latter flows across its mouth, seeming to bar it completely. It must not be supposed, from the change of name, that the Solimoens is anything more than the continuation of the Amazons; just as the so-called river Marañon is its continuation above Nauta, after crossing the Brazilian frontier. It is always the same gigantic stream, traversing the continent for its whole breadth; but it has received in its lower, middle, and upper course the three local names of the Amazons, the Solimoens, and the Marañon. At the point where the Brazilians give it the name of Solimoens it takes a sudden turn to the south, just where the Rio Negro enters it from the north, so that the two form a sharp angle.

We landed at Manaos and went at once to the house which Major Coutinho, with his usual foresight, has provided for us. As the day of our arrival was uncertain, the arrangements were not completed, and the house was entirely empty when we entered it. In about ten minutes, however, chairs and tables — brought, I believe, from the house of a friend — made their appearance, the rooms were promptly furnished, and presently assumed a very cosey and comfortable look, notwithstanding their brick floors and bare walls. We have some pleasant neighbors in a family living almost next door to us, old and intimate friends of Major Coutinho, who receive us for his sake as if we also had a claim on their affection. Here we rest from our wanderings, for a week at least, until the steamer sails for Tabatinga.

September 9th. — We have passed such quiet days here, so far as any variety of incident is concerned, that there is little to record. Work has gone on as usual; the whole collection of fishes, made since we left Pará, has been so repacked as to leave it in readiness to be shipped for that port. Our companions have rejoined us on their return from the Tapajoz, bringing with them considerable collections from that river also. They seem to have enjoyed their excursion greatly, and describe the river as scarcely inferior to the Amazons itself in breadth and grandeur, having wide sand-beaches where the waves roll in, when the wind is high, almost as upon a sea-shore. Mr. Agassiz has done nothing in the way of collecting here, with the exception of securing such fishes as are to be had in the immediate neighborhood; he reserves his voyage on the Rio Negro for our return. And, by the way, we are met here by another practical evidence of the good-will of the Brazilian government. On leaving Rio, the Emperor had offered Mr. Agassiz the use of a small government steamer to make explorations on the Negro and Madeira rivers. On our arrival at Pará he was told that the steamer had been found to be so much out of repair that she was considered unsafe. Under these circumstances, he supposed that we should be obliged to resort to the small boats generally used. But to-day an official communication informs him that, as the Piraja is found not to be serviceable, another steamer will be furnished, which will meet us at Manaos on our return from the Upper Amazons. The following letter, acknowledging this favor, to the President of Pará, through whom it was received, contains some account of the scientific results thus far, and may not be uninteresting.

MANAOS, 8 Septembre, 1865.

A Son Excellence M. Couto de Magalhães, Président du Pará.

MON CHER MONSIEUR :—Je vous remercie infiniment de l'aimable lettre que vous avez eu la bonté de m'écrire la semaine dernière et je m'empresse de vous faire part des succès extraordinaires qui continuent à couronner nos efforts. Il est certain dès-à-présent que le nombre des poissons qui peuplent l'Amazone excède de beaucoup tout ce que l'on avait imaginé jusqu'ici et que leur distribution est très limitée en totalité, bien qu'il y ait un petit nombre d'espèces qui nous suivent depuis Pará et d'autres pour une étendue plus ou moins considérable. Vous vous rappelez peut-être qu'en faisant allusion à mes espérances je vous dis un jour que je croyais à la possibilité de trouver deux cent cinquante à trois cents espèces de poissons dans tout le bassin de l'Amazone ; et bien aujourd'hui, même avant d'avoir franchi le tiers du cours principal du fleuve et remonté par ci par là seulement quelques lieues au delà de ses bords j'en ai déjà obtenu plus de trois cents. C'est inoui ; surtout si l'on considère que le nombre total connu des naturalistes ne va pas au tiers de ce que j'ai déjà recueilli. Ce resultat laisse à peine entrevoir ce qu'on découvrira un jour lorsqu'on explorera avec le même soin tous les affluents du grand fleuve. Ce serait une entreprise digne de vous de faire explorer l'Araguay dans tout son cours pour nous apprendre combien d'assemblages differents d'espèces distinctes se rencontrent successivement depuis ses sources jusqu'à sa jonction avec le Tocantins et plus bas jusqu'à l'Amazone Vous avez déjà une sorte de propriété scientifique sur ce fleuve à laquelle vous ajouteriez de nouveaux droits en fournissant à la science ces renseignements.

Permettez moi de vous exprimer toute ma gratitude pour l'intérêt que vous prenez à mon jeune compagnon de voyage. M. Ward le mérite également par sa grande jeunesse, son courage et son dévouement à la science. M. Epaminondas vient de me faire part de vos généreuses intentions à mon égard et de me dire que vous vous proposez d'expédier un vapeur à Manaos pour prendre la place du Piraja et faciliter notre exploration du Rio Negro et du Rio Madeira. Je ne sais trop comment vous remercier pour une pareille faveur ; tout ce que je puis vous dire dès-à-présent c'est que cette faveur me permettra de faire une exploration de ces fleuves qui me serait impossible sans cela. Et si le résultat de ces recherches est aussi favorable que je l'attends, l'honneur en reviendra avant tout à la libéralité du gouvernement Brésilien. Entraîné par les resultats que j'ai obtenus jusqu'ici, je pense que si les circonstances nous sont favorables en arrivant à Tabatinga, nous ferons une poussée jusque dans la partie inférieure du Pérou* tandis que mes compagnons exploreront les fleuves intermédiaires entre cette ville et Teffé ; en sorte que nous ne serons probablement pas de retour à Manaos avant la fin du mois d'Octobre.

Agréez, mon cher Monsieur, l'assurance de ma haute considération et de mon parfait dévouement.

L. AGASSIZ.†

---

* As will be seen hereafter, want of time and the engrossing character of his work in the Amazons, compelled Mr. Agassiz to renounce the journey into Peru, as also the ascent of the river Madeira.

† *To His Excellency M. Couto de Magalhães, President of Pará.*

MY DEAR SIR : — I thank you sincerely for the kind letter you were so good as to write me last week, and I hasten to inform you of the extraordinary success which continues to crown our efforts. It is certain from this time forth, that the number of fishes inhabiting the Amazons greatly exceeds all that has hitherto been imagined, and that their distribution is very limited on the whole,

There is little to be said of the town of Manaos. It consists of a small collection of houses, half of which seem going to decay, and indeed one can hardly help smiling at the tumble-down edifices, dignified by the name of public buildings, the treasury, the legislative hall, the post-

though a small number of species have followed us since we left Pará and others have a range more or less extensive. You remember, perhaps, that, when alluding to my hopes, I told you one day that I believed in the possibility of finding from two hundred and fifty to three hundred species of fish in the whole basin of the Amazons: even now, having passed over less than one third of the main stream, and only diverged here and there to some points beyond its shores, I have already obtained more than three hundred. It is incredible, above all, if one considers that the total number known to naturalists does not reach one third of what I have already collected. This result scarcely allows one to foresee the discoveries to be made whenever the affluents of the great river are explored with the same care. An exploration of the Araguay for its whole course, in order to teach us how many different combinations of distinct species occur in succession, from its sources to its junction with the Tocantins and lower down till it meets the Amazons, would be an enterprise worthy of you. You have already a sort of scientific property in this river, to which you would add new rights in furnishing science with this information.

Permit me to express to you all the gratitude I feel for the interest you take in my young travelling companion. Mr. Ward is worthy of it, alike from his youth, his courage, and his devotion to science. Mr. Epaminondas has just communicated to me your generous intentions towards myself, and your purpose of sending a steamer to Manaos to take the place of the Piraja, and facilitate our exploration of the Rio Negro and the Rio Madeira. I do not know how to thank you enough; all that I can say is, that this favor will allow me to make an exploration of these rivers which would be otherwise impossible. If the result of these researches be as favorable as my hopes, the honor will be due, in the first instance, to the liberality of the Brazilian government. Encouraged by the results thus far obtained, I think that, if the circumstances are favorable, on arriving at Tabatinga, we shall make a push into the lower part of Peru, while my companions will explore the rivers intermediate between this town and Teffé; so that we shall probably not return to Manaos before the end of October.

Accept, my dear Sir, the assurance of my high regard, &c., &c.

L. AGASSIZ.

office, the custom-house, the President's mansion, &c. The position of the city, however, at the junction of the Rio Negro, the Amazons, and the Solimoens, is commanding; and, insignificant as it looks at present, Manaos will no doubt be a great centre of commerce and navigation at some future time.*

But when we consider the vast extent of land covered by almost impenetrable forest and the great practical difficulties in the way of the settler here, arising from the climate, the insects, the obstacles to communication, the day seems yet far distant when a numerous population will cover the banks of the Amazons, when steamers will ply between its ports as between those of the Mississippi, and when all nations will share in the rich products of its valley.† One of my greatest pleasures in Manaos has been to walk toward the neighboring forest at nightfall, and see the water-carriers, Indian and negro, coming down from the narrow pathways with their great red earthen jars on their

---

* Some English travellers have criticised the position of the town, and regretted that it is not placed lower down, at the immediate junction of the Rio Negro with the Solimoens. But its actual situation is much better, on account of the more quiet port, removed as it is from the violent currents caused by the meeting of the two rivers. — L. A.

† When this was written there was hardly any prospect of the early opening of the Amazons to the free commerce of the world. The circumstance that since the 7th of September last this great fresh-water ocean has been made free to the mercantile shipping of all nations will, no doubt, immensely accelerate the development of civilization in these desert regions. No act could have exhibited more unequivocally the liberal policy which actuates the Brazilian government than this. To complete the great work, two things are still wanting, — a direct high road between the upper tributaries of the Rio Madeira and Rio Paraguay, and the abolition of the subsidies granted to privileged companies, that the colossal traffic of which the whole basin is susceptible may truly be thrown open to a fair competition. — L. A.

heads. They make quite a procession at morning and evening; for the river water is not considered good, and the town is chiefly supplied from pools and little streamlets in the woods. Many of these pools, very prettily situated and embowered in trees, are used as bathing-places; one, which is quite large and deep, is a special favorite; it has been thatched over with palm, and has also a little thatched shed adjoining, to serve as a dressing-room.

Yesterday we passed an interesting morning at a school for Indian children a little way out of the city. We were astonished at the aptness they showed for the arts of civilization so uncongenial to our North American Indians: it reminded one that they are the successors, on the same soil, of the races who founded the ancient civilizations of Peru and Mexico, so much beyond any social organization known to have existed among the more northern tribes. In one room they were turning out very nice pieces of furniture,— chairs, tables, book-stands, &c., with a number of smaller articles, such as rulers and paper-knives. In another room they were working in iron, in another making fine fancy articles of straw. Besides these trades, they are taught to read, write, and cipher, and to play on various musical instruments. For music they are said to have, like the negro, a natural aptitude. In the main building were the school-rooms, dormitories, store-rooms, kitchen, &c. We were there just at the breakfast hour, and had the satisfaction of seeing them sit down to a hearty meal, consisting of a large portion of bread and butter and a generous bowl of coffee. I could not help contrasting the expression of these boys, when they were all collected, with that of a number of negro children assembled together; the latter always so jolly and careless, the former shy, serious, almost sombre. They looked, however, very intelligent, and we were told that those of pure Indian descent were more so than the half-breeds. The school is supported by the province, but the fund is small, and the number of pupils is very limited. Our pleasure in this school was somewhat marred by hearing that, though it purports to be an orphan asylum, children who have parents loath to part with them are sometimes taken by force from the wild Indian tribes to be educated here. The appearance of a dark cell, barred up like the cell of a wild animal, which was used as a prison for refractory scholars, rather confirmed this impression. Whenever I have made inquiries about these reports, I have been answered, that, if such cases occur, it is only where children are taken from an utterly savage and degraded condition, and that it is better they should be civilized by main force than not civilized at all. It may be doubted, however, whether any providence but the providence of God is so wise and so loving that it may safely exercise a compulsory charity. Speaking of the education of the Indians reminds me that we have been fortunate enough to meet a French padre here who has furnished Mr. Agassiz with a package of simple elementary Portuguese books, which he has already sent to our literary Indian friend, José Maia. This kind priest offers also to take the boy, for whom Maia was so anxious to secure an education, into the seminary of which he is director, and where he receives charity scholars.

September 12*th*. — On Sunday we left Manaos in the steamer for Tabatinga, and are again on our way up the river. I insert here a letter which gives a sort of *résumé* of the scientific work up to this moment, and shows also how constantly we were attended by the good-will of the *employés* on the Amazonian line of steamers, and that of their excellent director, Mr. Pimenta Bueno.

Senhor Pimenta Bueno.

MANAOS, 8 Septembre, 1865.

MON CHER AMI : — Vous serez probablement surpris de recevoir seulement quelques lignes de moi après le temps qui s'est écoulé depuis ma dernière lettre. Le fait est que depuis Obydos je suis allé de surprise en surprise et que j'ai à peine eu le temps de prendre soin des collections que nous avons faites, sans pouvoir les étudier convenablement. C'est ainsi que pendant le semaine que nous avons passée dans les environs de Villa Bella, au Lago José Assú et Lago Maximo, nous avons recueilli cent quatre-vingts espèces de poissons dont les deux tiers au moins sont nouvelles et ceux de mes compagnons qui sont restés à Santarem et dans le Tapajoz en ont rapporté une cinquantaine, ce qui fait déjà bien au delà de trois cents espèces en comptant celles de Porto do Moz, de Gurupá, de Tajapurú et de Monte Alégre. Vous voyez qu'avant même d'avoir parcouru le tiers du cours de l'Amazone, le nombre des poissons est plus du triple de celui de toutes les espèces connues jusqu'à ce jour, et je commence à m'apercevoir que nous ne ferons qu'effleurer la surface du centre de ce grand bassin. Que sera-ce lorsqu'on pourra étudier à loisir et dans l'époque la plus favorable tous ses affluents. Aussi je prends dès-à-présent la résolution de faire de plus nombreuses stations dans la partie supérieure du fleuve et de prolonger mon séjour aussi long-temps que mes forces me le permettront. Ne croyez pas cependant que j'oublie à qui je dois un pareil succès. C'est vous qui m'avez mis sur la voie en me faisant connaitre les ressources de la forêt et mieux encore en me fournissant les moyens d'en tirer parti. Merci, mille fois, merci. Je dois aussi tenir grand compte de l'assistance que m'ont fournie les agents de la compagnie sur tous les points où nous avons touché. Notre aimable commandant s'est également évertué, et pendant que j'explorais les lacs des environs de Villa Bella il a fait lui-même une très belle collection dans l'Amazone même, où il a recueilli de nombreuses petites espèces que les pecheurs négligent toujours. A l'arrivée du Belem, j'ai reçu votre aimable lettre et une partie de l'alcohol que j'avais demandé à M. Bond. Je lui écris aujourd'hui pour qu'il m'en envoie encore une partie à Teffé et plus tard davantage à Manaos. Je vous remercie pour le catalogue des poissons du Pará ; je vous le restituerai à notre retour, avec les additions que je ferai pendant le reste du voyage. Adieu, mon cher ami.

Tout à vous,
L. AGASSIZ.*

* *Senahor Pimenta Bueno.*

MY DEAR FRIEND: — You will probably be surprised to receive only a few lines from me after the time which has elapsed since my last letter. The truth is, that, since Obydos, I have passed from surprise to surprise, and that I have scarcely had time to take care of the collections we have made, without being able to study them properly. Thus, during the week we spent in the environs of Villa Bella, at Lago José Assú and Lago Maximo, we have collected one hundred and eighty species of fishes, two thirds of which, at least, are new, while those of my companions who remained at Santarem and upon the Tapajoz have brought back some fifty more, making already more than three hundred species, including those of Porto do Moz, of Gurupá, of Tajapurú, and of Monte Alégre. You see that before having ascended the Amazons for one third of its course, the number of fishes is more than triple that of all the species known thus far, and I begin to perceive that we shall not do more than skim over the surface of the centre of this great basin. What will it be when it becomes possible to study all its affluents at leisure and in the

Although no longer on board an independent steamer, we are still the guests of the company, having government passages. Nothing can be more comfortable than the travelling on these Amazonian boats. They are clean and well kept, with good-sized state-rooms, which most persons use, however, only as dressing-rooms, since it is always more agreeable to sleep on the open deck in one's hammock. The table is very well kept, the fare good, though not varied. Bread is the greatest deficiency, but hard biscuit makes a tolerable substitute. Our life is after this fashion. We turn out of our hammocks at dawn, go down stairs to make our toilets, and have a cup of hot coffee below. By this time the decks are generally washed and dried, the hammocks removed, and we can go above again. Between then and the breakfast hour, at half past ten o'clock, I generally study Portuguese, though my lessons are somewhat interrupted by watching the

most favorable season! I have resolved to make more numerous stations in the upper part of the river and to stay as long as my strength and means will allow. Do not think, however, that I forget to whom I owe such a success. It is you who have put me on the path, by making known to me the resources of the forest, and, better still, by furnishing me with the means to profit by them. Thanks, a thousand times, thanks. I ought also to acknowledge the assistance afforded me by the agents of the Company, at all the points where we have touched. Our amiable commander has also exerted himself, and while I explored the lakes in the neighborhood of Villa Bella, he made a very fine collection in the Amazons, especially of the numerous small species always overlooked by fishermen. On the arrival of the Belem I received your kind letter and a part of the alcohol I had asked from Mr. Bond. I am writing to-day to ask him to send me a part to Teffé, and, somewhat later, more to Manaos. Thank you for the catalogue of Pará fishes; I shall give it back on our return, with the additions I shall make during the remainder of the voyage. Adieu, my dear friend.

Ever yours,
L. AGASSIZ.

shore and the trees, a constant temptation when we are coasting along near the banks. At half past ten or eleven o'clock breakfast is served, and after that the glare of the sun becomes trying, and I usually descend to the cabin, where we make up our journals, and write during the middle of the day. At three o'clock I consider that the working hours are over, and then I take a book and sit in my lounging-chair on deck, and watch the scenery, and the birds and the turtles, and the alligators if there are any, and am lazy in a general way. At five o'clock dinner is served, (the meals being always on deck,) and after that begins the delight of the day. At that hour it grows deliciously cool, the sunsets are always beautiful, and we go to the forward deck and sit there till nine o'clock in the evening. Then comes tea, and then to our hammocks; I sleep in mine most profoundly till morning.

To-day we stopped at a small station on the north side of the river called Barreira das Cudajas. The few houses stand on a bank of red drift, slightly stratified in some parts, and affording a support for the river-mud, shored up against it. Since then, in our progress, we have seen the same formation in several localities.

September 13*th.* — This morning the steamer dropped anchor at the little town of Coari on the Coari River, — one of the rivers of black water. We were detained at this place for some hours, taking in wood; so slow a process here, that an American, accustomed to the rapid methods of work at home, looks on in incredulous astonishment. A crazy old canoe, with its load of wood, creeps out from the shore, the slowness of its advance accounted for by the fact that of its two rowers one has a broken paddle, the other a long stick, to serve as apologies for oars. When the boat reaches the side of the steamer, a line of men is formed some eight or ten in number, and the wood is passed from hand to hand, log by log, each log counted as it arrives. Mr. Agassiz timed them this morning, and found that they averaged about seven logs a minute. Under these circumstances, one can understand that stopping to wood is a long affair. Since we left Coari we have been coasting along close to the land, the continental shore, and not that of an island. The islands are so large and numerous in the Amazons, that often when we believe ourselves between the northern and southern margins of the river, we are in fact between island shores. We have followed the drift almost constantly to-day, — the same red drift with which we have become so familiar in South America. Sometimes it rises in cliffs and banks above the mud deposit, sometimes it crops out through the mud, occasionally mingling with it and partially stratified, and in one locality it overlaid a gray rock in place, the nature of which Mr. Agassiz could not determine, but which was distinctly stratified and slightly tilted. The drift is certainly more conspicuous as we ascend the river; is this because we approach its source, or because the nature of the vegetation allows us to see more of the soil? Since we left Manaos the forest has been less luxuriant; it is lower on the Solimoens than on the Amazons, more ragged and more open. The palms are also less numerous than hitherto, but there is a tree here which rivals them in dignity. Its flat dome, rounded but not conical, towers above the forest, and, when seen from a distance, has an almost architectural character, so regular is its form. This majestic tree, called the Sumaumeira (Eriodendron Sumauma), is one of the few trees in this climate which shed their leaves periodically, and now it lifts its broad rounded summit above the green mass of vegetation around it, quite bare of foliage. Symmetrical as it is, the branches are greatly ramified and very knotty. The bark is white. It would seem that the season approaches when the Sumaumeiras should take on their green garb again, for a few are already beginning to put out young leaves. Beside this giant of the forest, the Imbauba (Cecropia), much lower here, however, than in Southern Brazil, and the Taxi, with its white flowers and brown buds, are very conspicuous along the banks. Close upon the shore the arrow-grass, some five or six feet in height, grows in quantity; it is called "frexas" here, being used by the Indians to make their arrows.

September 14*th*. — For the last day or two the shore has been higher than we have seen it since leaving Manaos. We constantly pass cliffs of red drift with a shallow beach of mud deposit resting against them; not infrequently a gray rock, somewhat like clay slate, crops out below the drift; this rock is very distinctly stratified, tilting sometimes to the west, sometimes to the east, always unconformable with the overlying drift.* The color of the drift changes occasionally, being sometimes nearly white in this neighborhood instead of red. We are coming now to that part of the Amazons where the wide sand-beaches occur, the breeding-places of the turtles and alligators. It is not yet quite the season for gathering the turtle-eggs, making the turtle-butter, &c., but we frequently see the Indian

---

* In the course of the investigation, I have ascertained that this slaty rock, as well as the hard sandstone seen along the river-banks at Manaos, forms part of the great drift formation of the Amazons, and that there is neither old red sandstone, nor trias, here, as older observers supposed. — L. A.

huts on the beaches, and their stakes set up for spreading and drying fish, which is one of the great articles of commerce here. This morning we have passed several hours off the town of Ega, or Teffé as the Brazilians call it. It takes its name from the river Teffé, but the town itself stands on a small lake, formed by the river just before it joins the Amazons. The entrance to the lake, which is broken by a number of little channels or igarapés, and the approach to the town, are exceedingly pretty. The town itself, with a wide beach in front, standing on the slope of a green hill, where sheep and cattle, a rare sight in this region, are grazing, looks very inviting. We examined it with interest, for some of the party at least will return to this station for the purpose of making collections.

September 15th. — For the last two or three days we have been holding frequent discussions as to the best disposition of our forces after reaching Tabatinga; — a source of great anxiety to Mr. Agassiz, the time we have to spend being so short, and the subjects of investigation so various and so important. Should he give up the idea of continuing, in person, his study of the fishes in the upper Amazons, leaving only some parties to make collections, and going himself into Peru, to visit at least the first spur of the Andes, with the purpose of ascertaining whether any vestiges of glaciers are to be found in the valleys, and also of making a collection of fishes from the mountain streams; or should he renounce the journey into Peru for the present, and, making a station somewhere in this region for the next month or two, complete, as far as may be, his investigation of the distribution and development of fishes in the Solimoens? Had the result of the Peruvian journey been more certain, the decision would have been easier; but it is more than likely that the torrential rains of this latitude have decomposed the surface and swept away all traces of glaciers, if they ever existed at so low a level. To go on, therefore, seemed a little like giving up a certain for an uncertain result. Earnestly desirous of making the best use of his time and opportunities here, this doubt has disturbed Mr. Agassiz's waking and sleeping thoughts for several days past. Yesterday morning, at Teffé, a most unexpected adviser appeared in the midst of our council of war. Insignificant in size, this individual, nevertheless, brought great weight to the decision. The intruder was a small fish with his mouth full of young ones. The practical plea was irresistible, — embryology carried the day. A chance of investigating so extraordinary a process of development, not only in this species but in several others said to rear their young in the same fashion, was not to be thrown away; and, besides, there was the prospect of making a collection and a series of colored drawings, from the life, of the immense variety of fishes in the river and lake of Teffé, and perhaps of studying the embryology of the turtles and alligators in their breeding season. Mr. Agassiz, therefore, decides to return to Teffé with his artist and two or three other assistants, and to make a station there for a month at least, leaving Mr. Bourget, with our Indian fisherman, at Tabatinga to collect in that region, and sending Mr. James and Mr. Talisman to the river Putumayo, or Içá, and afterwards to the Hyutahy for the same purpose. This dispersion of parties to collect simultaneously in different areas, divided from each other by considerable distances, will show how the fishes are distributed, and whether their combinations differ in these localities as they have been found to do in the Lower Amazons.

I insert here a letter to the Emperor on the subject of this curious fish, which happened to be one which Mr. Agassiz had formerly dedicated to him.

Teffé, 14 Septembre, 1865.

Sire: — En arrivant ici ce matin j'ai eu la surprise la plus agréable et la plus inattendue. Le premier poisson qui me fut apporté était l'Acara que votre Majesté a bien voulu me permettre de lui dédier et par un bonheur inoui c'était l'époque de la ponte et il avait la bouche pleine de petits vivants, en voie de développement. Voilà donc le fait le plus incroyable en ombryologie pleinement confirmé, et il ne me reste plus qu'à étudier en detail et à loisir tous les changements que subissent ces petits jusqu'au moment où ils quittent leur singulier nid, afin que je puisse publier un recit complet de cette singulière histoire. Mes prévisions sur la distribution des poissons se confirment ; le fleuve est habité par plusieurs faunes ichthyologiques très distinctes, qui n'ont pour lien commun qu'un très petit nombre d'espèces qu'on rencontre partout. Il reste maintenant à préciser les limites de ces régions ichthyologiques et peut-être me laisserai-je entrainer à consacrer quelque temps à cette étude, si je trouve les moyens d'y parvenir. Il y a maintenant une question qui devient fort intéressante, c'est de savoir jusqu'à quel point le même phénomène se reproduit dans chacun des grands affluents du Rio Amazonas, ou en d'autres termes si les poissons des régions supérieures du Rio Madeira et du Rio Negro, etc., etc., sont les mêmes que ceux du cours inférieur de ces fleuves. Quant à la diversité même des poissons du bassin tout entier mes prévisions sont de beaucoup dépassées. Avant d'arriver à Manaos j'avais déjà recueilli plus de trois cents espèces, c. à. d. le triple des espèces connues jusqu'à ce jour au moins. La moitié environ ont pu être peintes sur le vivant par M. Burkhardt ; ensorte que si je puis parvenir à publier tous ces documents, les renseignements que je pourrai fournir sur ce sujet dépasseront de beaucoup tout ce que l'on a publié jusqu'à ce jour.

Je serais bien heureux d'apprendre que Votre Majesté n'a pas rencontré de difficultés dans son voyage et qu'Elle a atteint pleinement le but qu'Elle se proposait. Nous sommes ici sans nouvelles du Sud, depuis que nous avons quitté Rio, et tout ce que nous avions appris alors était qu'après une traversée assez orageuse votre Majesté avait atteint le Rio Grande. Que Dieu protège et bénisse votre Majesté! Avec les sentiments du plus profond respect et de la reconnaissance la plus vive,

Je suis de votre Majesté
    le très humble et très obeissant serviteur,
                                        L. AGASSIZ.*

* TEFFÉ, 14 September, 1865.

SIRE : — On arriving here this morning I had the most agreeable and unexpected surprise. The first fish brought to me was the Acara, which your Majesty kindly permitted me to dedicate to you, and by an unlooked-for good fortune it was the breeding season, and it had its mouth full of little young ones in the process of development. Here, then, is the most incredible fact in embryology fully confirmed, and it remains for me only to study, in detail and at leisure, all the changes which the young undergo up to the moment when they leave their singular nest, in order that I may publish a complete account of this curious history. My anticipations as to the distribution of fishes are confirmed ; the river is inhabited by several very distinct ichthyological faunæ, which have, as a common link, only a very

The character of the banks yesterday and to-day continues unchanged; they are rather high, rising now and then in bluffs and presenting the same mixture of reddish drift and mud deposit, with the gray, slaty rock below, cropping out occasionally. This morning we are stopping to wood at a station opposite the village of Fonte Bôa. Here Mr. Agassiz has had an opportunity of going on shore and examining this formation. He finds a thick bed of ferruginous sandstone underlying a number of thinner beds of mud clay, resembling old clay slate with cleavage. These beds are overlaid by a bank of ochre-colored sandy clay (designated as drift above), with hardly any signs of stratification. Yesterday we passed several lakes, shut out from the river by mud-

small number of species to be met with everywhere. It remains now to ascertain with precision the limits of these ichthyological regions, and I may perhaps be drawn on to devote some time to this study, if I find the means of accomplishing it. There is a question which now becomes very interesting; it is to know how far the same phenomenon is reproduced in each one of the great affluents of the river Amazons, or, in other words, whether the fishes of the upper regions of the Rio Madeira, the Rio Negro, &c., &c., are the same as those of the lower course of these rivers. As to the diversity of fishes in the whole basin, my expectations are far surpassed. Before arriving at Manaos I had already collected more than three hundred species, that is to say, at least three times the number of species thus far known. About half have been painted from life by Mr. Burkhardt; if I can succeed in publishing all these documents, the information I shall be able to furnish on this subject will exceed all that has been thus far made known. I should be very glad to learn that your Majesty has not met with difficulties on the voyage, and has been able fully to accomplish the ends proposed. We are here without news from the South since we left Rio, and all we had learned then was, that after a very stormy passage your Majesty had reached the Rio Grande. May God protect and bless your Majesty!

With sentiments of the most profound respect and the liveliest gratitude, I am

Your Majesty's very humble and obedient servant,

L. AGASSIZ.

oars, and seemingly haunted by waterfowl. In one we saw immense flocks of what looked at that distance either like red Ibises or red spoonbills, and also numbers of gulls. Our sportsmen looked longingly at them, and are impatient for the time when we shall be settled on land, and they can begin to make havoc among the birds.

September 17*th*. — Last evening we took in wood from the shore some miles below the town of Tonantins. I sat watching the Indians on the bank, of whom there were some fifteen or twenty, men, women, and children ; the men loading the wood, the women and children being there apparently to look on. They had built a fire on the bank, and hung their nets or cotton tents, under which they sleep, on the trees behind. They made a wild group, passing to and fro in the light of the fire, the care of which seemed the special charge of a tall, gaunt, weird-looking woman, who would have made a good Meg Merrilies. She seemed to have but one garment, — a long, brown, stuff robe, girt round the waist; as she strode about the fire, throwing on fresh logs and stirring the dying embers, the flames blazed up in her face, lighting her tawny skin and long, unkempt hair, flickering over the figures of women and children about her, and shedding a warm glow over the forest which made the setting to the picture. This is the only very tall Indian woman I have seen ; usually the women are rather short of stature. When the Indians had made their preparations for the night, they heaped damp fuel on the fire till it smouldered down and threw out thick clouds of smoke, enveloping the sleeping-tents, and no doubt driving off effectually the clouds of mosquitoes, from which the natives seem as great sufferers as strangers. These upper stations on the Amazons are haunted by swarms of mosquitoes at night, and during the day by a little biting fly called Pium, no less annoying.

September 18th. — Another pause last evening at the village of San Paolo, standing on a ridge which rises quite steeply from the river and sinks again into a ravine behind. Throughout all this region the banks are eaten away by the river, large portions falling into the water at a time, and carrying the trees with them. These land-slides are so frequent and so extensive as to make travelling along the banks in small boats quite dangerous. The scenery of the Solimoens is by no means so interesting as that of the Lower Amazons. The banks are ragged and broken, the forest lower, less luxuriant, and the palm growth very fitful. For a day or two past we have scarcely seen any palms. One kind seems common, however, namely, the Paxiuba Barriguda — Pa-shee-oo-ba (Iriartea ventricosa), a species not unlike the Assai in dignity of port, but remarkable for the swelling of its stem at half height, giving it a sort of spindle shape. The cut of the foliage is peculiar also, each leaflet being wedge-shaped. The steamer is often now between the shores of the river itself instead of coasting along by the many lovely islands which make the voyage between Pará and Manaos so diversified ; what is thus gained in dimensions is lost in picturesqueness of detail. Then the element of human life and habitations is utterly wanting ; one often travels for a day without meeting even so much as a hut. But if men are not to be seen, animals are certainly plenty ; as our steamer puffs along, great flocks of birds rise up from the shore, turtles pop their black noses out of the water, alligators show themselves occasionally, and sometimes a troop of brown

Capivari scuttles up the bank, taking refuge in the trees at our approach. To-morrow morning we reach Tabatinga, and touch the farthest point of our journey.

September 20*th*. — On Monday evening we arrived at Tabatinga, remaining there till Wednesday morning to discharge the cargo, — a lengthy process, with the Brazilian method of working. Tabatinga is the frontier town between Brazil and Peru, and is dignified by the name of a military station, though when one looks at the two or three small mounted guns on the bank, the mud house behind them constituting barracks, with half a dozen soldiers lounging in front of it, one cannot but think that the fortification is not a very formidable one.* The town itself standing on a mud bluff, deeply ravined and cracked in many directions, consists of some dozen ruinous houses built around an open square. Of the inhabitants I saw but little, for it was toward evening when I went on shore, and they were already driven under shelter by the mosquitoes. One or two looked out from their doors and gave me a friendly warning not to proceed unless I was prepared to be devoured, and indeed the buzzing swarm about me soon drove me back to the

---

* At this point the Amazonian meets the Peruvian steamer, and they exchange cargoes. Formerly the Brazilian company of Amazonian steamers extended its line of travel to Laguna, at the mouth of the Huallaga. Now this part of the journey has passed into the hands of a Peruvian company, whose steamers run up to Urimaguas on the Huallaga. They are, however, by no means so comfortable as the Brazilian steamers, having little or no accommodation for passengers. The upper Marañon is navigable for large steamers as far as Jaen, as are also its tributaries, the Huallaga and Ucayali on the south, the Moronha, Pastazza, and Napo on the north, to a great distance above their junction with the main stream. There is reason to believe that all these larger affluents of the Amazons will before long have their regular lines of steamers like the great river itself. The opening of the Amazons, no doubt, will hasten this result. — L. A.

steamer. The mosquitoes by night and the Piums by day are said to render life almost intolerable here. Under these circumstances we could form little idea of the character of the vegetation in our short stay. But we made the acquaintance of one curious palm, the Tucum, a species of Astrocaryum, the fibre of which makes an excellent material for weaving hammocks, fishing-nets, and the like. It is gradually becoming an important article of commerce. The approach to Tabatinga, with two or three islands in the neighborhood, numerous igarapés opening out of the river, and the Hyavary emptying into it, is, however, one of the prettiest parts of the Solimoens. We found here four members of a Spanish scientific commission, who have been travelling several years in South and Central America, and whose track we have crossed several times without meeting them. They welcomed the arrival of the steamer with delight, having awaited their release at Tabatinga for two or three weeks. The party consisted of Drs. Almagro, Spada, Martinez, and Isern. They had just accomplished an adventurous journey, having descended the Napo on a raft, which their large collection of live animals had turned into a sort of Noah's ark. After various risks and exposures they had arrived at Tabatinga, having lost almost all their clothing, except what they wore, by shipwreck. Fortunately, their papers and collections were saved.* We are now on our way down the river again, having left Mr. Bourget at Tabatinga to pass a month in making collections in that region, and dropped Mr. James

* These gentlemen descended the river with us as far as Teffé, and we afterwards heard of their safe arrival in Madrid. They had, however, suffered much in health, and Mr. Isern died soon after his return to his native land.

and Mr. Talisman last evening at San Paolo, where they are to get a canoe and Indians for their further journey to the Iça. This morning, while stopping to wood at Fonte Bôa, Mr. Agassiz went on shore and collected a very interesting series of fossil plants in the lower mud deposit; he was also very successful in making a small collection of fishes, containing several new species, during the few hours we passed at this place.

September 25th.—Teffé. On Friday, the day after my last date, we were within two or three hours of Teffé; we had just finished packing our various effects, and were closing our letters to be mailed from Manaos, when the steamer came to a sudden pause with that dead, sullen, instantaneous stop which means mischief. The order to reverse the engines was given instantly, but we had driven with all our force into the bed of the river, and there we remained, motionless. This is sometimes rather a serious accident at the season when the waters are falling, steamers having been occasionally stranded for a number of weeks. It is not easily guarded against, the river bottom changing so constantly and so suddenly that even the most experienced pilots cannot always avoid disaster. They may pass with perfect safety in their upward voyage over a place where, on their return, they find a formidable bank of mud. During three hours the crew worked ineffectually, trying to back the steamer off, or sinking the anchor at a distance to drag her back upon it. At five o'clock in the afternoon the sky began to look black and lowering, and presently a violent squall, with thunder and rain, broke upon us. The wind did, in an instant, what man and steam together had failed to do in hours. As the squall struck the steamer on her side, she vibrated, veered and floated free. There was a general stir of delight at this sudden and unexpected liberation, for the delay was serious to all. One or two of the passengers were merchants, to whom it was important to meet the steamer of the 25th at Manaos, which connects with other steamers all along the coast; and the members of the Spanish scientific commission, if they could not at once transfer their effects to the other steamer, would not only miss the next European steamer, but must be at the expense and care of storing their various luggage and maintaining their live stock at Manaos for a fortnight. And lastly, to Mr. Agassiz himself it was a serious disappointment to lose two or three days out of the precious month for investigations at Teffé. Therefore, every face beamed when the kindly shock of the wind set us afloat again; but the work, so vainly spent to release us, was but too efficient in keeping us prisoners. The anchor, which had been sunk in the mud at some distance, was so deeply buried that it was difficult to raise it, and in the effort to do so we grounded again. Indeed, environed as we were by mud and sand, it was no easy matter to find a channel out of them. We now remained motionless all night, though the Captain was unremitting in his efforts and kept the men at work till morning, when, at about seven o'clock, the boat worked herself free at last, and we thought our troubles fairly over. But the old proverb "There's many a slip 'twixt the cup and the lip" never was truer; on starting once more we found that, in the strain and shock to which the ship had been submitted, the rudder was broken. In view of this new disaster, the passengers for Pará gave up all hope of meeting the steamer at Manaos, and the rest resigned themselves to waiting with such philosophy as they could muster. The whole of that day and the following night were spent in rigging up a new rudder, and it was not until eight o'clock on Sunday morning that we were once more on our way, arriving at Teffé at eleven o'clock.

CHAPTER VII.

LIFE IN TEFFÉ.

Aspect of Teffé. — Situation. — Description of Houses. — Fishing Excursion. — Astonishing Variety of Fishes. — Acara. — Scarcity of Laborers. — Our indoors Man. — Bruno. — Alexandrina. — Pleasant Walks. — Mandioca-shed in the Forest. — Indian Encampment on the Beach. — Excursion to Fishing Lodge on the Solimoens. — Amazonian Beaches. — Breeding-Places of Turtles, Fishes, etc. — Adroitness of Indians in finding them. — Description of a "Sitio." — Indian Clay-Eaters. — Cuieira-Tree. — Fish Hunt. — Forest Lake. — Water Birds. — Success in collecting. — Evening Scene in Sitio. — Alexandrina as "aide scientifique." — Fish Anecdote. — Relations between Fishes as shown by their Embryology. — Note upon the Marine Character of the Amazonian Faunæ. — Acara. — News from the Parties in the Interior. — Return of Party from the Içá. — Preparations for Departure. — Note on General Result of Scientific Work in Teffé. — Waiting for the Steamer. — Sketch of Alexandrina. — Mocuim. — Thunder-Storm. — Repiquete. — Geological Observations.

September 27th. — Of all the little settlements we have seen on the Amazons, Teffé looks the most smiling and pleasant. Just now the town, or, as it should rather be called, the village, stands, as I have said, above a broad sand-beach; in the rainy season, however, we are told that the river covers this beach completely, and even encroaches on the fields beyond, coming almost to the threshold of some of the dwellings. The houses are generally built of mud, plastered over and roofed with tiles, or thatched with palm. Almost all have a little ground about them, enclosed in a picket fence, and planted with orange-trees and different kinds of palms, — Cocoa-nut, Assais, and Pupunhas or peach-palms. The latter bears, in handsome clusters, a fruit not unlike the peach in size and coloring; it has a mealy character when cooked, and is very palatable, eaten

LIFE IN TEFFÉ. 213

with sugar. The green hill behind the town, on which cows and sheep are grazing,* slopes up to the forest, and makes a pretty background to the picture. In approaching the village, many little inlets of the lake and river give promise of pleasant canoe excursions. Through our friend Major Coutinho we had already bespoken lodgings, and to-day finds us as comfortably established as it is possible for such wayfarers to be. Our house stands on an open green field, running down to the water, and is enclosed only on two sides by buildings. In front, it commands a pretty view of the beach and of the opposite shore across the water. Behind, it has a little open ground planted with two or three orange-trees, surrounding a turtle-tank, which will be very convenient for keeping live specimens. A well-stocked turtle-tank is to be found in almost every yard, as the people depend largely upon turtles for their food. The interior of the house is very commodious. On the right of the flagged entry is a large room already transformed into a laboratory. Here are numerous kegs, cans, and barrels for specimens, a swinging-shelf to keep birds and insects out of the way of the ants, a table for drawing, and an immense empty packing-case, one side of which serves as a table for cleaning and preparing birds, while the open space beneath makes a convenient cupboard for keeping the instruments and materials of one sort and another, used in the process. After a little

---

* It is a curious fact, that though a large number of cows were owned in Teffé, and were constantly seen feeding about the houses, milk was among the unattainable luxuries. Indeed, milk is little used in Brazil, so far as our observation goes. It is thought unhealthy for children, and people will rather give coffee or tea to a two-year-old baby than pure milk. The cows are never milked regularly, but the quantity needed for the moment is drawn at any time.

practice in travelling one learns to improvise the conveniences for work almost without the accessories which seem indispensable at home. Opposite to the laboratory on the other side of the entry is a room of the same size, where

Veranda and Dining-room at Teffé.

the gentlemen have slung their hammocks; back of this is my room, from the window of which, looking into the court behind, I get a glimpse of some lovely Assai palms and one or two orange-trees in full flower; adjoining that is the dining-room, with a large closet leading out of it, used as a storage-place for alcohol, and serving at this moment as a prison-house for two live alligators who are awaiting execution there. The news of our arrival has already gone abroad, and the fishermen and boys of the village are bringing in specimens of all sorts, — alligators, turtles, fish, insects, birds. Enough is already gathered to show what a rich harvest may be expected in this neighborhood.

September 28th. — Yesterday afternoon, between sunset and moonlight, our neighbor Dr. Romualdo invited us to go with him and his friend Senhor João da Cunha on a fishing excursion into one of the pretty bayous that open out to the lake. As our canoe entered it, lazy alligators were lying about in the still glassy water, with their heads just resting above the surface; a tall, gray heron stood on the shore, as if watching his reflection, almost as distinct as himself, and a variety of water-birds sailed over our heads as we intruded upon their haunts. When we had reached a certain point, the Indians sprang up to their necks in the water, (which was, by the way, unpleasantly warm,) and stretched the net. After a few minutes, they dragged it into shore with a load of fish, which seemed almost as wonderful as Peter's miraculous draught. As the net was landed the fish broke from it in hundreds, springing through the meshes and over the edges, and literally covering the beach. The Indians are very skilful in drawing the net, going before it and lashing the water with long rods to frighten the fish and drive them in. Senhor da Cunha, who is a very ardent lover of the sport, worked as hard as any of the boatmen, plunging into the water to lend a hand at the net or drive in the fish, and, when the draught was landed on the beach, rushing about in the mud to catch the little fishes which jumped in myriads through the meshes, with an enthusiasm equal to that of Mr. Agassiz himself. The operation was repeated several times, always with the same success, and we returned by moonlight with a boat-load of fish, which Mr. Agassiz is examining this morning, while Mr. Burkhardt makes colored drawings of the rarer specimens. Here, as elsewhere in the Amazonian waters, the variety of species is bewildering. The collections already number more than four hundred, including those from Pará, and, while every day brings in new species, new genera are by no means infrequent. The following letter to Professor Milne Edwards, of the Jardin des Plantes, gives some account of the work in this department.

Teffé, le 22 Septembre, 1865.

Mon cher Ami et très honoré Confrère : — Me voici depuis deux mois dans le bassin de l'Amazone et c'est ici que j'ai eu la douleur de recevoir la nouvelle de la mort de mon vieil ami Valenciennes. J'en suis d'autant plus affecté que personne plus que lui n'aurait apprécié les résultats de mon voyage, dont je me réjouissais déjà de lui faire part prochainement. Vous concevrez naturellement que c'est à la classe des poissons que je consacre la meilleure partie de mon temps et ma récolte excède toutes mes prévisions. Vous en jugerez par quelques données. En atteignant Manaos, à la jonction du Rio Negro et de l'Amazonas, j'avais déjà recueilli plus de trois cents espèces de poissons, dont la moitié au moins ont été peintes sur le vivant c. à. d. d'après le poisson nageant dans un grand vase en verre devant mon dessinateur. Je suis souvent peiné de voir avec quelle légèreté on a publié des planches coloriées de ces animaux. Ce n'est pas seulement tripler le nombre des espèces connues, je compte les genres nouveaux par douzaines et j'ai cinq ou six familles nouvelles pour l'Amazone et une voisine des Gobioides entièrement nouvelle pour l'Ichthyologie. C'est surtout parmi les petites espèces que je trouve le plus de nouveautés. J'ai des Characins de cinq à six centimètres et au-dessous, ornés des teintes les plus élégantes, des Cyprinodontes, se rapprochant un peu de ceux de Cuba et des Etats-Unis, des Scomberésoces voisins du Bélone de la Méditerranée, un nombre considérable de Carapoides, des Raies de genres différents de ceux de l'océan, et qui par conséquent ne sont pas des espèces qui remontent le fleuve. Une foule de Goniodontes et de Chromides de genres et d'espèces inédits. Mais ce que j'apprécie surtout c'est la facilité que j'ai d'étudier les changements que tous ces poissons subissent avec l'âge et les différences de sexe qui existent entr'eux et qui sont souvent très considérables. C'est ainsi que j'ai observé une espèce de Geophagus dont le mâle porte sur le front une bosse très-saillante qui manque entièrement à la femelle et aux jeunes. Ce même poisson a un mode de reproduction des plus extraordinaires. Les œufs passent, je ne sais trop comment, dans la bouche dont ils tapissent le fond, entre les appendices intérieurs des arcs branchiaux et surtout dans une poche formée par les pharyngiens supérieurs qu'ils remplissent complètement. Là ils éclosent et les petits, libérés de leur coque, se développent jusqu'à ce qu'ils soient en état de fournir à leur existence. Je ne sais pas encore combien de temps cela va durer ; mais j'ai déjà rencontré des exemplaires dont les jeunes n'avaient plus de sac vitellaire, qui hébergeaient encore leur progéniture. Comme je passerai environ un mois à Teffé, j'espère pouvoir compléter cette observation. L'examen de la structure d'un grand nombre de Chromides m'a fait entrevoir des affinités entre ces poissons et diverses autres familles dont on ne s'est jamais avisé de les rapprocher. Et d'abord je me suis convaincu que les Chromides, répartis autrefois parmi les Labroides et les Sciènoides, constituent bien réellement un groupe naturel, reconnu à peu près en même temps et d'une manière indépendante par Heckel et J. Müller. Mais il y a plus; les genres Enoplosus, Pomotis, Centrarchus et quelques autres genres voisins, rangés parmi les Percoides par tous les Ichthyologistes, me paraissent, d'ici et sans moyen de comparaison directe, tellement voisins des Chromides que je ne vois pas comment on pourra les en séparer, surtout maintenant que je sais que les pharyngiens inférieurs ne sont pas toujours soudés chez les Chromides. Et puis l'embryologie et les métamorphoses des Chromides que je viens d'étudier m'ont convaincu que les "Poissons à branchies labyrinthiques" separés de tous les autres poissons par Cuvier comme une famille entièrement isolée, à raison de la structure étrange de ses organes respiratoires, se rattachent de très-près aux Chromides. Ce groupe devient ainsi par ses affinités variées, l'un des plus intéressants de la classe des poissons, et le bassin de l'Amazone parait être la vraie patrie de cette famille. Je ne veux pas vous fatiguer de mes recherches ichthyologiques ; permettez moi seulement d'ajouter que les poissons ne sont point uniformément répandus dans ce grand bassin. Déjà j'ai acquis la certitude qu'il faut y distinguer plusieurs faunes ichthyologiques, très-nettement charactérisées ; c'est ainsi que les espèces qui habitent la rivière du Pará, des bords de la mer jusque vers l'embouchure du Tocantins, diffèrent de celles que l'on rencontre dans le réseau d'anastomoses qui unissent la rivière de Pará à l'Amazone propre. Les espèces de l'Amazone, au-dessous du Xingu, diffèrent de celles que j'ai rencontrées plus haut ; celles du cours inférieur du Xingu, diffèrent de celles du cours inférieur du Tapajos. Celles des nombreux igarapés et lacs de Manaos diffèrent également de celles du cours principal du grand fleuve et de ses principaux affluents. Il reste maintenant à étudier les changements qui peuvent survenir dans cette distribution, dans le cours de l'année, suivant la hauteur des eaux et peut-être aussi suivant l'époque à laquelle les différentes espèces pondent leurs œufs. Jusqu'à présent je n'ai rencontré qu'un petit nombre d'espèces qui aient une aire de distribution très étendue. C'est ainsi que le Sudis gigas se trouve à-peu-près partout. C'est le poisson le plus important du fleuve ; celui qui comme aliment remplace le bétail pour les populations riveraines. Un autre problème à résoudre c'est de savoir jusqu'à quel point les grands affluents de l'Amazone répètent ce phénomène de la distribution locale des poissons. Je vais chercher à le résoudre en remontant le Rio Negro et le Rio Madeira et comme je reviendrai à Manaos, je pourrai comparer mes premières observations dans cette localité, avec celles d'une autre saison de l'année. Adieu, mon cher ami. Veuillez faire mes amitiés à M. Elie de Beaumont et me rappeler aux bons souvenirs de ceux de mes collègues de l'Académie qui veulent bien s'intéresser à mes travaux actuels. Faites aussi, je vous prie, mes amitiés à M. votre fils.

Tout à vous,
L. AGASSIZ.*

---

* TEFFÉ, September 22, 1865.

MY DEAR FRIEND AND HONORED COLLEAGUE : — Here I have been for two months in the basin of the Amazons, and it is here that I have heard with sorrow of the death of my old friend Valenciennes. I am the more

Mr. Agassiz has already secured quite a number of the singular type of Acarà, which carries its young in its mouth, affected by it, because no one would have appreciated more than he the results of my journey, which I had hoped soon to share with him. You will naturally understand that it is to the class of fishes I consecrate the better part of my time, and my harvest exceeds all my anticipations. You will judge of it by a few statements.

On reaching Manaos, at the junction of the Rio Negro and the Amazons, I had already collected more than three hundred species of fishes, half of which have been painted from life, that is, from the fish swimming in a large glass tank before my artist. I am often pained to see how carelessly colored plates of these animals have been published. Not only have we tripled the number of species, but I count new genera by dozens, and I have five or six new families for the Amazons, and one allied to the Gobioides entirely new to Ichthyology. Among the small species especially I have found novelties. I have Characines of five or six centimetres and less, adorned with the most beautiful tints, Cyprinodonts resembling a little those of Cuba and the United States, Scomberesoces allied to the Belone of the Mediterranean, a considerable number of Carapoides, and Rays of different genera from those of the ocean, and therefore not species which ascend the river; and a crowd of Goniodonts and Chromides of unpublished genera and species. But what I appreciate most highly is the facility I have for studying the changes which all these fishes undergo with age and the differences of sex among them; which are often very considerable. Thus I have observed a species of Geophagus in which the male has a very conspicuous protuberance on the forehead, wholly wanting in the female and the young. This same fish has a most extraordinary mode of reproduction. The eggs pass, I know not how, into the mouth, the bottom of which is lined by them, between the inner appendages of the branchial arches, and especially into a pouch, formed by the upper pharyngials, which they completely fill. There they are hatched, and the little ones, freed from the egg-case, are developed until they are in a condition to provide for their own existence. I do not yet know how long this continues; but I have already met with specimens whose young had no longer any vitelline sac, but were still harbored by the progenitor. As I shall still pass a month at Teffé I hope to be able to complete this observation. The examination of the structure of a great number of Chromides has led me to perceive the affinities between these fishes and several other families with which we have never thought of associating them. In the first place, I have convinced myself that the Chromides, formerly scattered among the Labroides and the Sciænoides, really constitute a natural group recognized nearly at the same time and in an indepen-

and he has gathered a good deal of information about its habits. The fishermen here say that this mode of caring

dent manner by Heckel and J. Müller. But, beside these, there are the genera Enoplosus, Pomotis, Centrarchus, and some other neighboring genera, classed among the Percoids by all Ichthyologists, which seem to me, from this distance and without means of direct comparison, so near the Chromides that I do not see how they can be separated, especially now that I know the lower pharyngials not to be invariably soldered in the Chromides. And then the embryology and metamorphoses of the Chromides, which I have just been studying, have convinced me that the fishes with labyrinthic branchiæ, separated from all other fishes by Cuvier, as a family entirely isolated on account of the strange structure of its respiratory organs, are closely related to the Chromides. Thus this group becomes, by its various affinities, one of the most interesting of the class of fishes, and the basin of the Amazons seems to be the true home of this family. I will not fatigue you with my ichthyological researches; let me only add, that the fishes are not uniformly spread over this great basin. I have already acquired the certainty that we must distinguish several ichthyological faunæ very clearly characterized. Thus the species inhabiting the river of Pará, from the borders of the sea to the mouth of the Tocantins, differ from those which are met in the network of anastomoses uniting the river of Pará with the Amazons proper. The species of the Amazons below the Xingu differ from those which occur higher up; those of the lower course of the Xingu differ from those of the lower course of the Tapajoz. Those of the numerous igarapés and lakes of Manaos differ as much from those of the principal course of the great river and of its great affluents. It remains now to study the changes which may take place in this distribution in the course of the year, according to the height of the waters, and perhaps also according to the epoch at which the different species lay their eggs. Thus far I have met but a small number of species having a very extensive area of distribution. One of those is the Sudis gigas, found almost everywhere. It is the most important fish of the river, that which, as food, corresponds to cattle for the population along the banks. Another problem to be solved is, how far this phenomenon of the local distribution of fishes is repeated in the great affluents of the Amazons. I shall try to solve it in ascending the Rio Negro and Rio Madeira, and as I return to Manaos I shall be able to compare my first observations in this locality with those of another season of the year. Adieu, my dear friend. Remember me to M. Elie de Beaumont and to those of my colleagues of the Academy who are interested in my present studies. My kind remembrance also to your son.

Always yours,
L. Agassiz

for the young prevails more or less in all the family of Acarà. They are not all born there, however; some lay their eggs in the sand, and, hovering over their nest, take up the little ones in their mouth, when they are hatched. The fishermen also add, that these fish do not always keep their young in the mouth, but leave them sometimes in the nest, taking them up only on the approach of danger.*

* We found that this information was incorrect, at least for some species, as will be seen hereafter. I let the statement stand in the text, however, as an instance of the difficulty one has in getting correct facts, and the danger of trusting to the observations even of people who mean to tell the real truth. No doubt some of these Acaras do occasionally deposit their young in the sand, and continue a certain care of them till they are able to shift for themselves. But the story of the fisherman was one of those half truths as likely to mislead, as if it had been wholly false. I will add here a few details concerning these Acaras, a name applied by the natives to all the oval-shaped Chromides. The species which lay their eggs in the sand belong to the genera Hydrogonus and Chætobranchus. Like the North American Pomotis, they build a kind of flat nest in the sand or mud, in which they deposit their eggs, hovering over them until the young are hatched. The species which carry their young in the mouth belong to several genera, formerly all included under the name of Geophagus by Heckel. I could not ascertain how the eggs are brought into the mouth, but the change must take place soon after they are laid, for I have found in that position eggs in which the embryo had just begun its development as well as those in a more advanced stage of growth. Occasionally, instead of eggs, I have found the cavity of the gills, as also the space enclosed by the branchiostegal membrane, filled with a brood of young already hatched. The eggs before hatching are always found in the same part of the mouth, namely, in the upper part of the branchial arches, protected or held together by a special lobe or valve formed of the upper pharyngeals. The cavity thus occupied by the eggs corresponds exactly to the labyrinth of that curious family of fishes inhabiting the East Indian Ocean, called Labyrinthici by Cuvier. This circumstance induces me to believe that the branchial labyrinth of the eastern fishes may be a breeding pouch, like that of our Chromides, and not simply a respiratory apparatus for retaining water. In the Amazonian fish a very sensitive network of nerves spreads over this marsupial pouch, the principal stem of which arises from a special nervous ganglion, back of the cerebellum, in the

Our household is now established on a permanent basis. We had at first some difficulty in finding servants; at this fishing season, when the men are going off to dry and salt fish, and when the season for hunting turtle-eggs and making turtle-butter is coming on, the town is almost deserted by the men. It is like haying-time in the country, when every arm is needed in the fields. Then the habits of the Indians are so irregular, and they care so little for money, finding, as they do, the means of living almost without work immediately about them, that even if one does engage a servant, he is likely to disappear the next day. An Indian will do more for good-will and a glass of cachaça (rum) than he will do for wages, which are valueless to him. The individual, who has been supplying the place of indoors man while we have been looking for a servant, is so original in his appearance that he deserves a special description. He belongs to a neighbor who has undertaken to provide our meals, and he brings them when they are prepared and waits on the table. He is rather an elderly Indian, and his dress consists of a pair of cotton drawers, originally white, but now of many hues and usually rolled up to the knees, his feet being bare; the upper part of his person is partially

medulla oblongata. This region of the central nervous system is strangely developed in different families of fishes, and sends out nerves performing very varied functions. From it arise, normally, the nerves of movement and sensation about the face; it also provides the organs of breathing, the upper part of the alimentary canal, the throat and the stomach. In the electric fishes the great nerves entering the electric battery arise from the same cerebral region, and now I have found that the pouch in which the egg of the Acara is incubated and its young nursed for a time, receives its nerves from the same source. This series of facts is truly wonderful, and only shows how far our science still is from an apprehension of the functions of the nervous system. — L. A.

(very partially) concealed by a blue rag, which I suppose in some early period of the world's history must have been a shirt; this extraordinary figure is surmounted by an old straw hat full of holes, bent in every direction, and tied under the chin by a red string. Had he not been a temporary substitute, we should have tried to obtain a more respectable livery for him; but to-day he gives place to an Indian lad, Bruno by name, who presents a more decent appearance, though he seems rather bewildered by his new office. At present his idea of waiting on the table seems to be to sit on the floor and look at us while we eat. However, we hope to break him in gradually. He looks as if he had not been long redeemed from the woods, for his face is deeply tattooed with black, and his lips and nose are pierced with holes, reminding one of the becoming vanities he has renounced in favor of civilization.* Besides Bruno we have a girl, Alexandrina by name, who, by her appearance, has a mixture of Indian and black blood in her veins. She promises very well, and seems to have the intelligence of the Indian with the greater pliability of the negro.

September 29*th*. — One of the great charms of our residence here is, that we have so many pleasant walks within easy reach. My favorite walk in the early morning is to the wood on the brow of the hill. From the summit, the sunrise is lovely over the village below, the lake with its many picturesque points and inlets, and the forests on the opposite shores. From this spot a little path through the bushes brings one at once into a thick, beautiful wood.

---

* It is a very general habit among the South American Indians to pierce the nose, ears, and lips with holes, in which they hang pieces of wood and feathers, as ornaments.

Here one may wander at will, for there are a great many paths, worn by the Indians, through the trees; and one is constantly tempted on by the cool, pleasant shade, and by the perfume of moss and fern and flower. The forest here is full of life and sound. The buzz of insects, the shrill cry of the cicadas, the chattering talk of the papagaios, and occasionally busy voices of the monkeys, make the woods eloquent. The monkeys are, however, very difficult of approach, and though I hear them often, I have not yet seen them on the trees; but Mr. Hunnewell told me that the other day, when shooting in this very wood, he came upon a family of small white monkeys sitting on a bough together, and talking with much animation. One of the prettiest of the paths, with which my daily walks made me familiar, leads over an igarapé to a house, or rather to a large thatched shed, in the forest, used for preparing mandioca. It is supplied with four large clay ovens, having immense shallow pans fitted on to the top, with troughs for kneading, sieves for straining, and all the apparatus for the various processes to which the mandioca is subjected. One utensil is very characteristic; the large, empty turtle-shells, which may be seen in every kitchen, used as basins, bowls, &c. I suppose this little establishment is used by a number of persons, for in my morning walks I always meet troops of Indians going to it, the women with their deep working baskets, — something like the Swiss "hotte," — in which they carry their tools, on their backs, supported by a straw band fastened across the forehead, and their babies astride on their hips, so as to leave their hands perfectly free. They always give me a cordial morning greeting and stop to look at the plants and flowers with which I am usually laden. Some of the women are quite pretty, but as a general thing the Indians in this part of the country do not look very healthy, and are apt to have diseases of the eyes and skin. It is a curious thing that the natives seem more liable to the maladies of the country than strangers. They are very subject to intermittent fevers, and one often sees Indians worn to mere skin and bone by this terrible scourge.

If the morning walk in the woods is delightful, the evening stroll on the beach in front of the house is no less so, when the water is dyed in the purple sunset, and the quiet of the scene is broken here and there by a fire on the sands, around which a cluster of Indians are cooking their supper. As Major Coutinho and I were walking on the shore last evening we came on such a group. They were a family who had come over from their home on the other side of the lake, with a boat-load of fish and turtle to sell in the village. When they have disposed of their cargo, they build their fire on the beach, eat their supper of salted or broiled fish, farinha, and the nuts of a particular kind of palm (Atalea), and then sleep in their canoe. We sat down with them, and, that they should not think we came merely out of curiosity, we shared their nuts and farinha, and they were soon very sociable. I am constantly astonished at the frank geniality of these people, so different from our sombre, sullen Indians, who are so unwilling to talk with strangers. The cordiality of their reception, however, depends very much on the way in which they are accosted. Major Coutinho, who has passed years among them, understands their character well, and has remarkable tact in his dealings with them. He speaks their language a little also, and this is important here where many of the Indians speak only the "lingua geral."

This was the case with several of the family whose acquaintance we made last evening, though some of them talked in Portuguese fluently enough, telling us about their life in the forest, their success in disposing of their fish and turtle, and inviting us to come to their house. They pointed out to us one of the younger girls, who they said had never been baptized, and they seemed to wish to have the rite performed. Major Coutinho promised to speak to the priest about it for them. So far as we can learn, the white population do little to civilize the Indians beyond giving them the external rites of religion. It is the old sad story of oppression, duplicity, and license on the part of the white man, which seems likely to last as long as skins shall differ, and which necessarily ends in the degradation of both races.

October 4th. — On Saturday morning at four o'clock, Major Coutinho, Mr. Agassiz, and myself left Teffé in company with our neighbor and landlord Major Estolano, on our way to his "sitio," a rough sort of Indian lodge on the other side of the Solimoens, where he goes occasionally with his family to superintend the drying and salting of fish, a great article of commerce here. It had rained heavily all night, but the stars were bright, and the morning was cool and fresh when we put off in the canoe. When we issued from Teffé lake it was already broad day, and by the time we entered the Solimoens we began to have admonitions that breakfast-time was approaching. There is something very pleasant in these improvised meals; the coffee tastes better when you have made it yourself, setting up the coffee-machine under the straw-roof of the canoe, dipping up the water from the river over the side of the boat, and cooking your own breakfast. One would think it a great bore at home, with all the necessary means and appliances; but with the stimulus of difficulty and the excitement of the journey it is quite pleasant, and gives a new relish to ordinary fare. After we had had a cup of hot coffee and a farinha biscuit, being somewhat cramped with sitting in the canoe, we landed for a walk on a broad beach along which we were coasting. There is much to be learned on these Amazonian beaches; they are the haunts and breeding-places of many different kinds of animals, and are covered by tracks of alligators, turtles, and capivari. Then there are the nests, not only of alligators and turtles, but of the different kind of fishes and birds that lay their eggs in the mud or sand. It is curious to see the address of the Indians in finding the turtle-nests; they walk quickly over the sand, but with a sort of inquiring tread, as if they carried an instinctive perception in their step, and the moment they set their foot upon a spot below which eggs are deposited, though there is no external evidence to the eye, they recognize it at once, and, stooping, dig straight down to the eggs, generally eight or ten inches under the surface. Besides these tracks and nests, there are the rounded, shallow depressions in the mud, which the fishermen say are the sleeping-places of the skates. They have certainly about the form and size of the skate, and one can easily believe that these singular impressions in the soft surface have been made in this way. The vegetation on these beaches is not less interesting than these signs of animal life. In the rainy season more than half a mile of land, now uncovered along the margins of the river, is entirely under water, the river rising not only to the edge of the forest, but penetrating far into it. At this time of the year, however, the shore consists, first of the beach, then of a broad band of tall grasses, beyond which are the lower shrubs and trees, leading up, by a sort of gradation, to the full forest growth. During this dry season the vegetation makes an effort to recover its lost ground; one sees the little Imbauba (Cecropia) and a kind of willow-tree (Salix humboldiana), the only familiar plant we met, springing up on the sand, and creeping down to the water's edge, only to be destroyed again with the next rise of the river. While we were walking, the boatmen were dragging the net, and though not with such astonishing success as the other day, yet it landed not only an ample supply of fresh fish for breakfast, but also a number of interesting specimens. At about eleven o'clock we turned from the Solimoens into the little river on which Mr. Estolano's fishing-lodge is situated, and in a few minutes found ourselves at the pretty landing, where a rough flight of steps led up to the house. In this climate a very slight shelter will serve as a house. Such a dwelling is indeed nothing but a vast porch; and a very airy, pleasant, and picturesque abode it makes. A palm-thatched roof to shed the rain and keep off the sun, covering a platform of split logs that one may have a dry floor under foot; these, with plenty of posts and rafters for the swinging of hammocks, are the essentials. It was somewhat after this fashion that Major Estolano's lodge was built. The back part of it consisted of one very large, high chamber, to which the family retired in the hottest part of the day, when the sun was most scorching; all the rest was roof and platform, the latter stretching out considerably beyond the former, thus leaving an open floor on one side for the stretching and drying of fish. The whole structure was lifted on piles about eight feet above the ground, to provide against the rising of the river in the rainy season. In front of the house, just on the edge of the bank, were several large, open, thatched sheds, used as kitchen and living-rooms for the negroes and Indians employed in the preparation of the fish. In one of these rooms were several Indian women who looked very ill. We were told they had been there for two months, and they were worn to skin and bone with intermittent fever. Major Coutinho said they were, no doubt, suffering in part from the habit so prevalent among these people of eating clay and dirt, for which they have a morbid love. They were wild-looking creatures, lying in their hammocks or squatting on the ground, often without any clothes, and moaning as if in pain. They were from the forest, and spoke no Portuguese.

We were received most cordially by the ladies of the family, who had gone up to the lodge the day before, and were offered the refreshment of a hammock, the first act of hospitality in this country, when one arrives from any distance. After this followed an excellent breakfast of the fresh fish we had brought with us, cooked in a variety of ways, broiled, fried, and boiled. The repast was none the less appetizing that it was served in picnic fashion, the cloth being laid on the floor, upon one of the large palm-mats, much in use here to spread over the uncarpeted brick floors or under the hammocks. For several hours after breakfast the heat was intense, and we could do little but rest in the shade, though Mr. Agassiz, who works at all hours if specimens are on hand, was busy in making skeletons of some fish too large to be preserved in alcohol. Towards evening it grew cooler, and we walked in the banana plantation near the house, and sat under an immense gourd-tree on the bank, which made a deep shade; for it was clothed not only by its own foliage, but the branches were covered with parasites, and with soft, dark moss, in contrast with which the lighter green, glossy fruit seemed to gain new lustre. I call it a gourd-tree, simply from the use to which the fruit is put. But it goes here by the name of the Cuieira-tree (Crescentia Cajeput), the cup made from the fruit being called a Cuia. The fruit is spherical, of a light green, shiny surface, and grows from the size of an apple to that of the largest melon. It is filled with a soft, white pulp, easily removed when the fruit is cut in halves; the rind is then allowed to dry. Very pretty cups and basins, of many sizes, are made in this way; and the Indians, who understand how to prepare a variety of very brilliant colors, are very skilful in painting them. It would seem that the art of making colors is of ancient date among the Amazonian Indians, for in the account of Francisco Orellana's journey down the Amazons in 1541, " the two fathers of the expedition declare that in this voyage they found all the people to be both intelligent and ingenious, which was shown by the works which they performed in sculpture and painting in bright colors." * Their paints are prepared from a particular kind of clay and from the juices of several plants which have coloring properties. In an Amazonian cottage one hardly sees any utensils for the table except such as the Indians have prepared and ornamented themselves from the fruits of the Cuieira-tree. I longed to extend my walk into the woods which surrounded us on all sides; but the forest is very tantalizing here, so tempting and so impenetrable. The ladies told me there were no paths cut in the neighborhood of the house.

* See " Expeditions into the Valley of the Amazons," published by the Hakluyt Society.

The next morning we were off early in the canoes on a fish hunt; I call it a hunt advisedly, for the fish are the captives of the bow and spear, not of the net and line. The Indians are very adroit in shooting the larger fish with the bow and arrow, and in harpooning some of the veritable monsters of their rivers, such as the Peixe-boi ("fish-cow"), Manatee or Dugon, with the spear. We made two parties this morning, some of us going in the larger canoe to drag a forest lake with the net, while some of the fishermen took a smaller, lighter boat, to be able to approach their larger prey. Our path lay through a pretty igarapé, where, for the first time, I saw monkeys in a tree by the water-side. On coming to the Amazons we expect to see monkeys as frequently as squirrels are seen at home; but, though very numerous, they are so shy that one rarely gets a fair view of them. After an hour's row we landed at a little point jutting out into the water, and went through the forest, the men cutting the way before us, clearing the path of branches, fallen trees, and parasitic vines which obstructed it. I was astonished to see the vigor and strength with which Dona Maria, the mother-in-law of our host, made her way through the tangled trees, helping to free the road, and lopping off branches with her great wood-knife. We imagine all the ladies in this warm country to be very indolent and languid; and in the cities, as a general thing, their habits are much less vigorous than those of our women. But here, in the Upper Amazons, the women who have been brought up in the country and in the midst of the Indians are often very energetic, bearing a hand at the oar or the fishing-net with the strength of a man. A short walk brought us out upon a shallow forest lake, or, as the Indians call it, "round water." The Indian names are often very significant. I have mentioned the meaning of igarapé, "boat path"; to this, when they wish to indicate its size more exactly, they affix either the word "assú" (large) or "mirim" (small). But an igarapé, whether large or small, is always a channel opening out of the main river and having no other outlet. For a channel connecting the upper and lower waters of the same river, or leading from one river to another, they have another word, "Paraná" (signifying river), which they modify in the same way, as Paraná-assú or Paraná-mirim. Paraná-assú, the big river, means also the sea. A still more significant name for a channel connecting two rivers is the Portuguese word "furo," meaning bore.

The lake was set in the midst of long, reed-like grass, and, as we approached it, thousands of white water-birds rustled up from the margin and floated like a cloud above us. The reason of their numbers was plain when we reached the lake: it was actually lined with shrimps; one could dip them out by the bucketful. The boatmen now began to drag the net, and perhaps nowhere, from any single lake or pond, has Mr. Agassiz made a more valuable collection of forest fishes. Among them was a pipe-fish, one of the Goniodont family, very similar to our ordinary Syngnathus in appearance, but closely related to Acestra, and especially interesting to him as throwing light on certain investigations of his, made when quite a young man. This specimen confirmed a classification by which he then associated the pipe-fish with the Garpikes and Sturgeons, a combination which was scouted by the best naturalists of the time, and is even now repudiated by most of them. Without self-glorification, it is impossible not to be gratified when the experience of later years confirms the premonitions of youth, and shows them to have been not mere guesses, but founded upon an insight into the true relations of things. Wearied after a while with watching the fishing in the sun, I went back into the forest, where I found the coffee-pot already boiling over the fire. It was pleasant to sit down on a fallen, moss-grown trunk, and breakfast in the shade. Presently the fishermen came back from the lake, and we found our way to the boats again, laden with an immense number of fishes. The gentlemen returned to the house in one of the smaller montarias, taking the specimens with them, and leaving me to return in the larger canoe with the Senhoras. It seemed to me strange on this Sunday morning, when the bells must be ringing and the people trooping to church under the bright October sky, in our far-off New England home, to be floating down this quiet igarapé, in a boat full of half-naked Indians, their wild, monotonous chant sounding in our ears as they kept time to their oars. In these excursions one learns to understand the fascination this life must have for a people among whom civilization is as yet but very incomplete; it is full of physical enjoyment, without any mental effort. Up early in the morning and off on their fishing or hunting excursions long before dawn, they return by the middle of the day, lie in their hammocks and smoke during the hours of greatest heat; cook the fish they have brought with them, and, unless sickness comes to them, know neither want nor care. We reached the house in time for a twelve o'clock breakfast of a more solid character than the lighter one in the forest, and by no means unacceptable after our long row. In the course of the day two "Peixe-bois" (Manatees) were brought in, also a Boto (porpoise), and some large specimens of Pirarucu (Sudis).

All these are too clumsy to preserve in alcohol, especially when alcohol is so difficult to obtain and so expensive as it is here; but Mr. Agassiz has had skeletons made of them, and will preserve the skins of the Peixe-bois for mounting. He obtained at the same time an entirely new genus of the Siluroid family. It is a fish weighing some ten pounds, called here the Pacamun, and of a bright canary color.

The evening scene at the " Sitio " was always very pretty. After dinner, when the customary " boa noite," the universal greeting at the close of the day, had been exchanged, the palm-mats, spread over the platforms, had each their separate group, Indians or negroes, children, members of the family or guests, the central figure being usually that of Major Coutinho, who was considered to be especially successful in the making of coffee and who generally had a mat to himself, where he looked, as the blue flame of his alcohol lamp flickered in the wind, not unlike a magician of old, brewing some potent spell. Little shallow cups, like open antique lamps, filled with oil and having a bit of wick hanging over the edge, were placed about the floors, and served to light the interior of the porch, though after a glimmering and uncertain fashion. On Monday morning we left the " Sitio " and returned to Teffé, where Mr. Agassiz had the pleasure of receiving all his collections, both those he had sent on before him and those which accompanied us, in good condition.

October 9th. — Alexandrina turns out to be a valuable addition to the household, not only from a domestic, but also from a scientific point of view. She has learned to prepare and clean skeletons of fish very nicely, and makes herself quite useful in the laboratory. Besides, she knows many paths in the forest, and accompanies me in all my botanizing excursions; with the keen perceptions of a person whose only training has been through the senses, she is far quicker than I am in discerning the smallest plant in fruit or flower, and now that she knows what I am seeking, she is a very efficient aid. Nimble as a monkey, she thinks nothing of climbing to the top of a tree to bring down a blossoming branch; and here, where many of the trees shoot up to quite a height before putting out their boughs, such an auxiliary is very important. The collections go on apace, and every day brings in new species; more than can be easily cared for, — far more than our artist can find time to draw. Yesterday, among other specimens, a hollow log was brought in, some two feet and a half in length, and about three inches in diameter, crowded with Anojas (a common fish here) of all sizes, from those several inches long to the tiniest young. The thing was so extraordinary that one would have been inclined to think it was prepared in order to be passed off as a curiosity, had not the fish been so dexterously packed into the log from end to end, that it was impossible to get them out without splitting it open, when they were all found alive and in perfectly good condition. They could not have been artificially jammed into the hollow wood, in that way, without injuring them. The fishermen say that this is the habit of the family; they are often found thus crowded into dead logs at the bottom of the river, making their nests as it were in the cavities of the wood.*

October 14*th*. — Mr. Agassiz has a corps of little boys

---

* This species belongs to one of the subdivisions of the genus Aucheniptorus; it is undescribed, and Mr. Burkhardt has made five colored sketches of a number of specimens of different sizes, varying in their markings. — L. A.

engaged in catching the tiniest fishes, so insignificant in size that the regular fishermen, who can never be made to understand that a fish which is not good to eat can serve any useful purpose, always throw them away. Nevertheless, these are among the most instructive specimens for the ichthyologist, because they often reveal the relations not only between parent and offspring, but wider relations between different groups. Mr. Agassiz's investigations on these little fish here have shown repeatedly that the young of some species resemble closely the adult of others. Such a fish, not more than half an inch long, was brought to him yesterday. It constitutes a new genus, Lymnobelus, and belongs to the bill-fish family, Scomberesoces, with Belone and others, — that long, narrow type, with a long beak, which has such a wide distribution over the world. In the Northern United States, as well as in the Mediterranean, it has a representative of the genus Scomberesox, in which the jaws of its long snout are gaping; in the Mediterranean, and almost everywhere in the temperate and torrid zones, Belones are found in which, on the contrary, the bill is closed; in Florida and on the Brazilian coast, as well as in the Pacific, species of Hemirhamphus occur in which the two jaws are unequal, the upper one being very short and the lower one enormously long, while the Amazonian bill-fish has a somewhat different cut of the bill from either of those mentioned above, though both jaws are very long, as in Belone. When, then, the young of this Amazonian species was brought to Mr. Agassiz, he naturally expected to find it like its parent. On the contrary, he found it far more like the species of Florida and the Brazilian coast, having the two jaws unequal, the upper one excessively short, the lower enormously long, showing that the Amazonian species, before taking on its own characteristic features, passes through a stage resembling the permanent adult condition of the Hemirhamphus. It is interesting to find that animals, which have their natural homes so far from each other that there is no possibility of any material connection between them, are yet so linked together by structural laws, that the development of one species should recall the adult form of another.* The story of the Acaras,

---

* When I attempted to record my impression of the basin of the Amazons, and characterized it as a fresh-water ocean with an archipelago of islands, I did not mean to limit the comparison to the wide expanse of water and the large number of islands. The resemblance extends much further, and the whole basin may be said to be oceanic also, in the character of its fauna. It is true, we are accustomed to consider the Chromides, the Characines, the Siluroids, and the Goniodonts, which constitute the chief population of this network of rivers, as fresh-water fishes; but in so doing we shut our eyes to their natural affinities, and remember only the medium in which they live. Let any one enter upon a more searching comparison, and he will not fail to perceive that, under the name of Chromides, fishes are united which in their form and general appearance recall several families of the class, only known as inhabitants of the sea. The genus Pterophyllum, for instance, might be placed side by side with the Chætodonts, without apparently violating its natural affinities, since even Cuvier considered it as a Platax. The genera Symphysodon and Uaru would not seem very much out of place, by the side of Brama. The genus Geophagus and allied forms recall at once the Sparoids, with which some of them were associated by earlier ichthyologists; while the genus Crenicichla forms a striking counterpart to the genus Malacanthus. Finally, the genus Acara and their kindred closely resemble the Pomacentroids. Indeed, had not the fresh-water genera Pomotis, Centrarchus, and the like, been erroneously associated with the Percoids, the intimate relations which bind them to the Chromides, and these again to the marine types mentioned above, would long ago have been acknowledged. The genus Monocirrus is a miniature Toxotes, with a barbel. Polycentrus, which is also found in the Amazons, stands nearest to Acara and Heros; it has only a larger number of anal spines. In this connection it ought not to be overlooked that these fishes are not pelagic, like the Scomberoids, but rather archipelagic, if I may use this word to designate fishes dwelling among low islands. If we discard the long-prevailing idea of a close relationship between the

the fish which carries its young in its mouth, grows daily more wonderful. This morning Mr. Agassiz was off before

Characines and Salmonides, based solely upon the presence of an adipose fin, we may at once perceive how manifold are the affinities between the Characines on one hand, and on the other the Scopelines and Clupeoids, all of which are essentially marine. These relations may be traced to the details of the genera; Gasteropelecus, from the family of Characines, is the pendant of Pristigaster among the Clupeoids, as Chalcinus recalls Pellona. In the same way may Stomias and Chauliodus be compared to Cynodon and the like; or Sudis and Osteoglossum to Megalops, and Erythrinus to Ophicephalus, &c., &c. The Goniodonts may at first sight hardly seem to have any kindred among marine fishes; but if we take into account the affinity which unquestionably links the genus Loricaria and its allies with Pegasus, and further remember that to this day all the ichthyologists, with the sole exception of C. Duméril, have united Pegasus in one order with the Pipe-fishes, it will no longer be doubted that the Goniodonts have at least a remarkable analogy with the Lophobranches, if they should not be considered as bearing a close structural relation to them. But this relation truly exists. The extraordinary mode of rearing their young, which characterizes the various representatives of the old genus Syngnathus, is only matched by the equally curious incubation of the eggs in Loricaria. And as to the other families represented in the basin of the Amazons, such as the Skates, the Sharks, the Tetraodonts, the Flat-fishes (Pleuronectides), the Bill-fishes (Scomberesoces), the Anchovis, Herrings, and other forms of the family of Clupeoids, the Muraenoids, the genuine Sciaenoids, the Gobioids, &c., &c., they are chiefly known as marine types; while the Cyprinodonts occur elsewhere both in salt and fresh water. The Gymnotines are thus far only known as fresh-water fishes, nor do I see any ground for comparing them to any marine type. They cannot be compared to the Muraenoids, with which they have thus far been associated. The only real affinity I can trace in them is with the Mormyri of the Nile and Senegal, and with the Notopteri of the Sunda Islands. Eel-shaped fishes are by no means all related to one another, and their elongated form, with a variety of patterns, is no indication of their relationship. It may, nevertheless, be inferred from what precedes, that the fishes of the Amazons have, as a whole, a marine character peculiarly their own, and not at all to be met with among the inhabitants of the other great rivers of the world.

These peculiarities extend to other classes besides fishes. Among the Bivalve shells, it has long been known that the Amazons nourishes genera of Naiades peculiar to its waters, or only found besides in the other great rivers of South dawn, on a fishing excursion with Major Estolano, and returned with numerous specimens of a new species of America; such as Hyria, Castalia, and Mycetopus, to which I would add another genus, founded upon slender, sickle-shaped Unios, common to North and South America. But what seems to have escaped the attention of conchologists is the striking resemblance of Hyria and Avicula, of Castalia and Arca, of Mycetopus and Solen, &c. Thus exhibiting another repetition of marine types in a family exclusively limited to fresh waters, and having structural characters of its own, entirely distinct from the marine genera, the appearance of which they so closely ape. In this connection I cannot suppress the remark, that it would be puerile to consider such mimicry as indicative of a community of origin. Some of the land shells even recall marine forms; such are some of the Bulimus tribe, which resemble the genus Phasianella and Littorina far more than their own relatives. The similarity of the fringes of the anterior margin of the foot is particularly striking. The Ampullariæ remind one also, in a measure, of the marine genera Struthiolaria, Natica, &c., and many fossils of the latter family have been confounded with fresh-water Ampularise.

The most noticeable feature of the Amazonian fauna, considered with reference to its oceanic character, is, however, the abundance of Cetaceans through its whole extent. Wherever I have navigated these waters, from Pará, where the tides still send the salt brine up the river, to Tabatinga on the borders of Peru, in all the larger and smaller tributaries of the great stream as well as in the many lakes connected with their ever-changing course, I have seen and heard them, gamboling at the surface and snoring rhythmically, when undisturbed in their breathing. At night, especially, when quietly at anchor in the river, you hardly ever fail to be startled by the noise they make, when reaching the surface to exhale forcibly the air they have long retained in their lungs while under water. I have noticed five different species of this order of animals in the waters of the Amazons, four of which belong to the family of Porpoises and one to that of Manatees. Mr. Burkhardt has drawn three of them from fresh specimens for me, and I hope before long to secure equally faithful representations of the others, when I shall describe them all comparatively. One of the Porpoises belongs to the genus Inia, and may be traced on the upper tributaries of the Amazons to Bolivia, another resembles more our common Porpoise, while still another recalls the Dolphin of the sea-coast; but I have been unable to ascertain whether any one of them is identical with the marine species. At all events, the black Porpoise of the bay of Marajo, frequently seen in the vicinity of Pará, is totally different from the gray species seen higher up the stream. — L. A.

that family. These specimens furnished a complete embryological series, some of them having their eggs at the back of the gills, between the upper pharyngeals and the branchial arches, others their young in the mouth in different stages of development, up to those a quarter of an inch long and able to swim about, full of life and activity, when removed from the gills and placed in water. The most advanced were always found outside of the gills, within the cavity formed by the gill-covers and the wide branchiostegal membrane. In examining these fishes Mr. Agassiz has found that a special lobe of the brain, similar to those of the Triglas, sends large nerves to that part of the gills which protects the young; thus connecting the care of the offspring with the organ of intelligence. The specimens of this morning seem to invalidate the statement of the fishermen, that the young, though often found in the mouth of the parent, are not actually developed there, but laid and hatched in the sand. The series, in these specimens, was too complete to leave any doubt that in this species at least the whole process of development is begun and completed in the gill-cavity.

October 17th. — Teffé. Yesterday, to our great pleasure, our companions, Mr. James and Mr. Talisman, returned from their canoe expedition on the rivers Iça and Hyutahy, bringing most valuable collections. Mr. Agassiz has felt some anxiety about their success, as, in consequence of their small supply of alcohol, for preserving specimens, which was, nevertheless, all he could spare from the common store, a great deal of judgment in the choice of specimens was required in order to make a truly characteristic collection. The commission could not have been better executed, and the result raises the number of species from the Amazonian waters to more than six hundred, every day showing more clearly how distinctly the species are localized, and that this immense basin is divided into numerous zoölogical areas, each one of which has its own combination of fishes. Our stay at Teffé draws to a close, and to-day begins the great work of packing, in preparation for the arrival of the steamer at the end of the week. These days are the most laborious of all; on leaving every station, all the alcoholic specimens have to be overhauled, their condition ascertained, the barrels, kegs, and cans examined, to make sure that the hoops are fast, and that there are no leakages. Fortunately, there are some of our party who are very dexterous as coopers and joiners, and at these times the laboratory is turned into a workshop. We were reminded of the labors of the day by a circular distributed at breakfast this morning: —

"Sir: — The 'United Coopers' Association' will meet in the laboratory after breakfast. You are particularly requested to attend.

"Teffé, Oct. 17th, 1865."

And at this moment the laboratory rings with click of hammer, and nails, and iron hoops. As usual, there are a number of uninvited spectators watching the breaking up of the scientific establishment, which has been, during the past month, a source of constant entertainment to the vagrant population of Teffé. In this country of open doors and windows one has not the same protection against intrusion as in a colder climate, and we have had a constant succession of curious visitors hanging about our premises.

I have dwelt especially on the fish collection; but we do not go away empty-handed in other respects. Mr. Dexter has prepared a large number of the forest birds for mounting, — papagaios, toucans, and a great variety of smaller species of very brilliant plumage, not to speak of the less showy water-birds. He has been often in the woods shooting, with Mr. Hunnewell and Mr. Thayer, and has employed several sportsmen of the place to assist him. Turtles, jacarés, and snakes are also largely represented in the collections; and Mr. Agassiz has obtained, by purchase, a large and well-preserved collection of insects, made by a Frenchman during a several years' residence in this little town. In Teffé and its neighborhood we constantly tread in the footsteps of the English naturalist, Mr. Bates, "Senhor Henrique." as the people call him here, whose charming book. "The Naturalist on the Amazons," has been a very pleasant companion to us in our wanderings.*

* As from the beginning our arrangements were made to stay at least a month in Teffé, it became possible to lay out our work in a more systematic form than during our rambling travels. It was here that I secured the largest number of fish skeletons and had several of the larger animals of the country prepared for the Museum; such as Manatees, Porpoises, Pirarucus, Sorubims, and the like. I also undertook here, for the first time, a regular search for the young of all the species of fishes that could be obtained. Here again my neighbors, and indeed all the inhabitants of the place, vied with one another in their efforts to procure specimens for me. Senhor João da Cunha and Dr. Romualdo made frequent fishing excursions for my benefit; and when I could not accompany them, a boatful of fish was nevertheless moored to the shore, in the evening, from which I could select whatever was useful or interesting. The grocer of the place, Mr. Pedro Mendez, who employed a skilful fisherman daily to supply his large family, gave directions that all the fishes caught should be brought in, and before the kitchen received its provisions, I had my choice of everything. This was a great favor, especially since the Indian fisherman, José, whom I had engaged in Manaos to accompany me through the rest of my journey, was now at Tabatinga, assisting Mr. Bourget, who had been left there when I returned to Teffé. An old Passé Indian, who was as familiar with the fishes of the waters as with the animals of the forest, and whom Major Continho had befriended for many years, rendered also great service in hunting particular kinds of fishes and reptiles, the haunts of which he alone seemed to know. The schoolmaster and his boys, in short, everybody

October 21*st*. — Since Thursday afternoon our canoe has been loaded, all the specimens, amounting to something more than thirty barrels, kegs, and boxes, packed and waiting the arrival of the steamer. We have paid our parting visits to friends and acquaintances here. I have taken my last ramble in the woods where I have had so

who knew how to catch fish or fowl, was out at work, and, with the assistance of my young friends Dexter, Hunnewell, and Thayer, and the co-operation of Major Coutinho and Mr. Burkhardt, our daily progress was unmistakable. They generally took care of the collections of land animals, while I reserved the fishes to myself, and Major Coutinho was busy with geological and meteorological observations. Even the servants helped in cleaning the skeletons. I made here a very extensive collection of fish brains, embracing most genera found in this locality, but it was unfortunately lost on arriving at Manaos. Aware of the difficulty of transporting preparations so delicate, I kept them always by my side, simply packed in an open barrel, in the hope of bringing them safely home, and also that I might, without difficulty, add to the number. In an unguarded moment, however, while landing, one of our attendants capsized the whole into the Rio Negro. It is the only part of my collections which was completely lost.

After setting my whole party well under way in Teffé, I made the very instructive excursion with Major Estolano, of which an account is given in the text, to the Lago do Boto, a small sheet of water, by the side of his sitio on the banks of the main course of the Amazons, where I had a fair opportunity of ascertaining how widely different the fishes may be that inhabit adjoining faunæ in the same hydrographic basin. To this day I have not yet recovered from my surprise at finding that shores which, from a geographic point of view, must be considered simply as opposite banks of the same stream, were, nevertheless, the abode of an essentially different ichthyological population. Among the most curious fishes obtained here, I would mention a new genus, allied to Phractocephalus, of which I know only a single very large species, remarkable for its uniform canary-yellow color. Doras, Acestra, Pterygoplichthys, &c., were particularly common. Small as this lake is, the largest animals known in the whole basin are found in it: such as Manatees Botos, — the Porpoise of the Amazons, which has given its name to the lake; Alligators, Pirarucus, — the Sudis gigas of systematic writers; Sorubims, the large flat-headed Hornpouts; Pacamums, the large, yellow Siluroid above alluded to, &c., &c. — L. A.

many pleasant walks, and now we are sitting in the midst of valises and carpet-bags, waiting to see the steamer round the wooded point in front of the house, before we turn the key on our four weeks' home, and close this chapter of our Amazonian life. In this country, where time seems to be

Head of Alexandrina.

of comparatively little importance, one is never sure whether the boat will leave or arrive on the appointed day. One has only to make the necessary preparations, and then practise the favorite Brazilian virtue, "paciencia." The adjoining sketch is a portrait of my little house-maid, Alexandrina, who, from her mixture of Negro and Indian blood, is rather a curious illustration of the amalgamation of races here. She consented yesterday, after a good deal of coy demur, to have her portrait taken. Mr. Agassiz wanted it especially on account of her extraordinary hair, which, though it has lost its compact negro crinkle, and acquired something of the length and texture of the Indian hair, retains, nevertheless, a sort of wiry elasticity, so that, when combed out, it stands off from her head in all directions as if electrified. In the examples of negro and Indian half-breeds we have seen, the negro type seems the first to yield, as if the more facile disposition of the negro, as compared with the enduring tenacity of the Indian, showed itself in their physical as well as their mental characteristics. A few remarks, gathered from Mr. Agassiz's notes on the general character of the population in this region may not be without interest.

"Two things are strongly impressed on the mind of the traveller in the Upper Amazons. The necessity, in the first place, of a larger population, and, secondly, of a better class of whites, before any fair beginning can be made in developing the resources of the country; and, as an inducement to this, the importance of taking off all restraint on the navigation of the Amazons and its tributaries, opening them to the ambition and competition of other nations. Not only is the white population too small for the task before it, but it is no less poor in quality than meagre in numbers. It presents the singular spectacle of a higher race receiving the impress of a lower one, of an educated class adopting the habits and sinking to the level of the savage. In the towns of the Solimoens the people who pass for the white gentry of the land, while they profit by the ignorance of the Indian to cheat and abuse him, nevertheless adopt his social habits, sit on the ground and eat with their fingers as he does. Although it is forbidden by law to enslave the Indian, there is a practical slavery by which he becomes as absolutely in the power of the master as if he could be bought and sold. The white man engages an Indian to work for him at a certain rate, at the same time promising to provide him with clothes and food until such time as he shall have earned enough to take care of himself. This outfit, in fact, costs the employer little; but when the Indian comes to receive his wages he is told that he is already in debt to his master for what has been advanced to him; instead of having a right to demand money, he owes work. The Indians, even those who live about the towns, are singularly ignorant of the true value of things. They allow themselves to be deceived in this way to an extraordinary extent, and remain bound to the service of a man for a lifetime, believing themselves under the burden of a debt, while they are, in fact, creditors. Besides this virtual slavery, an actual traffic of the Indians does go on: but it is so far removed from the power of the authorities that they cannot, if they would, put a stop to it. A better class of emigrants would suppress many of these evils. Americans or Englishmen might be sordid in their transactions with the natives; their hands are certainly not clean in their dealings with the dark-skinned races; but they would not degrade themselves to the social level of the Indians as the Portuguese do; they would not adopt his habits."

I cannot say good by to Teffé without a word in commemoration of one class of its inhabitants who have interfered very seriously with our comfort. There is a tiny creature called the Mocuim, scarcely visible except for its bright vermilion color, which swarms all over the grass and low growth here. It penetrates under the skin so that one would suppose a red rash had broken out over the body, and causes excessive itching, ending sometimes in troublesome sores. On returning from a walk it is necessary to bathe in alcohol and water, in order to allay the heat and irritation produced by these little wretches. Mosquitoes are annoying, piums are vexatious, but for concentrated misery commend me to the Mocuim.

October 23d. — We left Teffé on Saturday evening on board the Icamiaba, which now seems quite like a home to us; we have passed so many pleasant hours in her comfortable quarters since we left Pará. We are just on the verge of the rainy season here, and almost every evening during the past week has brought a thunder-storm. The evening before leaving Teffé we had one of the most beautiful storms we have seen on the Amazons. It came sweeping up from the east; these squalls always come from the east, and therefore the Indians say "the path of the sun is the path of the storm." The upper, lighter layer of cloud, travelling faster than the dark, lurid mass below, hung over it with its white, fleecy edge, like an avalanche of snow just about to fall. We were all sitting at the doorstep watching its swift approach, and Mr. Agassiz said that this tropical storm was the most accurate representation of an avalanche on the upper Alps he had ever seen. It seems sometimes as if Nature played upon herself, reproducing the same appearances under the most dissimilar circumstances. It is curious to mark the change in the river. When we reached Teffé it was rapidly falling at the rate of about a foot a day. It was easy to measure its retreat by the effect of the occasional rains on the beach. The shower of one day, for instance, would gully the sand to the water's edge, and the next day we would find the water about a foot below the terminus of all the cracks and ruts thus caused, their abrupt close showing the line at which they met the water the previous day. Ten days or a fortnight before we left, and during which we had heavy rains at the close of every day, continuing frequently through the night, those oscillations in the river began, which the people here call "repiquete," and which, on the Upper Amazons, precede the regular rise of the water during the winter. The first repiquete occurs in Teffé toward the end of October, accompanied by almost daily rains. After a week or so the water falls again; in ten or twelve days it begins once more to ascend, and sinks again after the same period. In some seasons there is a third rise and fall, but usually the third repiquete begins the permanent annual rise of the river. On board the steamer we were joined by Mr. Bourget, with his fine collections from Tabatinga. He, like both the other parties, has been hindered, by want of alcohol, from making as large collections as he might otherwise have done; but they are, nevertheless, very valuable, exceedingly well put up, and embracing a great variety of species, from the Marañon as well as from the Hyavary. Thus we have a rich harvest from all the principal tributaries of the Upper Amazons, within the borders of Brazil, above the Rio Negro, except the Purus, which must be left unexplored for want of time and a sufficient working force.

On leaving Teffé I should say something of the nature of the soil in connection with Mr. Agassiz's previous observations on this subject. Although he has been almost constantly occupied with his collections, he has, nevertheless, found time to examine the geological formations of the neighborhood. The more he considers the Amazons and its tributaries, the more does he feel convinced that the whole mass of the reddish, homogeneous clay, which he has called drift, is the glacial deposit brought down from the Andes and worked over by the melting of the ice which transported it. According to his view, the whole valley was originally filled with this deposit, and the Amazons itself, as well as the rivers connected with it, are so many channels worn through the mass, having cut their way just as the igarapé now wears its way through the more modern deposits of mud and sand. It may seem strange that any one should compare the formation of these insignificant forest-streams with that of the vast river which pours itself across a whole continent; but it is, after all, only a reversal of the microscopic process of investigation. We magnify the microscopically small in order to see it, and we must diminish that which transcends our apprehension by its great size, in order to understand it. The naturalist who wishes to compare an elephant with a Coni (Hyrax),* turns the diminishing end of his glass upon the former, and, reducing its clumsy proportions, he finds that the difference is one of size rather than structure. The essential features are the same. So the little igarapé, as it wears its channel through the forest to-day, explains the early history of the great river and feebly reiterates the past.

* It was Cuvier who first ascertained that the small Hyrax belongs to the same order as the elephant.

CHAPTER VIII.

RETURN TO MANAOS. — AMAZONIAN PICNIC.

ARRIVAL AT MANAOS. — NEW QUARTERS. — THE "IBICUHY." — NEWS FROM HOME. — VISIT TO THE CASCADE. — BANHEIRAS IN THE FOREST. — EXCURSION TO LAKE HYANUARY. — CHARACTER AND PROSPECTS OF THE AMAZONIAN VALLEY. — RECEPTION AT THE LAKE. — DESCRIPTION OF SITIO. — SUCCESSFUL FISHING. — INDIAN VISITORS. - INDIAN BALL. — CHARACTER OF THE DANCING. — DISTURBED NIGHT. — CANOE EXCURSION. — SCENERY. — ANOTHER SITIO. — MORALS AND MANNERS. — TALK WITH THE INDIAN WOMEN. — LIFE IN THE FOREST. — LIFE IN THE TOWNS. — DINNER-PARTY. — TOASTS. — EVENING ROW ON THE LAKE. — NIGHT SCENE. — SMOKING AMONG THE SENHORAS. — RETURN TO MANAOS.

October 24th. — Manaos. We reached Manaos yesterday. As we landed in the afternoon, and as our arrival had not been expected with any certainty, we had to wait a little while for lodgings; but before night we were fairly established, our corps of assistants and all our scientific apparatus, in a small house near the shore, Mr. Agassiz and myself in an old, rambling edifice, used when we were here before for the public treasury, which is now removed to another building. Our abode has still rather the air of a public establishment, but it is very quaint and pleasant inside, and, from its open, spacious character, is especially agreeable in this climate. The apartment in which we have taken up our quarters, making it serve both as drawing-room and chamber, is a long, lofty hall, opening by a number of doors and windows on a large, green enclosure, called by courtesy a garden, but which is, after all, only a ragged space overgrown with grass, and having a few trees in it. Nevertheless, it makes a pleasant background of shade and verdure. At the upper end of our airy room hang our hammocks, and here are disposed our trunks, boxes, &c.; in the other half are a couple of writing-tables, a Yankee rocking-chair that looks as if it might have come out of a Maine farmer's house, a lounging-chair, and one or two other pieces of furniture, which give it a domestic look and make it serve very well as a parlor. There are many other apartments in this rambling, rickety castle of ours, with its brick floors and its rat-holes, its lofty, bare walls, and rough rafters overhead; but this is the only one we have undertaken to make habitable, and to my eye it presents a very happy combination of the cosey and the picturesque. We have been already urged by some of our hospitable friends here to take other lodgings; but we are much pleased with our quarters, and prefer to retain them, at least for the present.

On our arrival we were greeted by the tidings that the first steamer of the line recently opened between New York and Brazil had touched at Pará on her way to Rio. According to all accounts, this has been made the occasion of great rejoicing; and, indeed, there appears to be a strong desire throughout Brazil to strengthen in every way her relations with the United States. The opening of this line seems to bring us nearer home, and its announcement, in connection with excellent news, public and private, from the United States, made the day of our return to Manaos a very happy one. A few hours after our own arrival the steamer "Ibicuhy," provided by the government for our use, came into port. To our great pleasure, she brings Mr. Tavares Bastos, deputy from Alagoas, whose uniform kindness to us personally ever since our arrival in Brazil, as well as his interest in the success of the expedition, make it a great pleasure to meet him again. This morning Mr. Agassiz received the official document placing the steamer at his disposition, and also a visit from her commander, Captain Faria.

October 26*th.* — Yesterday morning at six o'clock we made our first excursion to a pretty spot much talked of in Manaos on account of its attractions for bathing, picnics, and country enjoyments of all sorts. It is called the "little cascade," to distinguish it from a larger and, it is said, a much more picturesque fall, half a league from the city on the other side. Half an hour's row through a winding river brings you to a rocky causeway, over which the water comes brawling down in a shallow rapid. Here you land, and a path through the trees leads along the edge of the igarapé to a succession of "banheiras," as they call them here ; and they are indeed woodland bathing-pools fit for Diana and her nymphs, completely surrounded by trees, and so separated from each other by leafy screens, that a number of persons may bathe in perfect seclusion. The water rushes through them with a delicious freshness, forming a little cascade in each. The inhabitants make the most of this forest bathing establishment while it lasts ; the rise of the river during the rainy season overflows and effaces it completely for half the year. While we were bathing, the boatmen had lighted a fire, and when we returned to the landing we found a pot of coffee simmering very temptingly over the embers. Thus refreshed, we returned to town just as the heat of the day was beginning to be oppressive.

October 28*th.* — Yesterday morning, at about half past six o'clock, we left Manaos on an excursion to the Lake of Hyanuary on the western side of the Rio Negro. The morning was unusually fresh for these latitudes, and a strong wind was blowing up so heavy a sea in the river, that, if it did not make one actually sea-sick, it certainly called up very vivid and painful associations. We were in a large eight-oared custom-house barge, our company consisting of His Excellency Dr. Epaminondas, President of the province, his Secretary, Senhor Codicera, Senhor Tavares Bastos, Major Coutinho, Mr. Agassiz and myself, Mr. Burkhardt, Mr. Dexter, and Mr. James. We were preceded by a smaller boat, an Indian montaria, in which was our friend Senhor Honorio, who has been so kind as to allow us to breakfast and dine with him during our stay here, and who, having undertaken to provide for our creature comforts, had the care of a boatful of provisions. After an hour's row we left the rough waters of the Rio Negro, and, rounding a wooded point, turned into an igarapé which gradually narrowed up into one of those shaded, winding streams, which make the charm of such excursions in this country. A ragged drapery of long, faded grass hung from the lower branches of the trees, marking the height of the last rise of the river to some eighteen or twenty feet above its present level. Here and there a white heron stood on the shore, his snowy plumage glittering in the sunlight, and numbers of Ciganas (Opistocomus), the pheasants of the Amazons, clustered in the bushes; once a pair of large king vultures (Sarcorhamphus papa) rested for a moment within gunshot, but flew out of sight as our canoe approached; and now and then an alligator showed his head above water. As we floated along through this picturesque channel, so characteristic of the wonderful region to which we were all more or less strangers, Dr. Epaminondas and Senhor Tavares Bastos being here also for the first time, the conversation turned naturally enough upon the nature of this Amazonian valley, its physical conformation, its origin and resources, its history past and to come, both alike obscure, both the subject of wonder and speculation. Senhor Tavares Bastos, although not yet thirty years of age, is already distinguished in the politics of his country, and from the moment he entered upon public life to the present time the legislation of the Amazons, its relation to the future progress and development of the Brazilian Empire, have been the object of his deepest interest. He is a leader in that class of men who advocate the most liberal policy with regard to this question, and has already urged upon his countrymen the importance, even from selfish motives, of sharing their great treasure with the world. He was little more than twenty years of age when he published his papers on the opening of the Amazons, which have done more, perhaps, than anything else, of late years, to attract attention to the subject.* There are points where the researches of the statesman and the investigator meet, and natural science is not without a voice even in the practical bearings of this question. Shall this region be legislated for as sea or land? Shall the interests of agriculture or navigation prevail in its councils? Is it essentially aquatic or terrestrial? Such were some of the inquiries which came up in the course of the discussion. A region of country which stretches across a whole continent and is flooded for half the year, where there can never be railroads or highways, or even pedestrian travelling to any great extent, can hardly be

* The most accurate information upon the industrial resources of the Valley of the Amazons may be found in a work published by Senhor Tavares Bastos, on his return to Rio de Janeiro, after this journey, entitled " O Valle do Amazonas — Estudo sobre a livre Navegaçaõ do Amazonas, Estatistica, Producções, Commercio, Questões Fiscaes do Valle do Amazonas." Rio de Janeiro. 1866.

considered as dry land. It is true that in this oceanic river-system the tidal action has an annual instead of a daily ebb and flow, that its rise and fall obey a larger orb, and is ruled by the sun and not the moon; but it is, nevertheless, subject to all the conditions of a submerged district, and must be treated as such. Indeed, these semiannual changes of level are far more powerful in their influence on the life of the inhabitants than any marine tides. People sail half the year above districts where for the other half they walk, though hardly dry shod, over the soaked ground; their occupations, their dress, their habits are modified in accordance with the dry and wet seasons. And not only the ways of life, but the whole aspect of the country, the character of the landscape, are changed. The two picturesque cascades, at one of which we took our bath the other morning, and at this season such favorite resorts with the inhabitants of Manaos, will disappear in a few months, when the river rises for some forty feet above its lowest level. Their bold rocks and shady nooks will have become river bottom. All that we hear or read of the extent of the Amazons and its tributaries fails to give an idea of its immensity as a whole. One must float for months upon its surface, in order to understand how fully water has the mastery over land along its borders. Its watery labyrinth is rather a fresh-water ocean, cut up and divided by land, than a network of rivers. Indeed, this whole valley is an aquatic, not a terrestrial basin; and it is not strange, when looked upon from this point of view, that its forests should be less full of life, comparatively, than its rivers.

While we were discussing these points, talking of the

time when the banks of the Amazons will teem with a population more active and vigorous than any it has yet seen,—when all civilized nations will share in its wealth, when the twin continents will shake hands and Americans of the North come to help Americans of the South in developing its resources,—when it will be navigated from north to south as well as from east to west, and small steamers will run up to the head-quarters of all its tributaries,—while we were speculating on these things, we were approaching the end of our journey; and as we neared the lake, there issued from its entrance a small two-masted canoe, evidently bound on some official mission, for it carried the Brazilian flag, and was adorned with many brightly-colored streamers. As it drew near we heard music, and a salvo of rockets, the favorite Brazilian artillery on all festive occasions, whether by day or night, shot up into the air. Our arrival had been announced by Dr. Canavaro, of Manaos, who had come out the day before to make some preparations for our reception, and this was a welcome to the President on his first visit to the Indian village. When they came within speaking distance, a succession of hearty cheers went up for the President, for Tavares Bastos, whose character as the political advocate of the Amazons makes him especially welcome here, for Major Coutinho, already well known from his former explorations in this region, and for the strangers within their gates,—for the Professor and his party. After this reception they fell into line behind our boat, and so we came into the little port with something of state and ceremony.

This pretty Indian village is hardly recognized as a village at once, for it consists of a number of sitios scattered through the forest; and though the inhabitants look on each other as friends and neighbors, yet from our landing-place only one sitio is to be seen,—that at which we are staying. It stands on a hill sloping gently up from the lake-shore, and consists of a mud-house containing two rooms, besides several large, open palm-thatched rooms outside. One of these outer sheds is the mandioca kitchen, another is the common kitchen, and a third, which is just now used as our dining-room, serves on festal days and occasional Sundays as a chapel. It differs from the others in having the upper end closed in with a neat thatched wall, against which, in time of need, the altar-table may stand, with candles and rough prints or figures of the Virgin and saints. We were very hospitably received by the Senhora of the mud-house, an old Indian woman, whose gold ornaments, necklace, and ear-rings were rather out of keeping with her calico skirt and cotton waist. This is, however, by no means an unusual combination here. Beside the old lady, the family consists, at this moment, of her "afilhada"* (god-daughter), with her little boy, and several other women employed about the place; but it is difficult to judge of the population of the sitios now, because a great number of the men have been taken as recruits for the war with Paraguay and others are hiding in the forest for fear of being pressed into the same service. The situation of this sitio is exceedingly pretty, and as we sit around the table in our open, airy dining-room, surrounded by the forest, we command a view of the lake and wooded hillside opposite and of the little landing below, where are moored our

---

* This relation is a much nearer one throughout Brazil than with us. A god-child is treated as a member of their own family by its sponsors.

Dining Room at Hyantary.

barge with its white awning, the gay canoe, and two or three Indian montarias. After breakfast our party dispersed, some to rest in their hammocks, others to hunt or fish, while Mr. Agassiz was fully engaged in examining a large basket of fish, Tucanarés (Cichla), Acaras (Heros· and other genera), Curimatas (Anodus), Surubims (Platystoma), &c., just brought up from the lake for his inspection, and showing again, what every investigation demonstrates afresh, namely, the distinct localization of species in each different water basin, be it river, lake, igarapé, or forest pool.

One does not see much of the world between one o'clock and four, in this climate. These are the hottest hours of the day, and there are few who can resist the temptation of the cool, swinging hammock, slung in some shady spot within doors or without. After a little talk with our Indian hostess and her daughter, I found a quiet retreat by the lake-shore, where, though I had a book in my hand, the wind in the trees overhead, the water rippling softly around the montarias moored at my side, lulled me into that mood of mind when one may be lazy without remorse or ennui. The highest duty seems then to be to do nothing. The monotonous notes of a "Viola" came to me from a group of trees at a little distance, where our boatmen were resting in the shade, the red fringes of their hammocks giving to the landscape just the bit of color which it needed; occasionally a rustling flight of parroquets or ciganas overhead startled me for a moment, or a large pirarucu plashed out of the water, but except for these sounds nature was still, and animals as well as men seemed to pause in the heat and seek shelter. Dinner brought us all together again at the close of the afternoon. As we are with the President of the province, our picnic is of a much more magnificent character than our purely scientific excursions have been. Instead of our usual makeshifts, — teacups doing duty as tumblers, and empty barrels acting as chairs, — we have a silver soup-tureen, and a cook, and a waiter, and knives and forks enough to go round, and many other luxuries which such wayfarers as ourselves learn to do without. While we were dining, the Indians began to come in from the surrounding forest to pay their respects to the President, for his visit was the cause of great rejoicing, and there was to be a ball in his honor in the evening. They brought an enormous cluster of game as an offering. What a mass of color it was! — more like a gorgeous bouquet of flowers than a bunch of birds. It was composed entirely of Toucans, with their red and yellow beaks, blue eyes, and soft white breasts bordered with crimson; and of parrots, or papagaios as they call them here, with their gorgeous plumage of green, blue, purple, and red. When we had dined, we took coffee outside, while our places around the table were filled by the Indian guests, who were to have a dinner-party in their turn. It was pleasant to see with how much courtesy several of the Brazilian gentlemen of our party waited upon these Indian Senhoras, passing them a variety of dishes, helping them to wine, and treating them with as much attention as if they had been the highest ladies of the land. They seemed, however, rather shy and embarrassed, scarcely touching the nice things placed before them, till one of the gentlemen, who has lived a good deal among the Indians, and knows their habits perfectly, took the knife and fork from one of them, exclaiming,

"Make no ceremony, and don't be ashamed; eat with your fingers as your 're accustomed to do, and then you'll find your appetites and enjoy your dinner." His advice was followed, and I must say they seemed much more comfortable in consequence, and did more justice to the good fare. Although the Indians who live in the neighborhood of the towns have seen too much of the conventionalities of life not to understand the use of a knife and fork, no Indian will eat with one if he can help it.

When the dinner was over, the room was cleared of the tables and swept; the music, consisting of a viola, flute, and violin, was called in, and the ball was opened. The forest belles were rather shy at first in the presence of strangers; but they soon warmed up and began to dance with more animation. They were all dressed in calico or muslin skirts, with loose, cotton waists, finished around the neck with a kind of lace they make themselves by drawing the threads from cotton or muslin, so as to form an open pattern, sewing those which remain over and over to secure them. Some of this lace is quite elaborate and very fine. Many of the women had their hair dressed either with white jessamine or with roses stuck into their round combs, and several wore gold beads and ear-rings. The dances were different from those I saw in Esperança's cottage, and much more animated; but the women preserved the same air of quiet indifference which I noticed there. Indeed, in all the Indian dances I have seen the man makes the advances, while the woman is coy and retiring, her movements being very languid. Her partner throws himself at her feet, but does not elicit a smile or a gesture; he stoops and pretends to be fishing; making motions as if he were drawing her in with a line, he dances around her, snapping his fingers as if he were playing on castanets, and half encircling her with his arms, but she remains reserved and cold. Now and then they join together in something like a waltz, but this is only occasionally and for a moment. How different from the negro dances which we saw frequently in the neighborhood of Rio, and in which the advances generally come from the women, and are not always of the most modest character. The ball was gayer than ever at ten o'clock when I went to my room, — or rather to the room where my hammock was slung, and which I shared with Indian women and children, with a cat and her family of kittens, who slept on the edge of my mosquito-net and made frequent inroads upon the inside, with hens and chickens and sundry dogs, who went in and out. The music and dancing, the laughter and talking outside, continued till the small hours. Every now and then an Indian girl would come in to rest for a while, take a nap in a hammock, and then return to the dance. When we first arrived in South America we could hardly have slept soundly under such circumstances; but one soon becomes accustomed, on the Amazons, to sleeping in rooms with mud floors and mud walls, or with no walls at all, where rats and birds and bats rustle about in the thatch overhead, and all sorts of unwonted noises in the night suggest that you are by no means the sole occupant of your apartment. There is one thing, however, which makes it far pleasanter to lodge in the houses of the Indians here than in those of our poorer class at home. One is quite independent in the matter of bedding; nobody travels without his own hammock, and the net which in many places is a necessity on account of the mosquitoes. Beds and bedding are almost unknown; and there are none so poor as not to possess two or three of the strong and neat twine hammocks made by the Indians themselves from the fibres of the palm. Then the open character of the houses and the personal cleanliness of the Indians make the atmosphere fresher and purer in their houses than in those of our poor. However untidy they may be in other respects, they always bathe once or twice a day, if not oftener, and wash their clothes frequently. We have never yet entered an Indian house where there was any disagreeable odor, unless it might be the peculiar smell from the preparation of the mandioca in the working-room outside, which has, at a certain stage of the process, a slightly sour smell. We certainly could not say as much for many houses where we have lodged when travelling in the West, or even "Down East," where the suspicious look of the bedding and the close air of the room often make one doubtful about the night's rest.

This morning we were up at five o'clock, and at six we had had coffee and were ready for the various projects suggested for our amusement. Our sportsmen were already in the forest, others had gone off on a fishing excursion in a montaria, and I joined a party on a visit to a sitio higher up on the lake. Mr. Agassiz was obliged to deny himself all these parties of pleasure, for the novelty and variety of the fish brought in kept him and his artist constantly at work. In this climate the process of decomposition goes on so rapidly, that, unless the specimens are attended to at once, they are lost; and the paintings must be made while they are quite fresh, in order to give any idea of their vividness of tint. Mr. Burkhardt is indefatigable, always busy with his drawing, in spite of heat, mosquitoes, and other discomforts; occasionally he makes not less than twenty colored sketches of fishes in one day. Of course, made with such rapidity, they are mere records of color and outline; but they will be of immense service in working up the finished drawings.* Leaving Mr. Agassiz, therefore, busy with the preparation of his collections, and Mr. Burkhardt painting, we went up the lake through a strange, half-aquatic, half-terrestrial region, where land seemed at odds with water. Groups of trees rose directly from the lake, their roots hidden below its surface, while numerous blackened and decayed trunks stood up from the water in all sorts of picturesque and fantastic forms. Sometimes the trees had thrown down from their branches those singular aerial roots so common here, and seemed standing on stilts. Here and there, where we coasted along by the bank, we had a glimpse into the deeper forest, with its drapery of lianas and various creeping vines, and its parasitic sipos twining close around the trunks or swinging themselves from branch to branch like loose cordage. But usually the margin of the lake was a gently sloping bank, covered with a green so vivid and yet so soft, that it seemed as if the earth had been born afresh in its six months' baptism, and had come out like a new creation. Here and there a palm lifted its head above the line of forest, especially the light, graceful Assai, its crown of feathery leaves vibrating above the tall, slender, smooth stem with every breeze. Half an hour's row brought us to the landing of the sitio for which we were bound. Usually the sitios stand on the bank of the lake or river, a stone's throw from the shore, for convenience of fishing,

* In the course of our journey on the Amazons, Mr. Burkhardt made more than eight hundred paintings of fishes, more or less finished. — L. A.

bathing, &c. But this one was at some distance, with a very nicely kept path winding through the forest. It stood on the brow of a hill which dipped down on the other side into a wide and deep ravine; through this ravine ran an igarapé, beyond which the land rose again in an undulating line of hilly ground, most refreshing to the eye after the flat character of the Upper Amazonian scenery. The fact that this sitio, standing now on a hill overlooking the valley and the little stream at its bottom, will have the water nearly flush with the ground around it, when the igarapé is swollen by the rise of the river, gives an idea of the difference of aspect between the dry and wet seasons. The establishment consisted of a number of buildings, the most conspicuous being a large open room, which the Indian Senhora who did the honors of the house told me was their reception-room, and was often used, she said, by the "brancas" from Manaos and the neighborhood for an evening dance, when they came out in a large company and passed the night. A low wall, some three or four feet in height, ran along the sides, wooden benches being placed against them for their whole length. The two ends were closed from top to bottom with a wall made of palm-thatch, exceedingly pretty, fine, and smooth, and of a soft straw color. At the upper end stood an immense embroidery-frame, looking as if it might have served for Penelope's web, but in which was stretched an unfinished hammock of palm-thread, the Senhora's work. She sat down on a low stool before it and worked a little for my benefit, showing me how the two layers of transverse threads were kept apart by a thick, polished piece of wood, something like a long, broad ruler. Through the opening thus made the shuttle

12

is passed with the cross thread, which is then pushed down and straightened in its place by means of the same piece of wood. After we had rested for a while, hammocks of various color and texture being immediately brought and hung up for our accommodation, the gentlemen went down to bathe in the igarapé, while the Senhora and her daughter, a very pretty Indian woman, showed me the rest of the establishment. The elder of the two had the direction of everything now, as the master of the house was absent, having a captain's commission in the army.

In the course of our conversation I was reminded of a social feature which strikes us as the more extraordinary the longer we remain on the Amazons, on account of its generality. Here were people of gentle condition, although of Indian blood, lifted above everything like want, living in comfort and, as compared with people about them, with a certain affluence, — people from whom, therefore, in any other society, you might certainly expect a knowledge of the common rules of morality. Yet when I was introduced to the daughter, and naturally asked something about her father, supposing him to be the absent captain, the mother answered, smiling, quite as a matter of course, "Naõ tem pai ; é filha da fortúna," — " She has n't any father ; she is the daughter of chance." In the same way, when the daughter showed me two children of her own, — little fair people, many shades lighter than herself, — and I asked whether their father was at the war, like all the rest of the men, she gave me the same answer, "They have n't any father." It is the way the Indian or half-breed women here always speak of their illegitimate children ; and though they say it without an intonation of sadness or of blame, apparently as unconscious of any wrong or shame as if they said the father was absent or dead, it has the most melancholy significance ; it seems to speak of such absolute desertion. So far is this from being an unusual case, that among the common people the opposite seems the exception. Children are frequently quite ignorant of their parentage. They know about their mother, for all the care and responsibility falls upon her, but they have no knowledge of their father ; nor does it seem to occur to the woman that she or her children have any claim upon him.

But to return to the sitio. The room I have described stood on one side of a cleared and neatly swept ground, about which, at various distances, stood a number of little thatched "casinhas," as they call them, consisting mostly of a single room. But beside these there was one larger house, with mud walls and floor, containing two or three rooms, and having a wooden veranda in front. This was the Senhora's private establishment. At a little distance farther down on the hill was the mandioca kitchen and all the accompanying apparatus. Nothing could be neater than the whole area of this sitio, and while we were there two or three black girls were sent out to sweep it afresh with their stiff twig-brooms. Around lay the plantation of mandioca and cacao, with here and there a few coffee-shrubs. It is difficult to judge of the extent of these sitio plantations, because they are so irregular and comprise such a variety of trees, — mandioca, coffee, cacao, and often cotton, being planted pellmell together. But this one, like the whole establishment, seemed larger and better cared for than those usually seen. On the return of the gentlemen from the igarapé we took leave, though very warmly pressed to stay and breakfast. At parting, our Indian hostess presented me with a wicker-basket of fresh eggs and some abacatys, or alligator pears as we call them.* We reached the house just in time for a ten o'clock breakfast, which assembled all the different parties once more from their various occupations, whether of work or play. The sportsmen returned from the forest, bringing a goodly supply of toucans, papagaios, and parroquets, with a variety of other birds, and the fisherman brought in new treasures for Mr. Agassiz.

October 29th. — Yesterday, after breakfast, I retreated to the room where we had passed the night, hoping to find time and quiet for writing letters and completing my journal. But I found it already occupied by the old Senhora and her guests, who were lounging in the hammocks or squatting on the floor and smoking their pipes. The house is indeed full to overflowing, as the whole party assembled for the ball are to stay during the President's visit. But in this way of living it is an easy matter to accommodate any number of people, for if they cannot all be received under the roof, they can hang their hammocks under the trees outside. As I went to my room last evening, I stopped to look at a pretty picture of an Indian mother with her two little children asleep on either arm, all in one hammock, in the open air. My Indian friends were too much interested in my occupations to allow of my continuing them uninterruptedly. They were delighted with my books (I happened to have "The Naturalist on the Amazons" with me, in which I showed them some pictures of Amazonian scenery and insects), and asked me many questions about my country, my voyage, and my travels here. In return they gave me much information

* The fruit of the Persea gratissima.

about their own way of life. They said the present gathering of neighbors and friends was no unusual occurrence, for they have a great many festas, which, though partly religious in character, are also occasions of great festivity. These festas are celebrated at different sitios in turn, the saint of the day being carried, with all his ornaments, candles, bouquets, &c., to the house where the ceremony is to take place, and where all the people of the village congregate. Sometimes the festa lasts for several days, and is accompanied with processions, music, and dances in the evening. But the women said the forest was very sad now, because their men had all been taken as recruits, or were seeking safety in the woods. The old Senhora told me a sad story of the brutality exercised in recruiting the Indians. She assured me that they were taken wherever found, without regard to age or circumstances, women and children often being dependent upon them; and if they made resistance, were carried off by force, and frequently handcuffed or had heavy weights attached to their feet. Such proceedings are entirely illegal; but these forest villages are so remote, that the men employed to recruit may practice any cruelty without being called to account for it. If the recruits are brought in in good condition, no questions are asked. These women said that all the work of the sitios — the making of farinha, the fishing, the turtle-hunting — was stopped for want of hands. The appearance of things certainly confirms this, for we scarcely see any men in the villages, and the canoes we meet are mostly rowed by women.

Yet I must say that the life of the Indian woman, so far as we have seen it, seems enviable, in comparison with that of the Brazilian lady in the Amazonian towns. The former has a healthful out-of-door life; she has her canoe on the lake or river and her paths through the forest, with perfect liberty to come and go; she has her appointed daily occupations, being busy not only with the care of her house and children, but in making farinha or tapioca, or in drying and rolling tobacco, while the men are fishing and turtle-hunting; and she has her frequent festa-days to enliven her working life. It is, on the contrary, impossible to imagine anything more dreary and monotonous than the life of the Brazilian Senhora in the smaller towns. In the northern provinces especially the old Portuguese notions about shutting women up and making their home-life as colorless as that of a cloistered nun, without even the element of religious enthusiasm to give it zest, still prevail. Many a Brazilian lady passes day after day without stirring beyond her four walls, scarcely ever showing herself at the door or window; for she is always in a slovenly dishabille, unless she expects company. It is sad to see these stifled existences; without any contact with the world outside, without any charm of domestic life, without books or culture of any kind, the Brazilian Senhora in this part of the country either sinks contentedly into a vapid, empty, aimless life, or frets against her chains, and is as discontented as she is useless.

On the day of our arrival the dinner was interrupted by the entrance of the Indians with their greetings and presents of game to the President; yesterday it was enlivened by quite a number of appropriate toasts and speeches. I thought, as we sat around the dinner-table, there had probably never been gathered under the palm-roof of an Indian house on the Amazons just such a party before, combining so many different elements and objects. There was the President, whose chief interest was of course in administering the affairs of the province, in which the Indians shared largely his attention; there was the young statesman, whose whole heart is in the great national question of peopling the Amazons and opening it to the world, and the effect this movement is to have upon his country; there was the able engineer, much of whose scientific life has been passed in surveying the great river and its tributaries with a view to their future navigation; and there was the man of pure science, come to study the distribution of animal life in their waters, without any view to practical questions. The speeches touched upon all these different interests, and were received with enthusiasm, each one closing with a toast and music; for our little band of the night before was brought in to enliven the occasion. The Brazilians are very happy in their after-dinner speeches, expressing themselves with great facility, either from a natural gift or because speech-making is an art in which they have had much practice. The habit of drinking healths and giving toasts is very general throughout the country, and the most informal dinner among intimate friends does not conclude without some mutual greetings of this kind.

As we were taking coffee under the trees afterwards, having yielded our places, in the primitive dining-room, to the Indian guests, the President suggested a sunset row on the lake. The hour and the light were most tempting, and we were soon off in the canoe, taking no boatmen, the gentlemen preferring to row themselves. We went through the same lovely region, half water, half land, which we had passed in the morning, floating between patches of greenest grass, and by large forest trees, and blackened trunks standing out of the lake like ruins. We did not go very fast nor very far, for our amateur boatmen found the evening warm, and their rowing was rather play than work; they stopped, too, every now and then, to get a shot at a white heron or to shoot into a flock of parroquets or ciganas, whereby they wasted a good deal of powder to no effect. As we turned to come back we were met by one of the prettiest sights I have ever seen. The Indian women, having finished their dinner, had taken the little two-masted canoe, dressed with flags, which had been prepared for the President's reception, and had come out to meet us. They had the music on board and there were two or three men in the boat; but the women were some twelve or fifteen in number, and seemed, like genuine Amazons, to have taken things into their own hands. They were rowing with a will; and as the canoe drew near, with music playing and flags flying, the purple lake, dyed in the sunset and smooth as a mirror, gave back the picture. Every tawny figure at the oars, every flutter of the crimson and blue streamers, every fold of the green and yellow national flag at the prow, was as distinct below the surface as above it. The fairy boat — for so it looked — floating between glowing sky and water, and seeming to borrow color from both, came on apace; and as it approached, our friends greeted us with many a *Viva*, to which we responded as heartily. Then the two canoes joined company and we went on together, the guitar sometimes being taken into one canoe and sometimes into the other, while Brazilian and Indian songs followed each other. Anything more national, more completely imbued with tropical coloring and character than this evening scene on the lake, can hardly be conceived. When we reached the landing, the gold and rose-colored clouds were fading into soft masses of white and ashen gray, and moonlight was taking the place of sunset. As we went up the green slope to the sitio, a dance on the grass was proposed, and the Indian girls formed a quadrille; for thus much of civilization has crept into their native manners, though they throw into it so much of their own characteristic movements, that it loses something of its conventional aspect. Then we returned to the house, where the dancing and singing were renewed, while here and there groups sat about on the ground laughing and talking, the women smoking with as much enjoyment as the men. Smoking is almost universal among the common women here, yet is not confined to the lower classes. Many a Senhora (at least in this part of Brazil, for we must distinguish between the civilization on the banks of the Amazons and in the interior and that in the cities along the coast) enjoys her pipe, while she lounges in her hammock through the heat of the day.

October 30th. — Yesterday our party broke up. The Indian women came to bid us good-by after breakfast, and dispersed to their several homes, going off in various directions through the forest-paths in little groups, their babies, of whom there were a goodly number, astride on their hips, as usual, and the older children following. Mr. Agassiz passed the morning in packing and arranging his fishes, having collected in those two days more than seventy new species.* His studies have been the subject

* I was indebted to the President for many valuable specimens on this excursion, many of the birds and fishes brought in by the Indians for the table being turned over to the scientific collections. My young friends Dexter and James were also efficient, passing always a part of the day in the woods, and assisting me greatly in the preparation and preservation of the

of great curiosity to the people about the sitio; one or two were always hovering about to look at his work and to watch Mr. Burkhardt's drawing. They seemed to think it extraordinary that any one should care to take the portrait of a fish. The familiarity of these children of the forest with the natural objects about them — plants, birds, insects, fishes, etc. — is remarkable. They frequently ask to see the drawings; and in turning over a pile containing several hundred colored sketches of fishes, they scarcely make a mistake, — even the children giving the name instantly, and often adding, " É filho d'este," (it is the child of such an one,) thus distinguishing the young from the adult, and pointing out their relation.

We dined rather earlier than usual, our chief dish being a stew of parrots and toucans, and left the sitio at about five o'clock, in three canoes, the music accompanying us in the smaller boat. Our Indian friends stood on the shore as we left, giving us farewell greetings, waving their hats and hands, and cheering heartily. The afternoon row through the lake and igarapé was delicious; but the sun had long set as we issued from the little river, and the Rio Negro, where it opens broadly out into the Amazons, was a sea of silver. The boat with the music presently joined our canoe, and we had a number of the Brazilian " modinhas," as they call them, — songs which seem especially adapted for the guitar. These mo-

---

specimens. Among others we made a curious skeleton of a large black Doras, a species remarkable for the row of powerful scales extending along the side, each one provided with a sharp hook bent backward. It is the species I have described, in Spix and Martius's great work, under the name of Doras Humboldti. The anterior vertebræ form a bony swelling of a spongeous texture, resembling drums, on each side of the backbone. — L. A.

dinhas have a quite peculiar character. They are little graceful, lyrical snatches of song, with a rather melancholy cadence; even those of which the words are gay not being quite free from this undertone of sadness. This put us all into a somewhat dreamy mood, and we approached the end of our journey rather silently. But as we drew near the landing, we heard the sound of a band of brass instruments, effectually drowning our feeble efforts, and saw a crowded canoe coming towards us. They were the boys from the Indian school which we visited on our previous stay at Manaos. The canoe looked very pretty as it came towards us in the moonlight; it seemed full to overflowing, the children all dressed in white uniforms and standing up. This little band comes always on Sunday evenings and festa-days to play before the President's house. They were just going home, it being nearly ten o'clock; but the President called to them to turn back, and they accompanied us to the beach, playing all the while. Thus our pleasant three days' picnic ended with music and moonlight.

CHAPTER IX.

MANAOS AND ITS NEIGHBORHOOD.

Photographic Establishment. — Indian Portraits. — Excursion to the "Great Cascade." — Its Geological Formation. — Bathing Pool. — Parasitic Plants. — Return by the Igarapé. — Public Ball. — Severity in Recruiting, and its Effects. — Collecting Parties. — Scenes of Indian Life. — Fête Champêtre at the "Casa dos Educandos." — Prison at Manaos. — Prison Discipline on the Amazons. — Extracts from Presidential Reports on this Subject. — Prison at Teffé. — General Character of Brazilian Institutions. — Emperor's Birthday. — Illuminations and Public Festivities. — Return of Collecting Parties. — Remarks on the Races. — Leave Manaos for Mauhes.

Saturday, November 4th. — Manaos. This week has been rather uneventful. Mr. Agassiz is prevented from undertaking new expeditions by the want of alcohol. The next steamer will bring a fresh supply from Pará; and meanwhile, being interrupted in his collections, he is making a study of the various intermixture of races, Indians and Negroes, with their crossings, of which a great number are found here. Our picturesque barrack of a room, which we have left for more comfortable quarters in Mr. Honorio's house, serves as a photographic saloon, and here Mr. Agassiz is at work half the day with his young friend Mr. Hunnewell, who spent almost the whole time of our stay in Rio in learning photography, and has become quite expert in taking likenesses. The grand difficulty is found in the prejudices of the people themselves. There is a prevalent superstition among the Indians and Negroes that a portrait absorbs into itself something of the vitality of the sitter, and that any one is liable to die shortly after his picture is taken. This notion is so deeply rooted that it has been no easy matter to overcome it. However, of late the desire to see themselves in a picture is gradually gaining the ascendant, the example of a few courageous ones having emboldened the more timid, and models are much more easily obtained now than they were at first.

Yesterday our quiet life was interrupted by an excursion to the great cascade, where we went with a party of friends to breakfast and dine. We were called with the dawn, and were on the road at six o'clock, the servants following laden with baskets of provisions. The dewy walk through the woods in the early morning was very pleasant, and we arrived at the little house above the cascade before the heat of the day began. This house stands on a hill in a cleared ground entirely surrounded by forest; just below it the river comes rushing through the wood, and falls some ten feet over a thin platform of rock. By its formation, this cascade is a Niagara in miniature; that is, the lower layer of rock being softer than the upper, the water has worn it away until there now remains only a thin slab of harder rock across the river. Deprived of its support, this slab must break down eventually, as Table-rock has done, when the cascade will, of course, retreat by so much and begin the same process a little higher up. It has, no doubt, thus worn its way upward already from a distant point. The lower deposit is clay, the upper consists of the constantly recurring reddish sandstone, — in other words, drift worked over by water. Below the fall, the water goes tearing along through a narrow passage, over boulders, fallen trees, and decaying logs, which break it into rapids. At a little distance from the cascade there is a deep, broad basin in the wood, with a sand bottom, so overshadowed by great trees that it looks dark

even in tropical midday. The bathing here, as we found
by experience at a later hour, is most delicious. The
shade over the pool is so profound and the current runs
through it so swiftly that the water is exceedingly cold, —
an unusual thing here, — and it seems very refreshing to
those coming from the hot sun outside. At the side of this
pool I saw a very large parasitic plant in flower. Since we
have been on the Amazons most of these parasites have been
out of bloom, and, though we have seen beautiful collections
in private gardens, we have not met them in the woods.
This one was growing in the lofty notch of a great tree,
overhanging the water; a tuft of dark green leaves with
large violet and straw-colored blossoms among them. It
was quite out of reach, and the little garden looked so
pretty in its airy perch, that I was almost glad we had no
power to disturb it. After breakfast some of the guests,
and Mr. Agassiz among them, were obliged to return to
town on business. They rejoined us in time for a late
dinner, arriving in a canoe instead of coming on foot,
an experiment which we had been prevented from trying
in the morning, because we had been told that, as the
igarapé was low and the bottom very rocky, it would be
impossible to ascend the whole distance in a boat. They
came, however, in perfect safety, and were delighted with
the picturesque beauty of the row. After a very cheerful
dinner, closing with a cup of coffee in the open air, we
started at twilight for town, by different roads. Desirous
to see the lower course of the igarapé, which Mr. Agassiz
reported as so beautiful, and being assured that there was
no real danger, I returned in the little canoe with Mr.
Honorio. It was thought best not to overload it, so the
others took the forest road by which we had come in the

morning. I must say that as I went down the rough steps to the landing, in the very pool where we had bathed, it struck me that the undertaking was somewhat perilous; if this overshadowed nook was dark at noonday, it was black at nightfall, and the turbulent little stream, rushing along over rocks and logs, looked mischievous. The rest of the party went with us to the embarkation, and, as we disappeared in the darkness under the overhanging branches, one of them called after us, laughingly,

"Lasciate ogni speranza, voi che 'ntrate."

However, there was only danger enough to laugh at, none to give real concern, and I enjoyed the row through the narrow channel, where the trees met overhead, and where the boatmen were obliged to jump into the water to guide the canoe among the boulders and fallen trunks. We reached home in perfect safety, and in time to welcome the others when they arrived on foot.

November 8th. — Manaos has been in unwonted agitation, for the last few days, on the subject of a public ball to be given in honor of Mr. Tavares Bastos. Where it should take place, what should be the day and hour, and, among the Senhoras, what one should wear, have been the subjects of discussion. The doubtful questions were at last settled, and it was appointed for the fifth of the month, in the President's palace. "Palace" is the name always given to the residence of the President of the province, however little the house may be in keeping with the title. The night was not so auspicious as could have been wished; it was very dark, and, as no such luxury as a carriage is known here, the different parties might be seen groping through the streets at the appointed hour, lighted with lanterns. Every now and then, as we were on our way, a ball-dress would emerge from the darkness of an opposite corner, picking its way with great care along the muddy ruts. When we had all assembled, however, I did not see that any toilet had suffered seriously on the road. The dresses were of every variety, from silks and satins to stuff gowns, and the complexions of all tints, from the genuine negro through paler shades of Indian and negro to white. There is absolutely no distinction of color here; a black lady, always supposing her to be free, is treated with as much consideration and meets with as much attention as a white one. It is, however, rare to see a person in society who can be called a genuine negro; but there are many mulattoes and mamelucos, that is, persons having black or Indian blood. There is little ease in Brazilian society, even in the larger cities; still less in the smaller ones, where, to guard against mistakes, the conventionalities of town life are exaggerated. The Brazilians, indeed, though so kind and hospitable, are a formal people, fond of etiquette and social solemnities. On their arrival, all the Senhoras were placed in stiff rows around the walls of the dancing-room. Occasionally an unfortunate cavalier would stray in and address a few words to this formidable array of feminine charms; but it was not until the close of the evening, when the dancing had broken up the company into groups, that the scene became really gay. At intervals, trays of "doces" and tea were handed round, and at twelve there was a more solid repast, at which all the ladies were seated, their partners standing behind their chairs and waiting upon them. Then began the toasts and healths, which were given and received with great enthusiasm. After supper the dancing was renewed and continued till after midnight, when the steamer from Pará was seen coming into port, throwing up rockets and burning blue-lights as she advanced, to announce that she was the bearer of good tidings from the war. This, of course, gave general satisfaction, and the ball broke up in great hilarity. There were some who did not sleep at all that night, for many of the gentlemen went from the ball-room to the steamer in search of the papers, which brought the news of a decided victory over the Paraguayans, at Uruguayana, where the Emperor commanded in person. It is said that seven thousand prisoners were taken. The next night the ball was renewed in honor of this victory; so that Manaos, whose inhabitants complain of the life as very dull, has had a most unwonted rush of gayety this week.

November 9th. — The severity in recruiting, of which we heard so much at the Lake of Hyanuary, is beginning to bear its fruits in general discontent. Some of the recruits have made their escape, and, on Tuesday and Wednesday, before the steamer in which they were to go down to Pará sailed, the disturbance was so great among them that they were kept under lock and key. The impression seems to be general here that the province of the Amazonas has been called upon to bear more than its share of the burden, and that the defencelessness of the Indians in the scattered settlements has made them especially victims. As there was no other armed force here, several of the crew of the "Ibicuhy" were taken to go down to Pará as guard over the unruly troops. Partly in consequence of this, we have resolved to remain at Manaos till the end of the month; a delay which Mr. Agassiz does not regret, as it enables him to continue the comparison of the races which he has begun, and for which the circumstances here are unusually favorable. In the mean time the President has provided him with canoes and men for three separate expeditions, on which he sends off three parties this week: Mr. Talisman and Mr. Dexter to the Rio Negro and Rio Branco, to be absent six weeks; Mr. Thayer and Mr. Bourget to Lake Cudajas, to be gone ten days; Mr. James to Manacapuru, for about the same time. We feel the generosity of this conduct the more, knowing how greatly the administration stands in need of men and of all the resources at its command in the present disturbed state of things.

November 18*th.* — One can hardly walk in any direction out of the town without meeting something characteristic of the people and their ways of living. At seven o'clock, to-day, I took my morning walk through the wood near the house to an igarapé, which is the scene of much of the out-of-doors life here, — fishing, washing, bathing, turtle-shooting. As I returned along the little path leading by the side of the stream, two naked Indian boys were shooting fish with bow and arrows from a fallen tree which jutted out into the stream. Like bronze statues they looked, as they stood quiet and watchful, in attitudes full of grace and strength, their bows drawn ready to let the arrow fly the moment they should catch sight of the fish. The Indian boys are wonderfully skilful in this sport, and also in shooting arrows through long blow-pipes (Sarabatanas) to kill birds. This is no bad way of shooting, for the report of the gun startles the game so effectually in these thick forests, that after a few shots the sportsman finds the woods in his immediate neighborhood deserted; whereas the Indian boy creeps stealthily up to the spot from which he takes aim and discharges his noiseless arrow with such precision, that the bird or monkey drops down from among its companions, without their perceiving the cause of its disappearance. While I was watching the boys, a canoe came up the stream, paddled by women, and loaded with fruit and vegetables, on the top of which sat two bright green parrots. Two of the women were old and hideous, very wrinkled and withered, as these people usually are in old age; but the third was the handsomest Indian woman I have ever seen, with a tinge of white blood to be sure, for her skin was fairer and her features more regular than those of the Indians generally. They were coming from their sitio, as I learned afterwards. When they had moored their boat to a tree, the younger woman began to unload, tucking her petticoat about her hips, and wading to and fro with baskets of fruit and vegetables on her head. Her hair was dressed with flowers, as is usual with these women; however scanty their clothing, they seldom forget this ornament.

November 20th. — The President, Dr. Epaminondas, added yesterday to the many kindnesses by which he has rendered our stay here doubly pleasant, in giving an exceedingly pretty fête in honor of Mr. Agassiz. The place chosen was the asylum for Indian children already described, well adapted for the purpose on account of its large, airy rooms and beautiful situation; and the invitation was given out in the name of the "Province of the Amazonas." *

---

* I trust that the motive will not be misunderstood which induces me to add here a translation of the general cards of invitation distributed on this occasion. The graceful expression of a thought so kind, and the manner in which the President merges his own personality in the name of the Province of which he is the administrative head, are so characteristic of his mingled courtesy and modesty, that I am tempted to insert the note, notwithstanding its personal

The day was most propitious; a rain during the night had cooled the air, and a slightly overcast sky, combined with the freshness of the atmosphere, gave just the conditions most desirable for any such excursion in this climate. When we reached the beach from which we were to leave, people were beginning to assemble, and a number of canoes were already on their way, looking very gay with their white awnings above and the bright dresses inside. Twenty minutes' row brought us to our destination. The scene was very pretty; the path from the landing to the main house was lined with flags and

character. Unfortunately, I cannot always do full justice to the kindness shown Mr. Agassiz throughout our journey, or to the general appreciation of his scientific objects, without introducing testimonials into this narrative which it would perhaps be more becoming in me to suppress. But I do not know how otherwise to acknowledge our obligations, and I trust it will be attributed, by candid readers, to the true motive, — to gratitude and not to egotism.

"The scientific labors undertaken at this time by the learned and illustrious Professor Agassiz in this Province, merit from the Amazonenses the most sincere gratitude and acknowledgment, and elicit on our part a manifestation by which we seek to show due appreciation of his high intellectual merit. I wish that for this object I could dispose of more abundant resources, or that the Province had in readiness better means of showing the veneration and cordial esteem we all bear to him, the respect and admiration we feel for his scientific explorations. But the uncertainty of his stay among us obliges me to offer at once some proof, however insignificant, of our profound esteem for this most deserving American.

"To this end, the accomplishment of which I cannot longer defer, I invite all to join me in offering to Professor Agassiz and to his wife, in the name of the Province of the Amazonas, a modest rural breakfast (*almoço campestre*) in the Casa dos Educandos, on Sunday, the 18th of this month, at 11 o'clock in the morning. I hereby invite you and your family to be present, in order that this festival, great in the earnestness of our intentions, however small as compared with the importance of those to whom it is offered, should be gay and brilliant.

"ANTONIO EPAMINONDAS DE MELLO.

"*Palace of the Government at Manaos*, 13 *November*, 1865."

with palm-trees brought from the forest for the occasion, and the open sides of the large rooms outside, usually working-rooms, but now fitted up for the breakfast, were all filled in with green arches built of trees and flowers, so that the whole space was transformed, for the time being, into an arbor. We were received with music and conducted to the main building, where all the guests gradually assembled, some two hundred in number. At about one o'clock the President led the way to the green arcades which, as yet, we had seen only from a distance. Nothing could be more tasteful than the arrangements. The tables were placed around a hollow square, in the centre of which was the American flag, with the Brazilian on either side of it; while a number of other flags draped the room and made the whole scene bright with color. The landscape, framed in the open green arches, made so many pictures, pretty glimpses of water and wood, with here and there a palm-thatched roof among the trees on the opposite side of the river. A fresh breeze blew through the open dining-room, stirring the folds of the flags, and making a pleasant rustle in the trees, which added their music to that of the band outside. Since we are on the Amazons, a thousand miles from its mouth, it is worth while to say a word of the breakfast itself. There is such an exaggerated idea of the hardships and difficulty of a voyage on the Amazons, (at least so I infer from many remarks made to us, not only at home, but even in Rio de Janeiro by Brazilians themselves, when we were on the eve of departure for this journey,) that it will hardly be believed that a public breakfast, given in Manaos, should have all the comforts, and almost all the luxuries, of a similar entertainment in any other part of the world. It is true, that we had neither ices nor champagne, the former being of course difficult to obtain in this climate; but these two exceptions were more than compensated for by the presence of tropical fruits not to be had elsewhere at any price,—enormous Pineapples, green and purple Abacatys (alligator pears), crimson Pitangas, Attas (fruta do Conde), Abios, Sapotis, Bananas of the choicest kinds and in the greatest profusion, and a variety of Maracujas (the fruit of the passion-flower).* The breakfast was gay, the toasts were numerous, the speeches animated, and long after the Senhoras had left the table the room still echoed with Vivas, as health followed health. At the close of the dinner there was a little scene which struck us as very pretty; I do not know whether it is a custom here, but, as it excited no remark, I suppose it may be. When the gentlemen returned to the house, bringing the music with them, all the waiters assembled in line before the door, decanter and glass in hand, to finish the remains of the wine with a toast on their own account. The head-waiter then stood in front of them and gave the health, first, of the persons for whom the banquet was given, followed by that of the President, all of which were answered with Vivas as they filled their glasses. Then one of the gentlemen stepping forward gave, amid shouts of laughter, the health of the head-waiter

* As I do not wish to mislead, and this narrative may perhaps influence some one to make a journey in this region, I should add, that, while the above is strictly true, there are many things essential to the comfort of the traveller not to be had. There is not a decent hotel throughout the whole length of the Amazons, and any one who thinks of travelling there must provide himself with such letters as will secure accommodation in private houses. So recommended, he may safely depend upon hospitality, or upon such assistance from individuals as will enable him to find a private lodging.

himself, which was drank in a closing bumper with perhaps more animation than either of the others. The afternoon closed with dancing, and at sunset the canoes assembled and we returned to the city, all feeling, I believe, that the festival had been a very happy one. It certainly was so for those to whom it was intended to give pleasure, and could hardly fail to be likewise for those who had planned and executed it. It will seem strange to many of my readers that Sunday should be chosen for such a fête; but here, as in many parts of continental Europe, even in Protestant districts, Sunday is a holiday and kept as such.

November 27th. — Yesterday I visited the prison where the wife of the chief of police had invited me to see some of the carved articles, straw work, &c., made by the prisoners. I had expected to be pained, because I thought, from the retrograde character of things in general here, the prison system would be bad. But the climate in these hot countries regulates the prison life in some degree. Men cannot be shut up in close, dark cells, without endangering not only their own lives, but the sanitary condition of the establishment also. Therefore the prison is light and airy, with plenty of doors and windows, secured by bars, but not otherwise closed. I infer, however, from a passage on the prisons of the province, contained in one of the able reports of President Adolfo de Barros (1864), that within the last year there has been a great improvement, at least in the prison of Manaos. He says: "The state of the prisons exceeds all that can be said to their disadvantage. Not only is it true that there is not to be found throughout the province a prison which fulfils the conditions imposed by the law, but there is not one which deserves the name of prison with the exception of that in the capital. And even this one, while it does not possess one of the conditions exacted by similar institutions, contains so disproportionate a number of prisoners of all classes, so indiscriminately mingled, that, setting aside the other difficulties arising from this association, it is only by the mercy of Providence that the jail has not been converted into a focus of epidemics during the great heat prevailing in this city for a great part of the year. In four small rooms, insufficiently ventilated and lighted, are assembled forty prisoners (including the sick) of various classes and conditions. Without air, without cleanliness, almost without room to move in their smothered and damp enclosure, these unhappy beings, against all precepts of law and humanity, suffer far more than the simple and salutary rigor of punishment." These strictures must have led to a great amendment, for the prison does not now appear to be deficient in light or in ventilation, and there is a hospital provided apart for the sick. Some of the prisoners, especially those who were there for political offences, having been concerned in a recent revolt at Serpa, were very heavily ironed; but, excepting this, there were no signs, visible at least to the transient observer, of cruelty or neglect. After some remarks on the best modes of reforming these abuses and the means to be employed for that object, Dr. Adolfo goes on to speak of the ruinous condition of the prisons in other cities of the province. "Such is the state of the prison in the town of Teffé The edifice in which it is established is an old and crumbling house, belonging to the municipality, thatched with straw, and so ruinous, that it seemed to me, when I visited it, rather like a deserted habitation than like a building destined for the detention of criminals. There were but a few prisoners, some of whom were already condemned. I formed a favorable judgment of them all, for it seemed to me they must have either great confidence in their own innocence, or scruples as to compromising the few soldiers who acted as guards. In no other way could I explain the fact that they remained in prison, when flight seemed so easy." I well remember one evening when walking in Teffé seeing a number of men leaning against the wooden grating of a dimly lighted room in a ruinous thatched house, and being told that this was the prison. I asked myself the same question which presented itself to the President's mind, — why these wild-looking, half-naked creatures had not long ago made their escape from a prison whose bars and bolts would hardly have imposed restraint upon a child. The report continues: "A more decent and, above all, a more secure prison at this point, the most important in the whole Solimoens, is an urgent and even indispensable necessity. Of the sixteen prisons in the whole province, only two, that of the capital and of Barcellos, have their own buildings. With these exceptions, the prisoners occupy either a part of the houses of the legislative chambers, or are placed in private houses hired for the purpose, or in the quarters of the military detachments. In these different prisons 538 prisoners were received during the current year, inclusive of recruits and deserters." This last clause, "inclusive of recruits and deserters," and the association of the two classes of men together, as if equally delinquent, touches upon a point hardly to be overlooked by the most superficial observer, and which makes a very painful impression on strangers. The system of recruiting, or rather the utter want of system, leads to the most terrible abuse of authority in raising men for the army. I believe that the law provides for a constitutional draft levied equally on all classes, excluding men below or above a certain age, or having certain responsibilities at home. But if such a law exists it is certainly not enforced; recruiting parties, as bad as the old "press-gangs" of England, go out into the forest and seize the Indians wherever they can find them. All who resist this summary treatment or show any inclination to escape are put into prison till the steamer leaves, by which they are despatched to Pará and thence to the army. The only overcrowded room I saw at the prison was that where the recruits were confined. Coming from a country where the soldier is honored, where men of birth and education have shown that they are not ashamed to serve in the ranks if necessary, it seemed to me strange and sad to see these men herded with common criminals. The record of the province of the Amazonas will read well in the history of the present war, for the number of troops contributed is very large in proportion to the population. But as most of them are obtained in this way, it may be doubted whether the result is a very strong evidence of patriotism. The abuses mentioned above are not, however, confined to these remote regions.* It is not uncommon, even in the

* Much of what follows upon social abuses, tyranny of the local police, prison discipline, &c., though not quoted in his own words, has been gathered from conversations with Mr. Agassiz, or from discussions between him and his Brazilian friends. The way in which this volume has grown up, being as it were the result of a double experience, makes it occasionally difficult to draw the exact line marking the boundaries of authorship; the division being indeed somewhat vague in the minds of the writers themselves. But since criticisms of this sort would have little value, except as based upon larger opportunities for observation than fell to my share, I am the more anxious to refer them, wherever I can, to their right source.

more populous and central parts of Brazil, to meet recruits on the road, so-called volunteers, chained two and two by the neck like criminals, under an armed guard. When we first met a squad of men under these circumstances, on the Juiz de Fora road, we supposed them to be deserters, but the Brazilians who were with us, and who seemed deeply mortified at the circumstance, said that they were no doubt ordinary recruits, arrested without inquiry on the one side, or power of resistance on the other. They asserted that this mode of recruiting was illegal, but that their chains would be taken off before entering the city, and no questions asked. A Brazilian told me that he had known an instance in which a personal pique against an enemy had been gratified by pointing out its object to the recruiting officer, who had the man at once enlisted, though a large family was entirely dependent upon him. Our informant seemed to know no redress for tyranny like this.

The hospitality we have received in Brazil, the sympathy shown to Mr. Agassiz in his scientific undertakings, as well as our own sentiments of gratitude and affection for our many friends here, forbid us to enter into any criticism of Brazilian manners or habits which could have a personal application. Neither do I believe that a few months' residence in a country entitles any one to a judgment upon the national character of its people. Yet there are certain features of Brazilian institutions and polities which cannot but strike a stranger unfavorably, and which explain the complaints one constantly hears from foreign residents. The exceedingly liberal constitution, borrowed in great part from our own, prepares one to expect the largest practical liberty. To a degree this exists; there is no censorship of the press; there is no constraint upon the exercise of any man's religion; nominally, there is absolute freedom of thought and belief. But in the practical working of the laws there is a very arbitrary element, and a petty tyranny of the police against which there seems to be no appeal. There is, in short, an utter want of harmony between the institutions and the actual condition of the people. May it not be, that a borrowed constitution, in no way the growth of the soil, is, after all, like an ill-fitting garment, not made for the wearer, and hanging loosely upon him? There can be no organic relation between a truly liberal form of government and a people for whom, taking them as a whole, little or no education is provided, whose religion is administered by a corrupt clergy, and who, whether white or black, are brought up under the influence of slavery. Liberty will not abide in the laws alone; it must have its life in the desire of the nation, its strength in her resolve to have and to hold it. Another feature which makes a painful impression on the stranger is the enfeebled character of the population. I have spoken of this before, but in the northern provinces it is more evident than farther south. It is not merely that the children are of every hue; the variety of color in every society where slavery prevails tells the same story of amalgamation of race; but here this mixture of races seems to have had a much more unfavorable influence on the physical development than in the United States. It is as if all clearness of type had been blurred, and the result is a vague compound lacking character and expression. This hybrid class, although more marked here because the Indian element is added, is very numerous in all the cities and on the large plantations; perhaps the fact, so honorable to Brazil, that the free negro has full access to all the privileges of any free citizen, rather tends to increase than diminish the number.*

December 3d. — Yesterday was the Emperor's birthday, always kept as a holiday throughout Brazil, and this year with more enthusiasm than usual, because he has just returned from the army, and has made himself doubly dear to his people, not only by the success which attended his presence there, but by his humanity toward the soldiers. We had our illuminations, bouquets, music, &c., as well as the rest of the world; but as Manaos is not overflowing with wealth, the candles were rather few, and there were long lapses of darkness alternating with the occasional brilliancy. We went out in the evening to make a few calls, and listen to the music in the open ground dignified by the name of the public square. Here all the surrounding buildings were brightly illuminated; there was a very pretty tent in the centre, where the band of Indian children from the Casa dos Educandos was playing; preparations were making for the ascension of a

---

* Let any one who doubts the evil of this mixture of races, and is inclined, from a mistaken philanthropy, to break down all barriers between them, come to Brazil. He cannot deny the deterioration consequent upon an amalgamation of races, more widespread here than in any other country in the world, and which is rapidly effacing the best qualities of the white man, the negro, and the Indian, leaving a mongrel nondescript type, deficient in physical and mental energy. At a time when the new social status of the negro is a subject of vital importance in our statesmanship, we should profit by the experience of a country where, though slavery exists, there is far more liberality toward the free negro than he has ever enjoyed in the United States. Let us learn the double lesson: open all the advantages of education to the negro, and give him every chance of success which culture gives to the man who knows how to use it; but respect the laws of nature, and let all our dealings with the black man tend to preserve, as far as possible, the distinctness of his national characteristics, and the integrity of our own. — L. A.

lighted balloon at a later hour, and so on. But whenever we have been present at public festivities in Brazil, — and our observation is confirmed by other foreigners, — we have been struck with the want of gayety, the absence of merriment. There is a kind of lack-lustre character in their fêtes, so far as any demonstration of enjoyment is concerned. Perhaps it is owing to their enervating climate, but the Brazilians do not seem to work or play with a will. They have not the activity which, while it makes life a restless fever with our people, gives it interest also; neither have they the love of amusement of the continental Europeans.

December 6th. — Manaos. Mr. Thayer returned to-day from Lake Alexo, bringing a valuable collection of fish, obtained with some difficulty on account of the height of water; it is rapidly rising now, and the fish are in consequence daily scattered over a wider space. This addition with the collections brought in by Mr. Bourget and Mr. Thayer from Cudajas, by Mr. James from Manacapuru, and by Major Coutinho from Lake Hyanuary, José-Fernandez, Curupira, &c., &c., brings the number of Amazonian species up to something over thirteen hundred. Mr. Agassiz still carries out his plan of dispersing his working force in such a manner as to determine the limits of the distribution of species; to ascertain, for instance, whether those which are in the Amazons at one season may be in the Solimoens at another or at the same time, and also whether those which are found about Manaos extend higher up in the Rio Negro. For this reason, as we have seen, while at Teffé himself he kept parties above in various localities, — at Tabatinga and on the rivers Içá and Hyutahy; and now, while he and some of his assistants are collecting in the immediate neighborhood of Manaos, Mr. Dexter and Mr. Talisman are on the Rio Negro and Rio Branco. Following the same plan in descending the river, he intends to establish one station at Serpa, another at Obydos, another at Santarem, while he will go himself to the river Mauhes, which connects the Amazons with the Madeira.

December 10*th*. — To-day Mr. Dexter and Mr. Talisman returned from their canoe excursion to the Rio Branco. They are rather disappointed in the result of their expedition, having found the state of the waters most extraordinary for the season and very unfavorable for their purpose. The Rio Negro was so full that the beaches had entirely disappeared, and it was impossible to draw the nets; while on the Rio Branco the people stated that the water had not fallen during the whole year, — an unheard-of phenomenon, and unfortunate for the inhabitants, who were dreading famine for want of their usual supply of dried and salted fish, on which they so largely depend for food. This provision is always made when the waters are lowest, and when the large fish, driven into shallower and narrower basins, are easily caught. Though their collection of fish is therefore small, including only twenty-eight new species, Mr. Dexter and Mr. Talisman bring several monkeys, a very large alligator, some beautiful birds, among them the blue Mackaw, and a number of very fine palms. To-morrow we leave Manaos in the Ibicuhy, on an excursion to the little town of Mauhes, where we are to pass a week or ten days. Though we return for a day or two on our way to the Rio Negro, yet we feel that our permanent stay in Manaos is over. The six weeks we have passed here have been very valuable in scientific results. Not only has Mr. Agassiz largely increased his knowledge of the fishes, but he has had an opportunity of accumulating a mass of new and interesting information on the many varieties of the colored races, produced by the crossing of Indians, negroes, and whites, which he has recorded not only in notes, but in a very complete series of photographs. Perhaps nowhere in the world can the blending of types among men be studied so fully as in the Amazons, where mamelucos, cafuzos, mulattoes, cabocos, negroes, and whites are mingled in a confusion that seems at first inextricable. I insert below a few extracts from his notes on this subject, which he purposes to treat more in detail, should he find time hereafter to work up the abundant material he has collected.

"However naturalists may differ respecting the origin of species, there is at least one point on which they agree, namely, that the offspring from two so-called different species is a being intermediate between them, sharing the peculiar features of both parents, but resembling neither so closely as to be mistaken for a pure representative of the one or the other. I hold this fact to be of the utmost importance in estimating the value and meaning of the differences observed between the so-called human races. I leave aside the question of their probable origin, and even that of their number; for my purpose, it does not matter whether there are three, four, five, or twenty human races, and whether they originated independently from one another or not. The fact that they differ by constant permanent features is in itself sufficient to justify a comparison between the human races and animal species. We know that, among animals, when two individuals of different sex and belonging to distinct species produce an offspring, the latter does not closely resemble either parent, but shares the characteristics of both; and it seems to me of the highest significance that this fact is equally true of any two individuals of different sexes, belonging to different human races. The child born of negro and white parents is neither black nor white, but a mulatto; the child born of white and Indian parents is neither white nor Indian, but a mameluco; the child born of negro and Indian parents is neither a negro nor an Indian, but a cafuzo; and the cafuzo, mameluco, and mulatto share the peculiarities of both parents, just as the mule shares the characteristics of the horse and ass. With reference to their offspring, the races of men stand, then, to one another in the same relation as different species among animals; and the word *races*, in its present significance, needs only to be retained till the number of human species is definitely ascertained and their true characteristics fully understood. I am satisfied that, unless it can be shown that the differences between the Indian, negro, and white races are unstable and transient, it is not in keeping with the facts to affirm a community of origin for all the varieties of the human family, nor in keeping with scientific principles to make a difference between human races and animal species in a systematic point of view. In these various forms of humanity there is as much system as in anything else in nature, and by overlooking the thoughtful combinations expressed in them we place ourselves at once outside of the focus from which the whole may be correctly seen. In consequence of their constancy, these differences are so many limitations to prevent a complete melting of normal types into each other and consequent loss of their primitive features. That these different types are genetically foreign to one another, and do not run together by imperceptible, intermediate degrees, appears plain when their mixtures are compared. White and negro produce mulattoes, white and Indian produce mamelucos, negro and Indian produce cafuzos, and these three kinds of half-breeds are not connecting links between the pure races, but stand exactly in that relation to them in which all hybrids stand to their parents. The mameluco is as truly a half-breed between white and Indian, the cafuzo as truly a half-breed between negro and Indian, as is the mulatto, commonly so called, a half-breed between white and negro. They all share equally the peculiarities of both parents, and though more fertile than half-breeds in other families of the animal kingdom, there is in all a constant tendency to revert to the primary types in a country where three distinct races are constantly commingling, for they mix much more readily with the original stocks than with each other.* Children between mameluco and mameluco, or between cafuzo and cafuzo, or between mulatto and mulatto, are seldom met with where the pure races occur; while offspring of mulattoes with whites, Indians and negroes, or of mamelucos with whites, Indians, and negroes, or of cafuzos with whites, Indians, and negroes, form the bulk of these mixed populations. The natural result of an uninterrupted contact of half-breeds with one another is a class of men in which pure type fades away as completely as do all the good qualities, physical and moral, of the primitive races, engendering a mongrel crowd as repulsive as the mongrel dogs, which are apt to be their companions, and among which it is impossible to pick out a single specimen retaining the intelligence, the nobility, or the affectionateness of nature which makes

---

* For some remarks concerning the structural peculiarities of the Indians and Negroes, see Appendix No. V.

the dog of pure type the favorite companion of civilized man. The question respecting the relation of the human races to each other is complicated by the want of precision in the definition of species. Naturalists differ greatly in their estimation of the characters by which species are to be distinguished, and of their natural limitations. I have published elsewhere my own views on this subject. I believe the boundaries of species to be precise and unvarying, based upon a category of characters quite distinct from those on which the other groups of the animal kingdom, as genera, families, orders, and classes, are founded. This category of characters consists chiefly in the relation of individuals to one another and to their surroundings, and in the relative dimensions and proportions of parts. These characters are no less permanent and constant in the different species of the human family than in those of any other family in the animal kingdom, and my observations upon the cross-breeds in South America have convinced me that the varieties arising from contact between these human species, or so-called races, differ from true species just as cross-breeds among animals differ from true species, and that they retain the same liability to revert to the original stock as is observed among all so-called varieties or breeds."

Our visit to Manhes will be the pleasanter and doubtless the more successful, because Dr. Epaminondas, who has already done so much to facilitate the objects of the expedition, takes this opportunity of visiting a region with which, as President of the province, he is desirous of becoming acquainted. He is accompanied by our host, Mr. Honorio, whose house has been such a pleasant home for us during our stay in Manaos, and also by Mr. Michelis,

Lieutenant-Colonel of the National Guard of Mauhes, returning to his home there, after a stay of several weeks in Manaos. Besides these, our party consists of Major Coutinho, Mr. Burkhardt, and ourselves. The position of Mauhes, on the southern side of the Amazons, and its proximity to Manaos and Serpa, may make this excursion especially instructive, with reference to the study of the geographical distribution of the Fishes in the great network of rivers connecting the Rio Madeira and the Rio Tapajoz with the Amazons.

CHAPTER X.

EXCURSION TO MAUHES AND ITS NEIGHBORHOOD.

Leave Manaos. — On board the "Ibicuhy." — Navigation of the River Ramos. — Aspect of the Banks. — Arrival at Mauhes. — Situation of Mauhes. — Tupinambaranas. — Character of Population. — Appearance of the Villages of Mauhes. — Bolivian Indians — Guaraná. — Excursion to Mucaja-Tuba. — Mundurucu Indians — Aspect of Village. — Church. — Distribution of Presents. — Generosity of the Indians. — Their Indifference. — Visit to another Settlement. — Return to Mauhes. — Arrival of Mundurucus in the Village. — Description of Tattooing. — Collection. — Boto. — Indian Superstitions. — Palm Collection. — Walk in the Forest. — Leave Mauhes. — Mundurucu Indian and his Wife. — Their Manners and Appearance. — Indian Tradition. — Distinctions of Caste.

December 12th. — We left Manaos, according to our intention, on Sunday evening (the 10th), raising the anchor with military exactness at five o'clock, the very moment appointed, somewhat to the disappointment of a boatful of officials from the National Guard, who were just on their way to pay their parting compliments to the President, at the hour fixed for his departure. In Brazil it may safely be assumed that things will always be a little behind time; on this occasion, however, our punctuality was absolute, and the officers were forced to wave their adieux as we proceeded on our way, leaving their canoe behind. The hour was of good omen, — a cool breeze, the one blessing for which the traveller sighs in these latitudes, blowing up the Amazons; and as we left the Rio Negro, it lay behind us, a golden pathway to the setting sun, which was going down in a blaze of glory. We were received on board with all possible hospitality by the commander, Captain Faria. He has made every arrangement for our comfort which a vessel of war, not intended for passengers, can afford, giving up his own quarters for my accommodation. On deck he has arranged a little recess, sheltered by a tarpauling from the sun and rain, to serve as a dining-room, that we may take our meals in the fresh air instead of dining in the close cabin below decks intended for this purpose.

The morning following our departure was an interesting one, because we found ourselves at the mouth of the Ramos, unknown to steam navigation, and about which the Captain had some apprehensions, as he was by no means sure that he should find water enough for his vessel. It was, therefore, necessary to proceed with great caution, sounding at every step and sending out boats in advance, to ascertain the direction of the channel. Once within the river, we had depth of water enough to float much larger vessels. The banks of this stream are beautiful. The forest was gay with color, and the air laden with the rich perfume of flowers, which, when we came up the Amazons six months ago, were not yet in bloom. We were struck also with the great abundance and variety of the palms, so much more numerous on the lower course of the Amazons than on the Solimoens. The shores were dotted with thrifty-looking plantations, laid out with a neatness and care which bespeak greater attention to agriculture than we have seen elsewhere. Healthy-looking cattle were grazing about many of the sitios. As the puff of our steam was heard, the inhabitants ran out to gaze in amazement at the unwonted visitant, standing in groups on the shores, almost too much lost in wonder to return our greetings. The advent of a steamer in their waters should be to them a welcome harbinger of the time, perhaps not far distant, when, instead of their present tedious and uncertain canoe journeys to Serpa or Villa Bella, they will be able to transport their produce to either of these points in a few hours, in small steamboats, connecting all these settlements, and adapted to the navigation. Any such prophetic vision was, however, no doubt very far from their thoughts; if they had any idea as to the object of our coming, it was probably a fear lest we should be on a recruiting expedition. If so, it is certainly a very innocent one, fishes being the only recruits we aim at entrapping. From the Ramos we turned into the Mauhes, ascending to the town of the same name, where to-day we are enjoying the hospitality of Mr. Michelis.

If any of my readers are as ignorant as I was myself before making this voyage, a bit of geography may not be out of place here. As everybody knows, the river Madeira, that great affluent of the Amazons, all whose children are giants, except when compared with their royal father, enters the main stream on its southern side at a point nearly opposite Serpa. But this is not its only connection with the Amazons. The river Mauhes starting about twenty-five leagues from its mouth, runs from the river Madeira almost parallel with the Amazons until it joins the river Ramos, which continues its course in the same direction to a lower point, where it empties into the main stream. The district of land thus enclosed between four rivers, having the Madeira on the west, the Amazons on the north, and the Ramos and the Mauhes on the south, is known on the map as the island of Tupinambaranas. It is a network of rivers, lakes, and islands; one of those watery labyrinths which would be in itself an extensive river system in any other country, but is here absolutely lost in the world of waters of which it forms a part. Indeed, the vastness of the Amazons is not felt chiefly when following its main course, but rather on its lesser tributaries, where streams to which a place on the map is hardly accorded are found to be in fact large rivers.

The region of Mauhes is comparatively little known, because it is off the line of steam navigation; but, thanks to the efforts of its most prominent citizen, Mr. Michelis, who has made his home there for twenty-five years, and contributed, by his energy, intelligence, and honorable character, to raise the tone of the whole district, it is one of the most prosperous in the province. It is melancholy to see how little is done in other districts, when an instance like this shows what one man can do to improve the forest population along the banks of the Amazons. His example and its successful results should be an encouragement to all intelligent settlers on the Amazons. The little village of Mauhes stands on a sort of terrace, in front of which, at this season when the waters are still considerably below high-water mark, runs a broad, white beach, rendered all the prettier at the moment of our arrival by a large party of Bolivian Indians, who had built their camp-fires on its sands. We looked at these people with a kind of wonder, thinking of the perilous voyages they constantly make in their heavily-laden canoes, forced to unload their cargo over and over again as they shoot the cataracts of the Madeira on their way down, or drag their boats wearily up them on their return. It seems strange, when this river is the highway of commerce from Bolivia, Matto-Grosso, and through Matto-Grosso from Paraguay to the Amazons, that the suggestion made by Major Coutinho

in his interesting account of his journey on the Rio Madeira, has not been adopted. He says that a road carried along the shore of the river for a distance of forty leagues would obviate all the difficulty and danger of this arduous journey.

Mauhes is not a cluster of houses, but is built in line along a broad, grass-grown street running the length of the terrace formed by the top of the river-bank. In an open space, at one end of this village street, stands the church, a small but neat-looking building, with a wooden cross in front. Most of the houses are low and straw-thatched, but here and there a more substantial house, with tiled roof, like that of Mr. Michelis, breaks the ordinary level of the buildings. Notwithstanding the modest appearance of this little town, all who know something of its history speak of it as one of the most promising of the Amazonian settlements, and as having a better moral tone than usually prevails. One of its great staples is the Guaraná. This shrub, or rather vine, — for it is a trailing plant somewhat like our high-bush blackberry, — is about eight feet high when full grown, and bears a bean the size of a coffee-bean, two being enclosed in each envelope. This bean, after being roasted, is pounded in a small quantity of water, until it becomes, when thoroughly ground, a compact paste, and when dry is about the color of chocolate, though much harder. In this state it is grated, (the grater being always the rough tongue of the Pirarucu,) and when mixed with sugar and water it makes a very pleasant, refreshing drink. It is said to have medicinal properties also, and is administered with excellent effect in cases of diarrhœa. In certain parts of Brazil it is very extensively used as well as in Bolivia, and will, no doubt, have a wider distribution when its value is more generally known. The Indians display no little fancy in the manufacture of this article, moulding the paste into the shape of mounted soldiers, horses, birds, serpents, &c.

This morning I was attracted by voices in the street, and going to the window I saw the door of the house where the President is lodged besieged by a crowd of Bolivian Indians. They had brought some of their robes to sell, and it was not long before several of our party, among whom were ready purchasers, made their appearance in Bolivian costume. This dress is invariable; always the long robe, composed of two pieces, one hanging before, the other behind, belted around the waist and fastened on the shoulders, with an opening for the head to pass through. Such a robe, with a broad-brimmed, coarse straw hat, constitutes the whole dress of these people. Their ordinary working garb is made of bark; their better robe, for more festive occasions, consists of a twilled cotton of their own manufacture, exceedingly soft and fine, but very close and strong. These dresses may be more or less ornamented, but are always of the same shape. The Bolivian Indians seem to be more industrious than those of the Amazons, or else they are under more rigorous discipline.

December 14th. — At the settlement of Mucaja-Tuba. Mucaja signifies a particular kind of palm, very abundant here; Tuba means a place. Thus we are among the woods of Acrocomia. Yesterday we were to have left Maulies with the dawn on an excursion to this place, but at the appointed hour a flood of rain, such as is seen only in these latitudes, was pouring down in torrents, accompanied by thunder and lightning. The delay occasioned by this interruption, however, proved a good fortune in the end. By eleven o'clock the storm was over, but the sky continued overcast during the rest of the day. Our way lay up the river Mauhes, past the mouths of nameless streams and lakes,— broad sheets of water, perfectly unknown out of their immediate neighborhood. Night brought us to our destination, and at about eight o'clock we anchored before this little village. As we approached it a light or two was seen glimmering on the shore, and we could not help again wondering what was the feeling of the people who saw and heard for the first time one of these puffing steam monsters. This morning, with a boat-load of goods of all sorts, intended by the President as presents for the Indians, we put off for the shore. Landing on the beach we went at once to the house of the chief, a most respectable looking old man, who stood at the door to receive us. He was an old acquaintance of Major Coutinho, having formerly accompanied him on his exploration of the Rio Madeira. The inhabitants of this village are Mundurucu Indians, one of the most intelligent and kindly disposed of the Amazonian tribes. Although they are too civilized to be considered as illustrating in any way the wild life of the primitive Indians, yet, as it is the first time we have seen one of their isolated settlements, removed from every civilizing influence except the occasional contact of the white man, the visit was especially interesting to us. It is astonishing to see the size and solidity of their houses, with never a nail driven, the frame consisting of rough trunks bound together by withes made of long, elastic sipos, the cordage of the forest. Major Coutinho tells us that they know very well the use of nails in building, and say to one another derisively, when they want another sipo, "Hand me a nail." The ridge-pole of this chief's house could not have been less than twenty-five to thirty-eight feet high, and the room was spacious in proportion. Hammocks were hung in the corners, one of which was partitioned off by a low wall of palm-thatch; bows and arrows, guns and oars, hung on the walls or were leaning against them, and adjoining this central apartment was the mandioca kitchen. There were a number of doors and windows in the room, closed by large palm-mats. The house of the chief stood at the head of a line of houses differing from his only in being somewhat smaller; they made one side of an open square, on the opposite side of which was a corresponding row of buildings. With a few exceptions these houses were empty, for the population gather only three or four times in the course of the year, at certain festival seasons. Generally they are scattered about in their different sitios, attending to their plantations. But at these fêtes they assemble to the number of several hundred, all the dwellings are crowded with families, and the square in the centre is cleared of grass, swept and garnished for their evening dances. Such festivities last for ten days or a fortnight; then they all disperse to their working life again. At this time there are not more than thirty or forty persons in the village. The most interesting object we saw was their church, which stands at the head of the square, and was built entirely by the Indians themselves. It is quite a large structure, capable of holding an assembly of five or six hundred persons. The walls are of mud, very neatly finished inside, and painted in colors made by the Indians from the bark, roots, and fruits of certain trees, and also from a particular kind of clay. The front part of the church is wholly unfurnished, except for the rough wooden font standing just within the door. But the farther end is partitioned off to make a neat chancel, within which several steps lead up to the altar and niche above, where is placed the rude image of the Mother and the Child. Of course the architecture and the ornaments are of the coarsest description ; the painting consists only of stripes or lines of blue, red, and yellow, with here and there an attempt at a star or a diamond, or a row of scalloping; but there is something touching in the idea that these poor, uneducated people of the forest have cared to build themselves a temple with their own hands, lavishing upon it such ideas of beauty and taste as they have, and bringing at least their best to their humble altar. None of our city churches, on which millions have been expended, have power to move one like this church, the loving work of the worshippers themselves, with its mud walls so coarsely painted, its wooden cross before the door, and little thatched belfry at one side. It is sad that these people, with so much religious sensibility, are not provided with any regular service. At long intervals a priest, on his round of visitations, makes his way to them, but, except on such rare occasions, they have no one to administer the rites of burial or baptism, or to give religious instruction to them or to their children. And yet their church was faultlessly clean, the mud floor was strewn with fresh green leaves, and everything about the building showed it to be the object of solicitude and care. Their houses were very neat, and they themselves were decently dressed in the invariable costume of the civilized Indian,— the men in trousers and white cotton shirts, the women in calico petticoats, with short, loose chemises, either of cotton or calico, and their long, thick black hair drawn up and fastened on the top of their head by a semicircular comb, brought so far forward that the edge is about on a line with the forehead. A bunch of flowers is generally stuck under the comb on one side. I have never seen an Indian woman who did not wear one of these round combs ;. although of foreign manufacture, they find their way to the most isolated forest settlements, brought, I suppose, by the travelling pedlers, "regataõ." These gentry are known everywhere on the banks of the Amazons and its tributaries, and are said to be most unprincipled in their dealings with the Indians, who fall readily into the traps set for them by the wily traders. In one of the reports of Dr. Adolfo, who, during his short but able administration, exposed, and as far as it was in his power reformed, abuses in the province of the Amazonas, he says, after speaking of the great need of religious instruction in the more remote settlements: "To-day who goes to seek the Indian in the depth of his virgin forests along the shores of these endless rivers? No one, if it be not the 'regataõ,' less barbarous certainly than he, but much more corrupt; who spies upon him, depraves and dishonors him, under the pretext of trading." After our visit to the church, the whole population, men, women, and children, accompanied us down to the beach to receive their presents, distributed by the President in person : common jewelry, which they appreciate highly, calico dresses, beads, scissors, needles, and looking-glasses for the women ; knives, fish-hooks, hatchets, and other working tools for the men ; and a variety of little trinkets and playthings for the children. But though a cordial, kindly people, they have the impassiveness of the genuine Indian. I did not see a change of expression on any face or hear a word of acknowledgment or pleasure. The only smile was when, being tired with standing in the sun, I sat down among the women, and, as the things were passed rapidly around the circle, I was taken for one of them, and received a very gay gown for my share. This caused a general shout of laughter, and seemed to delight them greatly. We returned to the steamer to breakfast at ten o'clock, and in the afternoon the whole village came out to satisfy their curiosity about the vessel. They are a generous people. I never go among them without receiving some little present, which it would be an insult to refuse. Such as they have they offer to the stranger; it may be a fruit, or a few eggs, or a chicken, a cuia, a basket or a bunch of flowers, but their feelings would be wounded were you to go away empty-handed. On this occasion the daughter of the chief brought me a fine fat fowl, another woman gave me a basket, and another a fruit which resembles very much our winter squash, and is used in the same way. I was glad to have with me some large beads and a few little pictures of saints with which to acknowledge their gifts. But I believe they do not think of any return; it is simply a rite of hospitality with them to make their guest a present. They went over the vessel, heard the cannon fired off, and, as the captain took them on a little excursion, they saw the machine and the wheels in action; but they looked at all with the same calm, quiet air of acceptance, above, or perhaps one should rather say below, any emotion of surprise. For is not the readiness to receive new impressions, to be surprised, delighted, moved, one of the great gifts of the white race, as different from the impassiveness of the Indian as their varying complexion from the dark skin, which knows neither blush nor pallor? We could have but little conversation with these people, for, with the exception of the chief and one or two men who acted as interpreters, they spoke only the "lingua geral," and did not understand Portuguese.

December 15th. — After the Indians had left us yesterday, we proceeded on our way to another settlement, where we expected to find a considerable village. We arrived after dark, and some of the party went on shore; but they found only a grass-grown path and deserted houses. The whole population was in the forest. To-day, however, two or three canoesful of people have come off to the steamer to greet the President and receive their presents. Among them was an old woman who must have come originally from some more primitive settlement. The lower part of her face was tattooed in a bluish-black tint, covering the mouth and lower part of the cheeks to the base of the ears. Below this the chin was tattooed in a kind of network, no doubt considered very graceful and becoming in her day and generation. A black line was drawn across the nose, and from the outer corner of the eyes to the ears, giving the effect of a pair of spectacles. The upper part of the breast was tattooed in an open-work, headed by two straight lines drawn around the shoulders as if to represent a coarse lace finish, such as one constantly sees around the necks of their chemises. They left us at breakfast, and we are now on our way back to Maulies, after a most interesting excursion.

December 16th. — Maulies. We arrived here yesterday at midday, and, as it happened, we found in the village an Indian and his wife, who, as specimens of the genuine

EXCURSION TO MAUHES AND ITS NEIGHBORHOOD. 313

Mundurucus, were more interesting than those we had visited. They came on trading business from a distant settlement some twenty days' journey from Mauhes. The

Mundurucu Indian (Male).*

man's whole face is tattooed in bluish black, this singular mask being finished on the edge by a fine, open pattern, about half an inch broad, running around the

* I did not succeed in getting good likenesses of this Mundurucu pair. The above wood-cuts do no justice to their features and expression, though they give a faithful record of the peculiar mode of tattooing. — L. A.

14

jaws and chin. His ears are pierced with very large holes, from which, when his costume is complete, pieces of wood are suspended, and his whole body is covered with a neat and intricate network of tattooing. At present, however, being in civilized regions, he is dressed in

Mundurucu Indian (Female).

trousers and shirt. In the woman the mask of tattooing covers only the lowest part of the face, the upper part being free, with the exception of the line across the nose and eyes. Her chin and neck are also ornamented like that of the old woman we saw yesterday. They speak no Portuguese, and seem rather reluctant to answer the questions of the interpreter.

Mr. Agassiz has been very fortunate in collecting in this region. Although we are at so short a distance from Manaos, where he already knows the fishes tolerably well, he finds a surprising number of new genera and species about Mauhes and its neighborhood. As usual, wherever we go, everybody turns naturalist in his behalf. Our kind friend, the President, always ready to do everything in his power to facilitate his researches, has several boats out, manned by the best fishermen of the place, fishing for him. The commander, while his ship lies at anchor, has his men employed in the same way; and Mr. Michelis and his friends are also indefatigable. Occasionally, however, in the midst of his successes, he has to bear disappointments, arising from the ignorance and superstition of the working people. Ever since he came to the Amazons he has been trying to obtain a specimen of a peculiar kind of porpoise, native to these waters. It is, however, very difficult to obtain, because, being useless for food, there is nothing to induce the Indian to overcome the difficulty of catching it. Mr. Michelis has, however, impressed upon the fishermen the value of the prize, and, yesterday evening, just as we were rising from the dinner-table, it was announced that one was actually on its way up from the beach. Followed by the whole party of sympathizing friends, — for all had caught the infection, — Mr. Agassiz hastened out to behold his long-desired treasure; and there was his Boto, but sadly mutilated, for one Indian had cut off a piece of the fin as a cure for a sick person, another had taken out an eye as a love-charm, which, if it could be placed near the person of the girl he loved, would win him her favor, and so on. Injured as it was, Mr. Agassiz was, nevertheless, very glad to have the specimen; but he locked it up carefully for the night, not knowing what other titbits might be coveted by the superstitious inhabitants.

December 18*th*. — In the midst of the zoölogical work, the collection of palms, which is now becoming very considerable, is not forgotten. This morning we went into the forest for the purpose of gathering young palms to compare with the full-grown ones, already cut down and put up for transportation. In these woods a thousand objects attract the eye, beside that which you especially seek. How many times we stopped to wonder at some lofty tree which was a world of various vegetation in itself, parasites established in all its nooks and corners, sipos hanging from its branches or twining themselves so close against the bark that they often seem as if sculptured on its trunk; or paused to listen to the quick rustle of the wind in palm-leaves fifty feet above our heads, not at all like the slow, gathering rush of the wind in pine-trees at home, but like rapidly running water. Through the narrow path an immense butterfly, of that vivid blue which excites our wonder in collections of Brazilian insects, came sailing towards us. He alighted in our immediate neighborhood, folding all his azure glories out of sight, and looking, when still, like a great brown moth, spotted with white. We crept softly nearer, but the first leaf trodden under foot warned him, and he was off again, dazzling us with the beauty of his wonderful coloring as he opened his wings and, bidding us a gay goodby, vanished among the trees. The sailing motion of these Morphos, though rapid, contrasts strikingly with the more fluttering flight of the Heliconians. The former give broad, strong strokes with their wide wings, the latter beat the air with quick, impatient, tremulous movements.

December 20*th.* — This morning we left Mauhes, accompanied by our Mundurucu Indian and his wife. The President takes them to Manaos, in the hope of obtaining their portraits to enlarge Mr. Agassiz's collection. I am interested in watching the deportment of these people, which is marked by a striking propriety that wins respect. They have remained in the seat where the Captain has placed them, not moving, except to bring their little baggage, from which the woman has taken out her work and is now busy in sewing, while her husband makes cigarette envelopes from a bark used by the Indians for this purpose; — certainly very civilized occupations for savages. As they speak no Portuguese, we can only communicate with them through the interpreter or through Mr. Coutinho, who has considerable familiarity with the "lingua geral." They seem more responsive, more ready to enter into conversation now than when we first saw them; but the woman, when addressed, or when anything is offered to her, invariably turns to her husband, as if the decision of everything rested with him. It might be thought that the fantastic ornaments of these Indians would effectually disguise all pretence to beauty; but it is not so with this pair. Their features are fine, the build of the face solid and square, but not clumsy, and there is a passive dignity in their bearing which makes itself felt, spite of their tattooing. I have never seen anything like the calm in the man's face; it is not the stolidity of dulness, for his expression is sagacious and observant, but a look of such abiding tranquillity that you cannot imagine that it ever has been or ever will be different. The woman's face is more mobile; occasionally a smile lights it up, and her expression is sweet and gentle. Even her painted spectacles do not destroy the soft, drooping look in the eyes, very common among the Indian women here, and, as it would seem, characteristic of the women in the South American tribes; for Humboldt speaks of it in those of the Spanish provinces to the north.

Major Coutinho tells us that the tattooing has nothing to do with individual taste, but that the pattern is appointed for both sexes, and is invariable throughout the tribe. It is connected with their caste, the limits of which are very precise, and with their religion. The tradition runs thus, childish and inconsequent, like all such primitive fables. The first man, Caro Sacaibu, was also divine. Associated with him was his son, and an inferior being named Rairu, to whom, although he was as it were his prime minister and executed his commands, Caro Sacaibu was inimical. Among other stratagems he used to get rid of him was the following. He made a figure in imitation of a tatu (armadillo), and buried it partly in the earth, leaving only the tail exposed. He covered the tail with a kind of oil, which when touched adheres to the skin. He then commanded Rairu to drag the half-buried tatu out of its hole and bring it to him. Rairu seized it by the tail, but was of course unable to withdraw his hand, and the tatu, suddenly endowed with life by the Supreme Being, dived into the earth, dragging Rairu with him. The story does not say how Rairu found his way out of the earth again, but, being a spirit of great cunning and invention, he contrived to reach the upper air once more. On his return, he informed Caro Sacaibu that he had found in the earth a great many men and women, and that it would be an excellent thing to get them out to till the soil and make themselves useful above ground. This advice seems to have found favor in the sight of Caro Sacaibu, who forthwith planted a seed in the ground. From this seed sprang a cotton-tree, for into this fantastic tale is thus woven the origin of cotton. The tree throve and grew apace, and from the soft white contents of its pods Caro Sacaibu made a long thread, with one end of which Rairu descended once more into the earth by the same hole through which he had entered before. He collected the people together, and they were dragged up through the hole by means of the thread. The first who came out were small and ugly, but gradually they improved in their personal appearance, until at last the men began to be finely formed and handsome, and the women beautiful. Unfortunately, by this time the thread was much worn, and being too weak to hold them, the greater number of handsome people fell back into the hole and were lost. It is for this reason that beauty is so rare a gift in the world. Caro Sacaibu now separated the population he had thus drawn from the bowels of the earth, dividing them into different tribes, marking them with distinct colors and patterns, which they have since retained, and appointing their various occupations. At the end there remained over a residue, consisting of the ugliest, smallest, most insignificant representatives of the human race; to these he said, drawing at the same time a red line over their noses, "You are not worthy to be men and women,— go and be animals." And so they were changed into birds, and ever since, the Mutums, with their red beaks and melancholy wailing voices, wander through the woods

The tattooing of the Mundurucus is not only connected with this dim idea of a primitive creative command; it is also indicative of aristocracy. A man who neglected this distinction would not be respected in his tribe; and so strong is this traditional association, that, even in civilized settlements where tattooing is no longer practised, an instinctive respect is felt for this mark of nobility. A Mundurucu Indian, tattooed after the ancient fashion of his tribe, arriving in a civilized village, such as the one we visited, is received with the honor due to a person of rank. "Il faut souffrir pour être beau," was never truer than among these savages. It requires not less than ten years to complete the tattooing of the whole face and body; the operation being performed, however, only at intervals. The color is introduced by fine puncturings over the whole surface; a process which is often painful, and causes swelling and inflammation, especially on such sensitive parts as the eyelids. The purity of type among the Mundurucus is protected by stringent laws against close intermarriages. The tribe is divided into certain orders or classes, more or less closely allied; and so far do they carry their respect for that law, which, though recognized in the civilized world, is so constantly sinned against, that marriage is forbidden, not only between members of the same family, but between those of the same order. A Mundurucu Indian treats a woman of the same order with himself as a sister; any nearer relation between them is impossible. Major Coutinho, who has made a very careful study of the manners and habits of these people, assures us that there is no law more sacred among them, or more rigidly observed, than this one. Their fine physique, for which they are said to be remarkable, is perhaps owing to this. They are free from one great source of degeneration of type. It is to be hoped that Major Coutinho, who, while making his explorations as an engineer on the Amazonian rivers, has also made a careful study of the tribes living along their margins, will one day publish the result of his investigations. It is to him we owe the greater part of the information we have collected on this subject.

CHAPTER XI.

RETURN TO MANAOS. — EXCURSION ON THE RIO NEGRO. — LEAVE MANAOS.

CHRISTMAS EVE AT MANAOS. — CEREMONIES OF THE INDIANS. — CHURCHES ON THE AMAZONS. — LEAVE MANAOS FOR THE RIO NEGRO. — CURIOUS RIVER FORMATION. — ASPECT OF THE RIVER. — ITS VEGETATION. — SCANTY POPULATION. — VILLAGE OF TAUA PÉASSU. — PADRE OF THE VILLAGE. — PALMS. — VILLAGE OF PEDREIRA. — INDIAN CAMP. — MAKING PALM-THATCH. — SICKNESS AND WANT AT PEDREIRA. — ROW IN THE FOREST. — TROPICAL SHOWER. — GEOLOGY OF PEDREIRA. — INDIAN RECRUITS. — COLLECTION OF PALMS. — EXTRACTS FROM MR. AGASSIZ'S NOTES ON THE VEGETATION OF THE AMAZONS AND THE RIO NEGRO. — RETURN TO MANAOS. — DESOLATION OF THE RIO NEGRO. — ITS FUTURE PROSPECTS. — HUMBOLDT'S ANTICIPATIONS. — WILD FLOWERS. — DISTRIBUTION OF FISHES IN THE AMAZONIAN WATERS. — HOW FAR DUE TO MIGRATION. — HYDROGRAPHIC SYSTEM. — ALTERNATION BETWEEN THE RISE AND FALL OF THE SOUTHERN AND NORTHERN TRIBUTARIES.

December 25th. — Manaos. The Indians have a pretty observance here for Christmas eve. At nightfall, from the settlements at Hyanuary, two illuminated canoes come across the river to Manaos; one bearing the figure of Our Lady, the other of Saint Rosalia. They look very brilliant as they come towards the shore, all the light concentrated about the figures carried erect in the prows. On landing, the Indians, many of whom have come to the city in advance, form a procession, — the women dressed in white, and with flowers in their hair, the men carrying torches or candles; and they follow the sacred images, which are borne under a canopy in front of the procession, to the church, where they are deposited, and remain during Christmas week. We entered with them, and saw the kneeling, dusky congregation, and the two saints, — one a wooden, coarsely painted image of the Virgin, the other a gayly dressed doll, — placed on a small altar, where was also a figure of the infant Jesus, surrounded by flowers. At a later hour the midnight mass was celebrated; less interesting to me than the earlier ceremony, because not so exclusively a service of the Indians, though they formed a large part of the congregation; and the music, as usual, was performed by the band of Indian boys from the Casa dos Educandos. But there is nothing here to make the Catholic service impressive; the churches on the Amazons generally are of the most ordinary kind, and in a ruinous condition. There is a large unfinished stone church in Manaos, standing on the hill, and occupying a commanding position, which will make it a conspicuous object if it is ever completed; but it has stood in its present state for years, and seems likely to remain so for an indefinite length of time. It is a pity they have not the custom here of dressing their churches with green at Christmas, because they have so singularly beautiful and appropriate a tree for it in the palms. The Pupunha palm, for instance, so architectural in its symmetry, with its columnar-like stem, and its dark-green vault of drooping leaves, would be admirable for this purpose. To-morrow we leave Manaos in the "Ibicuhy," in order to ascend the Rio Negro as far as Pedreira, where the first granitic formation is said to occur.

December 27th. — On board the "Ibicuhy." There was little incident to mark our day yesterday, and yet it was one full of enjoyment. The day itself was such as rarely occurs in these regions; indeed, I should say it is the only time, during the whole six months we have passed on the Amazons, when we have had cool weather with a clear sky. Cool weather here is usually the result of rain. As soon as the sun shows his face the heat is great. But yesterday a strong wind was blowing down the Rio Negro; and its usually black, still waters were freshened to blue, and their surface broken by white caps. It is a curious fact in the history of this river, that, while tributary to the Amazons, it also receives branches from it. A little above its junction with the Solimoens, the latter sends several small affluents into the Rio Negro, the entrance to which we passed yesterday. The contrast between their milky-white waters and the clear, dark, amber tint of the main river makes them very conspicuous. It would seem that this is not a solitary instance of river formation in this gigantic fresh-water system; for Humboldt says, speaking of the double communication between the Cassiquiare and the Rio Negro, and the great number of branches by which the Rio Branco and the Rio Hyapura enter into the Rio Negro and the Amazons: "At the confluence of the Hyapura there is a much more extraordinary phenomenon. Before this river joins the Amazons, the latter, which is the principal recipient, sends off three branches, called Uaranapu, Manhama, and Avateparana, to the Hyapura, which is but a tributary stream. The Portuguese astronomer, Ribeiro, has proved this important fact. The Amazons gives waters to the Hyapura itself before it receives that tributary stream." So does it also to the Rio Negro.

The physiognomy of the Rio Negro is peculiar, and very different from that of the Amazons or the Solimoens. The shores jut out in frequent promontories, which, while they form deep bays between, narrow the river from distance to distance, and, as we advance towards them, look like the entrances to harbors or lakes. Indeed, we have already passed several large lakes; but great sheets of water so abound here that they are nameless, and hardly attract attention. The vegetation also is different from that of the Amazons. As yet we have seen few palms; and the forest is characterized by a great number of trees, the summits of which are evenly and gently arched, forming flattened domes. The most remarkable of these, on account of its lofty height and spreading foliage, is the Sumauméra, to which I have alluded before. But this umbrella-like mode of growth is by no means confined to one tree, but, like the buttressed trunks, characterizes a number of Brazilian trees. It is, however, more frequent here than we have seen it elsewhere. The shores seem very scantily inhabited; indeed, during our whole journey yesterday, we met but one canoe, which we hailed, in order to inquire our distance from the little hamlet of Taua Péassu, where we meant to drop anchor for the night. It was the boat of an Indian family going down the river. We were reminded that we were leaving inhabited regions, for the man who was rowing was quite naked; his wife and children peeped out from under the tolda in the stern of the boat. We received from them the welcome intelligence that we were not far from our destination, where we accordingly arrived soon after nightfall. At this hour we could form but little idea of the appearance of the place; yet, by the moonlight, we could see that its few houses (some eight or ten, perhaps) stood on a crescent-shaped terrace, formed by the bank of a little bay which puts in just at this point. The gentlemen went on shore, and brought back the padre of the village to tea. He seems a man of a good deal of intelligence, and was eloquent upon the salubrity of the village, its freedom from mosquitoes, piums, and all kinds of noxious insects. At first a life so remote and isolated seems a hard lot, and one would think only the greatest devotion could induce a man to undertake it. But there is hardly a corner so remote in Brazil as not to be reached by the petty local politics; and the padre is said to be a great politician, his campaign before election among the poor people with whom his lot is cast being as exciting to him as that of any man who canvasses in a more distinguished arena; the more satisfactory, perhaps, because he has the game very much in his own hands. We left Taua Péassu with the dawn, and are again on our way to Pedreira. The weather still continues most favorable for travelling,— an overcast sky and a cool breeze. But to-day the black river sleeps without a ripple; and, as we pass along, the trees meet the water, and are so perfectly reflected in it that we can hardly distinguish the dividing line. I have said that the forest is not characterized by palms, and yet we see many species which we have not met before; among these is the Jara-assú, with its tall, slender stem, and broom-like tuft of stiff leaves. Mr. Agassiz has just gone on shore in the montaria, to cut down some palms of another kind, new to him. As he returns, the little boat seems to have undergone some marvellous change; it looks like a green raft floating on the water, and we can hardly see the figures of the rowers for the beautiful crowns of the palm-trees.

December 29th. — Pedreira. I have said little about the insects and reptiles which play so large a part in most Brazilian travels, and, indeed, I have had much less annoyance from this source than I had expected. But I must confess the creature who greeted my waking sight this morning was not a pleasant object to contemplate. It was an enormous centipede close by my side, nearly a foot in length, whose innumerable legs looked just ready for a start, and whose two horns or feelers were protruded with a most venomous expression. These animals are not only hideous to look upon, but their bite is very painful, though not dangerous. I crept softly away from my sofa without disturbing my ugly neighbor, who presently fell a victim to science: being very adroitly caught under a large tumbler, and consigned to a glass jar filled with alcohol. Captain Faria says that centipedes are often brought on board with the wood, among which they usually lie concealed, seldom making their appearance, unless disturbed and driven out of their hiding-place. To less noxious visitors of this kind one gets soon accustomed. As I shake out my dress, I hear a cold flop on the floor, and a pretty little house-lizard, who has found a warm retreat in its folds, makes his escape with all celerity. Cockroaches swarm everywhere, and it would be a vigilant housekeeper who could keep her closets free of them. Ants are the greatest nuisance of all, and the bite of the fire-ant is really terrible. I remember once, in Esperança's cottage, having hung some towels to dry on the cord of my hammock; I was about to remove them, when suddenly my hand and arm seemed plunged into fire. I dropped the towels as if they had been hot coals, which for the moment they literally seemed to be, and then I saw that my arm was covered with little brown ants. Brushing them off in all haste, I called Laudigari, who found an army of them passing over the hammock, and out of the window, near which it hung. He said they were on their way somewhere, and, if left undisturbed, would be gone in an hour or two. And so it proved to be. We saw no more of them. Major Coutinho says that, in certain Amazonian tribes, the Indian bridegroom is subjected to a singular test. On the day of his marriage, while the wedding festivities are going on, his hand is tied up in a paper bag filled with fire-ants. If he bears this torture smilingly and unmoved, he is considered fit for the trials of matrimony.

Yesterday we arrived at Pedreira, a little village consisting of some fifteen or twenty houses hemmed in by forest. The place certainly deserves its name of the "place of stones," for the shore is fringed with rocks and boulders. We landed at once, and Mr. Coutinho and Mr. Agassiz spent the morning in geologizing and botanizing. In the course of our ramble we came upon an exceedingly picturesque Indian camp. The river is now so high that the water runs far up into the forest. In such an overflowed wood, a number of Indian montarias were moored; while, on a tract of dry land near by, the Indians had cleared a little grove, cutting down the inner trees, and leaving only the outer ones standing, so as to make a shady, circular arbor. Within this arbor the hammocks were slung; while outside were the kettles and water-jugs, and utensils of one sort and another. In this little camp were several Indian families, who had left their mandioca plantations in the forest, to pass the Christmas festa in the village. I asked the women what they did, they and their babies, of which there were a goodly number, when it rained; for a roof of foliage is poor shelter in these tropical rains, descending, not in- drops, but in sheets. They laughed, and, pointing to their canoes, said they crept under the tolda, the arched roof of palm-thatch which always encloses the stern of an Indian montaria, and were safe. Even this, in the open river, would not be a protection; but, moored as the boats are in the midst of a thick wood, they do not receive the full force of the showers. In returning from our walk we stopped at a house where an Indian was making palm-thatch from the leaflets of the Curua palm. When quite young, they are packed closely around the midrib. The Indians turn them down, leaving them attached to the axis by a few fibres only, so that, when the midrib is held up, they hang from it like so many straw-colored ribands, being, at that age, of a very delicate color. With these leaves they thatch their walls and roofs, setting the midrib, which is strong and sometimes four or five yards long, across, to serve as a support, and binding down the pendent leaves. Such a thatch will last for years, and is an excellent protection from rain as well as sun. I should add, that, in other parts of the country, different kinds of palms are used for this purpose.

On our return to the village we were met by the padre, who invited us to rest at his house, stopping on the way, at our request, to show us the church. The condition of a settlement is generally indicated by the state of the church. This one was sadly in want of repairs, the mud walls being pierced with more windows than they were originally intended to possess; but the interior was neat, and the altar prettier than one would expect to find in so poor a place as Pedreira appears to be. Perhaps the church was in better order than usual, being indeed in festival trim. Christmas week was not yet over, and the baby Christ lay on his green bed in a little arbor of leaves and flowers, evidently made expressly for the purpose.

The padre of this little village, Father Samuel, an Italian priest, who has passed many years of his life among the Indians of South America, partly in Bolivia and partly in Brazil, had not so much to say in favor of the healthfulness of his parish as the padre whom we had seen the night before in Taua Péassu. He told us that intermittent fever, from which he had suffered much himself, is frequent, and that the people are poorly and insufficiently fed. When they have had no recent arrival from Manaos neither coffee, sugar, tea, nor bread are to be had in the village. As there is no beach here, the fishing is done at a distance on the other side of the river; and when the waters are very high, fish are not obtained even there. At such times the Indians live exclusively on farinha d'agua and water. This meagre diet, though injurious to the health, satisfies the cravings of hunger with those accustomed to it; but the few whites in this solitary place suffer severely. What a comment is this scarcity of food on the indolence and indifference of the population in a region where an immense variety of vegetables might be cultivated with little labor, where the pasturage is excellent (as is attested by the fine condition of the few cows at Pedreira), and where coffee, cacao, cotton, and sugar have a genial climate and soil, and yield more copious crops than in many countries from which large exports of these productions are made! And yet, in this land of abundance, the people live in dread of actual want. The village consists, as I have said, of some fifteen or twenty houses, all of which are at this moment occupied; but Father Samuel tells us that we see the little place at its flood-tide, Christmas week having brought together the inhabitants of the neighborhood. They will disperse again, after a few days, to their palm-houses and mandioca plantations in the forest; and the padre says that, on many a Sunday throughout the year, his congregation consists only of himself and the boys who assist at the service.

After we had rested for half an hour at the priest's house, he proposed to send us to his little mandioca plantation at a short distance in the forest, where a particular kind of palm, which Mr. Agassiz greatly coveted, was to be obtained. Such a proposition naturally suggests a walk: but in this country of inundated surfaces land journeys, as will be seen, are often made by water. We started in a montaria, and, after keeping along the river for some time, we turned into the woods and began to navigate the forest. The water was still and clear as glass: the trunks of the trees stood up from it, their branches dipped into it; and as we wound in and out among them, putting aside a bough here and there, or stooping to float under a green arbor, the reflection of every leaf was so perfect that wood and water seemed to melt into each other, and it was difficult to say where the one began and the other ended. Silence and shade so profound brooded over the whole scene that the mere ripple of our paddles seemed a disturbance. After half an hour's row we came to dry land, where we went on shore, taking our boatmen with us; and the wood soon resounded with the sound of their hatchets, as the palms fell under their blows. We returned with a boat-load of palms, besides a number of plants of various kinds which we had not seen elsewhere. We reached the "Ibicuhy" just in time; for scarcely were we well on board and in snug quarters again, when the heavens opened and the floods came down. I am not yet accustomed to the miraculous force and profusion of these torrents of water, and every shower is a fresh surprise. Yet the rainy season is no such impediment to travelling and working as we had supposed it would be. The rain is by no means continuous, and there are often several days together of clear weather. Indeed, it no more rains all the time in the rainy season here than it snows all the time in the winter with us. One word of the geology. The Pedreira granite, of which we had heard, proves to be a granitoid mica-slate, — a highly metamorphic rock, indistinctly stratified, but resembling granite in its composition. It is in immediate contact with the red drift which rests above it.

This morning we had a melancholy proof of the brutality of recruiting here, of which we have already heard so much. Several Indians, who had been kept in confinement in Pedreira for some days, waiting for an opportunity to send them to Manaos, were brought out to the ship. These poor wretches had their feet passed through heavy blocks of wood, the holes being just large enough to fit around the ankles. Of course they could only move with the greatest difficulty; and they were half pushed, half dragged up the side of the vessel, one of them having apparently such a fit of ague upon him that, when he was fairly landed on his feet, I could see him shake from my seat at a distance of half the deck. These Indians can speak no Portuguese: they cannot understand why they are forced to go; they only know that they are seized in the woods and treated as if they were the worst criminals; punished with barbarity for no crime, and then sent to fight for the government which so misuses them. To the honor of our commander be it said, that he showed the deepest indignation at the condition in which these men were delivered into his hands: he caused the blocks of wood to be sawed off their feet immediately, gave them wine and food, and showed them every kindness. He protested that the whole proceeding was illegal, and contrary to the intentions of the central authority. It is, however, the way in which the recruiting is accomplished throughout this Indian district; and the defence made by those who justify it is, that the Indians, like any other citizens, must fight for the maintenance of the laws which protect them; that the government needs their services; and that this is the only way to secure them, as they are very unwilling to go, and very cunning and agile in escaping. Beside these three men, there were two others; one a volunteer, and the other from a better class, the pilot of the cataract on the Rio Branco. A man so employed ought, for the sake of the community, to be exempt from military service, as few persons understand the dangerous navigation of the river, where broken by cascades. He will doubtless be sent back when his case is represented to the President of the province.

December 31st. — Again on our way back to Manaos, having made, on our return, another short stay at Taua Péassu, where, during the two days of our absence, the padre of the village had prepared a large collection of palms for Mr. Agassiz. Our collection of palms is becoming quite numerous; and though they must of course, in the process of drying, lose all their beauty of coloring, we hope they may retain something of the grace and dignity of their bearing. But even should this not be the case, they will answer every purpose of study, as with each one specimens of its fruit and flowers are preserved in alcohol. A palm has just been brought on board — the Baccába, or wine-palm (Œnocarpus) — from which the flowers droop in long crimson cords, with bright-green berries from distance to distance along their length, like an immense coral tassel, flecked here and there with green, hanging from the dark trunk of the tree. The mode of flowering of the cocoa-nut palm, which we see everywhere though it is not indigenous here, is very beautiful. The flowers burst from the sheath in a long plume of soft, creamy-white blossoms: such a plume is so heavy with the weight of pendent flowers that it can hardly be lifted; and its effect is very striking, hanging high up on the trunk, just under the green vault of leaves. I think there is nothing among the characteristic features of tropical scenery of which one forms less idea at home than of the palms. Their name is legion; the variety of their forms, of their foliage, fruit, and flowers, is perfectly bewildering; and yet, as a group, their character is unmistakable. The following extracts are taken from Mr. Agassiz's notes on palms, written during this excursion on the Rio Negro.

"The palms, as a natural group, stand out among all other plants with remarkable distinctness and individuality. And yet this common character, uniting them so closely as a natural order, does not prevent the most striking difference between various kinds of palms. As a whole, no family of trees is more similar; generically and specifically none is more varied, even though other families include a greater number of species. Their differences seem to me to be determined in a great measure by the peculiar arrangement of their leaves; indeed, palms, with their colossal leaves, few in number, may be considered as ornamental diagrams of the primary laws according to which the leaves of all plants throughout the whole vegetable kingdom are arranged ; laws now recognized by the most advanced botanists of the day, and designated by them as Phyllotaxis. The simplest arrangement in these mathematics of the vegetable world is that of the grasses, in which the leaves are placed alternately on opposite sides of the stem, thus dividing the space around it in equal halves. As the stem of the grasses elongates, these pairs of leaves are found scattered along its length ; and it is only in ears or spikes of some genera that we find them growing so compactly on the axis as to form a

Fan Baccába (Œnocarpus distychius).

close head. Of this law of growth the palm known as the Baccába of Pará (Œnocarpus distychius) is an admirable illustration; its leaves being disposed in pairs one above another at the summit of the stem, but in such immediate contact as to form a thick crown. On account of this disposition of the leaves, its appearance is totally different from that of any other palm with which I am acquainted. I do not know any palm in which the leaves are arranged in three directions only, as in the reeds and sedges of our marshes, unless it be the Jacitara (Desmonchus), whose winding slender stem, however, makes the observation uncertain. An arrangement in five different directions is common in all those palms which, when young, have only a cluster of five fully developed leaves above the ground, with a spade-like sixth leaf rising from the centre. When full grown, they usually exhibit a crown of ten or fifteen leaves and more, divided into tiers of five, one above the other, but so close together that the whole appears like a rounded head. Sometimes, however, the crown is more open, as in the Maximiliana regia (Inaja), for instance, in which the stem is not very high, and the leaves, always in cycles of five, spread slightly, so as to form an open vase rising from a slender stem. The Assai (Euterpe edulis) has an eight-leaved arrangement, and has never more than a single cycle of leaves, though it may sometimes have seven leaves when the first of the old cycle has dropped, before the ninth, with which the new cycle begins, has opened; or nine, if the first leaf of the new cycle (the ninth in number) has opened, before the first of the old cycle has dropped. These leaves, of a delicate, pale green, are cut into a thousand leaflets, which tremble in the lightest breeze, and tell you that the air is stirring even when the heat seems breathless. A more elegant and attractive diagram of the Phyllotaxis of $\frac{3}{8}$ probably does not exist in nature. The common Cocoa-nut tree has its leaves arranged according to the fraction of $\frac{5}{13}$; but, though the crown consists of several cycles of leaves, they do not form a close head, because the older ones become pendent, while the younger are more erect. The Pupunha, or peach palm (Guilielma), follows the Phyllotaxis of $\frac{8}{21}$; but in this instance all the leaves are evenly arched over, so that the whole forms a deep-green vault, the more beautiful from the rich color of the foliage. When the heavy cluster of ripe, red fruit hangs under this dark vault, the tree is in its greatest beauty. As the leaves of this palm are not so closely set in the younger specimens as in the older ones, its aspect changes at different stages of growth; the leaves in the younger trees being distributed over a greater length of the trunk, while, in the adult taller ones, they are more compact. This arrangement is repeated in the Javari and Tucuma (Astrocaryum); but in these the closely-set leaves stand erect, broom-like, at the head of the long stalk. In the Mucaja (Acrocomia) the leaves are arranged according to the fraction $\frac{13}{34}$. Thus, under the same fundamental principle of growth, an infinite variety is introduced, among trees of one order, by the slight differences in the distribution and constitution of the leaves themselves. In the Musaceæ, or Scytamineæ, the Bananas, another order of the same class of plants, a diversity equally remarkable is produced in the same way, namely, by slight modifications of this fundamental law. What can differ more in appearance than the common Banana (Musa paradisiaca), with its large simple leaves, so loosely arranged around the stem, so graceful and easy in their movements, and the Banana of Madagascar (Ravenala madagascariensis), commonly known as the Traveller's tree, which, like the Baccába of Pará, has its leaves alternating regularly on opposite sides of the trunk, and so closely packed together as to form an immense flat fan on a colossal stem? Yet, in all these plants the arrangement of leaves obeys the same law, which is illustrated with equal distinctness by each one. This mathematical disposition of leaves is thus shown to be compatible with a great variety of essentially different structures; and though the law of Phyllotaxis prevails in all plants, being limited neither to class, orders, families, genera, nor species, but running in various combinations through the whole kingdom, I believe it can be studied to especial advantage in the group of palms, on account of the prominence of their few large leaves. The most abundant and characteristic palms of the Rio Negro are the Javari (Astrocaryum Javari), the Muru-Muru (Astrocaryum Murumuru), the Uauassu (Attalea speciosa), the Inaja (Maximiliana regia), the Baccába (Œnocarpus Baccába), the Paxiuba (Iriartea exorhiza), the Carana (Mauritia Carana), the Caranai (Mauritia horrida), the Ubim (Geonoma), and the Curua (Attalea spectabilis); of these the two latter are the most useful. The remarkable Piassaba (Leopoldinia Piassaba) occurs only far above the junction of the Rio Negro and Rio Branco. We obtained, however, a specimen that had been planted at Itatiassu. The many small kinds of Ubim (Geonoma), and Maraja (Bactris), and even the Jara (Leopoldinia), are so completely overshadowed by the larger trees that they are only noticed where clustered along the riverbanks. Bussus (Manicaria), Assais (Euterpe) Mucaja (Acrocomia), grow also on the Rio Negro, but it remains to be ascertained whether they are specifically identical with those of the Lower Amazons. So peculiar is the aspect of the different species of palms that, from the deck of the steamer, they can be singled out as easily as the live-oaks or pecean-nut trees, so readily distinguished on the lower course of the Mississippi, or the different kinds of oaks, birches, beeches, or walnut-trees which attract observation when sailing along the shores of our Northern lakes. It seems, however, impossible to discriminate between all the trees of this wonderful Amazonian forest ; partly because they grow in such heterogeneous associations. In the temperate zone we have oak-forests, pine-forests, birch, beech, and maple woods, the same kinds of trees congregating together on one soil. Not so here ; there is the most extraordinary diversity in the combination of plants, and it is a very rare thing to see the soil occupied for any extent by the same kind of tree. A large number of the trees forming these forests are still unknown to science, and yet the Indians, those practical botanists and zoölogists, are well acquainted, not only with their external appearance, but also with their various properties. So intimate is their practical knowledge of the natural objects about them, that I believe it would greatly contribute to the progress of science if a systematic record were made of all the information thus scattered through the land ; an encyclopædia of the woods, as it were, taken down from the tribes which inhabit them. I think it would be no bad way of collecting, to go from settlement to settleme sending the Indians out to gather all the plants they know, to dry and label them with the names applied to them in the locality, and writing out, under the heads of these names, all that may thus be ascertained of their medicinal and otherwise useful properties, as well as their botanical character. A critical examination of these collections would at once correct the information thus obtained, especially if the person intrusted with the care of gathering these materials had so much knowledge of botany as would enable him to complete the collections brought in by the Indians, adding to them such parts as might be wanted for a complete systematic description. The specimens ought not to be chosen, however, as they have hitherto been, solely with reference to those parts which are absolutely necessary to identify the species; the collections, to be complete, ought to include the wood, the bark, the roots, and the soft fruits in alcohol. The abundance and variety of timber in the Amazonian Valley strikes us with amazement. We long to hear the saw-mill busy in these forests, where there are several hundred kinds of woods, admirably suited for construction as well as for the finest cabinet-work; remarkable for the beauty of their grain, for their hardness, for the variety of their tints and their veining, and for their durability. And yet so ignorant are the inhabitants of the value of timber that, when they want a plank, they cut down a tree, and chop it to the desired thickness with a hatchet. There are many other vegetable products, besides those already exported from the Amazons, which will one day be poured into the market from its fertile shores. The clearest and purest oils are made from some of the nuts and palm fruits, while many of the palms yield the most admirable fibrous material for cordage, singularly elastic and resistant. Besides its material products, — and of these the greater part rot on the ground for want of hands to gather them, — the climate and soil are favorable for the growth of sugar, coffee, cocoa, and cotton; and I may add, that the spices of the East might be cultivated in the valley of the Amazons as well as in the Dutch possessions of Asia."

Sunday, 31st. — Manaos. We had wished exceedingly to extend our excursion on the Rio Negro to the mouth of the Rio Branco, but our pilot would not undertake to conduct the "Ibicuhy" beyond Pedreira, as he said the stones in the bed of the river were numerous and large and the channel at this season not very deep. We were, therefore, obliged to return without accomplishing the whole object of this voyage; but though short, it was nevertheless most interesting, and has left with us a vivid impression of the peculiar character of this great stream. Beautiful as are the endless forests, however, we could not but long, when skirting them day after day without seeing a house or meeting a canoe, for the sight of tilled soil, for pasture-lands, for open ground, for wheat-fields and haystacks,—for any sign, in short, of the presence of man. As we sat at night in the stern of the vessel, looking up this vast river, stretching many hundred leagues, with its solitary, uninhabited shores and impenetrable forests, it was difficult to resist an oppressive sense of loneliness. Though here and there an Indian settlement or a Brazilian village breaks the distance, yet the population is a mere handful in such a territory. I suppose the time will come when the world will claim it, when this river, where, in a six days' journey, we have passed but two or three canoes, will have its steamers and vessels of all sorts going up and down, and its banks will be busy with life; but the day is not yet. When I remember the poor people I have seen in the watch-making and lace-making villages of Switzerland, hardly lifting their eyes off their work from break of day till night, and even then earning barely enough to keep them above actual want, and think how easily everything grows here, on land to be had for almost nothing, it seems a pity that some parts of the world should be so overstocked that there is not nourishment for all, and others so empty that there are none to gather the harvest. We long to see a vigorous emigration pour into this region so favored by Nature, so bare of inhabitants. But things go slowly in these latitudes; great cities do not spring up in half a century, as with us. Humboldt, in his account of his South-American journey, writes: "Since my departure from the banks of the Orinoco and the Amazon, a new era has unfolded itself in the social state of the nations of the West. The fury of civil dissensions has been succeeded by the blessings of peace, and a freer development of the arts of industry. The bifurcations of the Orinoco, the isthmus of Tuamini, so easy to be made passable by an artificial canal, will erelong fix the attention of commercial Europe. The Cassiquiare, as broad as the Rhine, and the course of which is one hundred and eighty miles in length, will no longer form uselessly a navigable canal between two basins of rivers which have a surface of one hundred and ninety thousand square leagues. The grain of New Granada will be carried to the banks of the Rio Negro; boats will descend from the sources of the Napo and the Ucuyale, from the Andes of Quito and of Upper Peru, to the mouths of the Orinoco, — a distance which equals that from Timbuctoo to Marseilles." Such were the anticipations of Humboldt more than sixty years ago; and at this day the banks of the Rio Negro and the Cassiquiare are still as luxuriant and as desolate, as fertile and as uninhabited, as they were then.

January 8th. — Manaos. The necessity for some days of rest, after so many months of unintermitted work, has detained Mr. Agassiz here for a week. It has given us an opportunity of renewing our walks in the neighborhood of Manaos, of completing our collection of plants, and also of refreshing our memory of scenes which we shall probably never see again, and among which we have had a pleasant home for nearly three months. The woods are much more full of flowers than they were when I first became acquainted with their many pleasant paths. Passion-flowers are especially abundant. There is one kind which has a delicious perfume, not unlike Cape Jessamine. It hides itself away in the shade, but its fragrance betrays it; and if you put aside the branches of the trees, you are sure to find its large white-and-purple flowers, and dark, thick-leaved vine, climbing up some neighboring trunk. Another, which seems rather to court than avoid observation, is of a bright red; and its crimson stars are often seen set, as it were, in the thick foliage of the forest. But, much as I enjoy the verdure here, I appreciate, more than ever before, the marked passage of the seasons in our Northern hemisphere. In this unchanging, green world, which never alters from century to century, except by a little more or less moisture, a little more or less heat, I think with the deepest gratitude of winter and spring, summer and autumn. The circle of nature seems incomplete, and even the rigors of our climate are remembered with affection in this continual vapor-bath. It is literally true that you cannot move ten steps without being drenched in perspiration. However, this character of the heat prevents it from being scorching; and we have no reason to change our first impression, that, on the whole, the climate is much less oppressive than we expected to find it, and the nights are invariably cool.

At the end of this week we resume our voyage on board the "Ibicuhy," going slowly down to Pará, stopping at several points on the way. Our first station will be at Villa Bella, where Mr. Agassiz wishes to make another collection of fishes. It may seem strange that, after having obtained, nearly five months ago, very large collections from the Amazons itself at this point, as well as from the lakes in the neighborhood, he should return to the same locality, instead of choosing another region for investigation. Were his object merely or mainly to become acquainted with the endless diversity of fishes he now knows to exist in this immense fresh-water basin, such a repetition of specimens from the same locality would certainly be superfluous, since it is probable that a different point would be more prolific in new species. The mere accumulation of species is, however, entirely subordinate to the object which he has kept in view ever since he began his present researches, namely, that of ascertaining by direct observation the geographical range of the fishes, and determining whether their migrations are so frequent and extensive as they are said to be. I make an extract from Mr. Agassiz's notes on this subject.

"I have been frequently told here that the fishes were very nomadic, the same place being occupied at different seasons of the year by different species. My own investigations have led me to believe that these reports are founded on imperfect observations, and that the localization of species is more distinct and permanent in these waters than has been supposed; their migrations being, indeed, very limited, consisting chiefly in rovings from shallower to deeper waters, and from these to shoals again, at those seasons when the range of the shore in the same water-basin is affected by the rise and fall of the river;—that is to say, the fishes found at the bottom of a lake covering perhaps a square mile in extent, when the waters are lowest, will appear near the shores of the same lake when, at the season of high waters, it extends over a much wider area. In the same way, fishes which gather near the mouth of a rivulet, at the time of low waters, will be found as high as its origin at the period of high waters; while fishes which inhabit the larger igarapés on the sides of the Amazons when they are swollen by the rise of the river, may be found in the Amazons itself when the stream is low. There is not a single fish known to ascend from the sea to the higher courses of the Amazons at certain seasons, and to return regularly to the ocean. There is no fish here corresponding to the salmon, for instance, which ascends the streams of Europe and North America to deposit its spawn in the cool head-waters of the larger rivers, and then returns to the sea. The wanderings of the Amazonian fishes are rather a result of the alternate widening and contracting of their range by the rise and fall of the waters, than of a migratory habit; and may be compared to the movements of those oceanic fishes which, at certain seasons, seek the shoals near the shore, while they spend the rest of the year in deeper waters.

"Take our shad as an example. It is caught on the coast of Georgia in February, on the Carolina shores a little later; in March it may be found in Washington and Baltimore, next in Philadelphia and New York; and it does not make its appearance in the Boston market (except when brought from farther south) before the latter part of April, or the beginning of May. This sequence has led to the belief that the shad migrates from Georgia to New England. An examination of the condition of these fishes, during the months when they are sold in our markets, shows at once that this cannot be the case. They are always full of roe, and, being valued for the table at this period, they are

15 *

brought to market at each locality until the spawning season is over. Now, as they cannot breed twice within a few weeks, it is evident that the shad which make their appearance successively along the Atlantic coast from February to May are not the same. It is the spring which migrates northward, calling up the shoals of shad from the deeper sea, as it touches in succession different points along the shore. Such movements, if thus connected with the advancing spring along a whole coast, appear to be migrations from south to north, when they are, in fact, only the successive rising of the same species from deeper to shallower waters at the breeding season. In the same way it is probable that the inequality in the seasons of rise and fall, between the different tributaries of the Amazons and the various parts of its own course, may give a sequence to the appearance of the fish in certain localities, which seems like migration without being so, in fact.

"Keeping in view all the information I could obtain upon this subject, I have attempted, wherever it was possible to do so, to make collections simultaneously at different points of the Amazons: thus, while I was collecting at Villa Bella six months ago, some of my assistants were engaged in the same way at Santarem, and higher up on the Tapajoz; while I was working at Teffé, parties were busy in the Hyavary, the Içá, and the Hyutahy; and during my last stay at Manaos, parties have been collecting at Cudajas and at Manacaparu, and higher up on the Rio Negro, as well as at some lower points on the main river. At some of these stations I have been able to repeat my investigations at different seasons, though the intervals between the earlier and later collections made at the same localities have, of course, not been the same. Between the first collections made at Teffé and the last, hardly two months intervened, while those made on our first arrival at Manaos in September up to the present time cover an interval of four months; from the first to the last at Villa Bella more than five months will have elapsed. On this account I attach great importance to the renewal of my investigations at that place, as well as to the later collections from Obydos, Santarem, Monte Alegre, Porto do Moz, Gurupá, Tajapurú, and Pará. As far as these comparisons have gone, they show that the distinct faunæ of the above-named localities are not the result of migrations; for not only have different fishes been found in all these basins at the same time, but at different times the same fishes have been found to recur in the same basins, whenever the fishing was carried on, not merely in favored localities, but as far as possible over the whole area indiscriminately, in deep and shoal waters. Should it prove that at Pará, as well as at the intervening stations, after an interval of six months, the fishes are throughout the same as when we ascended the river, the evidence against the supposed extensive migrations of the Amazonian fishes will certainly be very strong. The striking limitation of species within definite areas does not, however, exclude the presence of certain kinds of fish simultaneously throughout the whole Amazonian basin. The Pirarucu, for instance, is found everywhere from Peru to Pará; and so are a few other species more or less extensively distributed over what may be considered distinct ichthyological faunæ. But these widespread species are not migratory; they have normally and permanently a wide range, just as some terrestrial animals have an almost cosmopolite character, while others are circumscribed within comparatively narrow limits. Though most quadrupeds of the United States, for instance, differ from those of Mexico and Brazil, constituting several distinct faunæ, there is one, the puma or red lion, the panther of the North, which is found on the east of the Rocky Mountains and the Andes, from Patagonia to Canada.

"The movement of the waters, which affects so powerfully the distribution of the fishes, forms in itself a very curious phenomenon. There is, as it were, a rhythmical correspondence in the rise and fall of the affluents on either shore of the Amazons, causing the great body of the water, in its semiannual tides, to sway alternately more to the north or to the south. On the southern side of the valley, the rains begin in the months of September and October. They pour down from the table-lands of Brazil and the mountains of Bolivia with cumulative force, gathering strength as the rainy season progresses, swelling the head-waters of the Purus, Madeira, Tapajoz, and other southern tributaries, and gradually descending to the main stream. The process is a slow one, however, and the full force of the new flood is not felt in the Amazons until February and March. During the month of March, in the region below the confluence of the Madeira, for instance, the rise of the Amazons averages a foot in twenty-four hours, so great is the quantity of water poured into it. At about the same period with the southern rains, or a little earlier, say in the months of August and September, the snows in the Andes begin to melt and flow down towards the plain. This contribution from the Cordilleras of Peru and Equador, coinciding with that from the highlands of Brazil and Bolivia, swells the Amazons in its centre and on its southern side to such an extent that the bulk of the water pushes northward, crowding upon its northern shore, and flowing even into the tributaries which open on that side of the river, and are now at their lowest ebb. Presently, however, the rains on the table-lands of Guiana, and on the northern spurs of the Andes, where the rainy season prevails chiefly in February and March, repeat the same process in their turn. During April and May the northern tributaries are rising, and they reach their maximum in June. Thus, at the end of June, when the southern rivers have already fallen considerably, the northern rivers are at their flood-tide. The Rio Negro, for instance, rises at Manaos to about forty-five feet above its lowest level. This mass of water from the north now presses against that in the centre, and bears it southward again. The rainy season along the course of the Amazons is from December till March, corresponding very nearly, in the time of the year and in duration, with our winter. It must be remembered that the valley of the Amazons is not a valley in the ordinary sense, bordered by walls or banks enclosing the waters which flow between. It is, on the contrary, a plain some seven or eight hundred miles wide and between two and three thousand miles long, with a slope so slight that it hardly averages more than a foot in ten miles. Between Obydos and the sea-shore, a distance of about eight hundred miles, the fall is only forty-five feet; between Tabatinga and the sea-shore, a distance of more than two thousand miles in a straight line, the fall is about two hundred feet. The impression to the eye is, therefore, that of an absolute plain; and the flow of the water is so gentle that, in many parts of the river, it is hardly perceptible. Nevertheless, it has a steady movement eastward, descending the gentle slope of this wide plain, from the Andes to the sea; this movement, aided by the interflow from the south and north at opposite seasons, presses the bulk of the water to its northernmost reach during our winter months, and to its southernmost limit during our summer months. In consequence of this, the bottom of the valley is constantly shifting, and there is a tendency to form channels from the main river to its tributaries, such as we have seen to exist between the Solimoens and the Rio Negro, — such as Humboldt mentions between the Hyapura and the Amazons. Indeed, all these rivers are bound together by an extraordinary network of channels, forming a succession of natural highways which will always make artificial roads, to a great degree, unnecessary. Whenever the country is settled, it will be possible to pass from the Purus, for instance, to the Madeira, from the Madeira to the Tapajoz, from the Tapajoz to the Xingu, and thence to the Tocantins, without entering the course of the main river. The Indians call these passes '*furo*,' literally, a bore, — a passage pierced from one river to another. Hereafter, when the interests of commerce claim this fertile, overflowed region, these channels will be of immense advantage for intercommunication."

CHAPTER XII.

DESCENDING THE RIVER TO PARÁ. — EXCURSIONS ON THE COAST.

Farewell Visit to the Great Cascade at Manaos. — Change in its Aspect. — Arrival at Villa Bella. — Return to the House of the Fisherman Maia. — Excursion to the Lago Maximo. — Quantity of Game and Waterfowl. — Victoria regia. — Leave Villa Bella. — Arrive at Obydos. — Its Situation and Geology. — Santarem. — Visit to the Church. — Anecdote of Martius. — A Row overland. — Monte Alégre. — Picturesque Scenery. — "Banheiras." — Excursion into the Country. — Leave Monte Alégre. — Anecdote of Indians. — Almeyrim. — New Geological Facts. — Porto do Moz. — Collections. — Gurupá. — Tajapurú. — Arrive at Pará. — Religious Procession. — Excursion to Marajo. — Sourés. — Jesuit Missions. — Geology of Marajo. — Buried Forest. — Vigia. — Igarapé. — Vegetation and Animal Life. — Geology. — Return to Pará. — Photographing Plants. — Extract from Mr. Agassiz's Notes on the Vegetation of the Amazons. — Prevalence of Leprosy.

January 15*th.* — To-day finds us on our way down the Amazons in the "Ibicuhy." The day before leaving Manaos we paid a last visit to the great cascade, bathed once more in its cool, delicious waters, and breakfasted by the side of the fall. Before many weeks are over, the cascade will have disappeared: it will be drowned out, as it were, for the igarapé is filling rapidly with the rise of the river, and will soon reach the level of the sandstone shelf over which the water is precipitated. Already the appearance of the spot is greatly changed since we were there before. The banks are overflowed; the rocks and logs which stood out from the water are wholly covered; and where there was only a brawling stream, so shallow that it hardly afforded depth for the smallest canoe, there is now a not insignificant river. Indeed, everywhere we see signs of the changes wrought by the "enchente." The very texture of the Amazons is changed; it is thicker and yellower than when we ascended it, and much more laden with floating wood, detached grasses, and *débris* of all sorts washed from the shore. Wild-flowers are also more abundant than they were when we came up the river in September; not delicate, small plants, growing low among moss and grass, as do our violets, anemones, and the like; but large blossoms, covering tall trees, and resembling exotics at home, by their rich color and powerful odor. Indeed, the flowers of the Amazonian forests always remind me of hot-house plants: and there often comes a warm breath from the depths of the woods, laden with moisture and perfume, like the air from the open door of a conservatory.

January 17*th*. — We reached Villa Bella at eight o'clock yesterday morning, but waited there only a few hours to make certain necessary arrangements, and then kept on to the mouth of the river Ramos, an hour's sail from the town, — the same river which we had ascended from its upper point of juncture with the Amazons, on our excursion to Mauhes. We anchored at a short distance from the entrance, before the house of our old acquaintances, the Maias, where, it may be remembered, we passed a few days when collecting in this neighborhood before. Fortunately, Maia himself was in Manaos when we left, employed as a soldier in the National Guard; and the President kindly gave him leave to accompany us, that Mr. Agassiz might have the advantage of his familiarity with the locality, and his experience in fishing. The man himself was pleased to have an opportunity of visiting his family, to whom his coming was an agreeable surprise. We went on shore this morning to make them a visit, taking with us some little souvenirs, such as beads, trinkets, knives, &c. We were received as old friends, and made welcome to all the house would afford ; but, though as clean as ever, it looked poorer than on our former visit. I saw neither dried fish nor mandioca nor farinha, and the woman told me that she found it very hard to support her large family, now that the husband and father was away.

The quantity of detached grass, shrubs, &c. carried past the vessel, as we lie here at anchor, is amazing, — floating gardens, sometimes half an acre in extent. Some of these green rafts are inhabited ; water-birds go sailing by upon them, and large animals are occasionally carried down the river in this way. The commander told me that, on one occasion, when an English vessel was lying at anchor in the Parana, one of these grassy gardens was seen coming down the river with two deer upon it. The current brought it directly against the ship, and the captain had only to receive on board the guests who arrived thus unexpectedly to demand his hospitality. In the same river another floating island brought with it a less agreeable inhabitant : a large tiger had possessed himself of it and was sailing majestically with the current, passing so near the shores that he was distinctly seen from the banks ; and people went out in montarias to get a nearer view of him, though keeping always at a respectful distance. The most conspicuous of the plants thus detached from the shore are the Canarana (a kind of wild cane), a variety of aquatic Aroides, Pistia among the number, Ecornia, and a quantity of graceful floating Marsileaceæ.

January 18th. — To-day we have been on a hunt after the Victoria regia. We have made constant efforts to see this famous lily growing in its native waters; but, though frequently told that it was plenty at certain seasons in the lakes and igarapés, we have never been able to find it. Yesterday some of the officers of the ship, who had been on an excursion to a neighboring lake, returned laden with botanical treasures of all sorts, and, among other plants, an immense lily-leaf, which, from its dimensions, we judged must be the Victoria regia, though it had not the erect edge so characteristic of it. This morning, accompanied by two or three of yesterday's party, who kindly undertook to be our guides, we went to visit the same lake. A short walk from the riverbank brought us to the shore of a large sheet of water, — the Lago Maximo, — which connects with the Ramos by a narrow outlet, but at a point so distant from our anchorage that it would have been necessary to make a great detour in order to reach it in a canoe. We found an old montaria, with one or two broken paddles, left, as it seemed, at the lake-shore for whom it might concern, and in that we embarked at once. The banks of this lake are bordered with beautiful forests, which do not, however, rise immediately from the water, but are divided from it by a broad band of grass. We saw many water-birds on this grassy edge, as well as on several dead trees, the branches of which were completely covered with gulls, all in exactly the same attitude, facing one way, to meet the wind which blew strongly against them. Ducks and ciganas were plenty; and once or twice we startled up from the woods small flocks of mackaws, — not only the gaudy red, green, and yellow species, but the far more beautiful blue mackaw. They flow by us, with their gorgeous plumage glittering in the sun, and disappeared again among the trees, seeking deeper and more undisturbed retreats. From the reedy grasses came also the deep note of the unicorn, so greatly prized in Brazil,— a large bird, half wader, half fowl, belonging to the genus Palamedea ; but as we were only prepared for a botanizing expedition, we could not avail ourselves of any of the opportunities thus offered ; and the birds, however near and tempting the shots, had little to fear from us. At the upper end of the lake we came upon the bed of water-lilies from which the trophies of yesterday had been gathered. The leaves were very large, many of them from four to five feet in diameter ; but, perhaps from having lost their first freshness and something therefore of their natural texture, the edge of the leaf was scarcely perceptibly raised, and in most instances lay perfectly flat upon the water. We found buds, but no perfect flower. In the afternoon, however, one of the daughters of our fisherman Maia, hearing that we wished to see one of the flowers, brought us a very perfect specimen from another more distant locality, which we had not time to visit. The Indians, by the way, have a characteristic name for the leaf. They call it "forno," on account of its resemblance to the immense shallow pans in which they bake their farinha over the mandioca ovens. The Victoria regia, with its formidable armor of spines, its gigantic leaves, and beautiful flowers, deepening in color from the velvety white outer leaves through every shade of rose to deepest crimson, and fading again to a creamy, yellowish tint in the heart of the flower, has been described so often that I hardly dare dwell upon it, for fear of wearying the reader. And yet we could not see it growing in its native waters — a type, as it were, of the luxuriance of tropical nature — without the deepest interest. Wonderful as it is when seen in the tank of a greenhouse, and perhaps even more impressive, in a certain sense, from its isolation, in its own home it has the charm of harmony with all that surrounds it, — with the dense mass of forest, with palm and parasite, with birds of glowing plumage, with insects of all bright and wonderful tints, and with fishes which, though hidden in the water beneath it, are not less brilliant and varied than the world of life above. I do not remember to have seen an allusion, in any description, to the beautiful device by which the whole immense surface of the adult leaf is contained within the smaller dimensions of the young one; though it is well worth notice, as one of the neatest specimens of Nature's packing. All know the heavy scaffolding of ribs by which the colossal leaf, when full grown, is supported on its under side. In the young leaf these ribs are comparatively small, but the whole green expanse of the adult leaf is gathered in between them in regular rows of delicate puffings. At this period, the leaf is far below the surface of the water, growing slowly up from the base of the stock from which it springs. Thus drawn up, it has the form of a deep cup or vase; but in proportion as the ribs grow, their ramifications stretching in every direction, the leaf lets out one by one its little folds, to fill the ever-widening spaces; till at last, when it reaches the surface of the water, it rests horizontally above it, without a wrinkle. Mr. Agassiz caused several stocks to be dragged up from the bottom (no easy matter, on account of the spines), and found the leaf-buds just starting between the roots, — little white caps, not more than half an inch in height. There was another lily growing in this lake, which, though diminutive by the side of the Victoria, would be a giant among our water-lilies. The leaf measured more than a foot in diameter, and was slightly scolloped around the edge. There were no open flowers, but the closed buds resembled those of our common white water-lilies, and were no larger. The stalk and ribs, unlike those of the Victoria, were quite smooth, and free from thorns. After our visit to the lilies, we paddled in among the trees along the overflowed margin of the lake, in order that the boatmen might cut down several palms new to us. While waiting under the trees in the boat, we had cause to admire the variety and beauty of the insects fluttering about us; the large blue butterflies (Morpho), and the brilliant dragonflies, with crimson bodies and burnished wings, glittering with metallic lustre.*

January 21*st*. — Obydos. We left Villa Bella yesterday with a large collection of fishes, and some valuable additions to the collection of palms. The general character of the fish collections, both from the river Ramos and the Lago Maximo, shows the faunæ to be the same now as when we were here five months ago. Certainly, during this interval, migration has had no perceptible influence upon the distribution of life in these waters. Leaving Villa Bella at night, we reached Obydos early this morning. This pretty town is one of the most picturesque in position, on the

---

* During my short stay in the neighborhood of Villa Bella and Obydos I was indebted to several residents of these towns for assistance in collecting; especially to Padre Torquato and to Padre Antonio Mattos. My friend, Mr. Honorio, who accompanied me to this point, with the assistance of the Delegado, at Villa Bella, made also a very excellent collection of fishes in this vicinity. At Obydos Colonel Bentos contributed a very large collection of fishes from the Rio Trombetas. — L. A.

Amazons. It stands on a steep bluff, commanding an extensive view of the river west and east, and is one of the few points at which the southern and northern shores are seen at the same time. The bluff of Obydos is crowned by a fortress, which has stood here for many years without occasion to test its power. It may be doubted whether it would be very effectual in barring the river against a hostile force, inasmuch as its guns, though they carry perfectly well to the opposite side, are powerless nearer home. The slope of the cliff on which the fortress stands intervenes between it and the water below, so that by keeping well in to shore the enemy could pass with impunity immediately under the guns. The hill consists entirely of the same red drift so constantly recurring on the banks of the Amazons and its tributaries. Here it is more full of pebbles than at Manaos or at Teffé; and we saw these pebbles disposed in lines or horizontal beds, such as are found in the same deposit along the coast and in the neighborhood of Rio. The city of Obydos is prettily laid out, its environs are very picturesque, its soil extremely fertile; but it has the same aspect of neglect and hopeless inactivity so painfully striking in all the Amazonian towns.

January 23*d*. Yesterday, in the early morning, we arrived at Santarem, and went on shore for a walk at half past seven. The town stands on a point of land dividing the black waters of the Tapajoz, on the one side, from the yellow flood of the Amazons on the other, and has a very attractive situation, enhanced by its background of hills stretching away to the eastward. Our first visit was to the church, fronting on the beach and standing invitingly open. We had, however, a special object in entering it. In 1819 Martius, the naturalist, on his voyage of exploration on the

Amazons, since made famous by his great work on the Natural History of Brazil, was wrecked off the town of Santarem, and nearly lost his life. In his great danger he took a vow to record his gratitude, should he live, by making a gift to the church of Santarem. After his return to Europe, he sent from Munich a full-length figure of Christ upon the cross, which now hangs against the wall, with a simple inscription underneath, telling in a few words the story of his peril, his deliverance, and his gratitude. As a work of art it has no special value, but it attracts many persons to the church who never heard of Martius or his famous journey; and to Mr. Agassiz it was especially interesting, as connected with the travels and dangers of his old friend and teacher.

After a walk through the town, which is built with more care, and contains some houses having more pretensions to comfort and elegance than we have seen elsewhere on the Amazons, we returned to the ship for breakfast. At a later hour we went on a very pleasant canoe excursion to the other side of the Tapajoz, again in search of the Victoria regia, said to grow in great perfection in this neighborhood. Our guide was Senhor Joachim Rodriguez, to whom Mr. Agassiz has been indebted for much personal kindness, as well as for a very valuable collection made since we stopped here on our way up the river, partly by himself and partly by his son, a bright boy of some thirteen years of age. Crossing to the opposite side of the river, we came upon a vast field of coarse, high grass, looking like an extensive meadow. To our surprise, the boatmen turned the canoe into this green field, and we found ourselves apparently navigating the land, for the narrow boat-path was entirely concealed by the long reedy grasses and tall mallow-plants with large pink blossoms rising on either side, and completely hiding the water below. This marshy, overflowed ground, above which the water had a depth of from four to six feet, was full of life. As the rowers pushed our canoe through the mass of grass and flowers, Mr. Agassiz gathered from the blades and stalks all sorts of creatures; small bright-colored toads of several kinds, grasshoppers, beetles, dragon-flies, aquatic snails, bunches of eggs, — in short, an endless variety of living things, most interesting to the naturalist. The harvest was so plentiful that we had only to put out our hands and gather it; the oarsmen, when they saw Mr. Agassiz's enthusiasm, became almost as interested as he was; and he had soon a large jar filled with objects quite new to him. After navigating these meadows for some time, we came upon open water-spaces where the Victoria regia was growing in great perfection. The specimens were much finer than those we had seen before in the Lago Maximo. One leaf measured five feet and a half in diameter, and another five feet, the erect edge being three inches and a half in height. A number of leaves grew from the same stalk; and seen thus together they are very beautiful, the bright rose-color of the outer edge contrasting with the vivid green of the inner surface of the leaf. As before, there were no open flowers to be seen; Senhor Rodriguez told us that they are cut by the fishermen almost as soon as they open. When Mr. Agassiz expressed a wish to get the roots, two of our boatmen plunged into the water with an alacrity which surprised me, as we had just been told that these marshes are the haunts of Jacarés. They took turns in diving to dig up the plants, and succeeded in bringing to the surface three large stalks, one with a flower-bud. We returned well pleased with our row overland.

Our live-stock is increasing as we descend the river, and we have now quite a menagerie on board; a number of parrots, half a dozen monkeys, two exquisite little deer from the region of Monte Alégre, and several Agamis, as tame and gentle as barn-yard fowls, stepping about the deck with graceful, dainty tread, and feeding from the hand. Their voices are singularly harsh, however, and out of keeping with their pretty looks and ways. Every now and then they raise their heads, stretch their long necks, and utter a loud, gurgling sound, more like the roll of a drum than the note of a bird. Last, but not least, we have a sloth on board, the most fascinating of all our pets to me, not certainly for his charms, but for his oddities. I am never tired of watching him, he looks so deliciously lazy. His head sunk in his arms, his whole attitude lax and indifferent, he seems to ask only for rest. If you push him, or if, as often happens, a passer-by gives him a smart tap to arouse him, he lifts his head and drops his arms so slowly, so deliberately, that they hardly seem to move, raises his heavy lids and lets his large eyes rest upon your face for a moment with appealing, hopeless indolence; then the lids fall softly, the head droops, the arms fold heavily about it, and he collapses again into absolute repose. This mute remonstrance is the nearest approach to activity I have seen him make. These live animals are not all a part of the scientific collections; many of them belong to the captain and officers. The Brazilians are exceedingly fond of pets, and almost every house has its monkeys, its parrots, and other tame animals and birds.

January 26th. — Monte Alégre. Leaving Santarem on Tuesday we arrived here on Wednesday morning, and, as on our former visit, were received most hospitably at the house of Senhor Manuel. Mr. Agassiz and Mr. Coutinho have gone on a geologizing excursion to the Serra d'Ereré, that picturesque range of hills bounding the campos, or open sandy plain, to the northwest of the town. They took different routes, Major Coutinho, with Captain Faria and one or two other friends, crossing the campos on horseback, while Mr. Agassiz went by canoe. They will meet at the foot of the Serra, and pass two or three days in that neighborhood. Little is as yet known of the geological structure of the Amazonian Serras, — those of Santarem, of Monte Alégre, and of Almeyrim. Generally they have been considered as prolongations either of the table-land of Guiana on the north, or that of Brazil on the south. Mr. Agassiz believes them to be independent of both, and more directly connected with the formation of the Amazonian Valley itself. The solution of this question is his special object, while Major Coutinho has taken barometers to determine the height of the range. In the mean time, I am passing a few quiet days here, learning to be more familiar with the scenery of a region very justly called one of the most picturesque on the borders of the Amazons. Not only are the views extensive, but the friable nature of the soil, so easily decomposed, combined with the heavy rains, has led to the formation of a variety of picturesque dells and hollows, some of which have springs running into them, surrounded by rocky banks and overhung with trees. One of these is especially pretty; the excavation is large, and has the form of an amphitheatre; its rocky walls are crowned with large foresttrees, palms, mimosas, etc., making a deep shade; and at one side the spring flows down from the top of the cliff, with a pleasant ripple. Here the negro or Indian servants come to fill their water-jars. They often have with them the children under their charge; and you may sometimes see the large red jars standing under the mouth of the spring above, while white babies and dark nurses splash about in the cool water-basin below. Although in the campos the growth is low, and the soil but scantily covered with coarse grass and shrubs, yet, in some localities, and especially in the neighborhood of the town, the forest is beautiful. We have seen nowhere larger and more luxuriant mimosas, sometimes of a green so rich and deep, and a foliage so close that it is difficult to believe, at a distance, that its dense mass is formed by the light, pinnate leaves of a sensitive plant. The palms are also very lofty and numerous, including some kinds which we have not met before.

January 28th. — Yesterday our kind host arranged an excursion into the country, for my especial pleasure, that I might see something of the characteristic amusements of Monte Alégre. One or two neighbors joined us, and the children, a host of happy little folks, for whom anything out of the common tenor of every-day life is "*festa*," were not left behind. We started on foot to walk out into a very picturesque Indian village called Surubiju. Here we were to breakfast, returning afterwards in one of the heavy carts drawn by oxen, the only conveyance for women and children in a country where a carriage-road and a side-saddle are equally unknown. Our walk was very pleasant, partly through the woods, partly through the campos; but as it was early in the day, we did not miss the shade when we chanced to leave the trees. We lingered by the wayside, the children stopping to gather wild fruits, of which there were a number on the road, and to help me in making a collection of plants. It was about nine o'clock when we reached the first straw-house, where we stopped to rest.

Though it has no longer the charm of novelty for me, I am always glad to visit an Indian cottage. You find a cordial welcome; the best hammock, the coolest corner, and a *cuia* of fresh water are ready for you. As a general thing, the houses of the Indians are also more tidy than those of the whites; and there is a certain charm of picturesqueness about them which never wears off.

After a short rest, we went on through the settlement, where the sitios are scattered at considerable distances, and so completely surrounded by trees that they seem quite isolated in the forest. Although the Indians are said to be a lazy people, and are unquestionably fitful and irregular in their habits of work, in almost all these houses some characteristic occupation was going on. In two or three the women were making hammocks, in one a boy was plaiting the leaves of the Curuà palm into a tolda for his canoe, in another the inmates were making a coarse kind of pottery; and in still another a woman, who is quite famous in the neighborhood for her skill in the art, was painting cuias. It was the first time I had seen the prepared colors made from a certain kind of clay found in the Serra. It is just the carnival season, and, as every one has a right to play pranks on his neighbors, we did not get off without making a closer acquaintance than was altogether pleasant with the rustic artist's colors. As we were leaving the cottage, she darted out upon us, her hands full of blue and red paints. If they had been tomahawks, they could not have produced a more sudden rout; and it was a complete *sauve qui peut* of the whole company across the little bridge which led to the house. As a stranger, I was spared; but all were not fortunate enough to escape, and some of the children carried their blue and red badges to the end of the day.

The prettiest of all these forest sitios was one at the bottom of a deep dell, reached by a steep, winding path through a magnificent wood abounding in palms. But though the situation was most picturesque, the sickly appearance of the children and the accounts of prevailing illness showed that the locality was too low and damp to be healthful. After a very pleasant ramble we returned to breakfast at our first resting-place, and at about one o'clock started for town in two ox-carts which had come out to meet us. They consist only of a floor set on very heavy, creaking wooden wheels, which, from their primitive, clumsy character, would seem to be the first wheels ever invented. On the floor a straw-mat was spread, an awning was stretched over a light scaffolding above, and we were soon stowed away in our primitive vehicle, and had a very gay and pleasant ride back to town. Yesterday evening Mr. Agassiz returned from his excursion to the Serra Ereré. I add here a little account of the journey, written out from his notes, and containing some remarks on the general aspect of the country, its vegetation and animals. A summary of the geological results of the excursion will be found in a separate chapter at the close of our Amazonian journey.

"I started before daylight; but as the dawn began to redden the sky large flocks of ducks, and of the small Amazonian goose, might be seen flying towards the lakes. Here and there a cormorant sat alone on the branch of a dead tree, or a kingfisher poised himself over the water, watching for his prey. Numerous gulls were gathered in large companies on the trees along the river-shore; alligators lay on its surface, diving with a sudden plash at the approach of our canoe; and occasionally a porpoise emerged from the water, showing himself for a moment and then disappearing again. Sometimes we startled a herd of capivaras, resting on the water's edge; and once we saw a sloth, sitting upon the branch of an Imbauba tree (Cecropia), rolled up in its peculiar attitude, the very picture of indolence, with its head sunk between its arms. Much of the river-shore consisted of low, alluvial land, and was covered with that peculiar and beautiful grass known as Capim; this grass makes an excellent pasturage for cattle, and the abundance of it in this region renders the district of Monte Alégre very favorable for agricultural purposes. Here and there, where the red-clay soil rose above the level of the water, a palm-thatched cabin stood on the low bluff, with a few trees about it. Such a house was usually the centre of a cattle-farm, and large herds might be seen grazing in the adjoining fields. Along the river-banks, where the country is chiefly open, with extensive low, marshy grounds, the only palm to be seen is the Maraja (Geonoma). After keeping along the Rio Gurupatuba for some distance, we turned to the right into a narrow stream, which has the character of an igarapé in its lower course, though higher up it drains the country between the serra of Ereré and that of Tajury, and assumes the appearance of a small river. It is named after the serra, and is known as the Rio Ereré. This stream, narrow and picturesque, and often so overgrown with capim that the canoe pursued its course with difficulty, passed through a magnificent forest of the beautiful fan-palm, called the Miriti (Mauritia flexuosa). This forest stretched for miles, overshadowing, as a kind of underbrush, many smaller trees and innumerable shrubs, some of which bore bright, conspicuous flowers. It seemed to me a strange spectacle,—

a forest of monocotyledonous trees with a dicotyledonous undergrowth ; the inferior plants thus towering above and sheltering the superior ones. Among the lower trees were many Leguminosæ, — one of the most striking, called Fava, having a colossal pod. The whole mass of vegetation was woven together by innumerable lianas and creeping vines, in the midst of which the flowers of the Bignonia, with its open, trumpet-shaped corolla, were conspicuous. The capim was bright with the blossoms of the mallow, growing in its midst ; and was often edged with the broad-leaved Aninga, a large aquatic Arum.

"Through such a forest, where the animal life was no less rich and varied than the vegetation, our boat glided slowly for hours. The number and variety of birds struck me with astonishment. The coarse, sedgy grasses on either side were full of water birds, one of the most common of which was a small chestnut-brown wading bird, the Jaçana (Parra), whose toes are immensely long in proportion to its size, enabling it to run upon the surface of the aquatic vegetation, as if it were solid ground. It was now the month of January, their breeding season : and at every turn of the boat we started them up in pairs. Their flat, open nests generally contained five flesh-colored eggs, streaked in zigzag with dark brown lines. The other waders were a snow-white heron, another ash-colored, smaller species, and a large white stork. The ash-colored herons were always in pairs ; the white ones always single, standing quiet and alone on the edge of the water, or half hidden in the green capim. The trees and bushes were full of small warbler-like birds, which it would be difficult to characterize separately. To the ordinary observer they might seem like the small birds of our woods ; but there was one species among them which attracted my attention by its numbers, and also because it builds the most extraordinary nest, considering the size of the bird itself, that I have ever seen. It is known among the country people by two names, as the Pedreiro or the Forneiro; both names referring, as will be seen, to the nature of its habitation. This singular nest is built of clay, and is as hard as stone (*pedra*), while it has the form of the round mandioca oven (*forno*) in which the country people prepare their farinha, or flour, made from the mandioca root. It is about a foot in diameter, and stands edgewise upon a branch, or in the crotch of a tree. Among the smaller birds I noticed bright Tanagers, and also a species resembling the Canary. Besides these, there were the wagtails; the black and white widow-finches; the hang-nests, or Japi, as they are called here, with their pendent, bag-like dwellings, and the familiar "Bem ti vi." Humming-birds, which we are always apt to associate with tropical vegetation, were very scarce. I saw but a few specimens. Thrushes and doves were more frequent, and I noticed also three or four kinds of woodpeckers, beside parrots and paroquets; of these latter there were countless numbers along our canoe path, flying overhead in dense crowds, and at times drowning every other sound in their high, noisy chatter.

"Some of these birds made a deep impression upon me. Indeed, in all regions, however far away from his own home, in the midst of a fauna and flora entirely new to him, the traveller is startled occasionally by the song of a bird or the sight of a flower so familiar that it transports him at once to woods where every tree is like a friend to him. It seems as if something akin to what in our own mental experience we call reminiscence or association existed in the workings of Nature; for though the organic combinations are so distinct in different climates and countries, they never wholly exclude each other. Every zoölogical and botanical province retains some link which binds it to all the others, and makes it part of the general harmony. The Arctic lichen is found growing under the shadow of the palm on the rocks of the tropical serra; and the song of the thrush and the tap of the woodpecker mingle with the sharp, discordant cries of the parrot and paroquet.

"Birds of prey, also, were not wanting. Among them was one about the size of our kite, and called the Red Hawk, which was so tame that, even when our canoe passed immediately under the low branch on which he was sitting, he did not fly away. But, of all the groups of birds, the most striking as compared with corresponding groups in the temperate zone, and the one which reminded me the most distinctly of the fact that every region has its peculiar animal world, was that of the gallinaceous birds. The most frequent is the Cigana, to be seen in groups of fifteen or twenty, perched upon trees overhanging the water, and feeding upon berries. At night they roost in pairs, but in the daytime are always in larger companies. In their appearance they have something of the character of both the pheasant and peacock, and yet do not closely resemble either. It is a curious fact, that, with the exception of some small partridge-like gallinaceous birds, all the representatives of this family in Brazil, and especially in the valley of the Amazons, belong to types which do not exist in other parts of the world. Here we find neither pheasants, nor cocks of the woods, nor grouse; but in their place abound the Mutum, the Jacu, the Jacami, and the Unicorn (Crax, Penelope,

Psophia, and Palamedea), all of which are so remote from the gallinaceous types found farther north that they remind one quite as much of the bustard, and other ostrich-like birds, as of the hen and pheasant. They differ also from northern gallinaceous birds in the greater uniformity of the sexes, none of them exhibiting those striking differences between the males and females which we see in the pheasants, the cocks of the woods, and in our barn-yard fowls, though the plumage of the young has the yellowish-mottled color distinguishing the females of most species of this family. While birds abounded in such numbers, insects were rather scarce. I saw but few and small butterflies, and beetles were still more rare. The most numerous insects were the dragon-flies, — some with crimson bodies, black heads, and burnished wings; others with large green bodies, crossed by blue bands. Of land-shells I saw but one, creeping along the reeds; and of water-shells I gathered only a few small Ampullariæ.

"Having ascended the river to a point nearly on a line with the serra, I landed, and struck across the campos on foot. Here I entered upon an entirely different region, — a dry, open plain, with scanty vegetation. The most prominent plants were clusters of Cacti and Curua palms, a kind of stemless, low palm, with broad, elegant leaves springing vase-like from the ground. In these dry, sandy fields, rising gradually toward the serra, I observed in the deeper gullies formed by the heavy rains the laminated clays which are everywhere the foundation of the Amazonian strata. They here presented again so much the character of ordinary clay-slates that I thought I had at last come upon some old geological formation. Instead of this I only obtained fresh evidence that, by baking them, the burning sun of the tropics may produce upon laminated clays of recent origin the same effect as plutonic agencies have produced upon the ancient clays, — that is, it may change them into metamorphic slates. As I approached the serra, I was again reminded how, under the most dissimilar circumstances, similar features recur everywhere in nature. I came suddenly upon a little creek, bordered with the usual vegetation of such shallow watercourses, and on its brink stood a sand-piper, which flew away at my approach, uttering its peculiar cry, so like what we hear at home that, had I not seen him, I should have recognized him by his voice. After an hour's walk under the scorching sun, I was glad to find myself at the hamlet of Ereré, near the foot of the serra, where I rejoined my companions. This is almost the only occasion in all my Amazonian journey when I have passed a day in the pure enjoyment of nature, without the labor of collecting, which in this hot climate, where specimens require such immediate and constant attention, is very great. I learned how rich a single day may be in this wonderful tropical world, if one's eyes are only open to the wealth of animal and vegetable life. Indeed, a few hours so spent in the field, in simply watching animals and plants, teaches more of the distribution of life than a month of closet study; for under such circumstances all things are seen in their true relations. Unhappily, it is not easy to present the picture as a whole; for all our written descriptions are more or less dependent on nomenclature, and the local names are hardly known out of the districts where they belong, while systematic names are familiar to few."

January 30th. — On board the "Ibicuhy." Yesterday we parted from our kind hosts, and bade good by to Monte Alégre. I shall long retain a picture, half pleasant, half sad, of its shady, picturesque walks and dells; of its wide green square, with the unfinished cathedral in the centre, where trees and vines mantle the open doors and windows, and grass grows thick over the unfrequented aisles; of its neglected cemetery, and the magnificent view it commands over an endless labyrinth of lakes on one side, beyond which glitter the yellow waters of the Amazons, while, on the other, the level campos is bordered by the picturesque heights of the distant Serra. I have never been able to explain quite to my own satisfaction the somewhat melancholy impression which this region, lovely as it unquestionably is, made upon me when I first saw it, — an impression not wholly destroyed by a longer residence. Perhaps it is the general aspect of incompleteness and decay, the absence of energy and enterprise, making the lavish gifts of Nature of no avail. In the midst of a country which should be overflowing with agricultural products, neither milk, nor butter, nor cheese, nor vegetables, nor fruit, are to be had. You constantly hear people complaining of the difficulty of procuring even the commonest articles of domestic consumption, when, in fact, they ought to be produced by every land-owner. The agricultural districts in Brazil are rich and fertile, but there is no agricultural population. The nomad Indian, floating about in his canoe, the only home to which he has a genuine attachment, never striking root in the soil, has no genius for cultivating the ground. As an illustration of the Indian character, it may not be amiss to record an incident which occurred yesterday when we were leaving Monte Alégre. On his journey to Ereré, Major Coutinho had been requested by an Indian and his wife, whose acquaintance he had made in former excursions there, to take one of their boys, a child about eight years of age, with him to Rio. This is very common among the Indians; they are not unwilling to give up their children, if they can secure a maintenance for them, and perhaps some advantages of education besides. On the day of departure, the mother and father and two sisters accompanied the child to the steamer, but I think, as the sequel showed, rather for the sake of seeing the ship, and having a day of amusement, than from any sentiment about parting with the child. When the moment of separation came, the mother, with an air of perfect indifference, gave the little boy her hand to kiss. The father seemed to be going off without remembering his son at all; but the little fellow ran after him, took his hand and kissed it, and then stood crying and broken-hearted on the deck, while the whole family put off in the canoe, talking and laughing gayly, without showing him the least sympathy. Such traits are said to be very characteristic of the Indians. They are cold in their family affections; and though the mothers are very fond of their babies, they seem comparatively indifferent to them as they grow up. It is, indeed, impossible to rely upon the affection of an Indian, even though isolated cases of remarkable fidelity have been known among them. But I have been told over and over again, by those who have had personal experience in the matter, that you may take an Indian child, bring him up, treat him with every kindness, educate him, clothe him, and find him to be a useful and seemingly faithful member of the household; one day he is gone, you know not where, and in every probability you will never hear of him again. Theft is not one of their vices. On the contrary, such an Indian, if he deserts the friend who has reared him and taken care of him, is very likely to leave behind him all his clothes, except those he has on, and any presents he may have received.

The only thing he may be tempted to take will be a canoe and a pair of oars: with these an Indian is rich. He only wants to get back to his woods; and he is deterred by no sentiment of affection, or consideration of interest.

To-day we are passing the hills of Almeyrim. The last time we saw them it was in the glow of a brilliant sunset; to-day, ragged edges of clouds overhang them, and they are sombre under a leaden, rainy sky. It is delightful to Mr. Agassiz, in returning to this locality, to find that phenomena, which were a blank to him on our voyage up the river, are perfectly explicable now that he has had an opportunity of studying the geology of the Amazonian Valley. When we passed these singular flat-topped hills before, he had no clew to their structure or their age,— whether granite, as they have been said to be, or sandstone or limestone; whether primitive, secondary, or tertiary: and their strange form made the problem still more difficult. Now he sees them simply as the remnants of a plain which once filled the whole valley of the Amazons, from the Andes to the Atlantic, from Guiana to Central Brazil. Denudations on a colossal scale, hitherto unknown to geologists, have turned this plain into a labyrinth of noble rivers, leaving only here and there, where the formation has resisted the rush of waters, low mountains and chains of hills to tell what was its thickness.*

February 1st. — On Tuesday evening we reached Porto do Moz, on the river Xingú, where we had expected to be detained several days, as Mr. Agassiz wished especially to obtain the fishes from this river, and, if possible, from its upper and lower course, between which rapids intervene. He found, however, his harvest ready to his hand. Senhor Vinhas, with whom, when stopping here for a few hours on

---

* See Chapter XIII., on the Physical History of the Amazons.

his voyage up the river, he had had some conversation respecting the scientific objects of his visit to the Amazons, has made during our absence one of the finest collections obtained in the whole course of our journey, containing, in separate lots, the fishes from above and below the cascade. By means of this double collection, which Mr. Agassiz has already examined carefully, he ascertains the fact that the faunæ on either side of the falls are entirely distinct from each other, as are those of the upper and lower courses of the Amazons, and also those of its tributaries, lakes, and igarapés. This is a most important addition to the evidence already obtained of the distinct localization of species throughout the waters of the Amazonian Valley. We regretted that, on account of the absence of Senor Vinhas from the town, we could not thank him in person for this valuable contribution. Finding that the efforts of this gentleman had really left nothing to be done in this locality, unless, indeed, we could have stayed long enough to make collections in all the water-basins connected with the Xingu, we left early in the morning and reached Gurupá yesterday. This little town stands on a low cliff some thirty feet above the river. On a projecting point of this cliff there is an old, abandoned fort; and in the open place adjoining it stands a church of considerable size, and seemingly in good repair. But the settlement is evidently not prosperous. Many of its houses are ruinous and deserted, and there is even less of activity in the aspect of the place than in most of the Amazonian villages. We heard much of its insalubrity, and found very severe cases of intermittent fever in one or two of the houses we entered. While Mr. Agassiz made a call upon the subdelegado, who was himself confined to his room with fever, I was invited to rest in the open veranda of a neighboring house, which looked pretty and attractive enough; for it opened into a sunny garden, where bananas and oranges and palm-trees were growing. But the old woman who received me complained bitterly of the dampness, to which, indeed, her hoarse cough and rheumatism bore testimony; and a man was lying in his hammock, slung under the porch, who was worn to mere skin and bone with fever. Here also we received some valuable specimens, collected, since our previous visit, by the subdelegado and one or two other residents.

February 3d. — On Thursday we reached Tajapuru, where we were detained for two days on account of some little repair needed on the steamer. The place is interesting as showing what may be done on the Amazons in a short time by enterprise and industry. A settler in these regions may, if he has the taste and culture to appreciate it, surround himself with much that is attractive in civilized life. Some seventeen years ago Senhor Sepeda established himself at this spot, then a complete wilderness. He has now a very large and pleasant country-house, with a garden in front and walks in the forest around. The interior of the house is commodious and tasteful; and we could not but wish, while we enjoyed Senhor Sepeda's hospitality, that his example might be followed, and that there might be many such homes on the banks of the Amazons. This morning we are again on our way down the river.

February 4th. — We reached Pará to-day, parting, not without regret, from the "Ibicuhy," on board of which we have spent so many pleasant weeks. Before we left the vessel, Captain Faria ordered the carpenter to take down our little pavilion on deck. It had been put up for our accommodation, and had served as our dining-room and our working-room, our shelter from the sun, and our snug retreat in floods of rain.* On arriving in Pará we found ourselves at once at home in the house of our kind friend, Senhor Pimenta Bueno, where we look forward to a pleasant rest from our wanderings. I insert here a letter to the Emperor, written two or three weeks later, and containing a short summary of the scientific work on the Amazons.

Pará, 23 Février, 1866.

Sire: — En arrivant à Pará, au commencement de ce mois j'ai eu le bonheur d'y trouver l'excellente lettre de Votre Majesté, qui m'attendait depuis quelques jours. J'aurais dû y répondre immédiatement ; mais je n'étais pas en état de le faire, tant j'étais accablé de fatigue. Il y a trois ou quatre jours seulement que je commence de nouveau à m'occuper de mes affaires. J'avouerai même que le pressentiment des regrets qui m'auraient poursuivi le reste de mes jours m'a seul empêché de retourner directement aux Etats-Unis. Aujourd'hui encore j'ai de la peine à vaquer aux occupations les plus simples. Et cependant je ne suis pas malade ; je suis seulement épuisé par un travail incessant et par la contemplation tous les jours plus vive et plus impressive des grandeurs et des beautés de cette nature tropicale. J'aurais besoin pour quelque temps de la vue monotone et sombre d'une forêt de sapins.

Que vous êtes bon, Sire, de penser à moi au milieu des affaires vitales qui absorbent votre attention et combien vos procédés sont pleins de délicatesse. Le cadeau de nouvel-an que vous m'annoncez m'enchante. La perspec-

* It is but fitting that I should express here my thanks to Captain Faria for the courteous manner in which he accomplished the task assigned him by the government. He was not only a most hospitable host on board his vessel, but he allowed me to encumber his deck with all kinds of scientific apparatus, and gave me very efficient assistance in collecting. — L. A.

tive de pouvoir ajouter quelques comparaisons des poissons du bassin de l'Uruguay à celles que j'ai déjà faites des espèces de l'Amazone et des fleuves de la côte orientale du Brésil a un attrait tout particulier. Ce sera le premier pas vers la connaissance des types de la zône tempérée dans l'Amérique du Sud. Aussi est-ce avec une impatience croissante que je vois venir le moment où je pourrai les examiner. En attendant, permettez-moi de vous donner un aperçu rapide des résultats obtenus jusqu'à ce jour dans le voyage de l'Amazone.

Je ne reviendrai pas sur ce qu'il y a de surprenant dans la grande variété des espèces de poissons de ce bassin, bien qu'il me soit encore difficile de me familiariser avec l'idée que l'Amazone nourrit à peu-près deux fois plus d'espèces que la Méditerrannée et un nombre plus considérable que l'Océan Atlantique d'un pôle à l'autre. Je ne puis cependant plus dire avec la même précision quel est le nombre exact d'espèces de l'Amazone que nous nous sommes procurées, parceque depuis que je reviens sur mes pas, en descendant le grand fleuve, je vois des poissons prêts à frayer que j'avais vus dans d'autres circonstances et vice versâ, et sans avoir recours aux collections que j'ai faites il y a six mois et qui ne me sont pas accessibles aujourd'hui, il m'est souvent impossible de déterminer de mémoire si ce sont les mêmes espèces ou d'autres qui m'avaient échappé lors de mon premier examen. J'estime cependant que le nombre total des espèces que je possède actuellement dépasse dix-huit cents et atteint peut-être à deux mille. Mais ce n'est pas seulement le nombre des espèces qui surprendra les naturalistes ; le fait qu'elles sont pour la plupart circonscrites dans des limites restreintes est bien plus surprenant encore et ne laissera pas que d'avoir une influence directe sur les idées qui se répandent de nos jours sur l'origine des êtres vivants. Que dans un fleuve comme le Mississippi, qui, du Nord au Sud, passe successivement par les zones froide, tempérée et chaude, qui roule ses eaux tantôt sur une formation géologique, tantôt sur une autre, et traverse des plaines couvertes au Nord d'une végétation presque arctique et au Sud d'une flore subtropicale,—que dans un pareil bassin on rencontre des espèces d'animaux aquatiques différentes, sur différents points de son trajet, ça se comprend dès qu'on s'est habitué à envisager les conditions générales d'existence et le climat en particulier comme la cause première de la diversité que les animaux et les plantes offrent entre eux, dans les différentes localités ; mais que, de Tabatinga au Pará, dans un fleuve où les eaux ne varient ni par leur température, ni par la nature de leur lit, ni par la végétation qui les borde, que dans de pareilles circonstances on rencontre, de distance en distance, des assemblages de poissons complètement distincts les uns des autres, c'est ce qui a lieu d'étonner. Je dirai même que dorénavant cette distribution, qui peut être vérifiée par quiconque voudra s'en donner la peine, doit jeter beaucoup de doute sur l'opinion qui attribue la diversité des êtres vivants aux influences locales.

Un autre côté de ce sujet, encore plus curieux peut-être, est l'intensité avec laquelle la vie s'est manifestée dans ces eaux. Tous les fleuves de l'Europe réunis, depuis le Tage jusqu'au Volga, ne nourissent pas cent cinquante espèces de poissons d'eau douce ; et cependant, dans un petit lac des environs de Manaos, nommé Lago Hyanuary, qui a à peine quatre ou cinq-cents mètres carrés de surface, nous avons découvert plus de deux-cents espèces distinctes, dont la plupart n'ont pas encore été observées ailleurs. Quel contraste !

L'étude du mélange des races humaines qui se croisent dans ces régions m'a aussi beaucoup occupé et je me suis procuré de nombreuses photographies de tous les types que j'ai pu observer. Le principal résultat auquel je suis arrivé est que les *races* se comportent les unes vis-à-vis des autres comme des espèces distinctes ; c. à. d. que les hybrides qui naissent du croisement d'hommes de race différente sont toujours un mélange des deux types primitifs et jamais la simple reproduction des caractères de l'un ou de l'autre des progéniteurs, comme c'est le cas pour les *races* d'animaux domestiques.

Je ne dirai rien de mes autres collections qui ont pour la plupart été faites par mes jeunes compagnons de voyage, plutôt en vue d'enrichir notre musée que de résoudre quelques questions scientifiques. Mais je ne saurais laisser passer cette occasion sans exprimer ma vive reconnaissance pour toutes les facilités que j'ai dues à la bienveillance de Votre Majesté, dans mes explorations. Depuis le Président jusqu'au plus humbles employés des provinces que j'ai parcourues, tous ont rivalisé d'empressement pour me faciliter mon travail et la Compagnie des vapeurs de l'Amazone a été d'une libéralité extrême à mon égard. Enfin, Sire, la générosité avec laquelle vous avez fait mettre un navire de guerre à ma disposition m'a permis de faire des collections qui seraient restées inaccessibles pour moi, sans un moyen de transport aussi vaste et aussi rapide. Permettez-moi d'ajouter que de toutes les faveurs dont Votre Majesté m'a comblé pour ce voyage, la plus précieuse a été la présence du Major Coutinho, dont la familiarité avec tout ce qui regarde l'Amazone a été une source intarissable de renseignements importants et de directions utiles pour éviter des courses oiseuses et la perte d'un temps précieux. L'étendue des connaissances de Coutinho, en ce qui touche l'Amazone, est vraiment encycopédique, et je crois que ce serait un grand service à rendre à la science que de lui fournir l'occasion de rédiger et de publier tout ce qu'il a observé pendant ses visites répétées et prolongées dans cette partie de l'Empire. Sa coopération pendant ce dernier voyage a été des plus laborieuses ; il s'est mis à la zoologie comme si les sciences physiques n'avaient pas été l'objet spécial de ses études, en même temps qu'il a fait par devers lui de nombreuses observations thermométriques, barométriques, et astronomiques, qui ajouteront de bons jalons à ce que l'on possède déjà sur la météorologie et la topographie de ces provinces. C'est ainsi que nous avons les premiers porté le baromètre au milieu des collines d'Almeyrim, de Monte Alégre, et d'Ereré et mesuré leurs sommets les plus élevés.

L'étude de la formation de la vallée de l'Amazone m'a naturellement occupé, bien que secondairement, dès le premier jour que je l'ai abordée.

. . . . . .

Mais il est temps que je finisse cette longue épitre en demandant pardon à Votre Majesté d'avoir mis sa patience à une aussi rude épreuve.

De Votre Majesté le serviteur le plus dévoué et le plus affectueux,

L. AGASSIZ.*

* PARÁ, February 23, 1866.

SIRE :— On arriving at Pará in the beginning of this month, I had the pleasure to find your Majesty's kind letter, which had been awaiting me for several days. I ought to have acknowledged it immediately, but I was not in a condition to do so, being overcome by fatigue. It is only during the last

February 24*th.* — Pará, Nazareth. Our time has passed so quietly here that it gives me nothing to record. Mr. Agassiz has found himself in such absolute need of rest, after having arranged and put in order for transportation to

two or three days that I begin once more to occupy myself as usual. I confess that nothing but the presentiment of regrets which would have pursued me to the end of my days has prevented me from returning directly to the United States. Even now I find it difficult to take up the most simple occupations. And yet I am not ill; I am only exhausted by incessant work, and by the contemplation, each day more vivid and impressive, of the grandeur and beauty of this tropical nature. I need to look for a time upon the sombre and monotonous aspect of a pine forest.

How good you are, Sire, to think of me in the midst of the vital affairs which absorb your attention, and how considerate are your acts! The New Year's present you announce enchants me.* The prospect of being able to add some comparisons of the fishes from the basin of the Uruguay to such as I have already made between the Amazonian species and those of the rivers on the eastern coast of Brazil has a special attraction for me. It will be the first step towards a knowledge of the types of the temperate zone in South America. I wait with increasing impatience for the moment when I shall be able to examine them. In the mean while allow me to give you a rapid sketch of the results thus far obtained in my voyage on the Amazons.

I will not return to the surprising variety of species of fishes contained in this basin, though it is very difficult for me to familiarize myself with the idea that the Amazons nourishes nearly twice as many species as the Mediterranean, and a larger number than the Atlantic, taken from one pole to the other. I can no longer say, however, with precision, what is the exact number of species which we have procured from the Amazons, because, on retracing my steps as I descended the great river, I have seen fishes about to lay their eggs which I had seen at first under other conditions, and *vice versâ*; and without consulting the collections made six months ago, and which are not now accessible to me, it is often impossible for me to determine from memory whether they are the same species, or different ones which escaped my observation in my first examination. However, I estimate the total number of species which I actually possess at eighteen hundred, and it may be

* The Emperor had written to Mr. Agassiz that, during the time when he took command of the Brazilian army on the Rio Grande, he had caused collections of fishes to be made for him from several of the southern rivers.

the United States the collections accumulated, that our intended trip to the island of Marajo has been postponed day after day. Yesterday I witnessed a religious procession in two thousand.* But it is not only the number of species which will astonish naturalists; the fact that they are for the most part circumscribed within definite limits is still more surprising, and cannot but have a direct influence on the ideas now prevalent respecting the origin of living beings. That in a river like the Mississippi, which from the north to the south passes successively through cold, temperate, and warm zones, — whose waters flow sometimes over one geological formation, sometimes over another, and across plains covered at the north by an almost arctic vegetation, and at the south by a sub-tropical flora, — that in such a basin aquatic animals of different species should be met at various points of its course is easily understood by those who are accustomed to consider general conditions of existence, and of climate especially, as the first cause of the difference between animals and plants inhabiting separate localities. But that from Tabatinga to Pará, in a river where the waters differ neither in temperature nor in the nature of their bed, nor in the vegetation along their borders, — that under such circumstances there should be met, from distance to distance, assemblages of fishes completely distinct from each other, is indeed astonishing. I would even say that henceforth this distribution, which may be verified by any one who cares to take the trouble, must throw much doubt on the opinion which attributes the diversity of living beings to local influences. Another side of this subject, still more curious perhaps, is the intensity with which life is manifested in these waters. All the rivers of Europe united, from the Tagus to the Volga, do not nourish one hundred and fifty species of fresh-water fishes; and yet, in a little lake near Manaos, called Lago Hyannuary, the surface of which covers hardly four or five hundred square yards, we have discovered more than two hundred distinct species, the greater part of which have not been observed elsewhere. What a contrast!

The study of the mixture of human races in this region has also occupied me much, and I have procured numerous photographs of all the types which I have been able to observe. The principal result at which I have arrived is, that the *races* bear themselves towards each other as do distinct species; that is to say, that the hybrids, which spring from the crossing of men of different

* To-day I cannot give a more precise account of the final result of my survey. Though all my collections are safely stored in the Museum, every practical zoölogist understands that a critical examination of more than eighty thousand specimens cannot be made in less than several years. — L. A.

Pará, — one of the many festas said to be gradually dying out, and to be already shorn of much of their ancient glory. It represented a scene from the passion of Christ. The

races, are always a mixture of the two primitive types, and never the simple reproduction of the characters of one or the other progenitor, as is the case among the *races* of domestic animals.

I will say nothing of my other collections, which have been made for the most part by my young companions, rather with a view to enrich our Museum than to solve scientific questions. But I cannot allow this occasion to pass without expressing my lively gratitude for all the facilities, in my explorations, which I have owed to the kindness of your Majesty. From the President to the most humble employés of the provinces I have visited, all have competed with each other to render my work more easy; and the steamship company of the Amazons has shown an extreme liberality towards me. Finally, Sire, the generosity with which you have placed at my disposition a vessel of war has allowed me to make collections which, with less ample and rapid means of transport, must have remained utterly inaccessible to me. Permit me to add, that, of all the favors with which your Majesty has crowned this voyage, the most precious has been the presence of Major Coutinho, whose familiarity with all which concerns the Amazons has been an inexhaustible source of important information and of useful directions; by means of which the loss of time in unremunerative excursions has been avoided. His co-operation during this journey has been most laborious; he has applied himself to zoölogy as if the physical sciences had not hitherto been the special object of his study, while at the same time he has made numerous thermometric, barometric, and astronomical observations, which will furnish important additions to what is already known concerning the meteorology and topography of these provinces. We have, for instance, been the first to carry the barometer into the midst of the hills of Almeyrim, of Monte Alégre and Ereré, and to measure their highest summits. The study of the formation of the valley of the Amazons has naturally occupied me, though in a secondary degree, from the first day of my arrival.*

. . . .

But it is time that I should close this long letter, begging your Majesty to pardon me for putting your patience to so hard a trial.

Your Majesty's most humble and most affectionate servant,

L. AGASSIZ.

* The rest of this letter is omitted, as its substance is contained in Chapter XIII., on the Physical History of the Amazons.

life-size figure of the Saviour, sinking under the cross, is borne on a platform through the streets. Little girls, dressed as angels, walk before it, and it is accompanied by numerous dignitaries of the Church. Altars are illuminated in the different churches; the populace, even down to the children, are dressed in black; and the balconies of every house filled with figures in mourning, waiting for the sad procession to pass by.

February 28th. — Off Marajo, in the steamer Tabatinga. All great rivers, as the Nile, the Mississippi, the Ganges, the Danube, have their deltas; but the largest river in the world, the Amazons, is an exception to this rule. What, then, is the geological character of the great island which obstructs its opening into the ocean? This is the question which has made a visit to Marajo of special interest to Mr. Agassiz. Leaving Pará at midnight, we reached the little town of Sourés early this morning. It is a village lying on the southeastern side of the island, and so far seaward that, in the dry season, when the diminished current of the Amazonian waters is overborne by the tides, the water is salt enough to afford excellent sea-bathing, and is resorted to for that purpose by many families from Pará. At this moment, however, the water has not even a brackish character. The only building of any interest in the town is the old Jesuit church, a remnant of the earliest chapter in the civilization of South America. However tinged with ambition and a love of temporal power, the work of the Jesuits in Brazil tended toward the establishment of an organized system of labor, which one cannot but wish had been continued. All that remains of the Jesuit missions goes to prove that they were centres of industry. These men contrived to impart, even to the wandering Indian, some faint reflection of their own persistency and steadfastness of purpose. Farms were connected with all the Indian missions; under the direction of the fathers, the Indians learned something of agriculture, which the Jesuits readily saw to be one of the great civilizing influences in a country so fertile. They introduced a variety of vegetables and grains, and had herds of cattle where cattle now are hardly known. Humboldt, speaking of the destruction of the Jesuit missions, says, in reference to the Indians of Atures, on the Orinoco: "Formerly, being excited to labor by the Jesuits, they did not want for food. The fathers cultivated maize, French beans, and other European vegetables. They even planted sweet oranges and tamarinds round the villages; and they possessed twenty or thirty thousand head of cows and horses in the savannas of Atures and Carichana. . . . . Since the year 1795, the cattle of the Jesuits have entirely disappeared. There now remain as monuments of the ancient cultivation of these countries, and the active industry of the first missionaries, only a few trunks of the orange and tamarind in the savannas, surrounded by wild trees." *

Our walk through the little village of Sourés brought us to the low cliffs on the shore, which we had already seen from the steamer. The same formations prevail all along the coast of this island that we have found everywhere on the banks of the Amazons. Lowest, a well-stratified, rather coarse sandstone, immediately above which, and conformable with it, are finely laminated clays, covered by a crust. Upon this lies the highly ferruginous sandstone, in which an irregular cross stratification frequently alternates with the regular beds; above this, following all the undulations

---

* Humboldt's Personal Narrative, Bohn's Scientific Library, Vol. II. Chap. XX. p. 267.

of its surface, is the well-known reddish sandy clay, with quartz pebbles scattered through its mass, and only here and there faint traces of an indistinct stratification. This afternoon Mr. Agassiz has been again on shore, examining the formation of both banks of the Igarapé Grande, the river at the mouth of which stands the town of Sourés. He has returned delighted with the result of his day's work, having not only obtained the most complete evidence that the geological formation of Marajo corresponds exactly with that of the Amazonian Valley, but having also obtained some very important data with respect to the present encroachments of the sea upon the shore. He found upon the beach, partially covered by sea-sand, the remains of a forest which evidently grew in a peat-bog, and which the ocean is gradually laying bare.

February 20th. — Early this morning we crossed the Pará River, and anchored at the entrance of the bay within which stands the town of Vigia. We landed, and while the boatmen were dragging the net, we wandered along the beach, which is bordered by thick forest, now full of flowers. Here we found the same geological formations as on the Marajo shore, and on the beach the counterpart of the ancient forest which Mr. Agassiz unearthed yesterday on the opposite coast. There can hardly be more convincing evidence that the rivers which empty into the Amazons near its mouth, like all those higher up, as well as the main stream itself, have cut their way through identical formations, which were once continuous. Evidently these remains of forests on the beaches of Vigia Bay and at the mouth of the Igarapé Grande are parts of one forest, formerly uninterrupted and covering the whole of the intervening space now filled by the so-called Pará River. We followed the beach to the entrance of an igarapé, which here opens into the river, and which looked most tempting with the morning shadows darkening its cool recesses. As the boatmen had not been very successful in fishing, I proposed we should put their services to better use and row up this inviting stream. To this day, though I have become accustomed to these forest water-paths and have had so many excursions in them, they have lost none of their charm. I never see one without longing to follow its picturesque windings into the depths of the wood; and to me the igarapé remains the most beautiful and the most characteristic feature of the Amazonian scenery. This one of Vigia was especially pretty. Clumps of the light, exquisitely graceful Assai palm shot up everywhere from the denser forest; here and there the drooping bamboo, never seen in the higher Amazons, dipped its feathery branches into the water, covered sometimes to their very tips with purple bloom of convolvulus; yellow Bignonias carried their golden clusters to the very summits of some of the more lofty trees; while white-flowering myrtles and orange-colored mallows bordered the stream. Life abounded in this quiet retreat. Birds and butterflies were numerous; and we saw an immense number of crabs of every variety of color and size upon the margin of the water. However, it was not so easy to catch them as it seemed. They would sit quietly on the trunks of all the old trees or decaying logs projecting from the bank, apparently waiting to be taken; but the moment we approached them, however cautiously, they vanished like lightning either under the water or into some crevice near by. Notwithstanding their nimbleness, however, Mr. Agassiz succeeded in making a considerable collection. We saw also an immense army of caterpillars, evidently following some concerted plan of action. They were descending the trunk of a large tree in a solid phalanx about two handbreadths in width, and six or eight feet in length; no doubt coming down to make their chrysalids in the sand. We returned to the steamer at ten o'clock; and, after breakfast, finding our anchorage-ground somewhat rough as the tide came in, we went a little higher up, and entered the Bahia do Sul. Here again we went on shore to see the net drawn, this time more successfully. We should have had a delightful walk on the beach again, had it not been for hosts of minute flies which hovered about us, and had a power of stinging quite disproportionate to their size. On returning we met with an unforeseen difficulty. The tide had been falling during our walk, and the canoe could not approach the beach within several yards. The gentlemen plunged in, and walked out over knees in water; while the boatmen made a chair of their arms and carried me through the surf.

March 5th. — Our excursion in the harbor closed with a visit to the small island of Tatuatuba, distant about six miles from Pará. In order to examine the shores, we made the circuit of the island on foot. Here again the same geological structure presented itself; and there was one spot in particular where the sharp, vertical cut of the bank facing the beach presented an admirable section of the formations so characteristic of the Amazonian Valley; the red, sandy clay of the upper deposit filling in all the undulations and inequalities of the sandstone below, the surface of which was remarkably irregular. The sea is making great encroachments on the shore of this island. Senhor Figueiredo, who lives here with his family and by whom we were received with much hospitality, told us that during the last eighteen or twenty years, the beach had receded considerably in some places; the high-water line being many yards beyond its former limit. The result of this excursion has shown that, with the exception of some low mud-islands nearly level with the water, all the harbor islands lying in the mouth of the Amazons are, geologically speaking, parts of the Amazonian Valley, having the same structure. They were, no doubt, formerly continuous with the shore, but are separated now, partly by the fresh waters cutting their way through the land to the ocean, partly by the progress of the sea itself.

March 24th.— Our quiet life at Nazareth, though full of enjoyment for tired travellers, affords little material for a journal. A second excursion along the coast has furnished Mr. Agassiz with new evidence of the rapid changes in the outline of the shore, produced by the encroachment of the sea. So fast is this going on that some of the public works near the coast are already endangered by the advance of the ocean upon the land. During the past week he has been especially occupied in directing the work of a photographist employed by Senhor Pimenta Bueno, who, with his usual liberality towards the scientific objects of the expedition, is collecting in this way the portraits of some remarkable palms and other trees about his house and grounds. One of the most striking is a huge Sumauméra, with buttressed trunk. These buttresses start at a distance of about eight or ten feet from the ground, spreading gradually toward the base; they are from ten to twelve feet in depth. The lower part of the trunk is thus divided into open compartments, sometimes so large that two or three persons can stand within them. This disposition to throw out flanks or wings is not confined to one kind of tree, but occurs in many families; it seems, indeed, a characteristic feature of forest vegetation here. Occasionally the buttresses partially separate from the main trunk, remaining attached to it only at the point from which they start, so that they look like

Buttressed Tree (Eriodendrum Sumauma).

distinct supports propping the tree. I copy here an extract from Mr. Agassiz's notes upon the vegetation of the Amazons, in which allusion is made to the Sumaumèra.

"Any one coming from the North to the Tropics, if he has been in the habit of observing the vegetation about him, even without having made botany a special study, is, in a measure, prepared to appreciate the resemblances and the differences between plants of the tropical and those of the temperate regions. An acquaintance with the Robinia (Locust-trees), for instance, or with the large shrub-like Lotus, and other woody Leguminosæ, will enable him to recognize the numerous representatives of that family, forming so large a part of the equatorial vegetation; and, even should he never have seen specimens of the Mimosa in gardens or hot-houses, their delicate, susceptible foliage will make them known to him; he cannot fail to be struck with the inexhaustible combinations and forms of their pinnate leaves, as well as with the variety in their tints of green, the diversity in their clusters of leaves and in their pods and seeds. But there are families with which he fancies himself equally familiar, the tropical representatives of which will never seem to him like old acquaintances. Thus the tree which furnishes the Indian rubber belongs to the Milk-weed family. Every one knows the Milk-weeds of the North, to be seen, as humble herbs, all along the roadsides, on the edges of our woods and in the sands of our beaches. Yet on the Amazons, the Euphorbiaceæ, so small and unobtrusive with us, assume the form of colossal trees, constituting a considerable part of its strange and luxuriant forest-growth. The giant of the Amazonian woods, whose majestic flat crown towers over all other trees, while its white trunk stands out in striking relief from the surrounding mass of green (the Sumauméra), is allied to our mallows. Some of the most characteristic trees of the river-shore belong to these two families. Our paleontologists who attempt to restore the forests of older geological times should keep in mind this fact of the striking contrasts presented under different latitudes by the same families. Of course the equatorial regions teem with plants and trees belonging to families either entirely unknown or but poorly represented in more temperate latitudes; and these distinct groups naturally arrest the attention of the botanist, and perhaps awaken his interest more than those with which he is already familiar under other forms. But, while these different families are recognized as distinct, and no doubt deserve to be considered by themselves as natural groups, I believe that much might be learned of the deeper relations of plants by studying, not only the representatives of the same families in different latitudes, such as the Mimosas and the Milk-weeds, but also what I may call botanical equivalents,—groups which balance each other in the different climatic zones. This idea is suggested to me by my zoölogical studies in the Amazons, which have led me to perceive new relations between the animals of the temperate and the tropical zone: it seems probable that corresponding relations should exist in the vegetable world also. Struck, for instance, by the total absence of sturgeons, perches, pickerels, trouts, carps and other white fishes, cusks, sculpins, &c., I have asked myself, while studying the fishes of the Amazons, what analogy could exist between those of our Western rivers and those of the tropics, as well as between the latter and those of the intermediate latitudes. Looking at them with this view, I have been surprised to find how closely related the Goniodonts are to the Sturgeons; so much so, that the Loricariæ may be considered as genuine Sturgeons, with more extensive shields upon the body. I am satisfied also that the Cychla is a perch to all intents and purposes, that the Acaras are Sunfishes, the Xiphorhamphus (Pirá pucu) Pickerels, and the Curimatas genuine Carps. Now, may not a similar relation exist between the families of plants belonging to the North and those forming the most prominent vegetation of the South? What are the tropical trees which take the place of our elms, maples, lindens? By what families are our oaks, chestnuts, willows, poplars, represented under the burning sun of the equinoctial regions? The Rosaceæ in the temperate and the Myrtaceæ in the tropical regions seem to me such botanical equivalents. The family of Rosaceæ gives to the North its pears, its apples, its peaches, its cherries, its plums, its almonds; in short, all the most delicious fruits of the Old World, as well as its most beautiful flowers. The trees of this family, by their foliage, play a distinguished part in the vegetation of the temperate zone, and impart to it a character of their own. The Myrtaceæ give to the South its guavas, its pitangas, its araçàs, the juicy plum-like fruit of the swamp-myrtles, many of its nuts, and other excellent fruits. This family, including the Melastomaceæ, abounds in flowering shrubs, like the purple Queresma and many others not less beautiful; and some of its representatives, such as the Sapucaia and the Brazilian nut-tree, rise to the height of towering trees. Both of these families sink to insignificance in the one zone, while they assume a dignified port and perform an important part in the other. If this investigation be extended to the shrubs and humbler plants, I believe the botanist who undertakes it will reap a rich harvest."

The day after to-morrow we leave Pará in the Santa Cruz for Ceará. It will be like leaving a sort of home to say good by to our kind friends in the Rua de Nazareth. We have become attached to this neighborhood also from its beauty. The wide street, bordered for two or three miles with mangueiras, leads into the wooded country, where many a narrow green path in the forest tempts one to long rambles. One of these paths has been a favorite walk of mine on account of the beauty and luxuriance of the vegetation, making some parts of it shady even at noonday. I have often followed it for two or three miles in the early morning, between six and eight o'clock, when the verdant walls on either side are still fresh and dewy. Beautiful as it is, it leads to one of the saddest of all abodes. For a long time I could not understand why this lane was always in such good condition, the heavy rains making unfrequented forest-paths almost impassable in the wet season. I found on inquiry that it led to a hospital for lepers, and was kept in good repair because the various stores and supplies for the hospital were constantly carried over it. The prevalence of leprosy has made it necessary to provide separate establishments for its victims; and both at Pará and Santarem, where it is still more common, there are hospitals devoted exclusively to this purpose. This terrible disease is not confined wholly to the lower classes, and where it occurs in families whose circumstances are good the invalid is often kept at home under the care of his own friends. Bates states that leprosy is supposed to be incurable, and also adds that, during his eleven years' residence on the Amazons, he has never known a foreigner to be attacked by it. We have, however, been told by a very intelligent German physician in Rio de Janeiro, that he has known several cases of it among his own countrymen there, and has been so fortunate as to effect permanent cures in some instances. He says it is a mistake to suppose that it does not yield to treatment when taken in time, and the statistics of the disease show that, where there are good physicians, it is found to be gradually disappearing.

We must not leave Pará without alluding to our evening concerts from the adjoining woods and swamps. When I first heard this strange confusion of sounds, I thought it came from a crowd of men shouting loudly, though at a little distance. To my surprise, I found that the rioters were the frogs and toads in the neighborhood. I hardly know how to describe this Babel of woodland noises; and if I could do it justice, I am afraid my account would hardly be believed. At moments it seems like the barking of dogs, then like the calling of many voices on different keys, but all loud, rapid, excited, full of emphasis and variety. I think these frogs, like ours, must be silent at certain seasons of the year; for, on our first visit to Pará, we were not struck by this singular music, with which the woods now resound at nightfall.

NOTE. — Before leaving the Amazons, I wish to acknowledge attentions received from several friends, whose names do not appear in the narrative.

To Senhor Danin, Chef de Police at Pará, I was indebted for valuable Indian curiosities, and for specimens of other kinds; to Doctor Malcher for a collection of birds; to Senhor Penna for important additions to my collection of fishes; to Senhor Laitaō da Cunha for aid in collecting, and for many introductions to persons of influence along our route; and to Mr. Kaulfuss, a German resident at Pará, for fossils from the Andes.

I have to thank Mr. James Bond, United States Consul at Pará, for unwearied efforts in my behalf during the whole time of my stay in the Amazons. He supplied me with alcohol; received the collections on their arrival at Pará; examined the cases and barrels, causing those which were defective to be repaired, that they might reach their destination in safety, and finally despatched them to the United States, free of charge, on board sailing-vessels in which he had an interest. We owe it in great degree to him that our immense Amazonian collections arrived in Cambridge in good condition, suffering little loss or injury in the process of transportation. — L. A.

CHAPTER XIII.

PHYSICAL HISTORY OF THE AMAZONS.

DRIFT ABOUT RIO DE JANEIRO. — DECOMPOSITION OF UNDERLYING ROCK. — DIFFERENT ASPECT OF GLACIAL PHENOMENA IN DIFFERENT CONTINENTS. — FERTILITY OF THE DRIFT. — GEOLOGICAL OBSERVATIONS OF MESSRS. HARTT AND ST. JOHN. — CORRESPONDENCE OF DEPOSITS ALONG THE COAST WITH THOSE OF RIO AND THOSE OF THE VALLEY OF THE AMAZONS. — PRIMITIVE FORMATION OF THE VALLEY. — FIRST KNOWN CHAPTER OF ITS HISTORY. — CRETACEOUS FOSSIL FISHES. — FORMER EXTENT OF THE SOUTH-AMERICAN COAST. — CRETACEOUS FOSSILS FROM THE RIO PURUS. — COMPARISON BETWEEN NORTH AND SOUTH AMERICA. — GEOLOGICAL FORMATIONS ALONG THE BANKS OF THE AMAZONS. — FOSSIL LEAVES. — CLAYS AND SANDSTONES. — HILLS OF ALMEYRIM. — MONTE ALÉGRE. — SITUATION AND SCENERY. — SERRA ERERÉ. — COMPARISON WITH SWISS SCENERY. — BOULDERS OF ERERÉ. — ANCIENT THICKNESS OF AMAZONIAN DEPOSITS. — DIFFERENCE BETWEEN DRIFT OF THE AMAZONS AND THAT OF RIO. — INFERENCES DRAWN FROM THE PRESENT CONDITION OF THE DEPOSITS. — IMMENSE EXTENT OF SANDSTONE FORMATION. — NATURE AND ORIGIN OF THESE DEPOSITS. — REFERRED TO THE ICE-PERIOD. — ABSENCE OF GLACIAL MARKS. — GLACIAL EVIDENCE OF ANOTHER KIND. — CHANGES IN THE OUTLINE OF THE SOUTH-AMERICAN COAST. — SOURÉ. — IGARAPÉ GRANDE. — VIGIA. — BAY OF BRAGANZA. — ANTICIPATION.

A FEW days before we left Pará, Senhor Pimenta Bueno invited his friends and acquaintances, who had expressed a wish to hear Mr. Agassiz's views on the geological character of the Amazonian Valley, to meet at his house in the evening for that purpose. The guests were some two hundred in number, and the whole affair was very unceremonious, assuming rather the character of a meeting for conversation or discussion than that of an audience collected to hear a studied address. The substance of this talk or lecture, as subsequently written out by Mr. Agassiz, afterward appeared in the Atlantic Monthly, and is inserted here, with some few alterations under the head of a separate chapter. The reader will find occasional repetitions of facts already stated in the earlier part of the narrative; but they are retained for the sake of giving a complete and consistent review of the subject at this point of our journey, where it became possible to compare the geological structure of the Amazonian Valley with that of the southern provinces of Brazil and of those bordering on the Atlantic coast.

The existence of a glacial period, however much derided when first announced, is now a recognized fact. The divergence of opinion respecting it is limited to a question of extent; and after my recent journey in the Amazons, I am led to add a new chapter to the strange history of glacial phenomena, taken from the southern hemisphere, and even from the tropics themselves.

I am prepared to find that the statement of this new phase of the glacial period will awaken among my scientific colleagues an opposition even more violent than that by which the first announcement of my views on this subject was met. I am, however, willing to bide my time; feeling sure that, as the theory of the ancient extension of glaciers in Europe has gradually come to be accepted by geologists, so will the existence of like phenomena, both in North and South America, during the same epoch, be recognized sooner or later as part of a great series of physical events extending over the whole globe. Indeed, when the ice-period is fully understood, it will be seen that the absurdity lies in supposing that climatic conditions so different could be limited to a small portion of the world's surface. If the geological winter existed at all, it must have been cosmic; and it is quite as rational to look for its traces in the Western as in the Eastern hemisphere, to the south of the equator as to the north of it. Impressed by this wider view of the subject, confirmed by a number of unpublished investigations which I have made during the last three or four years in the United States, I came to South America, expecting to find in the tropical regions new evidences of a bygone glacial period, though, of course, under different aspects. Such a result seemed to me the logical sequence of what I had already observed in Europe and in North America.

On my arrival in Rio de Janeiro, — the port at which I first landed in Brazil, — my attention was immediately attracted by a very peculiar formation consisting of an ochraceous, highly ferruginous, sandy clay. During a stay of three months in Rio, whence I made many excursions into the neighboring country, I had opportunities of studying this deposit, both in the province of Rio de Janeiro and in the adjoining province of Minas Geraes. I found that it rested everywhere upon the undulating surfaces of the solid rocks in place, was almost entirely destitute of stratification, and contained a variety of pebbles and boulders. The pebbles were chiefly quartz, sometimes scattered indiscriminately throughout the deposit, sometimes lying in a seam between it and the rock below; while the boulders were either sunk in its mass, or resting loosely on the surface. At Tijuca, a few miles out of the city of Rio, among the picturesque hills lying to the southwest of it, these phenomena may be seen in great perfection. Near Bennett's Hotel there are a great number of erratic boulders, having no connection whatever with the rock in place; and also a bluff of this superficial deposit studded with boulders, resting above the partially stratified metamorphic rock.* Other excellent opportunities for observing this formation, also within easy reach from the city, are afforded along the whole line of the Dom Pedro Segundo Railroad, where the cuts expose admirable sections, showing the red, unstratified, homogeneous mass of sandy clay resting above the solid rock, and often divided from it by a thin bed of pebbles. There can be no doubt, in the mind of any one familiar with similar facts observed in other parts of the world, that this is one of the many forms of drift connected with glacial action. I was, however, far from anticipating, when I first met it in the neighborhood of Rio, that I should afterwards find it spreading over the surface of the country from north to south and from east to west, with a continuity which gives legible connection to the whole geological history of the continent.

It is true that the extensive decomposition of the underlying rock, penetrating sometimes to a considerable depth, makes it often difficult to distinguish between it and the drift; and the problem is made still more puzzling by the fact that the surface of the drift, when baked by exposure to the hot sun, often assumes the appearance of decomposed rock, so that great care is required for a correct interpretation of the facts. A little practice, however, trains the eye to read these appearances aright; and I may say that I have learned to recognize everywhere the limit between the two formations. There is indeed one safe guide, namely, the un-

---

* See Chapter III. p. 86.

dulating line, reminding one of *roches moutonnées*,* and marking the irregular surface of the rock on which the drift was accumulated; whatever modifications the one or the other may have undergone, this line seems never to disappear. Another deceptive feature, arising from the frequent disintegration of the rocks and from the brittle character of some of them, is the presence of loose fragments, which simulate erratic boulders, but are in fact only detached masses of the rock in place. A careful examination of their structure, however, will at once show the geologist whether they belong where they are found, or have been brought from a distance to their present resting-place.

But, while the features to which I have alluded are unquestionably drift phenomena, they present in their wider extension, and especially in the northern part of Brazil, some phases of glacial action hitherto unobserved. Just as the investigation of the ice-period in the United States has shown us that ice-fields may move over open level plains, as well as along the slopes of mountain valleys, so does a study of the same class of facts in South America reveal new and unlooked-for features in the history of the ice-period. Some will say that the fact of the advance of ice-fields over an open country is by no means established, inasmuch as many geologists believe all the so-called glacial traces — viz. striæ, furrows, polish, etc., found in the United States — to have been made by floating icebergs at a time when the continent was sub-

---

* The name consecrated by De Saussure to designate certain rocks in Switzerland which have had their surfaces rounded under the action of the glaciers. Their gently swelling outlines are thought to resemble sheep resting on the ground, and for this reason the people in the Alps call them *roches moutonnées*.

z

merged. To this I can only answer that, in the State of Maine, I have followed, compass in hand, the same set of furrows, running from north to south in one unvarying line, over a surface of one hundred and thirty miles, from the Katahdin Iron Range to the sea-shore.* These furrows follow all the inequalities of the country, ascending ranges of hills varying from twelve to fifteen hundred feet in height, and descending into the intervening valleys only two or three hundred feet above the sea, or sometimes even on a level with it. I take it to be impossible that a floating mass of ice should travel onward in one rectilinear direction, turning neither to the right nor to the left, for such a distance. Equally impossible would it be for a detached mass of ice, swimming on the surface of the water, or even with its base sunk considerably below it, to furrow in a straight line the summits and sides of the hills, and the bottoms of the intervening valleys. It would be carried over the inequalities of the country without touching the lowest depressions. Instead of ascending the mountains, it would remain stranded against any elevation which rose greatly above its own base, and, if caught between two parallel ridges, would float up and down between them. Moreover, the action of solid, unbroken ice, moving over the ground in immediate contact with it, is so different from that of floating ice-rafts or icebergs that, though the latter have unquestionably dropped erratic boulders, and made furrows and striæ on the surface where they happened to be grounded, these phenomena will easily be distinguished from the more connected tracks of glaciers, or extensive sheets of ice, resting directly upon the face of the country and advancing over it.

* See "Glacial Phenomena in Maine," Atlantic Monthly, 1866.

There seems thus far to be an inextricable confusion in the ideas of many geologists as to the respective action of currents, icebergs, and glaciers. It is time that they should learn to distinguish between classes of facts so different from each other, and so easily recognized after the discrimination has once been made. As to the southward movement of an immense field of ice, extending over the whole North, it seems inevitable, the moment we admit that snow may accumulate around the pole in such quantities as to initiate a pressure radiating in every direction. Snow, alternately thawing and freezing, must, like water, find its level at last. A sheet of snow ten or fifteen thousand feet in thickness, extending all over the northern and southern portions of the globe, must necessarily lead, in the end, to the formation of a northern and southern cap of ice, moving toward the equator.

I have spoken of Tijuca and the Dom Pedro Railroad as favorable localities for studying the peculiar southern drift; but one meets it in every direction. A sheet of drift, consisting of the same homogeneous, unstratified paste, and containing loose materials of all sorts and sizes, covers the country. It is of very uneven thickness, — sometimes thrown into relief, as it were, by the surrounding denudations, and rising into hills; sometimes reduced to a thin layer; sometimes, as, for instance, on steep slopes, washed entirely away, leaving the bare face of the rock exposed. It has, however, remained comparatively undisturbed on some very abrupt ascents; as may be seen on the Corcovado, along the path leading up the mountain, where there are some very fine banks of drift, the more striking from the contrast of their deep-red color with the surrounding vegetation. I have myself followed this sheet of drift from Rio de Janeiro to the top of the Serra do Mar, where, just outside the pretty town of Petropolis, the river Piabanha may be seen flowing between banks of drift, in which it has excavated its bed; thence I have traced it along the beautiful macadamized road leading to Juiz de Fora in the province of Minas Geraes, and beyond this to the farther side of the Serra da Babylonia. Throughout this whole tract of country the drift may be seen along the roadside, in immediate contact with the native crystalline rock. The fertility of the land, also, is a guide to the presence of drift. Wherever it lies thickest over the surface, there are the most flourishing coffee-plantations; and I believe that a more systematic regard to this fact would have a most beneficial influence upon the agricultural interests of the country. No doubt the fertility arises from the great variety of chemical elements contained in the drift, and the kneading process it has undergone beneath the gigantic ice-plough, — a process which makes glacial drift everywhere the most fertile soil. Since my return from the Amazons, my impression as to the general distribution of these phenomena has been confirmed by the reports of some of my assistants, who have been travelling in other parts of the country. Mr. Frederick C. Hartt, accompanied by Mr. Copeland, one of the volunteer aids of the expedition, has been making collections and geological observations in the province of Spiritu Santo, in the valley of the Rio Doce, and afterwards in the valley of the Mucury. He informs me that he has found everywhere the same sheet of red, unstratified clay, with pebbles and occasional boulders overlying the rock in place. Mr. Orestes St. John, who, taking the road through the interior, has visited, with the same objects in view, the valleys of the Rio San Francisco and the Rio das Velhas, and also the valley of Piauhy, gives the same account, with the exception that he found no erratic boulders in these more northern regions. The rarity of erratic boulders, not only in the deposits of the Amazons proper, but in those of the whole region which may be considered as the Amazonian basin, is accounted for, as we shall see hereafter, by the mode of their formation. The observations of Mr. Hartt and Mr. St. John are the more valuable, because I had employed them both, on our first arrival in Rio, in making geological surveys of different sections on the Dom Pedro Railroad, so that they had a great familiarity with those formations before starting on their separate journeys. Recently, Mr. St. John and myself met in Pará on our return from our respective explorations, and I have had an opportunity of comparing on the spot his geological sections from the valley of the Piauhy with the Amazonian deposits. There can be no doubt of the absolute identity of the formations in these valleys.

Having arranged the work of my assistants, and sent several of them to collect and make geological examinations in other directions, I myself, with the rest of my companions, proceeded up the coast to Pará. I was surprised to find at every step of my progress the same geological phenomena which had met me at Rio. It was my friend, Major Coutinho, already an experienced Amazonian traveller, who first told me that this formation continued through the whole valley of the Amazons, and was also to be found on all of its affluents which he had visited, although he had never thought of referring it to so recent a period. And here let me say that the facts I now state are by no means exclusively the result of my own investigations. They are in great part due to Major

Coutinho, a member of the Brazilian government corps of engineers, who, by the kindness of the Emperor, was associated with me in my Amazonian expedition. I can truly say that he has been my good genius throughout the whole journey, saving me; by his previous knowledge of the ground, from the futile and misdirected expenditure of means and time often inevitable in a new country, where one is imperfectly acquainted both with the people and their language. We have worked together in this investigation; my only advantage over him being my greater familiarity with like phenomena in Europe and North America, and consequent readiness in the practical handling of the facts and in perceiving their connection. Major Coutinho's assertion, that on the banks of the Amazons I should find the same red, unstratified clay as in Rio and along the southern coast, seemed to me at first almost incredible, impressed as I was with the generally received notions as to the ancient character of the Amazonian deposits, referred by Humboldt to the Devonian, and by Martius to the Triassic period, and considered by all travellers to be at least as old as the Tertiaries. The result, however, confirmed his report, at least so far as the component materials of the formation are concerned; but, as will be seen hereafter, the mode of their deposition, and the time at which it took place, have not been the same at the north and south; and this difference of circumstances has modified the aspect of a formation essentially the same throughout. At first sight, it would indeed appear that this formation, as it exists in the valley of the Amazons, is identical with that of Rio; but it differs from it in the rarity of its boulders, and in showing occasional signs of stratification. It is also everywhere underlaid by coarse, well-stratified deposits, resembling somewhat the *Recife* of Bahia and Pernambuco; whereas the unstratified drift of the south rests immediately upon the undulating surface of whatever rock happens to make the foundation of the country, whether stratified or crystalline. The peculiar sandstone on which the Amazonian clay rests exists nowhere else. Before proceeding, however, to describe the Amazonian deposits in detail, I ought to say something of the nature and origin of the valley itself.

The valley of the Amazons was first sketched out by the elevation of two tracts of land; namely, the plateau of Guiana on the north, and the central plateau of Brazil on the south. It is probable that, at the time these two table-lands were lifted above the sea-level, the Andes did not exist, and the ocean flowed between them through an open strait. It would seem (and this is a curious result of modern geological investigations) that the portions of the earth's surface earliest raised above the ocean have trended from east to west. The first tract of land lifted above the waters in North America was also a long continental island, running from Newfoundland almost to the present base of the Rocky Mountains. This tendency may be attributed to various causes, — to the rotation of the earth, the consequent depression of its poles, and the breaking of its crust along the lines of greatest tension thus produced. At a later period, the upheaval of the Andes took place, closing the western side of this strait, and thus transforming it into a gulf, open only toward the east. Little or nothing is known of the earlier stratified deposits resting against the crystalline masses first uplifted along the borders of the Amazonian Valley. There is here no sequence, as in North

America, of Azoic, Silurian, Devonian, and Carboniferous formations, shored up against each other by the gradual upheaval of the continent; although, unquestionably, older palæozoic and secondary beds underlie, here and there, the later formations. Indeed, Major Coutinho has found palæozoic deposits, with characteristic Brachiopods, in the valley of the Rio Tapajos, at the first cascade, and carboniferous deposits have been noticed along the Rio Guaporé and the Rio Mamoré. But the first chapter in the valley's geological history about which we have connected and trustworthy data is that of the cretaceous period. It seems certain, that, at the close of the secondary age, the whole Amazonian basin became lined with a cretaceous deposit, the margins of which crop out at various localities on its borders. They have been observed along its southern limits, on its western outskirts along the Andes, in Venezuela along the shore-line of mountains, and also in certain localities near its eastern edge. I well remember that one of the first things which awakened my interest in the geology of the Amazonian Valley was the sight of some cretaceous fossil fishes from the province of Ceará. These fossil fishes were collected by Mr. George Gardner, to whom science is indebted for the most extensive information yet obtained respecting the geology of that part of Brazil. In this connection, let me say that I shall speak of the provinces of Ceará, Piauhy, and Maranham as belonging geologically to the valley of the Amazons, though their shore is bathed by the ocean and their rivers empty directly into the Atlantic. But I entertain no doubt that, at an earlier period, the northeastern coast of Brazil stretched much farther seaward than in our day; so far, indeed, that in those times the rivers of all these provinces must have been tributaries of the Amazons in its eastward course. The evidence for this conclusion is substantially derived from the identity of the deposits in the valleys belonging to these provinces with those of the valleys through which the actual tributaries of the Amazons flow; as, for instance, the Tocantins, the Xingu, the Tapajos, the Madeira, etc. Besides the fossils above alluded to from the eastern borders of this ancient basin, I have had recently another evidence of its cretaceous character from its southern region. Mr. William Chandless, on his return from a late journey on the Rio Purus, presented me with a series of fossil remains of the highest interest, and undoubtedly belonging to the cretaceous period. They were collected by himself on the Rio Aquiry, an affluent of the Rio Purus. Most of them were found in place between the tenth and eleventh degrees of south latitude, and the sixty-seventh and sixty-ninth degrees of west longitude from Greenwich, in localities varying from four hundred and thirty to six hundred and fifty feet above the sea-level. There are among them remains of Mosasaurus, and of fishes closely allied to those already represented by Faujas in his description of Maestricht, and characteristic, as is well known to geological students, of the most recent cretaceous period.

Thus in its main features the valley of the Amazons, like that of the Mississippi, is a cretaceous basin. This resemblance suggests a further comparison between the twin continents of North and South America. Not only is their general form the same, but their framework, as we may call it, — that is, the lay of their great mountain-chains and of their table-lands, with the extensive intervening depressions, — presents a striking similarity. Indeed, a zoölogist, accustomed to trace a like structure under variously modified animal forms, cannot but have his homological studies recalled to his mind by the coincidence between certain physical features in the northern and southern parts of the Western hemisphere. And yet here, as throughout all nature, these correspondences are combined with a distinctness of individualization which leaves its respective character, not only to each continent as a whole, but also to the different regions circumscribed within its borders. In both, however, the highest mountain-chains, the Rocky Mountains and the Western Coast Range, with their wide intervening table-land in North America, and the chain of the Andes, with its lesser plateaux in South America, run along the western coast; both have a great eastern promontory, Newfoundland in the Northern continent, and Cape St. Roque in the Southern: and though the resemblance between the inland elevations is perhaps less striking, yet the Canadian range, the White Mountains, and the Alleghanies may very fairly be compared to the table-lands of Guiana and Brazil, and the Serra do Mar. Similar correspondences may be traced among the river-systems. The Amazons and the St. Lawrence, though so different in dimensions, remind us of each other by their trend and geographical position; and while the one is fed by the largest river-system in the world, the other drains the most extensive lake surfaces known to exist in immediate contiguity. The Orinoco, with its bay, recalls Hudson's Bay and its many tributaries, and the Rio Magdalena may be said to be the South-American Mackenzie; while the Rio de la Plata represents geographically our Mississippi, and the Paraguay recalls the Missouri. The Parana may be compared to the Ohio; the Pilcomayo,

Vermejo, and Salado rivers, to the river Platte, the Arkansas, and the Red River in the United States; while the rivers farther south, emptying into the Gulf of Mexico, represent the rivers of Patagonia and the southern parts of the Argentine Republic. Not only is there this general correspondence between the mountain elevations and the river-systems, but as the larger river-basins of North America — those of the St. Lawrence, the Mississippi, and the Mackenzie — meet in the low tracts extending along the foot of the Rocky Mountains, so do the basins of the Amazons, the Rio de la Plata, and the Orinoco join each other along the eastern slope of the Andes.

But while in geographical homology the Amazons compares with the St. Lawrence, and the Mississippi with the Rio de la Plata, the Mississippi and the Amazons, as has been said, resemble each other in their local geological character. They have both received a substratum of cretaceous beds, above which are accumulated more recent deposits, so that, in their most prominent geological features, both may be considered as cretaceous basins, containing extensive deposits of a very recent age. Of the history of the Amazonian Valley during the periods immediately following the Cretaceous, we know little or nothing. Whether the Tertiary deposits are hidden under the more modern ones; or whether they are wholly wanting, the basin having, perhaps, been raised above the sea-level before that time; or whether they have been swept away by the tremendous inundations in the valley, which have certainly destroyed a great part of the cretaceous deposit, — they have never been observed in any part of the Amazonian basin. Whatever Tertiary deposits are represented in geological maps of this region are so marked in consequence of an incorrect identification of strata belonging, in fact, to a much more recent period.

A minute and extensive survey of the valley of the Amazons is by no means an easy task, and its difficulty is greatly increased by the fact that the lower formations are only accessible on the river margins during the *vasante*, or dry season, when the waters shrink in their beds, leaving a great part of their banks exposed. It happened that the first three or four months of my journey (August, September, October, and November) were those when the waters are lowest, — reaching their minimum in September and October, and beginning to rise again in November, — so that I had an excellent opportunity, in ascending the river, of observing its geological structure. Throughout its whole length, three distinct geological formations may be traced, the two lower of which have followed in immediate succession, and are conformable with one another, while the third rests unconformably upon them, following all the inequalities of the greatly denudated surface presented by the second formation. Notwithstanding this seeming interruption in the sequence of these deposits, the third, as we shall presently see, belongs to the same series, and was accumulated in the same basin. The lowest set of beds of the whole series is rarely visible; but it seems everywhere to consist of sandstone, or even of loose sands well stratified, the coarser materials lying invariably below, and the finer above. Upon this lower set of beds rests everywhere an extensive deposit of fine laminated clays, varying in thickness, but frequently dividing into layers as thin as a sheet of paper. In some localities they exhibit, in patches, an extraordinary variety of beautiful colors, — pink, orange, crimson, yellow, gray, blue, and also black and white. It is from these beds that the Indians prepare their paints. These clay deposits assume occasionally a peculiar appearance, and one which might mislead the observer as to their true nature. When their surface has been long exposed to the action of the atmosphere and to the heat of the burning sun, they look so much like clay-slates of the oldest geological epochs that, at first sight, I took them for primary slates, my attention being attracted to them by a regular cleavage as distinct as that of the most ancient clay-slates. And yet at Tonantins, on the banks of the Solimoens, in a locality where their exposed surfaces had this primordial appearance, I found in these very beds a considerable amount of well-preserved leaves, the character of which proves their recent origin. These leaves do not even indicate as ancient a period as the Tertiaries, but resemble so closely the vegetation of to-day that I have no doubt, when examined by competent authority, they will be identified with living plants. The presence of such an extensive clay formation, stretching over a surface of more than three thousand miles in length and about seven hundred in breadth, is not easily explained under any ordinary circumstances. The fact that it is so thoroughly laminated shows that, in the basin in which it was formed, the waters must have been unusually quiet, containing identical materials throughout, and that these materials must have been deposited over the whole bottom in the same way. It is usually separated from the superincumbent beds by a glazed crust of hard, compact sandstone, almost resembling a ferruginous quartzite.

Upon this follow beds of sand and sandstone, varying in the regularity of their strata, reddish in color, often highly ferruginous, and more or less nodulous or porous. They present frequent traces of cross-stratification, alternating with regularly stratified horizontal beds, with here and there an intervening layer of clay. It would seem as if the character of the water-basin had now changed, and as if the waters under which this second formation was deposited had vibrated between storm and calm, had sometimes flowed more gently, and again had been tossed to and fro, giving to some of the beds the aspect of true torrential deposits. Indeed, these sandstone formations present a great variety of aspects. Sometimes they are very regularly laminated, or assume even the appearance of the hardest quartzite. This is usually the case with the uppermost beds. In other localities, and more especially in the lowermost beds, the whole mass is honeycombed, as if drilled by worms or boring shells, the hard parts enclosing softer sands or clays. Occasionally the ferruginous materials prevail to such an extent that some of these beds might be mistaken for bog-ore, while others contain a large amount of clay, more regularly stratified, and alternating with strata of sandstone, thus recalling the most characteristic forms of the Old Red or Triassic formations. This resemblance has, no doubt, led to the identification of the Amazonian deposits with the more ancient formations of Europe. At Monte Alégre, of which I shall presently speak more in detail, such a clay bed divides the lower from the upper sandstone. The thickness of these sandstones is extremely variable. In the basin of the Amazons proper, they hardly rise anywhere above the level of high water during the rainy season; while at low water, in the summer months, they may be observed everywhere along the river-banks. It will be seen, however, that the limit between high and low water gives no true measure of the original thickness of the whole series.

In the neighborhood of Almeyrim, at a short distance from the northern bank of the river, and nearly parallel with its course, there rises a line of low hills, interrupted here and there, but extending in evident connection from Almeyrim through the region of Monte Alégre to the heights of Obydos. These hills have attracted the attention of travellers, not only from their height, which appears greater than it is, because they rise abruptly from an extensive plain, but also on account of their curious form; many of them being perfectly level on top, like smooth tables, and very abruptly divided from each other by low, intervening spaces.* Nothing has hitherto been known of the geological structure of these hills, but they have been usually represented as the southernmost spurs of the table-land of Guiana. On ascending the river, I felt the greatest curiosity to examine them; but at the time I was deeply engrossed in studying the distribution of fishes in the Amazonian waters, and in making large ichthyological collections, for which it was very important not to miss the season of low water, when the fishes are most easily obtained. I was, therefore, obliged to leave this most interesting geological problem, and content myself with examining the structure of the valley so far as it could be seen on the river-banks and in the neighborhood of my different collecting stations. On my return, however, when my collections were completed, I was free to pursue this investigation, in which Major Coutinho was as much interested as myself. We determined to select Monte Alégre as the centre of our exploration, the serra in that region being higher than elsewhere. As I was detained by

---

* The atlas in Martins's "Journey to Brazil," or the sketch accompanying Bates's description of these hills in his "Naturalist on the Amazons,' will give an idea of their aspect.

indisposition at Manaos for some days at the time we had appointed for the excursion, Major Coutinho preceded me, and had already made one trip to the serra, with some very interesting results, when I joined him, and we took a second journey together. Monte Alégre lies on a side arm of the Amazons, a little off from its main course. This side arm, called the Rio Gurupatuba, is simply a channel, running parallel with the Amazons, and cutting through from a higher to a lower point. Its dimensions are, however, greatly exaggerated in all the maps thus far published, where it is usually made to appear as a considerable northern tributary of the Amazons. The town stands on an elevated terrace, separated from the main stream by the Rio Gurupatuba and by an extensive flat, consisting of numerous lakes divided from each other by low, alluvial land, and mostly connected by narrow channels. To the west of the town this terrace sinks abruptly to a wide sandy plain called the Campos, covered with a low forest-growth, and bordered on its farther limit by the picturesque serra of Ereré. The form of this mountain is so abrupt, its rise from the plains so bold and sudden, that it seems more than twice its real height. Judging by the eye and comparing it with the mountains I had last seen, — the Corcovado, the Gavia, and Tijuca range in the neighborhood of Rio, — I had supposed it to be three or four thousand feet high, and was greatly astonished when our barometric observations showed it to be somewhat less than nine hundred feet in its most elevated point. This, however, agrees with Martius's measurement of the Almeyrim hills, which he says are eight hundred feet in height.

We passed three days in the investigation of the Serra of Ereré, and found it to consist wholly of the sandstone deposits already described, and to have exactly the same geological constitution. In short, the Serra of Monte Alégre, and of course all those connected with it on the northern side of the river, lie in the prolongation of the lower beds forming the banks of the river, their greater height being due simply to the fact that they have not been worn to the same low level. The opposite range of Santarem, which has the same general outline and character, shares, no doubt, the same geological structure. In one word, all these hills were formerly part of a continuous formation, and owe their present outline and their isolated position to a colossal denudation. The surface of the once unbroken strata, which in their original condition must have formed an immense plain covered by water, has been cut into ravines or carried away over large tracts, to a greater or less depth, leaving only such portions standing as, from their hardness, could resist the floods which swept over it. The longitudinal trend of these hills is to be ascribed to the direction of the current which caused the denudation, while their level summits are due to the regularity of the stratification. They are not all table-topped, however; among them are many of smaller size, in which the sides have been gradually worn down, producing a gently rounded surface. Of course, under the heavy tropical rains this denudation is still going on, though in a greatly modified form.

I cannot speak of this Serra without alluding to the great beauty and extraordinary extent of the view to be obtained from it. Indeed, it was here that for the first time the geography of the country presented itself to my mind as a living reality in all its completeness. Insignificant as is its actual height, the Serra of Ereré commands a wider prospect than is to be had from many a more imposing mountain; for the surrounding plain, covered with forests and ploughed by countless rivers, stretches away for hundreds of leagues in every direction, without any object to obstruct the view. Standing on the brow of the Serra, with the numerous lakes intersecting the lowlands at its base, you look across the valley of the Amazons, as far as the eye can reach, and through its centre you follow for miles on either side the broad flood of the great river, carrying its yellow waters to the sea. As I stood there, panoramas from the Swiss mountains came up to my memory, and I fancied myself on the Alps, looking across the plain of Switzerland instead of the bed of the Amazons; the distant line of the Santarem hills on the southern bank of the river, and lower than the northern chain, representing the Jura range. As if to complete the comparison, Alpine lichens were growing among the cacti and palms, and a crust of Arctic cryptogamous growth covered rocks, between which sprang tropical flowers. On the northern flank of this Serra I found the only genuine erratic boulders I have seen in the whole length of the Amazonian Valley from Pará to the frontier of Peru, though there are many detached masses of rock, as, for instance, at Pedreira, near the junction of the Rio Negro and Rio Branco, which might be mistaken for them, but are due to the decomposition of the rocks in place. The boulders of Ereré are entirely distinct from the rock of the Serra, and consist of masses of compact hornblende.

It would seem that these two ranges skirting a part of the northern and southern banks of the Lower Amazons are not the only remnants of this arenaceous formation in its primitive altitude. On the banks of the Rio Japura, in the Serra of Cupati, Major Coutinho has found the same beds rising to the same height. It thus appears, by positive evidence, that over an extent of a thousand miles these deposits had a very considerable thickness, in the present direction of the valley. How far they extended in width has not been ascertained by direct observation; for we have not seen how they sink away to the northward, and towards the south the denudation has been so complete that, except in the very low range of hills in the neighborhood of Santarem, they do not rise above the plain. But the fact that this formation once had a thickness of more than eight hundred feet within the limits where we have had an opportunity of observing it, leaves no doubt that it must have extended to the edge of the basin, filling it to the same height throughout its whole extent. The thickness of the deposits gives a measure for the colossal scale of the denudations by which this immense accumulation was reduced to its present level. Here, then, is a system of high hills, having the prominence of mountains in the landscape, produced by causes to whose agency inequalities on the earth's surface of this magnitude have never yet been ascribed. We may fairly call them denudation mountains.

At this stage of the inquiry we have to account for two remarkable phenomena, — first, the filling of the Amazonian bottom with coarse arenaceous materials and finely laminated clays, immediately followed by sandstones rising to a height of more than eight hundred feet above the sea, the basin meanwhile having no rocky barrier towards the ocean on its eastern side; secondly, the wearing away and reduction of these formations to their present level by a denudation more extensive than any thus far recorded in the annals of geology, which has given rise to all the most prominent hills and mountain-chains along the northern bank of the river. Before seeking an explanation of these facts, let us look at the third and uppermost deposit.

This deposit is essentially the same as the Rio drift; but in the north it presents itself under a somewhat different aspect. As in Rio, it is a clayey deposit, containing more or less sand, and reddish in color, though varying from deep ochre to a brownish tint. It is not so absolutely destitute of stratification here as in its more southern range, though the traces of stratification are rare, and, when they do occur, are faint and indistinct. The materials are also more completely comminuted, and, as I said above, contain hardly any large masses, though quartz pebbles are sometimes scattered throughout the deposit, and occasionally a thin seam of pebbles, exactly as in the Rio drift, is seen resting between it and the underlying sandstone. In some places this bed of pebbles intersects even the mass of the clay, giving it, in such instances, an unquestionably stratified character. There can be no doubt that this more recent formation rests unconformably upon the sandstone beds beneath it; for it fills all the inequalities of their denudated surfaces, whether they be more or less limited furrows, or wide, undulating depressions. It may be seen everywhere along the banks of the river, above the stratified sandstone, sometimes with the river-mud accumulated against it; at the season of the *enchente*, or high water, it is the only formation left exposed above the water-level. Its thickness is not great; it varies from twenty or thirty to fifty feet, and may occasionally rise nearly to a hundred feet in height, though this is rarely the case. It is evident that this formation also was once continuous, stretching over the whole basin at one level. Though it is now worn down in many places, and has wholly disappeared in others, its connection may be readily traced; since it is everywhere visible, not only on opposite banks of the Amazons, but also on those of all its tributaries, as far as their shores have been examined. I have said that it rests always above the sandstone beds. This is true, with one exception. Wherever the sandstone deposits retain their original thickness, as in the hills of Monte Alégre and Almeyrim, the red clay is not found on their summits, but occurs only in their ravines and hollows, or resting against their sides. This shows that it is not only posterior to the sandstone, but was accumulated in a shallower basin, and consequently never reached so high a level. The boulders of Ereré do not rest on the stratified sandstone of the Serra, but are sunk in the unstratified mass of the clay. This should be remembered, as it will presently be seen that their position associates them with a later period than that of the mountain itself. The unconformability of the ochraceous clay and the underlying sandstones might lead to the idea that the two formations belong to distinct geological periods, and are not due to the same agency acting at successive times. One feature, however, shows their close connection. The ochraceous clay exhibits a remarkable identity of configuration with the underlying sandstones. An extensive survey of the two, in their mutual relations, shows clearly that they were both deposited by the same water-system within the same basin, but at different levels. Here and there the clay formation has so pale and grayish a tint that it may be com-founded with the mud deposits of the river. These latter, however, never rise so high as the ochraceous clay, but are everywhere confined within the limits of high and low water. The islands also, in the main course of the Amazons, consist invariably of river-mud; while those arising from the intersection and cutting off of portions of the land by diverging branches of the main stream always consist of the well-known sandstones, capped by the ochre-colored clay.

It may truly be said that there does not exist on the surface of the earth a formation known to geologists resembling that of the Amazons. Its extent is stupendous; it stretches from the Atlantic shore, through the whole width of Brazil, into Peru, to the very foot of the Andes. Humboldt speaks of it " in the vast plains of the Amazons, in the eastern boundary of Jaen de Bracamoros," and says, "This prodigious extension of red sandstone in the low grounds stretching along the east of the Andes is one of the most striking phenomena I observed during my examination of rocks in the equinoctial regions." *
When the great natural philosopher wrote these lines, he had no idea how much these deposits extended beyond the field of his observations. Indeed, they are not limited to the main bed of the Amazons; they have been fol-

---

* Bohn's edition of Humboldt's Personal Narrative, Chap. II. p. 134. Humboldt alludes to these formations repeatedly: it is true that he refers them to the ancient conglomerates of the Devonian age, but his description agrees so perfectly with what I have observed along the banks of the Amazons and the Rio Negro that there can be no doubt he speaks of the same thing. He wrote at a time when many of the results of modern geology were unknown, and his explanation of the phenomena was then perfectly natural. The passage from which the few lines in the text are taken shows that these deposits extend even to the Llanos.

lowed along the banks of its tributaries to the south and north as far as these have been ascended. They occur on the margins of the Huallaga and the Ucayale, on those of the Iça, the Hyutahy, the Hyurua, the Hyapura, and the Purus. On the banks of the Hyapura, where Major Coutinho has traced them, they are found as far as the Cataract of Cupati. I have followed them along the Rio Negro to its junction with the Rio Branco; and Humboldt not only describes them from a higher point on this same river, but also from the valley of the Orinoco. Finally, they may be tracked along the banks of the Madeira, the Tapajos, the Xingu, and the Tocantins, as well as on the shores of the Guatuma, the Trombetas, and other northern affluents of the Amazons. The observations of Martius, those of Gardner, and the recent survey above alluded to, made by my assistant, Mr. St. John, of the valley of the Rio Guruguea and that of the Rio Paranahyba, show that the great basin of Piauhy is also identical in its geological structure with the lateral valleys of the Amazons. The same is true of the large island of Marajo, lying at the mouth of the Amazons. And yet I believe that even this does not cover the whole ground, and that some future writer may say of my estimate, as I have said of Humboldt's, that it falls short of the truth; for, if my generalizations are correct, the same formation will be found extending over the whole basin of the Paraguay and the Rio de la Plata, and along their tributaries, to the very heart of the Andes.

Such are the facts. The question now arises, How were these vast deposits formed? The easiest answer, and the one which most readily suggests itself, is that of a submersion of the continent at successive periods, to allow the accumulation of these materials, and its subsequent elevation. I reject this explanation for the simple reason that the deposits show no sign whatever of a marine origin. No sea-shells, nor remains of any marine animal, have as yet been found throughout their whole extent, over a region several thousand miles in length and from five to seven hundred miles in width. It is contrary to all our knowledge of geological deposits to suppose that an ocean basin of this size, which must have been submerged during an immensely long period in order to accumulate formations of such a thickness, should not contain numerous remains of the animals formerly inhabiting it.* The only fossil remains of any kind truly belonging to it, which I have found in the formation, are leaves taken from the lower clays on the banks of the Solimoens at Tonantins; and these show a vegetation similar in general character to that which prevails there, to-day. Evidently, then, this basin was a fresh-water basin; these deposits are fresh-water deposits. But as the valley of

---

* I am aware that Bates mentions having heard that at Obydos calcareous layers, thickly studded with marine shells, had been found interstratified with the clay, but he did not himself examine the strata. The Obydos shells are not marine, but are fresh-water Unios, greatly resembling Aviculas, Solens, and Arcas. Such would-be marine fossils have been brought to me from the shore opposite to Obydos, near Santarem, and I have readily recognized them for what they truly are, — fresh-water shells of the family of Naiades. I have myself collected specimens of these shells in the clay-beds along the banks of the Solimoens, near Teffé, and might have mistaken them for fossils of that formation had I not known how Naiades burrow in the mud. Their resemblance to the marine genera mentioned above is very remarkable, and the mistake as to their true zoölogical character is as natural as that by which earlier ichthyologists, and even travellers of very recent date, have confounded some fresh-water fishes from the Upper Amazons, of the genus Pterophyllum (Heckel), with the marine genus Platax.

the Amazons exists to-day, it is widely open to the ocean on the east, with a gentle slope from the Andes to the Atlantic, determining a powerful seaward current. When these vast accumulations took place, the basin must have been closed; otherwise the loose materials would constantly have been carried down to the ocean.

It is my belief that all these deposits belong to the ice-period in its earlier or later phases, and to this cosmic winter, which, judging from all the phenomena connected with it, may have lasted for thousands of centuries, we must look for the key to the geological history of the Amazonian Valley. I am aware that this suggestion will appear extravagant. But is it, after all, so improbable that, when Central Europe was covered with ice thousands of feet thick; when the glaciers of Great Britain ploughed into the sea, and when those of the Swiss mountains had ten times their present altitude; when every lake in Northern Italy was filled with ice, and these frozen masses extended even into Northern Africa; when a sheet of ice, reaching nearly to the summit of Mount Washington in the White Mountains (that is, having a thickness of nearly six thousand feet), moved over the continent of North America, — is it so improbable that, in this epoch of universal cold, the valley of the Amazons also had its glacier poured down into it from the accumulations of snow in the Cordilleras, and swollen laterally by the tributary glaciers descending from the table-lands of Guiana and Brazil? The movement of this immense glacier must have been eastward, determined as well by the vast reservoirs of snow in the Andes as by the direction of the valley itself. It must have ploughed the valley-bottom over and over again, grinding all the materials beneath it into a fine powder or reducing them to small pebbles, and it must have accumulated at its lower end a moraine of proportions as gigantic as its own; thus building a colossal sea-wall across the mouth of the valley. I shall be asked at once whether I have found here also the glacial inscriptions, — the furrows, striæ, and polished surfaces so characteristic of the ground over which glaciers have travelled. I answer, not a trace of them; for the simple reason that there is not a natural rock-surface to be found throughout the whole Amazonian Valley. The rocks themselves are of so friable a nature, and the decomposition caused by the warm torrential rains and by exposure to the burning sun of the tropics so great and unceasing, that it is hopeless to look for marks which in colder climates and on harder substances are preserved through ages unchanged. With the exception of the rounded surfaces so well known in Switzerland as the *roches moutonnées* heretofore alluded to, which may be seen in many localities, and the boulders of Ereré, the direct traces of glaciers as seen in other countries are wanting in Brazil. I am, indeed, quite willing to admit that, from the nature of the circumstances, I have not here the positive evidence which has guided me in my previous glacial investigations. My conviction in this instance is founded, first, on the materials in the Amazonian Valley, which correspond exactly in their character to materials accumulated in glacier bottoms; secondly, on the resemblance of the upper or third Amazonian formation to the Rio drift,* of the

---

* As I have stated in the beginning, I am satisfied that the unstratified clay deposit of Rio and its vicinity is genuine glacial drift, resulting from the grinding of the loose materials interposed between the glacier and the solid rock in place, and retaining to this day the position in which it was left by the ice. Like all such accumulations, it is totally free from stratification. If this

glacial origin of which there cannot, in my opinion, be any doubt; thirdly, on the fact that this fresh-water basin must have been closed against the sea by some powerful barrier, the removal of which would naturally give an outlet to the waters, and cause the extraordinary denudations, the evidences of which meet us everywhere throughout the valley.

On a smaller scale, phenomena of this kind have long been familiar to us. In the present lakes of Northern Italy, in those of Switzerland, Norway, and Sweden, as well as in those of New England, especially in the State of Maine, the waters are held back in their basins by moraines. In the ice-period these depressions were filled with glaciers, which, in the course of time, accumulated at their lower end a wall of loose materials. These walls still remain, and serve as dams to prevent the escape of the waters. But for their moraines, all these lakes would be open valleys. In the Roads of Glen Roy, in Scotland, we have

be so, it is evident, on comparing the two formations, that the ochraceous sandy clay of the valley of the Amazons has been deposited under different circumstances; that, while it owes its resemblance to the Rio drift to the fact that its materials were originally ground by glaciers in the upper part of the valley, these materials have subsequently been spread throughout the whole basin and actually deposited under the agency of water. A survey of the more southern provinces of Brazil, extending to the temperate zone, where the combined effects of a tropical sun and of tropical rains must naturally be wanting, will, I trust, remove all the difficulties still attending this explanation. The glacial phenomena, with all their characteristic features, are already known to cover the southernmost parts of South America. The intervening range, between 22° and 36° of south latitude, cannot fail to exhibit the transition from the drift of the cold and temperate zone to the formations of a kindred character described above from the tropical zone. The knowledge of these deposits will definitely settle the question; and either prove the correctness of my generalizations or show their absurdity. I feel no anxiety as to the result. I only long for a speedy removal of all doubts.

an instance of a fresh-water lake, which has now wholly disappeared, formed in the same manner, and reduced successively to lower and lower levels by the breaking down or wearing away of the moraines which originally prevented its waters from flowing out. Assuming then that, under the low temperature of the ice-period, the climatic conditions necessary for the formation of land-ice existed in the valley of the Amazons, and that it was actually filled with an immense glacier, it follows that, when these fields of ice yielded to a gradual change of climate, and slowly melted away, the whole basin, then closed against the sea by a huge wall of *débris*, was transformed into a vast fresh-water lake. The first effect of the thawing process must have been to separate the glacier from its foundation, raising it from immediate contact with the valley bottom, and thus giving room for the accumulation of a certain amount of water beneath it; while the valley as a whole would still be occupied by the glacier. In this shallow sheet of water under the ice, and protected by it from any violent disturbance, those finer triturated materials always found at a glacier bottom, and ground sometimes to powder by its action, would be deposited, and gradually transformed from an unstratified paste containing the finest sand and mud, together with coarse pebbles and gravel, into a regularly stratified formation. In this formation the coarse materials would of course fall to the bottom, while the most minute would settle above them. It is at this time and under such circumstances that I believe the first formation of the Amazonian Valley, with the coarse, pebbly sand beneath, and the finely laminated clays above, to have been accumulated.

I shall perhaps be reminded here of my fossil leaves,

and asked how any vegetation would be possible under such circumstances. But it must be remembered, that, in considering all these periods, we must allow for immense lapses of time and for very gradual changes; that the close of this first period would be very different from its beginning; and that a rich vegetation springs on the very borders of the snow and ice fields in Switzerland. The fact that these were accumulated in a glacial basin would, indeed, at once account for the traces of vegetable life, and for the absence, or at least the great scarcity, of animal remains in these deposits. For while fruits may ripen and flowers bloom on the very edge of the glaciers, it is also well known that the fresh-water lakes formed by the melting of the ice are singularly deficient in life. There are, indeed, hardly any animals to be found in glacial lakes.

The second formation belongs to a later period, when, the whole body of ice being more or less disintegrated, the basin contained a larger quantity of water. Beside that arising from the melting of the ice, this immense valley bottom must have received, then as now, all which was condensed from the atmosphere above, and poured into it in the form of rain or dew at present. Thus an amount of water equal to that flowing in from all the tributaries of the main stream must have been rushing towards the axis of the valley, seeking its natural level, but spreading over a more extensive surface than now, until, finally gathered up as separate rivers, it flowed in distinct beds. In its general movement toward the central and lower part of the valley, the broad stream would carry along all the materials small enough to be so transported, as well as those so minute as to remain suspended in the waters. It would gradually deposit them in the valley bottom in horizontal beds more or less regular, or here and there, wherever eddies gave rise to more rapid and irregular currents, characterized by torrential stratification. Thus has been consolidated in the course of ages the continuous sand formation spreading over the whole Amazonian basin, and attaining a thickness of eight hundred feet.

While these accumulations were taking place within this basin, it must not be forgotten that the sea was beating against its outer wall, — against that gigantic moraine which I suppose to have closed it at its eastern end. It would seem that, either from this cause, or perhaps in consequence of some turbulent action from within, a break was made in this defence, and the waters rushed violently out. It is very possible that the waters, gradually swollen at the close of this period by the further melting of the ice, by the additions poured in from lateral tributaries, by the rains, and also by the filling of the basin with loose materials, would overflow, and thus contribute to destroy the moraine. However this may be, it follows from my premises that, in the end, these waters obtained a sudden release, and poured seaward with a violence which cut and denuded the deposits already formed, wearing them down to a much lower level, and leaving only a few remnants standing out in their original thickness, where the strata were solid enough to resist the action of the currents. Such are the hills of Monte Alégre, of Obydos, Almeyrim, and Cupati, as well as the lower ridges of Santarem. This escape of the waters did not, however, entirely empty the whole basin; for the period of denudation was again followed by one of quiet accumulation, during which was deposited the ochraceous sandy clay resting upon the denudated surfaces of the underlying sandstone. To this period I refer the boulders of Ereré, sunk as they are in the clay of this final deposit. I suppose them to have been brought to their present position by floating ice at the close of the glacial period, when nothing remained of the ice-fields except such isolated masses, — ice-rafts as it were ; or perhaps by icebergs dropped into the basin from glaciers still remaining in the Andes and on the edges of the plateaus of Guiana and Brazil. From the general absence of stratification in this clay formation, it would seem that the comparatively shallow sheet of water in which it was deposited was very tranquil. Indeed, after the waters had sunk much below the level which they held during the deposition of the sandstone, and the currents which gave rise to the denudation of the latter had ceased, the whole sheet of water would naturally become much more placid. But the time arrived when the water broke through its boundaries again, perhaps owing to the further encroachment of the sea and consequent destruction of the moraine.* In this second drainage, however, the waters, carrying away a considerable part of the new deposit, furrowing it to its very foundation, and even cutting through it into the underlying sandstone, were, in the end, reduced to something like their present level, and confined within their present beds. This is shown by the fact that in this ochre-colored clay, and penetrating to a greater or less depth the sandstone below, are dug, not only the great

---

* I would here remind the reader of the terraces of Glen Roy, which indicate successive reductions of the barrier encasing the lake, similar to those assumed to have taken place at the mouth of the Amazons.

longitudinal channel of the Amazons itself, but also the lateral furrows through which its tributaries reach the main stream, and the network of anastomosing branches flowing between them; the whole forming the most extraordinary river system in the world.

My assumption that the sea has produced very extensive changes in the coast of Brazil — changes more than sufficient to account for the disappearance of the glacial wall which I suppose to have closed the Amazonian Valley in the ice period — is by no means hypothetical. This action is still going on to a remarkable degree, and is even now rapidly modifying the outline of the shore. When I first arrived at Pará, I was struck with the fact that the Amazons, the largest river in the world, has no delta. All the other rivers which we call great, though some of them are insignificant as compared with the Amazons, — the Mississippi, the Nile, the Ganges, and the Danube, — deposit extensive deltas, and the smaller rivers also, with few exceptions, are constantly building up the land at their mouths by the materials they bring along with them. Even the little river Kander, emptying into the lake of Thun, is not without its delta. Since my return from the Upper Amazons to Pará, I have made an examination of some of the harbor islands, and also of parts of the coast, and have satisfied myself that, with the exception of a few small, low islands, never rising above the sea-level, and composed of alluvial deposit, they are portions of the main-land detached from it, partly by the action of the river itself, and partly by the encroachment of the ocean. In fact, the sea is eating away the land much faster than the river can build it up. The great island of Marajo was originally a continuation of the valley of the Amazons, and is identical with it in every detail of its geological structure. My investigation of the island itself, in connection with the coast and the river, leads me to suppose that, having been at one time an integral part of the deposits described above, at a later period it became an island in the bed of the Amazons, which, dividing in two arms, encircled it completely, and then, joining again to form a single stream, flowed onward to the sea-shore, which in those days lay much farther to the eastward than it now does. I suppose the position of the island of Marajo at that time to have corresponded very nearly to the present position of the island of Tupinambaranas, just at the junction of the Madeira with the Amazons. It is a question among geographers whether the Tocantins is a branch of the Amazons, or should be considered as forming an independent river system. It will be seen that, if my view is correct, it must formerly have borne the same relation to the Amazons that the Madeira River now does, joining it just where Marajo divided the main stream, as the Madeira now joins it at the head of the island of Tupinambaranas. If in countless centuries to come the ocean should continue to eat its way into the Valley of the Amazons, once more transforming the lower part of the basin into a gulf, as it was during the cretaceous period, the time might arrive when geographers, finding the Madeira emptying almost immediately into the sea, would ask themselves whether it had ever been indeed a branch of the Amazons, just as they now question whether the Tocantins is a tributary of the main stream or an independent river. But to return to Marajo, and to the facts actually in our possession.

The island is intersected, in its southeastern end, by a considerable river called the Igarapé Grande. The cut made through the land by this stream seems intended to serve as a geological section, so perfectly does it display the three characteristic Amazonian formations above described. At its mouth, near the town of Souré, and at Salvaterra, on the opposite bank, may be seen, lowest, the well-stratified sandstone, with the finely laminated clays resting upon it, overtopped by a crust; then the cross-stratified, highly ferruginous sandstone, with quartz pebbles here and there; and, above all, the well-known ochraceous, unstratified sandy clay, spreading over the undulating surface of the denudated sandstone, following all its inequalities, and filling all its depressions and furrows. But while the Igarapé Grande has dug its channel down to the sea, cutting these formations, as I ascertained, to a depth of twenty-five fathoms, it has thus opened the way for the encroachments of the tides, and the ocean is now, in its turn, gaining upon the land. Were there no other evidence of the action of the tides in this locality, the steep cut of the Igarapé Grande, contrasting with the gentle slope of the banks near its mouth, wherever they have been modified by the invasion of the sea, would enable us to distinguish the work of the river from that of the ocean, and to prove that the denudation now going on is due in part to both. But besides this, I was so fortunate as to discover, on my recent excursion, unmistakable and perfectly convincing evidence of the onward movement of the sea. At the mouth of the Igarapé Grande, both at Souré and at Salvaterra, on the southern side of the Igarapé, is a submerged forest. Evidently this forest grew in one of those marshy lands constantly inundated, for between the stumps is accumulated the loose, felt-like peat characteristic of such grounds, and containing about as much mud as vegetable matter. Such a marshy forest, with the stumps of the trees still standing erect in the peat, has been laid bare on both sides of the Igarapé Grande by the encroachments of the ocean. That this is the work of the sea is undeniable, for all the little depressions and indentations of the peat are filled with sea-sand, and a ridge of tidal sand divides it from the forest still standing behind. Nor is this all. At Vigia, immediately opposite to Souré, on the continental side of the Pará River, just where it meets the sea, we have the counterpart of this submerged forest. Another peat-bog, with the stumps of innumerable trees standing in it, and encroached upon in the same way by tidal sand, is exposed here also. No doubt these forests were once all continuous, and stretched across the whole basin of what is now called the Pará River.

Since I have been pursuing this inquiry, I have gathered much information to the same effect from persons living on the coast. It is well remembered that, twenty years ago, there existed an island, more than a mile in width, to the northeast of the entrance of the Bay of Vigia, which has now entirely disappeared. Farther eastward, the Bay of Braganza has doubled its width in the last twenty years, and on the shore, within the bay, the sea has gained upon the land for a distance of two hundred yards during a period of only ten years. The latter fact is ascertained by the position of some houses, which were two hundred yards farther from the sea ten years ago than they now are. From these and the like reports, from my own observations on this part of the Brazilian coast, from some investigations made by Major Coutinho at the mouth of the Amazons on its northern continental shore near Macapa, and from the reports of Mr. St. John respecting the formations in the valley of the Paranahyba, it is my belief that the changes I have been describing are but a small part of the destruction wrought by the sea on the northeastern shore of this continent. I think it will be found, when the coast has been fully surveyed, that a strip of land not less than a hundred leagues in width, stretching from Cape St. Roque to the northern extremity of South America, has been eaten away by the ocean. If this be so, the Paranahyba and the rivers to the northwest of it, in the province of Maranham, were formerly tributaries of the Amazons; and all that we know thus far of their geological character goes to prove that this was actually the case. Such an extensive oceanic denudation must have carried away not only the gigantic glacial moraine here assumed to have closed the mouth of the Amazonian basin, but the very ground on which it formerly stood. Although the terminal moraine has disappeared, there is, however, no reason why parts of the lateral moraines should not remain. And I expect in my approaching visit to Ceará to find traces of the southern lateral moraine in that neighborhood.

During the last four or five years I have been engaged in a series of investigations, in the United States, upon the subject of the denudations connected with the close of the glacial period there, and the encroachments of the ocean upon the drift deposits along the Atlantic coast. Had these investigations been published in detail, with the necessary maps, it would have been far easier for me to explain the facts I have lately observed in the Amazonian Valley, to connect them with facts of a like character on the continent of North America, and to show how remarkably they correspond with facts accomplished during the same period in other parts of the world. While the glacial epoch itself has been very extensively studied in the last half-century, little attention has been paid to the results connected with the breaking up of the geological winter and the final disappearance of the ice. I believe that the true explanation of the presence of a large part of the superficial deposits lately ascribed to the agency of the sea, during temporary subsidences of the land, will be found in the melting of the ice-fields. To this cause I would refer all those deposits which I have designated as remodelled drift. When the sheet of ice, extending from the Arctic regions over a great part of North America and coming down to the sea, slowly melted away, the waters were not distributed over the face of the country as they now are. They rested upon the bottom deposits of the ice-fields, upon the glacial paste, consisting of clay, sand, pebbles, boulders, etc., underlying the ice. This bottom deposit did not, of course, present an even surface, but must have had extensive undulations and depressions. After the waters had been drained off from the more elevated ridges, these depressions would still remain full. In the lakes and pools thus formed, stratified deposits would be accumulated, consisting of the most minutely comminuted clay, deposited in thin laminated layers, or sometimes in considerable masses, without any sign of stratification; such differences in the formation being determined by the state of the water, whether perfectly stagnant or more or less agitated. Of such pool deposits overlying the drift there are many instances in the Northern United States. By the overflowing of some of these lakes, and by the emptying of the higher ones into those on a lower level, channels would gradually be formed between the depressions. So began to be marked out our independent river-systems, — the waters always seeking their natural level, gradually widening and deepening the channels in which they flowed, as they worked their way down to the sea. When they reached the shore, there followed that antagonism between the rush of the rivers and the action of the tides, — between continental outflows and oceanic encroachments, — which still goes on, and has led to the formation of our Eastern rivers, with their wide, open estuaries, such as the James, the Potomac, and the Delaware. All these estuaries are embanked by drift, as are also, in their lower course, the rivers connected with them. Where the country was low and flat, and the drift extended far into the ocean, the encroachment of the sea gave rise, not only to our large estuaries, but also to the sounds and deep bays forming the most prominent indentations of the continental coast, such as the Bay of Fundy, Massachusetts Bay, Long Island Sound, and others. The unmistakable traces of glacial action upon all the islands along the coast of New England, sometimes lying at a very considerable distance from the main-land, give an approximate, though a minimum, measure of the former extent of the glacial drift seaward, and the subsequent advance of the ocean upon the land. Like those of the harbor of Pará, all these islands have the same geological structure as the continent, and were evidently continuous with it at some former period. All the rocky islands along the coast of Maine and Massachusetts exhibit the glacial traces wherever their surfaces are exposed by the washing away of the drift; and where the drift remains, its character shows that it was once continuous from one island to another, and from all the islands to the main-land.

It is difficult to determine with precision the ancient limit of the glacial drift, but I think it can be shown that it connected the shoals of Newfoundland with the continent; that Nantucket, Martha's Vineyard, and Long Island made part of the main-land; that, in like manner Nova Scotia, including Sable Island, was united to the southern shore of New Brunswick and Maine, and that the same sheet of drift extended thence to Cape Cod, and stretched southward as far as Cape Hatteras; — in short, that the line of shallow soundings along the whole coast of the United States marks the former extent of glacial drift. The ocean has gradually eaten its way into this deposit, and given its present outlines to the continent. These denudations of the sea no doubt began as soon as the breaking up of the ice exposed the drift to its invasion; in other words, at a time when colossal glaciers still poured forth their load of ice into the Atlantic, and fleets of icebergs, far larger and more numerous than those now floated off from the Arctic seas, were launched from the northeastern shore of the United States. Many such masses must have stranded along the shore, and have left various signs of their presence. In fact, the glacial phenomena of the United States and elsewhere are due to two distinct periods: the first of these was the glacial epoch proper, when the ice was a solid sheet; while to the second belongs the breaking up of this epoch, with the gradual disintegration and dispersion of the ice. We talk of the theory of glaciers and the theory of icebergs in reference to these phenomena, as if they were exclusively due to one or the other, and whoever accepted the former must reject the latter, and *vice versa*. When geologists have combined these now discordant elements, and consider these two periods as consecutive, — part of the phenomena being due to the glaciers, part to the icebergs and to freshets consequent on their breaking up, — they will find that they have covered the whole ground, and that the two theories are perfectly consistent with each other. I think the present disputes upon this subject will end somewhat like those which divided the Neptunic and Plutonic schools of geologists in the early part of this century; the former of whom would have it that all the rocks were due to the action of water, the latter that they were wholly due to the action of fire. The problem was solved, and harmony restored, when it was found that both elements have been equally at work in forming the solid crust of the globe. To the stranded icebergs alluded to above, I have no doubt, is to be referred the origin of the many lakes without outlets existing all over the sandy tract along our coast, of which Cape Cod forms a part. Not only the formation of these lakes, but also that of our salt marshes and cranberry-fields, I believe to be connected with the waning of the ice period.

I hope at some future time to publish in detail, with the appropriate maps and illustrations, my observations upon the changes of our coast, and other phenomena connected with the close of the glacial epoch in the United States. To give results without an account of the investigations which have led to them, inverts the true method of science; and I should not have introduced the subject here except to show that the fresh-water denudations and the oceanic encroachments which have formed the Amazonian Valley, with its river system, are not isolated facts, but that the process has been the same in both continents. The extraordinary continuity and uniformity of the Amazonian deposits are due to the immense size of the basin enclosed, and the identity of the materials contained in it.

A glance at any geological map of the world will show the reader that the Valley of the Amazons, so far as an attempt is made to explain its structure, is represented as containing isolated tracts of Devonian, Triassic, Jurassic, cretaceous, tertiary, and alluvial deposits. This is wholly inaccurate, as is shown by the above sketch, and whatever may be thought of my interpretation of the actual phenomena, I trust that, in presenting for the first time the formations of the Amazonian basin in their natural connection and sequence, as consisting of three uniform sets of comparatively recent deposits, extending throughout the whole valley, the investigations here recorded have contributed something to the results of modern geology.

CHAPTER XIV.

CEARÁ.

LEAVING PARÁ. — FAREWELL TO THE AMAZONS. — EASE OF TRAVELLING ON THE AMAZONS. — ROUGH PASSAGE. — ARRIVAL AT CEARÁ. — DIFFICULTY OF LANDING. — ASPECT OF THE TOWN. — RAINY SEASON. — CONSEQUENT SICKLINESS. — OUR PURPOSE IN STOPPING AT CEARÁ. — REPORT OF DR. FELICE ABOUT MORAINES. — PREPARATIONS FOR JOURNEY INTO THE INTERIOR. — DIFFICULTIES AND DELAYS IN GETTING OFF. — ON THE WAY. — NIGHT AT ARANCHO. — BAD ROADS. — CARNAUBA PALM. — ARRIVAL AT MONGUBA. — KIND RECEPTION BY SENHOR FRANKLIN DE LIMA. — GEOLOGY OF THE REGION. — EVENING GAMES AND AMUSEMENTS. — PACATUBA. — TRACES OF ANCIENT GLACIERS. — SERRA OF ARATANHA. — CLIMB UP THE SERRA. — HOSPITALITY OF SENHOR DA COSTA. — PICTURESQUE VIEWS. — THE SERTAŌ. — DROUGHT AND RAINS. — EPIDEMICS. — RETURN TO MONGUBA. — DETAINED BY EXTRAORDINARY RAINS. — RETURN TO CEARÁ. — OVERFLOWED ROADS. — DIFFICULTY OF FORDING. — ARRIVAL AT CEARÁ. — LIBERALITY OF THE PRESIDENT OF THE PROVINCE TOWARD THE EXPEDITION.

April 2d. — Ceará. We left Pará on the 26th of March, in the evening, feeling for the first time that we were indeed bidding good by to the Amazons. Our pleasant voyages on its yellow waters, our canoe excursions on its picturesque lakes and igarapés, our lingerings in its palm-thatched cottages, belonged to the past; except in memory, our Amazonian travels were over. When we entered upon them, what vague anticipations, what visions of a new and interesting life, not, as we supposed, without its dangers and anxieties, were before us. So little is known, even in Brazil, of the Amazons, that we could obtain only very meagre and, usually, rather discouraging information concerning our projected journey. In Rio, if you say you are going to ascend their great river, your Brazilian friends look at you with compassionate wonder. You are threatened with sickness, with intolerable heat, with the absence of any nourishing food or suitable lodgings, with mosquitoes, with Jacarés and wild Indians. If you consult a physician, he gives you a good supply of quinine, and tells you to take a dose every other day as a preventive against fever and chills; so that if you escape intermittent fever you are at least sure of being poisoned by a remedy which, if administered incautiously, may cause a disease worse than the one it cures. It will take perhaps from the excitement and novelty of Amazonian travelling to know that the journey from Pará to Tabatinga may be made with as much ease as a reasonable traveller has a right to expect, though of course not without some privations, and also with no more exposure to sickness than the traveller incurs in any hot climate. The perils and adventures which attended the voyages of Spix and Martius, or even of more recent travellers, like Castelnau, Bates, and Wallace, are no longer to be found on the main course of the Amazons, though they are met at every step on its great affluents. On the Tocantins, on the Madeira, on the Purus, on the Rio Negro, the Trombetas, or any of the large tributaries, the traveller must still work his way slowly up in a canoe, scorched by the sun or drenched by the rain; sleeping on the beach, hearing the cries of the wild animals in the woods around him, and waking perhaps in the morning, to find the tracks of a tiger in unpleasant proximity to his hammock. But along the course of the Amazons itself, these days of romantic adventure and hair-breadth escapes are over; the wild beasts of the forest have disappeared before the puff of the engine; the canoe and the encampment on the beach at night have given place to the prosaic conveniences of the steamboat. It is no doubt true of the Amazons, as of other tropical regions, that a long residence may reduce the vigor of the constitution, and perhaps make one more liable to certain diseases; but during our journey of eight months none of our large company suffered from any serious indisposition connected with the climate, nor did we see in any of our wanderings as many indications of intermittent fever as are to be met constantly on our Western rivers. The voyage on the Amazons proper has now become accessible to all who are willing to endure heat and mosquitoes for the sake of seeing the greatest river in the world, and the magnificent tropical vegetation along its shores. The best season for the journey is from the close of June to the middle of November, — July, August, September, and October being the four driest months of the year, and the most salubrious throughout that region.

We had a rough and boisterous passage from Pará to Ceará, with unceasing rain, in consequence of which the decks were constantly wet. Indeed, the cabins were not free from water, and it was only by frequent bailing that the floor of our state-room was kept tolerably dry. At Maranham we had the relief of a night on shore; and Mr. Agassiz and Major Coutinho profited by the occasion the following morning to examine the geology of the coast more carefully than they had formerly done. They found the structure identical with that of the Amazonian Valley, except that the formations were more worn down and disturbed. We arrived before Ceará at two o'clock on Saturday, March 31st, expecting to go on shore at once; but the sea ran high, the tide was unfavorable, and during the day not even a "jangada," those singular rafts that here take the place of boats, ventured out to our steamer as she lay rocking in the surf. Ceará has no harbor, and the sea drives in with fearful violence on the long sand-beach fronting the town, making it impossible, at certain states of the tide and in stormy weather, for any boat to land, unless it be one of these jangadas (catamarans), over which the waves break without swamping them. At about nine o'clock in the evening a custom-house boat came out, and, notwithstanding the lateness of the hour and the rough sea, we determined to go on shore, for we were told that in the morning the tide would be unfavorable, and if the wind continued in the present quarter it might be still more difficult, if not impossible, to land. It was not without some anxiety that I stood waiting my turn to enter the boat; for though at one moment it rose, on the swell of the sea, close to the stair, in the twinkling of an eye it was a couple of yards away. Some presence of mind and agility were needed in order to make the leap just at the right instant; and I was glad to find myself in the boat and not in the water, the chances being about even. As we rode in over the breakers, the boatmen entertained us with so many stories of the difficulty of landing, the frequent accidents, and especially of one which had occurred a few days before when three Englishmen had been drowned, that I began to think reaching the shore must be more perilous than leaving the ship. As we approached the town the scene was not without its picturesque charm. The moon, struggling through gray, watery clouds, threw a fitful light over the long sand-beach, on which the crested waves were driving furiously. A number of laden boats were tossing in the surf, and the roar of the breakers mingled with the cries of the black porters, as they waded breast high through the water, unloading the cargoes and carrying their burdens to the shore on their heads. We were landed much in the same way, the boatmen carrying us over the surf. This is the ordinary mode of embarking or landing passengers; it is but rarely, and at particular states of the tide, that it is possible to disembark at the pier which has been thrown out from the shore. Major Coutinho had written to a friend to engage lodgings for us, and we found a house ready. I was glad to sink into my comfortable hammock, to exchange the pitching and rolling of the steamer for its gentle rocking, to be out of reach of the hungry waves, and yet to hear their distant rush on the shore as I fell asleep.

The next morning was rainy, but in the afternoon it cleared, and toward evening we took a long drive with our host, Dr. Felice. I like the aspect of Ceará. I like its wide, well-paved, cleanly streets, which are bright with color, for the substantial houses on either side are of many hues. If it chance to be a Sunday or a festa day, every balcony is filled with gayly-dressed girls, while groups of men sit smoking and talking on the sidewalks before the doors. This town has not the stagnant, inanimate look of many Brazilian towns. It tells of movement, life, prosperity.* Beyond the city the streets stretch out into the campos, bordered on its inland side by beautiful serras; the Serra Grande and the Serra de Baturité. In front of the city stretches the broad sand-beach, and the murmur of the surf comes up into the heart of the town. It seems as if, so lying between sea and mountain, Ceará should be a healthy place, and it is usually so reputed. But at this moment, owing, it is thought, to the unusual continuance of the dry season and the extraordinary violence of the rains, now that they have begun, the town

---

* The prosperous province of Ceará has found in Senator Pompeo a worthy exponent of its interests; not only does he represent the province at Rio de Janeiro, but, by the publication of careful statistics, has largely contributed to its progress. — L. A.

is very sickly. Yellow-fever is prevalent, and there have been a good many deaths from it recently, though it is said not to have assumed the character of an epidemic as yet. Still more fatal is the malignant dysentery, which has been raging both in town and country for the last two months.

We are trying to hasten the arrangements for our inland journey, but do not find it very easy. Mr. Agassiz's object in stopping here is to satisfy himself by direct investigation of the former existence of glaciers in the serras of this province, and, if possible, to find some traces of the southern lateral moraine, marking the limit of the mass of ice which he supposes to have filled the Amazonian basin in the glacial period. In the Amazonian Valley itself he has seen that all the geological phenomena are connected with the close of the glacial period, with the melting of the ice and the immense freshets consequent upon its disappearance. On leaving the Amazons, the next step in the investigation was to seek the masses of loose materials left by the glacier itself. On arriving here he at once made inquiries to this effect, from a number of persons who have travelled a great deal in the province, and are therefore familiar with its features. The most valuable information he has obtained,—valuable from the fact, that the precision with which it is given shows that it may be relied upon,—is from Dr. Felice. His occupation as land-surveyor has led him to travel a great deal in the region of the Serra Grande. He has made a valuable map of this portion of the province, and he tells Mr. Agassiz that there is a wall of loose materials, boulders, stones, &c., running from east to west for a distance of some sixty leagues from the Rio Aracaty-Assù to Bom Jesu, in the Serra Grande. From his account, this wall resembles greatly the "Horsebacks" in Maine, those remarkable ridges accumulated by the ancient glaciers, and running sometimes uninterruptedly for thirty or forty miles. The horsebacks are, however, covered with soil and turf, whereas Dr. Felice describes this wall as rough and bare. Mr. Agassiz has no doubt that this accumulation or dike of loose materials, the position and direction of which corresponds exactly with his conjecture based upon the evidence obtained in the Amazonian Valley, is a portion of the lateral moraine, marking the southeastern limit of the great Amazonian glacier. Unhappily, it is impossible for him to visit it himself, for even could he devote the time necessary for so long a journey in the interior, we are told that at this season the state of the roads makes it almost impossible. He must therefore leave the identification of this colossal moraine to some younger and more fortunate investigator, and content himself with a direct examination of the next link in the chain of evidence, namely, the traces of local glaciers in the serras in the more immediate neighborhood of Ceará. If the basin of the Amazons was actually filled with ice, all the mountains lying outside of its limits in the neighboring provinces must have had their glaciers also. It is in search of these local glaciers that we undertake our present journey, hoping to reach the Serra of Baturité.

April 6th. — Pacatuba (at the foot of the Serra of Aratanha). After endless delays and difficulties about horses, servants, and other preparations for our journey, we succeeded in getting off on the afternoon of the 3d. The mode of travelling in the interior as well as the character of the people, makes it almost impossible to accomplish any journey with promptness and punctuality. While the preparations for our excursion were going on, neighbors and acquaintances would stroll in to see how things were advancing; one would propose that we should postpone our departure till the day after to-morrow, on account of some trouble about the horses; another that we should wait a week or two for more favorable weather. Evidently it did not occur to any one that it could be of much importance whether we started to-day or to-morrow, or next week or next month. The lotus-eaters in the "land in which it seemed always afternoon" could not have been more happily indifferent to the passage of time. Now this calm superiority to laws obeyed by the rest of mankind, this ignoring of the great dictum "*tempus fugit*," is rather exasperating to a man who has only the fortnight intervening between two steamers in which to accomplish his journey, and knows the time to be all too short for the objects he has in view. These habits of procrastination are much less marked in those parts of Brazil where railroad and steam travel have been introduced; though it cannot be said that promptness and despatch are anywhere familiar qualities in this country. Our delays in this particular instance were in no way owing to any want of interest in our plans; on the contrary, we met here, as everywhere, the most cordial sympathy with the objects of the expedition, and the President of the province, as well as other persons, were ready to give every assistance in their power. But a stranger cannot of course expect the habits of the people to be changed to suit his convenience, and we did but share in the general slowness of movement. However, we were at last on the way; our party consisting of Major Coutinho, Senhor Pompeo, Government Engineer of the province, whom the President had kindly detailed to accompany us, Mr. Agassiz, and myself. We had a servant, also provided by the President, one of his guard, and two men, with a couple of pack-mules for baggage and provisions. We started so late in the day, that our first ride was but a league or so out of the town; short as it was, however, we did not escape several showers, always to be expected at this season. Yet the ride was pleasant; a smell as of huckleberry meadows came from the low growth of shrubs covering the fields for miles around, and the very earth was fragrant from the rain. As we left the city, low clouds, full of distant showers, hung over the serras, and gave them a sombre beauty, more impressive, if less cheerful, than their sunshine look. At six o'clock we reached Arancho, a village where we were to pass the night. As we rode in at dusk, it seemed to me only a little cluster of low mud-houses; but I found, by daylight, there were one or two buildings of more pretentious character. We stopped at the end of the principal street, before the venda (village inn). At the door, which opened across the middle, allowing its lower half to serve as a sort of gate, stood the host, little expecting guests on this dark, rainy night. He was a fat old man, with a head as round as a bullet, covered with very short white curly hair, and a face beaming with good nature, but reddened also by many potations. He was dressed in white cotton drawers with a shirt hanging loose over them; his feet were stockingless, but he had on a pair of the wooden-soled slippers, down at heel, of which you hear the "clack, clack" in every town and village during the rainy season. He opened the gate and admitted us into a small room furnished with a hammock, a sofa, and a few chairs, the mud walls adorned with some coarse prints, of which the old gentleman seemed very proud. He said if we could be satisfied with such accommodation as he had, the gentlemen to sling their hammocks in the sitting-room with him, the Senhora to sleep with his wife and the children in the only other room he had to offer, he should be happy to receive us. I confess that the prospect was not encouraging; but I was prepared to meet with inconveniences, knowing that even a short journey into the interior involved discomforts, and when the hostess presently entered and made me heartily welcome to a corner of her apartment, I thanked her with such cordiality as I could muster. She was many years younger than her husband, and still very handsome, with an Oriental kind of beauty, rather enhanced by her dress. She wore a red muslin wrapper, somewhat the worse for wear, but still brilliant in color; and her long black hair hung loose and unbraided over her shoulders. An hour or two later supper was announced. We had brought the greater part of it with us from the city, but we invited all the family to sup with us, according to the fashion of the country. The old gentleman completed his toilet by adding to it a gaudy-flowered cotton dressing-gown, and seating himself at the table, contemplated the roast-chickens and claret with no little satisfaction. From the appearance of things, such a meal must have been a rarity in his house. The mud floor of the kitchen where we supped was sloppy, and its leaky roof and broken walls were but dimly lighted by the coarse guttering candles made from the Carnauba palm. I presently heard a loud gobbling close by my side; and, looking down, saw by the half-light a black pig feeding at a little table with the two children, assisted also by the dog and the cat.

Supper over, I proposed to go to the common sleeping apartment, preferring to be in advance of my companions. It was a little room, some ten feet square, behind the one where we had been received, and without any window. This is not, however, so great an objection here, where the roofs are so open that a great deal of air comes from above. Once ensconced in my hammock I began to watch the arrival of my room-mates with some curiosity. First entered a young girl and her little sister, who stowed themselves away in one of the beds; then came the servant-maid and hung herself up in her hammock in a corner; and lastly arrived the landlady, who took possession of the other bed, and completed the charms of the scene by lighting her pipe to have a quiet smoke before she went to sleep. I cannot say the situation was favorable to rest; the heavy showers which rattled on the tiles throughout the night penetrated the leaky roof, and, however I changed my position in the hammock, it rained into my face; fleas were abundant; the silence was occasionally broken by the crying of the children, or the grunting of the pig at the door, and for my part I was very glad when five o'clock called us all to get up, our plan being to start at six and ride three leagues before breakfast. However, on a journey of this kind, it is one thing to intend going anywhere at a particular time and quite another to accomplish it. When we met at six o'clock in readiness for our journey, two of the horses were not to be found; they had strayed away during the night. Though accidents of this kind are a constant subject of complaint, it does not seem to occur to any one to secure the horses for the night; it is indeed far easier to let them roam about and provide for themselves. The servants were sent to look for them, and we sat waiting, and losing the best hours of the morning, till, in their own good time, men and beasts reappeared. We were at last on the road at half past eight o'clock ; but, unhappily, it was just during our two hours of inaction that the rain, which had been pouring in torrents all night, had ceased for a time. We had scarcely started when it began again, and accompanied us for a great part of the way on our long three leagues' ride. We came now for the first time on the Carnauba palm (Copernicia cerifera), so invaluable for its many useful properties. It furnishes an admirable timber, strong and durable, from which the rafters of all the houses in this region are made ; it yields a wax which, if the process of refining and bleaching it were understood, would make an excellent candle, and which, as it is, is used for light throughout the province ; from its silky fibre very strong thread and cordage are manufactured ; the heart of the leaves, when cooked, makes an excellent vegetable, resembling delicate cabbage ; and, finally, it provides a very nourishing fodder for cattle. It is a saying in the province of Ceará, that where the Carnauba palm abounds a man has all he needs for himself and his horse. The stem is tall, and the leaves so arranged around the summit as to form a close spherical crown, entirely unlike that of any other palm.*

If we had to lament the rain, we were fortunate in not having the sun on our journey, for the forest is low and affords but little shade. The road was in a terrible condition from the long-continued rains, and though there

---

* For a very interesting treatise on this palm, and the various branches of industry it may be made to subserve, see "Notice sur le Palmier Carnauba," par M A. de Macedo, Paris, 1867, 8º.

are no rivers of any importance between the town and the Serra of Monguba, to which we were bound, yet in several places the little streams were swollen to a considerable depth; and, owing to the broken condition of the bottom, full of holes and deep ruts, they were by no means easy to ford. After a fatiguing ride of four hours, during which we inquired, two or three times, how far we had still to go, and always received the same answer, "uma legua," that league never seeming to diminish with our advance, we were delighted to find ourselves at the little bridle-path which turned off from the main road and led us to the fazenda of Senhor Franklin de Lima. The traveller is always welcome who asks hospitality at a Brazilian country house, but Major Coutinho had already stayed at this fazenda on previous journeys, and we shared the welcome given to him as an old friend. The hospitality of our excellent hosts repaid us for all the fatigues of our journey, and our luggage being still on the road, their kindness supplied the defects of our toilet, which was in a lamentable condition after splashing through muddy water two or three feet deep. Mr. Agassiz, however, could not spare time to rest; we had followed a morainic soil for a great part of our journey, had passed many boulders on the road, and he was anxious to examine the Serra of Monguba, on the slope of which Senhor Franklin has his coffee plantation, and at the foot of which his house stands. He was, therefore, either on foot or on horseback the greater part of this day and the following one, examining the geological structure of the mountain, and satisfying himself that, here too, all the valleys have had their glaciers, and that these valleys have brought down from the hill-sides into the plains boulders, pebbles, and *débris* of all sorts. In this pleasant home, in the midst of the bright, intelligent circle composing the family of Senhor Franklin, we passed two days. After breakfast we dispersed to our various occupations, the gentlemen being engaged in excursions in the neighborhood; the evening brought us together again, and was enlivened with music, dancing, and games. The Brazilians are fond of games, and play them with much wit and animation. One of their favorite games is called "the market of saints"; it is very amusing when there are two or three bright people to act the prominent parts. One person performs the salesman, another the padre who comes to purchase a saint for his chapel; the company enact the saints, covering their faces with their handkerchiefs, and remaining as motionless as possible. The salesman brings in the padre, and, taking him from one to another in turn, describes all their extraordinary miraculous qualities, their wonderful lives and pious deaths. After a few introductory remarks on the subject of the purchase, the handkerchief is drawn off, and if the saint keeps his countenance and remains immovable during all the ridiculous things that are said about him, he comes off scot free; but if he laughs he is subject to a forfeit. There are indeed few who stand the test; for if the salesman has any tact in the game, he knows how to seize upon any funny incident or characteristic quality connected with the individual, and give it prominence. Perhaps the reader, knowing something of our hunt for glaciers, may guess this saint, Major Coutinho being salesman. "This, Senhor Padre, is rather a stout saint, but still of most pious disposition, and, O meu Padre! a wonderful worker of miracles; he can fill these valleys with ice, he covers the mountains with snow in the hottest days, he brings the stones from the top of the serra to the bottom, he finds animals in the bowels of the earth and brings out their bones." "Ah!" replies the padre, "a wonderful saint, truly! such an one as I need for my chapel; let me look upon his face." Handkerchief withdrawn, and the saint in question of course loses his forfeit. Yesterday, after breakfast, we left our pleasant friends and came on to the little village of Pacatuba, a league farther inland, and most picturesquely situated at the foot of the Serra of Aratanha. Here we are fortunate in finding an empty "sobrada" (two-storied house), in which we shall establish ourselves for the two or three days we mean to spend in this neighborhood. We have had it swept out, have hung our hammocks in the vacant rooms, which, with the exception of a straw sofa and a few chairs, are innocent of furniture; and if we find it rather forlorn within doors, we have at least beautiful views from all our windows.

April 7th. — Pacatuba. We have already ascertained that our exploration must be confined to the serras in the midst of which we find ourselves; for every one tells us that, in the present state of the roads, it would be impossible to go to Baturité and return in the short time we have at our disposal. However, Mr. Agassiz is not disappointed; for he says a farther journey could only give him glacial phenomena on a larger scale, which he finds here immediately about him in the greatest perfection. On this very Serra of Aratanha, at the foot of which we happen to have taken up our quarters, the glacial phenomena are as legible as in any of the valleys of Maine, or in those of the mountains of Cumberland in England. It had evidently a local glacier, formed by the meeting of two arms, which descended from two depressions spreading right and left on the upper part of the serra, and joining below in the main valley. A large part of the medial moraine formed by the meeting of these two arms can still be traced in the central valley. One of the lateral moraines is perfectly preserved, the village road cutting through it; while the village itself is built just within the terminal moraine, which is thrown up in a long ridge in front of it. It is a curious fact that, in the centre of the medial moraine, formed by a little mountain stream making its way through the ridge of rocks and boulders, is a delicious bathing pool, overgrown by orange-trees and palms. As Mr. Agassiz came down from the serra yesterday, heated with his hunt after glaciers under a tropical sun, he stopped to bathe in this pool. He said, as he enjoyed its refreshing coolness, he could not but be struck with the contrast between the origin of this basin and the vegetation which now surrounds it; to say nothing of the odd coincidence that he, a naturalist of the nineteenth century, should be bathing under the shade of palms and orange-trees on the very spot where he sought and found the evidence of a cold so intense that it heaped the mountains with ice.

April 9th. — Yesterday, at seven o'clock in the morning, we left Pacatuba for the house of Senhor da Costa, lying half-way up the serra, at a height of about eight hundred feet above the level of the sea. The path up the serra is wild and picturesque, lined with immense boulders, and shaded with large trees; while here and there a little cascade comes brawling down over the rocks. In this climate, a road so broken by boulders is especially beautiful, on account of the luxuriance of the vegetation. Exquisite vines, shrubs, and even trees spring up wherever they can find the least soil in which to strike root; and many of these isolated rocks are gardens in themselves. One immense boulder in the path is split, and from its centre springs a palm all draperied in vines. Of the native trees, the Genipapu (Genipa braziliensis), the Imbauba (Cecropia), the Carnauba (Copernicia cerifera), the Catolé (Attalea humilis), and the Paõ d'Arco (Tecoma speciosa) are most prominent. The latter is so named because the Indians make their bows from its tough, elastic wood. Though not native to the soil, bananas, cocoa-nut palms, orange-trees, as well as cotton and coffee shrubs, are abundant. The cultivation of coffee, which thrives admirably on the slopes of all the serras, is the great source of prosperity here; but, at least in the sitios we have visited, it is difficult to judge of the extent of the plantations on account of the irregular manner of planting. The crops are, however, very large, and the coffee superior in quality. I found the climb up the precipitous serra exceedingly fatiguing. The people who live on the mountain come and go constantly, even with their children, on horseback; but as our horses were from the city, and unaccustomed to mountain paths, we had preferred ascending on foot, especially as the rains had made the road more rough and broken than usual. A mountain scramble in this country is very different from the same thing in temperate climates. The least exertion induces excessive perspiration; and if, when thus drenched to the skin, you stop to rest, you are chilled by the slightest breeze. I was very glad when, after about an hour's climbing, we reached the sitio of Senhor da Costa, on the slope of the serra. Donna Maria laughed at me for coming up on foot, and said I should have mounted like a man, as she does, and ascended the serra on horseback. Indeed, I think a lady who is obliged to make a journey in the interior of Brazil should dress Bloomer-fashion and mount *en cavalier*. A lady's seat on horseback is too insecure for dangerous mountain roads, or for fording streams; and her long skirt is another inconvenience.

Nothing can be more picturesque than the situation of this sitio. It is surrounded by magnificent masses of rock, which seem embedded in the forest, as it were; and by its side a cascade comes leaping down through the trees, so hidden by them that, though you hear the voice of the water constantly, you only see its glimmer here and there among the green foliage. The house itself stands on a fine specimen of moraine, flanked on one side by a bank of red morainic soil, overtopped by boulders. It is so built in among huge masses of rock that its walls seem half natural. At the foot of the mountain spreads the Sertaõ, stretching level for the most part to the ocean, though broken here and there by billowy hills rising isolated from its surface. Beyond it many miles away may be seen the yellow lines of the sand-dunes on the shore, and the white glitter of the sea. The Sertaõ (desert) is beautifully green now, and spreads out like a verdant prairie below. But in the dry season it justifies its name and becomes a very desert indeed, being so parched that all vegetation is destroyed. The drought is so great during eight months of the year, that the country people living in the Sertaõ are often in danger of famine from the drying up of all the crops.* After this long dry season the rains often set in with terrible violence,

---

* But for the existence of a shrub allied to our hawthorn, and known to botanists as Zizyphus Joazeiro, the cattle would suffer excessively during the drought. This shrub is one of the few plants common to this latitude which does not lose its foliage during the dry season, and, happily for the inhabitants, all the herbivorous domesticated animals delight to feed upon it.—L. A.

and it is at this time that epidemics are developed, such as prevail now. It rains day and night for weeks at a time, till everything is penetrated with dampness; and when the hot sun comes out upon the soaked and steaming earth, it is far more injurious than in the dry season. One cannot wonder at the prevailing sickness, for the humidity seems to permeate everything with subtle power. The walls, the floors, the very furniture, — your hammock at night and your clothes in the morning, — feel damp and have a sort of clammy chill; and the sun comes out with such fitful gleams, that, intense as is its heat while it lasts, nothing becomes thoroughly dried.

Toward nightfall we went to see the sunset from a boulder of enormous size, which seems to have stopped inexplicably on the steep descent. It juts out from the mountainside, and commands even a more extensive view than the house above. I could not help thinking, as we stood on the edge of this immense mass of rock, that, as it seemed to have stopped for no particular reason, it might start again at any minute, and bring one to the bottom of the serra with unpleasant rapidity.

April 10*th.* — Yesterday afternoon we returned to Pacatuba, descending the serra much more rapidly and with far less fatigue than we had ascended. We would gladly have availed ourselves longer of the pleasant hospitality of our hosts, who very graciously urged us to stay; but time is precious, and we are anxious not to miss the next steamer. Donna Maria's kindness followed us down the mountain, however, for scarcely had we reached the house before an excellent dinner — stewed fowls, beef, vegetables, etc. — arrived, borne on the heads of two negroes. When I saw the load these men had brought so steadily down the same path over which I had come rolling, pitching, tumbling, sliding,—any way, in short, but walking,—I envied their dexterity, and longed to be as sure-footed as these shoeless, half naked, ignorant blacks. To-day we leave Pacatuba for the house of Senhor Franklin, on our way back to Ceará.

April 12*th*.—On the 10th we returned to Monguba, where we passed that day and the following night at the fazenda of our friends, the Franklins. The next morning we had intended to start at six o'clock on our way to the city. No sooner were the horses at the door, however, and the pack-mules ready, than a pouring rain began. We waited for it to pass, but it was followed by shower after shower, falling in solid sheets. So the day wore on till twelve o'clock, when there was a lull, with a prospect of fine weather, and we started. I could not help feeling some anxiety, for I remembered the streams we had forded in coming, and wondered what they would be after these torrents. Fortunately, before we reached the first of them, we met two negroes, who warned us that there was a great deal of water on the road. We hired them to come on with us, and guide my horse. When we reached the spot it really looked appalling. The road was inundated to a considerable distance, and the water rushed across it with great violence, having in many places a depth of four or five feet, and a strong current. If there had been a sound bottom to rely upon, the wetting would have been nothing; but the road, torn up by the rains, was full of holes and deep gullies, so that the horses, coming unexpectedly on these inequalities, would suddenly flounder up to their necks in water, and recover their footing only by kicking and plunging. We crossed four such streams, one man leading my horse while the gentlemen followed close behind, and the second negro walking in front to see where it was possible to pass without getting completely out of depth. These streams, not quite deep enough to allow the horse to swim, and with such a broken bottom that he is in constant danger of falling, are sometimes more difficult of passage than a river. We met with only one accident, however, which, as it did no harm, was rather ludicrous than otherwise. The negroes had left us, saying there was no more deep water in the road, and when we came presently to a shallow stream we entered it quite confidently. It was treacherous, however, for just on its edge was a soft, adhesive bog-mud. In entering, the horses stepped across this quagmire, but their hind legs were instantly caught in it. Major Coutinho, who was riding at my side, seized my bridle, and, spurring his own horse violently, both the animals extricated themselves at once by a powerful effort. Our servant, who followed behind, was not so fortunate; he was mounted on a small mule, which seemed likely to be swallowed up bodily for a moment, so suddenly did it disappear in the mire; the man fell off, and it was some minutes before he and his animal regained the road, a mass of mud and dripping with water. We reached Ceará at five in the afternoon, having made a journey of five leagues. Every one tells us that the state of the roads is most unusual, such continuous rains not having been known for many years. The sickness in the city continues unabated, and a young man who was attacked with yellow-fever in the next house before we left has died in our absence. Everywhere on our journey we have heard the same complaints of prevalent epidemics, and the authorities are beginning to close the schools in the town on account of them. The steamer is due in a day or two, and we are making our preparations for departure. We should not bid good by to Ceará without acknowledging the sympathy shown by the President of the Province, Senhor Homem de Mello, in the objects of the expedition. Mr. Agassiz has received a collection of palms and fishes, the directions for which he had given before starting for the Serra, but the expenses of which are defrayed by the President, who insists upon their being received as a contribution from the province. Mr. Agassiz is also greatly indebted to Senhor Felice, at whose house we have lodged, for efficient help in collecting, and to Senhor Cicero de Lima for a collection of fishes and insects from the interior. I conclude this chapter with a few passages from notes made by Mr. Agassiz during his examination of the Serra of Aratanha and the site of Pacatuba.

"I spent the rest of the day in a special examination of the right lateral moraine, and part of the front moraine of the glacier of Pacatuba; my object was especially to ascertain whether what appeared a moraine at first might not, after all, be a spur of the serra, decomposed in place. I ascended the ridge to its very origin, and there crossed into an adjoining depression, immediately below the Sitio of Captain Henriquez, where I found another glacier bottom of smaller dimensions, the ice of which probably never reached the plain. Everywhere in the ridges encircling these depressions the loose materials and large boulders are so accumulated and embedded in clay or sand that their morainic character is unmistakable. Occasionally, where a ledge of the underlying rock crops out, in places where the drift has been removed by denudation, the difference between the moraine and the rock decomposed in place is recognized at once. It is equally easy to distinguish the boulders which here and there have rolled down from the mountain and stopped against the moraine. The three things are side by side, and might at first be easily confounded; but a little familiarity makes it easy to distinguish them. Where the lateral moraine turns toward the front of the ancient glacier, near the point at which the brook of Pacatuba cuts through the former, and a little to the west of the brook, there are colossal boulders leaning against the moraine, from the summit of which they have probably rolled down. Near the cemetery the front moraine consists almost entirely of small quartz pebbles; there are, however, a few larger blocks among them. The medial moraine extends nearly through the centre of the village, while the left-hand lateral moraine lies outside of the village, at its eastern end, and is traversed by the road leading to Ceará. It is not impossible that eastwards a third tributary of the serra may have reached the main glacier of Pacatuba. I may say, that in the whole valley of Hasli there are no accumulations of morainic materials more characteristic than those I have found here, — not even about the Kirchet; neither are there any remains of the kind more striking about the valleys of Mount Desert in Maine, where the glacial phenomena are so remarkable, nor in the valleys of Lough Fine, Lough Augh, and Lough Long in Scotland, where the traces of ancient glaciers are so distinct. In none of these localities are the glacial phenomena more legible than in the Serra of Aratanha. I hope that before long some members of the Alpine Club, thoroughly familiar with the glaciers of the Old World, not only in their present, but also in their past condition, will come to these mountains of Ceará and trace the outlines of their former glaciers more extensively than it has been possible for me to do in this short journey. It would be an easy excursion, since steamers from Liverpool and Bordeaux reach Pernambuco in about ten days, arriving twice a month, while

Brazilian steamers make the trip from Pernambuco to Ceará in two days. The nearest serra in which I have observed traces of ancient glaciers is reached from Ceará in one day on horseback. The best season for such a journey would be June and July, at the close of the rainy season, and before the great droughts of the dry season have began."

CHAPTER XV.

PUBLIC INSTITUTIONS OF RIO DE JANEIRO. — ORGAN MOUNTAINS.

VOYAGE FROM CEARÁ. — FRESHETS AT PERNAMBUCO. — ARRIVAL AT RIO. — COLLECTIONS. — VEGETATION ABOUT RIO AS COMPARED WITH THAT ON THE AMAZONS. — MISERICORDIA HOSPITAL. — CHARITIES CONNECTED WITH IT. — ALMSGIVING IN BRAZIL. — INSANE ASYLUM. — MILITARY SCHOOL. — THE MINT. — ACADEMY OF FINE ARTS. — HEROISM OF A NEGRO. — PRIMARY SCHOOL FOR GIRLS. — NEGLECTED EDUCATION OF WOMEN IN BRAZIL. — BLIND ASYLUM. — LECTURES. — CHARACTER OF THE BRAZILIAN AUDIENCE. — ORGAN MOUNTAINS. — WALK UP THE SERRA. — THERESOPOLIS — VISIT TO THE "ST. LOUIS" FAZENDA. — CLIMATE OF THERESOPOLIS. — DESCENT OF THE SERRA. — GEOLOGY OF THE ORGAN MOUNTAINS. — THE LAST WORD.

May 29th. — We arrived in Rio more than a month ago, having left Ceará on the 16th of April. There was nothing worth recording in our voyage down the coast, except that at Pernambuco we found the country even more overflowed by the recent rains than it had been at Ceará. Going to breakfast with our friends, Mr. and Mrs. R——, only four or five miles from the city, we passed through portions of the road where the water was nearly level with the floor of the carriage; and temporary ferries were established by negroes, who were plying rafts and canoes between the shores for the benefit of foot-passengers. A mile or two beyond Mr. R——'s house we were told that the road, though one of the most frequented in the neighborhood of the city, had become quite impassable. We saw many overflowed gardens and houses abandoned because the water was already above the windows of the ground-floor.

We had a warm welcome back to the beautiful bay of Rio, on board the "Susquehanna," just then in the harbor.

Captain Taylor sent his boat at once to our steamer, and we were soon on his deck, received so cordially by him and his officers, and by a party of American friends who were making a visit to his ship, that it seemed like an anticipation of our arrival at home. There is nothing so pleasant as an unexpected meeting with one's own fellow-citizens on coming into a foreign port, and this was a delightful surprise to us.

We are again in our old quarters in the Rua Direita, and, except that our fellow-travellers are all scattered, it would seem as if we had stepped back a year. Since our return, Mr. Agassiz has been arranging and despatching to the United States the numerous specimens which have been sent in during our absence. Among them is the large and very complete collection made for him by the Emperor last summer, when in command of the army at the South. It contains fishes from several of the southern fresh-water basins, and includes a great number of new species. Taken in connection with the Amazonian collections and those from the interior, it affords material for an extensive comparison of the faunæ of the southern and northern fresh-waters in Brazil.

Our excursions since our return have been only in the neighborhood of the city to Petropolis and the Dom Pedro Railroad. We are surprised, on returning to this road while our Amazonian impressions are fresh in our minds, to find that the vegetation, the richness of which amazed us when we first arrived in Brazil, looks almost meagre in comparison to that with which we have since been familiar. It is dwarfed, to our eye, by the still more luxuriant growth of the north.

Yesterday was Mr. Agassiz's birthday, again made very

bright to us by the cordial testimony of kind feeling and sympathy from his friends and countrypeople. In the evening we were pleasantly surprised by a torchlight procession in his honor, formed by the German and Swiss residents of Rio de Janeiro. The festivities concluded with a serenade under our windows by the German club.

June 4th. — When we were in Rio de Janeiro last year, Mr. Agassiz was so much occupied with the plans of the expedition that he was unable to visit the schools of the city, its charitable institutions, and the like. Being unwilling to leave Brazil without knowing something of the public works in its largest capital, we are now engaged in "sight-seeing." This morning we visited the Misericordia Hospital. Perhaps it will give a better idea of this institution, and of the influences under which it at present exists, to speak of it first as it was formerly. Nearly forty-years ago there was in Rio de Janeiro a hospital called "De la Misericordia." Its wards were low, its entries were confined and close, its staircases steep and narrow. According to the accounts of physicians who were medical students there in those days, its internal organization was as sordid as its general aspect. The floors were wet and dirty, the beds wretched, the linen soiled; and the absence of a system of ventilation made itself the more felt on account of the want of general cleanliness. The corpses awaited burial in a room where the rats held high festival; and a physician, who has since occupied a distinguished position in Rio de Janeiro, told us that when, as a student, he went to seek there the materials for his anatomical studies, he often found life stirring in this chamber of the dead, and startled away these unseemly visitors. Such, in brief, was the Misericordia Hospital at the time when Brazil secured her independence.

Let us see what it is now. On the same spot, though occupying a much larger space, stands the present hospital. When completed, it will consist of three parallel buildings, long in proportion to their breadth, connected by cross corridors enclosing courts between them. The central edifice, intended for male patients, has been long in use. The front building, looking on the bay, is nearly completed, and is to be devoted to the stores, to accommodations for hospital physicians, nurses, &c. The rear building, not yet begun, will be for the use of women and children, who now occupy the old hospital. Let us look first at the central division. We enter a spacious hall tiled with marble. A smaller hall, leading out of it, connects with one or two reception-rooms, where visitors are received, and medicines given out gratis to poor applicants. A broad staircase of dark wood brings us to the wide corridors, on which the wards open, and which look out upon green gardens enclosed between the buildings, where convalescents may be seen strolling about, or resting in the shade. At the first ward we are received by a Sister of Charity, who, in the absence of the Superior, is to show us the establishment. A description of one ward will answer for all, since they are identical. It is a long, lofty room, the beds in rows on either side, facing outward, and having a broad, open space down the centre. The beds are arranged two and two in pairs, each pair being divided by a door or window. Between every two beds is a little niche in the wall, with a shelf to draw out underneath. In the niche are one or two pitchers or goblets holding the patient's drink; on the shelf is his mug, ready to his hand. To a height of some six or eight feet the wall is wainscoted with blue-and-white porcelain tiles. They are easily washed, do not contract dampness, and look very cool and fresh. The floor is made of the dark Brazilian wood, partly inlaid, and waxed carefully; not a stain is to be seen anywhere on its shining surface. The bedding consists of a well-stuffed straw-mattress below, with a thick hair-mattress above. The sheets and pillow-cases are spotless. Indeed, everything in this fresh, well-aired, spacious room bespeaks an exquisite order and neatness. The bath-rooms are in convenient relation to the wards, furnished with large marble bath-tubs, and with hot and cold water in abundance. From the public wards we pass into large corridors, upon which open private apartments for the use of persons who, not having convenient arrangements at home, or being strangers in the city, prefer, in case of illness, to go to the hospital. The rent of these chambers is exceedingly moderate; — for a room to one's self, $1.50 a day; for a room shared with one other person, $1 a day; for a bed in a larger room occupied by half a dozen, but withdrawn from the general throng, 75 cents. These charges include medical attendance, nursing, and food. From the wards devoted to ordinary diseases, fevers and the like, we went to the surgical wards. It need not be said that here the same neatness and care prevailed; the operating rooms, the surgery lined with cases containing instruments, lint, bandages, &c. were all in faultless order.

From this building — looking, as we went, into the kitchen, where the contents of the great shiny copper kettles smelt very invitingly — we passed through a paved court to the old hospital, in which are the wards for women and children. This gave us an opportunity of comparing, at least in its general arrangement, the ancient establishment with the modern one. The neatness and order prevailing throughout make even this part of the hospital attractive and cheerful; but one feels at once the difference between the high, airy rooms and open corridors of the new building and the more confined quarters of the old one. In both parts of the hospital the mingling of color impresses the stranger. Blacks and whites lie side by side, and the proportion of negroes is considerable, both among the men and women.

The charity of the Misericordia is a very comprehensive one; it includes not only maladies susceptible of cure, but has also its ward for old and infirm persons, who will never leave it except for their last home. The day before our visit a very aged woman had been buried thence, who had lived under this roof for seventeen years. There is also a provision for children whose parents die in the hospital, and who have no natural protector. They remain there, receive an elementary education, being taught to read, write, and cipher; and are not turned into the world until they are of age to marry or to enter into service. There is a chapel connected with the hospital, and many of the wards are furnished with an altar at one end, above which is placed a statue of the Virgin, a crucifix, or a picture of some saint. I could not help asking myself if regular religious services would not be a wise addition to all charitable institutions of this kind, whether Protestant or Catholic. To the respectable poor, their church is a great deal. Many a convalescent would be glad to hear the Sunday hymn, to join in the prayer put up for his recovery; and would think himself the better, body and soul, because he had listened to a sermon. To be sure, in our country, where creeds are so various, and almost every patient might have his own doctrinal speciality, there might be some difficulties which do not exist where there is a state religion, and one form of service is sure to suit all. Still, many would be comforted and consoled, and would come without asking whether the clergyman were of this or that denomination, if they felt him to be genuine and truly devout.

I have presented the old hospital and the present one in direct contrast, because the comparison gives a measure of the progress which, in some directions at least, has taken place during the last thirty or forty years in Rio de Janeiro. It is true, that all their institutions have not advanced in proportion to their benevolent establishments; charity, like hospitality, may be said to be a national virtue among the Brazilians. They hold almsgiving a religious duty, and are more liberal to their churches and to the public charities connected with them than to their institutions of learning. Unhappily, a great deal of their liberality of this kind is expended upon church festas, street processions, saint days, and the like, more calculated to feed superstition than to stimulate pure religious sentiment.

We should not leave the Misericordia without some allusion to the man to whom it chiefly owes its present character. José Clemente Pereira would have been gratefully remembered by the Brazilians as a statesman of distinguished merit, who was intimately associated with more than one of the most important events in their history, even had he no other claim on their esteem. He was born in Portugal, and distinguished himself as a young man in the Peninsular war. Though he was already twenty-eight years of age when he left Europe, he seems to have been as true a lover of Brazil as if born on her soil. His merit was soon recognized in his adopted country, and he occupied, at different times, some of the highest offices of the realm. The early part of his political career fell upon the stormy times when Brazil was struggling for her national existence as an independent Empire ; but during the more tranquil close of his life he seems to have been chiefly occupied in works of benevolence, in founding charitable institutions, and even in personal attendance upon the sick and suffering.

The name of this benevolent Brazilian is associated not only with the Misericordia hospital, but also with the admirable asylum for the insane at Botafogo, which bears the name of the present Emperor. A great part of the funds for this establishment were obtained in an original way, which shows that Pereira knew how to turn the weaknesses of his countrymen to good account. The Brazilians are addicted to titles, and the government offered distinctions of this kind to wealthy citizens who would endow the insane asylum. They were to be either commendadores or barons, the importance of the title being in proportion to the magnitude of their donations. Large sums were actually obtained in this way, and several of the titled men of Rio thus purchased their patents of nobility. When I first arrived in Rio de Janeiro, mere chance led me to visit this asylum. Entering as a stranger, I saw only the outer rooms, listened to the evening service in the chapel for a few moments, and was struck with the order and quiet which seemed to prevail. It certainly never would have occurred to me that I was in an insane hospital. To-day Mr. Agassiz and myself, accompanied by our friend Dr. Pacheco da Silva, passed several hours there, and saw the whole establishment in detail. The building faces upon Botafogo Bay, having the beach immediately before it; on its right the picturesque gap, one side of which is made by the Paõ de Assucar, and on its left the beautiful valley running up toward Corcovado. Thus, looking on the sea and surrounded by mountains, it commands exquisite views on every side. The plan of the building, in its general arrangement, is not unlike that of the Misericordia. It is a handsome solid stone-structure, rather long in proportion to its height, and consists of two parallel buildings, connected by cross corridors. These corridors enclose courts, planted with trees and flowers, and making very pleasant gardens. The entrance hall is in the centre, and has on either side the statues of Pinel and Esquirol, the two French masters in the treatment of mental diseases. The statues have no merit as works of art; but it was pleasant to see them there, as showing a recognition of what these men have done for science and for humanity. A broad, low staircase of dark wood leads up to the chapel. Here we looked with interest at the ornaments on the altar, because they are the work of the patients, who take great pleasure in making artificial flowers and other decorations for the church. On the same floor with the chapel is a large hall, where stands the statue of the youthful Emperor Dom Pedro Segundo. Opposite to it is that of Pereira. It is worthy of note that this statue was presented by the Emperor, and at his request placed opposite his own. The face, quite in keeping with the history of the man, is expressive both of great benevolence and remarkable decision. Connected with this hall are several reception-halls, parlors, and antechambers; indeed, too much room is assigned to mere state apartments in an establishment where space must be precious. One of this suite of rooms was devoted to the various fancy-work made by the patients,

—embroidery of all sorts, artificial flowers and the like. Thence we passed to the wards. As in the Misericordia, the rooms are very large and high, wainscoted with tiles, and opening upon wide corridors, which look out into the enclosed gardens. Some of the dormitories have fifteen or twenty beds, but many of the sleeping-rooms are smaller, it being better, no doubt, to separate the patients at night. We saw but little indication of suffering or distress among them. There were one or two cases of religious melancholy, with the look of fixed, absorbed sadness characteristic of that form of insanity. We were met once or twice by the vacant stare, and heard the senseless chatter and laugh always to be found in these saddest of all asylums for human suffering. But, on the whole, an air of cheerfulness prevailed ; with few exceptions all the patients were occupied, the women with plain sewing or embroidery, the men with carpentering, shoemaking, or tailoring, making cigars for the use of the establishment, or picking over old cordage. The Superior told us that occupation was found to be the most efficient remedy, and that though work was not compulsory, with few exceptions all the patients preferred to share in it. The whole service of the house — washing, sweeping, waxing the floors. cleaning the chambers and putting them in order — is performed by them. Sunday is found to be the most difficult day, because much of the ordinary occupation is suspended, and the patients become unruly in proportion as they are unemployed. From these apartments, where all were busy and comparatively quiet, we passed to a corridor enclosing a large court, where some of the lunatics, too restless for employment, were walking about, gesticulating and talking loudly. The corridor was lined on its inner side with chambers devoted to the use of those whose violence made it necessary to confine them. The doors and windows were grated, the rooms empty of furniture, but well lighted, spacious, and airy; not at all like cells, except in being so strongly secured. They were mostly without occupants; but as we passed one of them a man rushed to the door, and called out to us that he was not a prisoner because he was mad, but that he had killed Lopez, and was now the rightful Emperor of Brazil. This corridor led us to the bath-rooms, which are really on a magnificent scale. A number of immense marble tubs are sunk in the tiled floors. They are of different depths, adapted for standing, sitting, or lying down, and have every variety of arrangement for douche, shower, or sponge baths.

This hospital, like the Misericordia, is under the care of the Sisters of Charity, and is a model of neatness and order. The Superior has a face remarkable for its serenity, expressive at once of sweetness and good sense. From her we learned some interesting facts respecting insanity in this country. She says furious maniacs are rare, and that violence generally yields readily to treatment. She also told us that insanity is more common among the poor than among the better classes. Though the asylum contains apartments for private patients, there are seldom more than eight or ten persons of this description to occupy them. This is not because they have any choice of establishments, for there is no other insane hospital in Rio de Janeiro, though there are one or two "Maisons de Santé" where insane persons are received. There were more blacks among the patients than we had expected to see, the general impression being that insanity is rare among the negroes. We left this hospital impressed by its superiority. A country which has so high a standard of excellence in its charities can hardly fail, sooner or later, to bring its institutions of learning and its public works generally up to the same level. Excellence in one department leads to excellence in all.

From the hospital we continued our walk to the military school, some quarter of a mile farther. It stands in the gap between the Paō de Assucar and the opposite range of hills, and has the Botafogo Bay on one side, the Praia Vermelha on the other. Here, as elsewhere in the public schools of Rio de Janeiro, there is a progressive movement; but old and theoretical methods still prevail to a great degree. The maps are poor; there are no bas-reliefs, no large globes, few dissections or chemical analyses, no philosophical experiments, and no library deserving the name. The school, however, has been in efficient operation only six years, and improvements in the building, as well as in the apparatus for instruction, are made daily. So far as its domestic economy is concerned, the appointments of the establishment are excellent; indeed, one is rather inclined to criticise it as over-luxurious for boys educated to be soldiers. The school-rooms and dormitories, as well as the dining-room, where the tables were laid with a nice service of crockery and glass, and also the kitchens, were clean and orderly. We cannot but wonder that the streets of Rio de Janeiro should be dirtier and more offensive than those of any other city we have visited, when we see the scrupulous neatness characteristic of all its public establishments. The observance of cleanliness in this respect shows that the Brazilians recognize its importance, and it seems strange that they should tolerate nuisances in their streets which make it almost impossible to pass through many of them on foot.

June 7th. — Yesterday we visited the Mint, the Academy of Fine Arts, and a primary school for girls. Of the Mint it is scarcely fair to judge in its present condition; a new building is nearly completed, and all improvements in machinery are wisely deferred until the establishment is removed. When this change takes place, much that is antiquated will be improved, and its many deficiencies supplied.

There is little knowledge of, or interest in, art in Brazil. Pictures are as rare as books in a Brazilian house; and though Rio de Janeiro has an Academy of Fine Arts, including a school of design and sculpture, it is still in too elementary a condition to warrant criticism. The only interesting picture in the collection derives its attraction wholly from the circumstances connected with it, not at all from any merit in the execution. It is a likeness of a negro who, in a shipwreck off the coast, saved a number of lives at the risk of his own. When he had brought several passengers to the shore, he was told that two children remained in the ship. He swam back once more and brought them safely to the beach, but sank down himself exhausted, and was seized with hemorrhage. A considerable sum was raised for him in the city of Rio, and his picture was placed in the Academy to commemorate his heroism.

Of the public school for girls not much can be said. The education of women is little regarded in Brazil, and the standard of instruction for girls in the public schools is low. Even in the private schools, where the children of the better class are sent, it is the complaint of all teachers that they are taken away from school just at the time when their minds begin to develop. The majority of girls in Brazil who go to school at all are sent at about seven or eight years of age, and are considered to have finished their education at thirteen or fourteen. The next step in their life is marriage. Of course there are exceptions; some parents wisely leave their children at school, or direct their instruction at home, till they are seventeen or eighteen years of age, and others send their girls abroad. But usually, with the exception of one or two accomplishments, such as French or music, the education of women is neglected, and this neglect affects the whole tone of society. It does not change the general truth of this statement, that there are Brazilian ladies who would be recognized in the best society as women of the highest intelligence and culture. But they are the exceptions, as they inevitably must be under the present system of instruction, and they feel its influence upon their social position only the more bitterly.

Indeed, many of the women I have known most intimately here have spoken to me with deep regret of their limited, imprisoned existence. There is not a Brazilian senhora, who has ever thought about the subject at all, who is not aware that her life is one of repression and constraint. She cannot go out of her house, except under certain conditions, without awakening scandal. Her education leaves her wholly ignorant of the most common topics of a wider interest, though perhaps with a tolerable knowledge of French and music. The world of books is closed to her; for there is little Portuguese literature into which she is allowed to look, and that of other languages is still less at her command. She knows little of the history of her own country, almost nothing of that of others, and she is hardly aware that there is any religious faith except the uniform one of Brazil; she has probably never heard of the Reformation, nor does she dream that there is a sea of thought surging in the world outside, constantly developing new phases of national and individual life; indeed, of all but her own narrow domestic existence she is profoundly ignorant.

On one occasion, when staying at a fazenda, I took up a volume which was lying on the piano. A book is such a rare sight, in the rooms occupied by the family, that I was curious to see its contents. As I stood turning over the leaves (it proved to be a romance), the master of the house came up, and remarked that the book was not suitable reading for ladies, but that here (putting into my hand a small volume) was a work adapted to the use of women and children, which he had provided for the senhoras of his family. I opened it, and found it to be a sort of text-book of morals, filled with commonplace sentiments, copy-book phrases, written in a tone of condescending indulgence for the feminine intellect, women being, after all, the mothers of men, and understood to have some little influence on their education. I could hardly wonder, after seeing this specimen of their intellectual food, that the wife and daughters of our host were not greatly addicted to reading. Nothing strikes a stranger more than the absence of books in Brazilian houses. If the father is a professional man, he has his small library of medicine or law, but books are never seen scattered about as if in common use; they make no part of the daily life. I repeat, that there are exceptions. I well remember finding in the sitting-room of a young girl, by whose family we had been most cordially received, a well-selected library of the best literary and historical works in German and French; but this is the only instance of the kind we met with during our year in Brazil. Even when the Brazilian women have received the ordinary advantages of education, there is something in their home-life so restricted, so shut out from natural contact with external influences, that this in itself tends to cripple their development. Their amusements are as meagre and scanty as their means of instruction.

In writing these things I but echo the thought of many intelligent Brazilians, who lament a social evil which they do not well know how to reform. If among our Brazilian friends there are some who, familiar with the more progressive aspect of life in Rio de Janeiro, question the accuracy of my statements, I can only say that they do not know the condition of society in the northern cities and provinces. Among my own sex, I have never seen such sad lives as became known to me there, — lives deprived of healthy, invigorating happiness, and intolerably monotonous, — a negative suffering, having its source, it is true, in the absence of enjoyment rather than in the presence of positive evils, but all the more to be deplored because so stagnant and inactive.

Behind all defects in methods of instruction, there lies a fault of domestic education, to be lamented throughout Brazil. This is the constant association with black servants, and, worse still, with negro children, of whom there are usually a number in every house. Whether the low and vicious habits of the negroes are the result of slavery or not, they cannot be denied ; and it is singular to see persons, otherwise careful and conscientious about their children, allowing them to live in the constant companionship of their blacks, waited upon by the older ones, playing all day with the younger ones. It shows how blind we may become, by custom, to the most palpable dangers. A stranger observes at once the evil results of this contact with vulgarity and vice, though often unnoticed by the parents. In the capital, some of these evils are fast disappearing; indeed, those who remember Rio de Janeiro forty years ago have witnessed, during that short period, a remarkable change for the better in the state of society. Nor should it be forgotten that the highest authority in the community is exerted in the cause of a liberal culture for women. It is well known that the education of the Imperial princesses has been not only superintended, but in a great measure personally conducted, by their father.

June 8th. — I was prevented yesterday from going to the Blind Asylum with Mr. Agassiz, but I transcribe his notes upon this, as well as upon the Marine Arsenal, which he also visited without me.

"The building is old and in a ruinous condition. I was not allowed to go over it, everything being brought to the reception-room for my inspection, though I told the director that I did not care about the external arrangements, but simply wished to know by what means the privations of the blind were alleviated in his establishment. The same processes of routine prevail here as in other schools and colleges I have seen in Rio. This, however, is not peculiar to Portuguese or Brazilian habits of instruction. The old habit of overrating memory, and neglecting the more active and productive faculties of the mind, still prevails more or less in education everywhere. I learned little of the general system pursued. The teachers were more anxious to show off the ability of special pupils in reading, writing from dictation, and music, than to explain their methods of instruction. Vocal and instrumental music seemed the favorite occupation; but though it is very pathetic to hear the blind deplore their misfortune and express their craving for light in harmonious sounds, it does not, after all, give much information as to the way in which their calamity is relieved. I should add, that their musical performance is excellent, and does great credit to their German professor. It struck me that very little use was made of object-teaching, such as is so much in vogue for children in Germany. There are not as many models in the whole establishment as would be found in any nursery in certain parts of Germany. The maps also are very poor.

"One of the most interesting of the public establishments at Rio de Janeiro is the Marine Arsenal. From the Gulf of Mexico to Cape Horn there is not to be found on the Atlantic coast another port where a vessel of war, or even a merchant vessel of large tonnage, could undergo important repairs. The machine-shops and saw-mills are well directed, and are deficient in none of the improvements belonging to modern establishments of the kind. The dock is large and constructed of granite. A considerable number of large vessels have been built at this shipyard during the last few years, and all its appointments have been constantly improving under the direction of several successive ministers of the navy. Such an establishment is, in fact, a necessity for Brazil; possessing as she does eleven hundred leagues of coast, it is impossible for her to depend upon other countries for her maritime supplies. The Marine Arsenal sends out from its school and shipyard many able engineers and clever artisans, who carry into ordinary branches of industry the ability they have acquired in the public service. Indeed, this establishment may be considered as a sort of school of industrial arts, furnishing the country with good workmen in various departments of labor."

This week Mr. Agassiz has concluded another course of six lectures given at the College of Dom Pedro II.; the subject, "The Formation of the Amazonian Valley, and its Productions." It is worthy of remark, that the appearance of ladies on such occasions no longer excites comment. There were many more senhoras among the listeners than at the previous lectures, when their presence was a novelty. A Brazilian audience is very sympathetic; in this they resemble a European assembly more than our own quiet, undemonstrative crowds. There is always a little stir, a responsive thrill, when anything pleases them, and often a spoken word of commendation or criticism.

June 10th. — Theresopolis. Yesterday, accompanied by Mr. Glaziou, Director of the Passeio Publico, and Dr. Nägeli, we started on an excursion to the Organ Mountains, leaving Rio in the boat for Piedade, and stopping on our way at the little island of Paquetá. This is one of the prettiest islands of the harbor, abounding in palms, populous with pleasant country-houses, and having a very picturesque shore, broken into bays and inlets. We reached the little cluster of houses called Piedade about five o'clock, and took the omnibus to the foot of the serra. The hours of public conveyance on this road seem ingeniously arranged to prevent the traveller from seeing its beauties. The greater part of the four hours' drive is made after nightfall; and the return offers no compensation, the second journey taking place before daybreak. We passed the night at the foot of the serra, and started at seven o'clock the next morning to walk up the mountain. It is impossible to describe the beauty of this walk, especially on such a day as we were favored with, varying between sunshine and shade, and with a fresh breeze which saved us any discomfort from the heat. The road winds gently up the serra, turning sometimes with so sharp an angle that below we could see all the ground we had travelled over. On one hand is the mountain-side, clothed with a vegetation of surpassing beauty, bright with crimson parasites, with the rich purple flowers of the Quaresma and the delicate blue blossoms of the Utricularia, as fragile and as graceful as the harebell. On the other hand, we looked down sometimes into narrow gorges, clothed with magnificent forest, from which huge masses of rock projected here and there; sometimes into wider valleys opening out into the plain below, and giving a distant view of the harbor and its archipelago of islands surrounded by mountains, the whole scene glittering in the sunshine, or veiled by shadows, as the fitful day showed it to us.

The ascent may be easily accomplished on foot in three or four hours. We had nothing to urge us forward, however, except a growing desire for breakfast, appeased every now and then by an orange, of which we had a good supply in the tin case for plants, and many a slow train of laden mules passed us in their upward march, and left us far behind as we loitered along, though not lazily. On the contrary, Mr. Agassiz and his friends found plenty of occupation in botanizing and geologizing. They stopped constantly to gather parasites, to study ferns and mosses, to break boulders, to collect insects and the little land-shells found here and there along the road. We saw one most beautiful insect, hardly larger than a lady-bug, but of the most exquisite colors and gleaming like a jewel on the leaf where it had alighted. In breaking the stones along the roadside Mr. Agassiz found many evidences of erratics, several of them being Diorite, entirely distinct from the rock in place. The surfaces of the boulders were universally decomposed and covered with a uniform crust, so that it was necessary to split them in order to ascertain their true nature. From distance to distance along the road were immense fragments of rock, sometimes twenty or thirty feet in height. These huge

Garrafaõ, among the Organ Mountains.

masses were frequently seen hanging on the brink of steep declivities, as if, having broken off from the heights above, and rolled down, they had been prevented from advancing farther by some obstacle, and had become gradually embedded in the soil. Many of these boulders were clothed in soft, thick reindeer moss, so like the reindeer moss of the Arctics that, if specifically distinct, the difference could not be detected except by the most careful examination. It suggests the question whether there are any representatives of the tropical flora among the lichens and pines of the high north. As we advanced, the character of the vegetation changed considerably, and we began to feel, by the increasing freshness of the air, that we were getting into higher regions. The near view became more beautiful as we approached the heart of the mountains, coming under the shadow of their strange peaks, which looked sharp and attenuated from a distance, but changed into wonderful masses of bare rock, very grand in their effect, as we drew closer to them. We reached the hotel at Theresopolis at about two o'clock. After our long walk, the answer we received to our inquiry about breakfast at the little grocery adjoining the inn was rather discouraging. What could they give us on short notice? "Only four eggs and some sausage." However, the master of the hotel made his appearance, opened his house, where, to judge from its closed doors and windows, the advent of guests is rare, and comforted us with the information that breakfast "pode se arranjar." Indeed, from the dish of eggs which made its appearance soon afterwards, we might have supposed that all the hens in the village had been called upon to contribute, and we enjoyed a breakfast for which mountain air and exercise had supplied the best sauce.

The village of Theresopolis is very prettily situated, lying in a dip between the mountains and commanding a magnificent view of the peaks, one of which stands out like a tall, narrow tower against the sky. Near it is another sharp summit, on the extreme point of which a large boulder is placed. It looks as if a touch would dislodge it; and yet for how many a long year has it held its place there through storm and sunshine! We looked up at this huge fragment of rock on its dizzy height, and wondered whether it was erratic, or simply an effect of decomposition on the spot,— a point impossible of decision at that distance. If the latter, it seems strange that the weather should have worn and excavated such a mass underneath, without destroying its upper surface, thus detaching it from the mountain, till it stands, as now, in bold relief, only supported by a single point of attachment on the extreme summit. We spent the rest of the day in a walk to a very pretty cascade which comes rushing down through the wood a mile or two from the village.

June 11th. — We left the inn at half past seven this morning, to pass the day again in rambling. Following the main road for a quarter of a mile or so beyond the village, we presently turned to the left into a narrow, shady pathway. It led us through the woods to the edge of a deep basin sunk between the mountains, on the slopes of which were strewn many immense boulders. A curious feature of the Organ Mountains which we have observed repeatedly even in this short excursion is, that between their strangely fantastic forms the country sinks down into well-defined basins, which usually have no outlet. Following the brink of such a basin for a couple of miles, and crossing an intervening ridge, we came out upon a kind of plateau overhanging another depression of the same character, and commanding a magnificent view of the chain, in the very centre of which it seems to be, for the mountains rise tier upon tier around it on every side. On this plateau stands the fazenda called St. Louis, belonging to Mr. d'Escragnolle. The exquisite beauty of the site and the hospitality of its owner have made this fazenda a favorite resort for travellers. The grounds are laid out with much taste, and Mr. d'Escragnolle's success in raising many of the European fruits and vegetables, as well as those of his own country, makes it the more to be regretted that this beautiful region should be so little cultivated. Pears, peaches, strawberries, thrive admirably, as also do green peas, asparagus, artichokes, and cauliflowers. The climate strikes a happy medium between the heat in the neighborhood of Rio de Janeiro, which brings these products to too rapid a development, drying them up before they have time to mature, and the sharp cold of higher mountain regions. But though at so short a distance from the capital, the transport is so difficult and expensive that Mr. d'Escragnolle, instead of sending the produce of his farm to the city market, as he would gladly do, feeds his pigs with cauliflowers. We passed the rest of the day most delightfully in this charming country place. Mr. Agassiz and Mr. Glaziou ascended one of the near mountain summits, but did not gain so extensive a view as they had hoped, on account of an intervening spur. They were able to distinguish three parallel ridges, however, separated by intervening depressions. Toward evening, while the mountains were still bright with the purple glory of the sunset, though shadows were settling over the valleys, we started on our return, bidding good by with great regret to our kind host, who warmly pressed us to stay. The path we had followed in the morning, without giving a thought to its irregularities, seemed quite broken and difficult by night. The slopes along which it ran were changed, in the dim light, to

21*

sudden precipices, and we picked our steps with care between rocks and over fallen logs and rivulets. It was bright starlight as we came out of the woods upon the high road. The village lay below, its lights twinkling cheerily, and the peaks and towers behind it drawn with strange distinctness against the night sky.

Organ Mountains.

June 12*th.* — Barreira. This morning at seven o'clock we were on our way down the serra. Mr. Agassiz deplores the necessity which obliges him to leave this region after so short an examination of its striking features. A naturalist might pass months here, and find every day rich in results. As we left the hotel the sun was just gilding the highest summits, while white clouds rose softly from the valleys, and, floating upward, broke into fleecy fragments against the mountain-sides. Having the day before us, we descended as slowly as we had mounted the serra, stopping almost at every step to gather plants, to examine rocks, to wonder at the strange position of the immense boulders hanging often just on the brow of some steep declivity. I wandered on beyond the others and sat down to wait for them on the low stone wall, forming a parapet on the edge of the road. Directly before me rose the bare, rocky surface of one of the great peaks; a vapory white cloud hung midway upon it; shadows floated over it. On the other side I looked down upon wooded valleys and mountains in strange confusion, while far below, stretching out to the sea, lay the billowy plain tossed into endless soft green waves. The stillness made the scene more impressive, the silence being only occasionally broken by the click of hoofs, as a train of mules came cautiously down the flagged road. While I sat there a liteira passed me slung between mules; a mode of travelling fast disappearing with the improvements of the roads, but still in use for women and children in certain parts of the country. We stopped to breakfast at a little venda about half-way down the serra; here the boulders are most remarkable from their great size and singular position. We reached the inn at the bottom of the serra between two and three o'clock, and are now sitting in the little piazza, while a drenching rain, which fortunately did not begin till we were under shelter, swells the stream near by, and is fast changing it to a rapid torrent. I will add here such observations respecting the geological structure of this mountain range as Mr. Agassiz has been able to make in our short excursion.

"The chain is formed by the sharp folding up of strata, sometimes quite vertically, in other instances with a slope more or less steep, but always rather sudden. To one standing on the hill to the east of Theresopolis, the whole range presents itself in a perfect profile; the axis, on either side of which dip the almost vertical beds of metamorphic rocks composing the chain, occupies about the centre of the range. To the north, though very steeply inclined, the beds are not so vertical as in the southern prolongation of the range. The consequence of this difference is the formation of more massive and less disconnected summits on the north side; while on the south side, where the strata are nearly or quite vertical, the harder sets of beds alone have remained standing, the softer intervening beds having been gradually disintegrated. By this process have been formed those strange peaks which appear from a distance like a row of organ-pipes, and have suggested the name by which the chain is known. They consist of vertical beds isolated from the general mass in consequence of the disappearance of contiguous strata. The aspect of these mountains from Rio is much the same as from Theresopolis, only that from the two points of view — one being to the northeast, the other to the southwest of the range — their summits present themselves in the reverse order. When seen in complete profile their slender appearance is most striking. Viewed from the side, the broad surfaces of the strata, though equally steep, exhibit a triangular form rather than that of vertical columns. It is strange that the height of the Organ Mountain peaks, so conspicuous a feature in the landscape of Rio de Janeiro, should not have been accurately measured. The only precise indication I have been able to find is recorded by Liais, who gives 7,000 feet as the maximum height observed by him.

"These abrupt peaks frequently surround closed basins, very symmetrical in shape, but without any outlet. On account of this singular formation, the glacial phenomena which abound in the Organ Mountains are of a peculiar character. At first, I was at a loss to explain how loose masses of rock, descending from the heights above, should be caught on the edges of these basins, instead of rolling to the bottom. But their position becomes quite natural when we remember that the ice must have remained in these depressions long after it had disappeared, or nearly disappeared, from the slopes above. Hindered from advancing, these huge masses of rock have become gradually embedded in the soil, and are now solidly fixed in positions which would be perfectly inexplicable, unless we suppose the basin to have been formerly filled with something which offered an obstacle to their farther descent. Moraines also abut upon these depressions, coming to an abrupt close upon their margin. Morainic soil — that is, masses of drift with all sorts of loose materials buried in it — abounds everywhere in this region; but, on the whole, the glacial phenomena are difficult to study, because the heavy growth of forest has covered all inequalities of the soil, and, except where sections have been made or ground has been cleared, the outlines are lost."

This was our final excursion in Brazil. The next morning we returned to the city; and the few remaining days were spent in preparations for departure, and in bidding farewell to the friends who had made Rio de Janeiro almost like a home to us. Among the pleasant incidents of this last week, was a breakfast given by Mr. Ledgerwood, who was then conducting the business of the American legation in the temporary absence of our Minister, General Webb. This occasion, at which Mr. Agassiz was invited to meet several members of the Brazilian administration, gave him an opportunity of expressing his sense of their uniform kindness and consideration in furthering to the utmost the scientific objects which had brought him to Brazil. On the following day (the 2d of July), we sailed for the United States, carrying with us to our northern home a store of pleasant memories and vivid pictures to enrich our life hereafter with tropical warmth and color.

CHAPTER XVI.

GENERAL IMPRESSIONS OF BRAZIL.

RELIGION AND CLERGY. — EDUCATION. — LAW, MEDICAL, AND SCIENTIFIC SCHOOLS. — HIGH AND COMMON SCHOOLS. — PUBLIC LIBRARY AND MUSEUM IN RIO DE JANEIRO. — HISTORICAL AND GEOGRAPHICAL INSTITUTE. — SOCIAL AND DOMESTIC RELATIONS. — PUBLIC FUNCTIONARIES. — AGRICULTURE. — ZONES OF VEGETATION. — COFFEE. — COTTON. — TIMBER AND OTHER PRODUCTS OF THE AMAZONS. — CATTLE. — TERRITORIAL SUBDIVISION OF THE GREAT VALLEY. — EMIGRATION. — FOREIGNERS. — PARAGUAYAN WAR.

I CANNOT close this book, written for the most part by another hand, without a few words as to my general impressions of Brazil. No one will expect from me an essay on the social and political aspects of the whole country, even had I remained there long enough to acquire the right of judgment on these matters. I am so unaccustomed to dealing with them that my opinions would be entitled to little weight. There is, however, another point of view, more general, but perhaps more comprehensive also, from which every intelligent man may form an estimate of the character of a people which, if sincere, will be in the main sound and just, without including an intimate knowledge of their institutions, or the practical working of their laws. My scientific life has brought me into relations with a world wholly unknown to me before; under conditions more favorable than were possible for my predecessors in the same region, I have studied this tropical nature, so rich, so grandiose, so instructive; I have seen a great Empire founded in the midst of unlimited material resources, and advancing to higher civilization under the inspiration of a sovereign as enlightened as he is humane. I must have been blind to everything except my science, had I not a word to say of Brazil as a nation,— of her present condition and her future prospects.

There is much that is discouraging in the aspect of Brazil, even for those who hope and believe as I do, that she has before her an honorable and powerful career. There is much also that is very cheering, that leads me to believe that her life as a nation will not belie her great gifts as a country. Should her moral and intellectual endowments grow into harmony with her wonderful natural beauty and wealth, the world will not have seen a fairer land. At present there are several obstacles to this progress; obstacles which act like a moral disease upon the people. Slavery still exists among them. It is true that it is on the wane; true that it has received a mortal blow; but the natural death of slavery is a lingering illness, wasting and destroying the body it has attacked. Next to this I would name, among the influences unfavorable to progress, the character of the clergy. In saying this I disclaim any reference to the national religion. It is of the character of the clergy I speak, not of the church they represent. Whatever be the church organization in a country where instruction is still so intimately linked with a state religion as it is in Brazil, it is of infinite importance that the clergy themselves should not only be men of high moral character, but of studious, thoughtful lives. They are the teachers of the people, and as long as they believe that the mind can be fed with tawdry street processions, with lighted candles, and cheap bouquets; and as long as the people accept this kind of instruction, they will be debased and enfeebled by it. Shows of this kind are of almost daily occurrence in all the large cities of Brazil. They interfere with the ordinary occupations, and make working days the exception rather than the rule. It must be remembered that in Brazil there is no laborious, cultivated class of priests, such as have been an honor to ecclesiastical literature in the Old World; there are no fine institutions of learning connected with the Church. As a general thing, the ignorance of the clergy is universal, their immorality patent, their influence very extensive and deep-rooted. There are honorable exceptions, but they are not numerous enough to elevate the class to which they belong. But if their private life is open to blame, the Brazilian priests are distinguished for their patriotism. At all times they have occupied high public stations, serving in the Legislative Assembly, in the Senate, and even nearer to the throne; yet their power has never been exerted in favor of Ultramontane tendencies. Independent religious thought seems, however, rare in Brazil. There may perhaps be scepticism; but I think this is not likely to be extensively the case, for the Brazilians are instinctively a believing people, tending rather to superstition than to doubt. Oppression in matters of faith is contrary to the spirit of their institutions. Protestant clergymen are allowed to preach freely; but, as a general thing, Protestantism does not attract the Southern nations, and it may be doubted whether its advocates will have a very wide-spread success. However this may be, every friend to Brazil must wish to see its present priesthood replaced by a more vigorous, intelligent, and laborious clergy.

In order to form a just estimate of the present condition of education in Brazil, and its future prospects, we must not consider it altogether from our own stand-point. The truth is that all steady progress in Brazil dates from her declaration of independence, and that is a very recent fact in her history. Since she has passed from colonial to national life her relations with other countries have enlarged, antiquated prejudices have been effaced, and with a more intense individual existence she has assumed also a more cosmopolitan breadth of ideas. But a political revolution is more rapidly accomplished than the remoulding of the nation which is its result,— its consequence rather than its accompaniment. Even now, after half a century of independent existence, intellectual progress in Brazil is manifested rather as a tendency, a desire, so to speak, giving a progressive movement to society, than as a positive fact. The intellectual life of a nation when fully developed has its material existence in large and various institutions of learning, scattered throughout the country. Except in a very limited and local sense, this is not yet the case in Brazil.

I did not visit San Paolo, and I cannot therefore speak from personal observation of the Faculty which stands highest in general estimation; I can, however, testify to the sound learning and liberal culture of many of its graduates whom it has been my good fortune to know, and whose characters as gentlemen and as students bear testimony to the superior instruction they have received at the hands of their Alma Mater. I was told that the best schools, after those of San Paolo, were those of Bahia and Pernambuco. I did not visit them, as my time was too short; but I should think that the presence of the professional faculties established in both these cities would tend to raise the character of the lower grades of education. The regular faculties embrace only medical and legal studies. The instruction in both is thorough, though perhaps limited; at least I felt that, in the former, in which my own studies have prepared me to judge, those accessory branches which, after all, lie at the foundation of a superior medical education, are either wanting or are taught very imperfectly. Neither zoölogy, comparative anatomy, botany, physics, nor chemistry is allowed sufficient weight in the medical schools. The education is one rather of books than of facts. Indeed, as long as the prejudice against manual labor of all kinds exists in Brazil, practical instruction will be deficient; as long as students of nature think it unbecoming a gentleman to handle his own specimens, to carry his own geological hammer, to make his own scientific preparations, he will remain a mere dilettante in investigation. He may be very familiar with recorded facts, but he will make no original researches. On this account, and on account of their personal indolence, field studies are foreign to Brazilian habits. Surrounded as they are by a nature rich beyond comparison, their naturalists are theoretical rather than practical. They know more of the bibliography of foreign science than of the wonderful fauna and flora with which they are surrounded.

Of the schools and colleges in Rio de Janeiro I have more right to judge than of those above mentioned. Several of them are excellent. The Ecole Centrale deserves a special notice. It corresponds to what we call a scientific school, and nowhere in Brazil have I seen an educational institution where improved methods of teaching were so highly appreciated and so generally adopted. The courses of mathematics, chemistry, physics, and the natural sciences are comprehensive and thorough. And yet even in this institution I was struck with the scantiness of means for practical illustration and experiment; its professors do not yet seem to understand that it is impossible to teach any of the physical sciences wholly or mainly from text-books. The facilities granted to pupils in this school, and perhaps still more in the military school, are very great. The instruction is entirely gratuitous, and in the military school the students are not only fed and clothed, etc.; they are even paid for their attendance, being considered as belonging to the army from the time they enter the school.

The Dom Pedro Segundo College is the best school of that class I have seen in Brazil. It may be compared to our New England high schools, and fully deserves the reputation it enjoys.

Of the common schools I saw little. Of course, in a country where the population is sparsely scattered over very extensive districts, it must be difficult to gather the children in schools, outside of the large cities. Where such schools have been organized the instruction is gratuitous; but competent teachers are few, the education very limited, and the means of instruction scanty. Reading, writing, and ciphering, with the least possible smattering of geography, form the groundwork of all these schools. The teachers labor under great difficulties, because they have not the strong support of the community. There is little general appreciation of the importance of education as the basis without which all higher civilization is impossible. I have, however, noticed throughout Brazil a disposition to give a practical education, a training in some trade, to the poor children. Establishments of this kind exist in almost all the larger cities. This is a good sign; it shows that they attach a proper value to labor, at least for the lower classes, and aim at raising a working population. In these schools blacks and whites are, so to speak, industrially united. Indeed, there is no antipathy of race to be overcome in Brazil, either among the laboring people or in the higher walks of life. I was pleased to see pupils, without distinction of race or color, mingling in the exercises.

It is surprising that, in a country so rich in mineral wealth, there should exist no special Mining School, and that everything connected with the working of the mines should be under the immediate supervision of the Minister of Public Works, without the assistance of a special office for the superintendence of mining operations. Nothing would more speedily increase the value of the mineral lands of the whole country than a regular geological survey, which has not yet been begun.*

The Imperial Library at Rio de Janeiro should not be omitted from an enumeration of its educational establishments. It is very fairly supplied with books in all departments of learning, and is conducted in a very liberal spirit, suffering no limitation from religious or political prejudice. In fact, tolerance and benevolence are common characteristics of the institutions of learning in Brazil. The Imperial Museum of Natural History in the Capital is antiquated; to any one acquainted with Museums which are living and progressive, it is evident that the collections it contains have been allowed to remain for years in their present con-

---

* I deeply regret that I could not visit the mining districts of Brazil. Especially would I have liked to examine for myself the Cascalho, in which the diamonds are found. From collections which I owe to the kindness of Dr. Vieira de Mattos in Rio de Janeiro, and Senhor Antonio de Lacerda in Bahia, I am prepared to find that the whole diamond-bearing formation is glacial drift. I do not mean the rocks in which the diamonds occur in their primary position, but the secondary agglomerations of loose materials from which they are washed.

dition, without additions or improvements. The mounted animals, mammalia and birds, are faded; and the fishes, with the exception of a few beautifully stuffed specimens from the Amazons, give no idea of the variety to be found in the Brazilian waters. A better collection might be made any morning in the fish-market. The Museum contains some very fine fossil remains from the valley of the San Francisco and from Ceará, but no attempt has as yet been made to arrange them.

The only learned society deserving a special mention is the Historical and Geographical Institute. Its Transactions are regularly published, and form already a series of many volumes, full of valuable documents, chiefly relative to the history of South America. The meetings are held in the Imperial Palace of Rio, and are habitually presided over by his Majesty the Emperor.

I cannot close what I have to say of instruction in Brazil without adding that, in a country where only half the nation is educated, there can be no complete intellectual progress. Where the difference of education makes an intelligent sympathy between men and women almost impossible, so that their relation is necessarily limited to that of the domestic affections, never raised except in some very exceptional cases to that of cultivated companionship, the development of the people as a whole must remain imperfect and partial. I believe, however, that, especially in this direction, a rapid reform may be expected. I have heard so many intelligent Brazilians lament the want of suitable instruction for women in their schools, that I think the standard of education for girls will steadily be raised. Remembering the antecedents of the Brazilians, their inherited notions as to what is becoming in the privacy and restraint of a woman's life, we are not justified, however false these ideas may seem to us, in considering the present generation as responsible for them ; they are also too deeply rooted to be changed in a day.

On several occasions I have alluded in terms of praise to the working of the institutions of Brazil. Nothing can be more liberal than the Constitution of the land ; every guaranty is therein secured to the freest assertion of all the natural rights of man. And yet there are some features in the habits of the people, probably the results of an antiquated social condition, which impede the progress of the nation. It should not be forgotten that the white population of Brazil is chiefly descended from the Portuguese, and that of all Europe Portugal is the country which at the time of the discovery and settlement of Brazil, had least been affected by the growth of our modern civilization. Indeed, the great migrations which convulsed Europe in the Middle Ages, and the Reformation, upon which the new social order chiefly rests, have scarcely affected Portugal ; so that Roman ways, Roman architecture, and a degenerate Latin were still flourishing when her Transatlantic colonies were founded ; and, as in all colonies, the conditions of the mother country were but slowly modified. No wonder, therefore, that the older structures of Rio de Janeiro should recall, in the most surprising manner, the architecture of ancient Rome, as disclosed by the excavations of Herculaneum and Pompeii, and that the social condition of Brazil should remind us of the habits of a people among whom women played so subordinate a part. It seems to me that even now the administration of the provinces, as in the Roman civilization, is calculated to enforce the law, rather than to develop the material resources of the country. I have been surprised to find young lawyers almost invariably at the head of the administration of the provinces, where practical men, conversant with the interests of agriculture, commerce, and the mechanical arts, would, in my opinion, have been better adapted to the pressing duty of stimulating all pursuits connected with the active life of a young and aspiring nation.

The exaggerated appreciation of political employment prevailing everywhere is a misfortune. It throws into the shade all other occupations, and loads the government with a crowd of paid officials who uselessly encumber the public service and are a drain upon the public funds. Every man who has received an education seeks a political career, as at once the most aristocratic and the easiest way of gaining a livelihood. It is but recently that gentlemen have begun to engage in mercantile pursuits.

It seems to me, that, though the character and habits of the Brazilians are not those of an agricultural people, Brazil is an essentially agricultural country, and some occurrences in her recent history confirm this view. Brazil had formerly a great variety of agricultural products, but now the number of plants under culture is rather limited. Agricultural operations are at present centred upon coffee, cotton, sugar, tobacco, mandioca, some cereals, beans, and cocoa. Owing to her climate and her geographical position, the vegetable zones of Brazil are not so marked as those of other countries. It would not be difficult to divide the whole Empire, with reference to its productions, into three great regions. The first of these, stretching from the borders of Guiana to Bahia, along the great rivers, is more especially characterized by the wild products of the forest: Indian-rubber, cocoa, vanilla, sarsaparilla, and an infinite variety of gums, resins, barks, and textile fibres still unknown to commerce in Europe and the United States. To these Brazil might add spices, the monopoly of which belongs now to the Sunda Islands. The second region, extending from Bahia to Santa Catarina, is that of coffee. The third, from Santa Catarina to Rio Grande, and in the interior of the high plateaux, is that of the grains; and, in connection with their culture, the raising of cattle. Rice, which is easily grown throughout Brazil, and cotton, which yields magnificent crops in all the provinces, bind together these three zones, sugar and tobacco following in their train. An important step with reference to agriculture, which has scarcely been thought of as yet, is the cultivation of the heights of the Organ Mountains, as well as those of the Serra do Mar and the Serra do Mantiqueira. On these high lands might be raised all the products characteristic of the warmer portions of the temperate zones, and Rio de Janeiro would receive daily from the mountains in her immediate neighborhood all those vegetables and garden fruits which she now procures in small quantities and at high prices from the provinces bordering on the La Plata. The slopes of these Serras might also be covered with plantations of cascarilla, and, as the production of quinine must sooner or later be greatly diminished by the devastation of the Cinchona-trees on the upper Amazonian tributaries, it is the more important that their culture should be introduced upon the largest scale on the heights above Rio. The attempts of Mr. Glaziou in that direction deserve every encouragement.

The sugar-cane has long been the chief object of cultivation in Brazil, and the production of sugar is still

22

considerable; but within several years the planting of sugar-cane has given way in many districts to that of coffee. I have taken pains to ascertain the facts respecting the culture of coffee during the last fifty years; (the immense development of this branch of industry and the rapidity of the movement, especially in a country where labor is so scarce, is among the most striking economical phenomena of our century.) Thanks to their perseverance and to the favorable conditions presented by the constitution of their soil, the Brazilians have obtained a sort of monopoly of coffee. More than half the coffee consumed in the world is of Brazilian growth. And yet the coffee of Brazil has little reputation, and is even greatly underrated. Why is this? Simply because a great deal of the best produce of Brazilian plantations is sold under the name of Java or Mocha, or as the coffee of Martinique or Bourbon. Martinique produces only six hundred sacks of coffee annually; Guadaloupe, whose coffee is sold under the name of the neighboring island, yields six thousand sacks, not enough to provide the market of Rio de Janeiro for twenty-four hours, and the island of Bourbon hardly more. A great part of the coffee which is bought under these names, or under that of Java coffee, is Brazilian, while the so-called Mocha coffee is often nothing but the small round beans of the Brazilian plant found at the summits of the branches and very carefully selected. If the fazendeiros, like the Java planters, sold their crops under a special mark, the great purchasers would learn with what merchandise they have to deal, and the agriculture of Brazil would be greatly benefited. But there intervenes between the fazendeiro and the exporter a class of merchants — half bankers, half brokers — known as commissarios, who, by mixing different harvests, lower the standard of the crop, thus relieving the producer of all responsibility and depriving the product of its true characteristics.

If the provinces adjacent to Rio de Janeiro offer naturally the most favorable soil for the culture of coffee, it must not be forgotten that coffee is planted with advantage in the shade of the Amazonian forest, and even yields two annual crops wherever pains are taken to plant it. In the province of Ceará, where the coffee is of a superior quality, it is not planted on the plains, or in the low grounds, or in the shadow of the forest, as in the valley of the Amazons, but on the slopes of the hills and on the mountain heights, to an elevation of from fifteen hundred to two thousand feet and more above the level of the sea, in the Serras of Aratanha and Baturité and in the Serra Grande. The channels opened to these products should augment their importance, and should give rise to numerous establishments in the valley of the Amazons.

The increased exportation of cotton from Brazil during the last few years is a still more marked feature in its industrial history than the large coffee crops. When, towards the close of the last century, cotton began to assume in England an importance which has ever since been increasing, Brazil naturally became one of the great providers of the English market. But it soon lost this advantage, because our Southern States acquired, with an extraordinary rapidity, an almost complete monopoly of this product. Favored by exceptional circumstances, North America succeeded, about the year 1846, in furnishing cotton at such low rates that all competition became impossible, and the culture of cotton was almost abandoned in other countries. Brazil, however, persisted. Her annual production showed a slow but steady progress; even the cessation of the slave-trade did not interrupt this advance. Indeed, it is a striking fact, which may well be mentioned in this connection, that the statistics of Brazilian agriculture have been steadily rising ever since the abolition of the slave-trade. When the Rebellion broke out in our Southern States, Brazil thus found herself prepared to give a considerable impulse to the cultivation of a product as much sought for as bread in time of famine. Spite of the want of population, which is an obstacle to all industrial enterprises in Brazil, she found labor, and, what was still more important, free labor, for this object. It seemed as if it were a point of national honor to show what could be done. Provinces like San Paolo, where a foot of ground had never before been planted with cotton; others, as for instance Alagoas, Parahyba do Norte, Ceará, where the cultivation of cotton had been abandoned, produced extraordinary quantities, — so large, indeed, that two lines of steamers were established, and have prospered, between Liverpool and the above-mentioned ports, chiefly for the transport of this crop. It will be remembered that during the whole of this time Brazil was in want of laborers, that she received no foreign capital for this undertaking, that she imported neither Coolies nor Chinese, that almost immediately after the movement began her war with Paraguay broke out, and yet her production of cotton has quadrupled and quintupled. This fact assumed such importance in the estimate of industrial interests at the late Paris Exposition, that an exceptional prize was awarded to Brazil, on the ground that, in supplying the European market so largely with this indispensable staple, she had rendered it independent of the former monopoly of the United States. If is true that the same prize was also granted to Algeria and to Egypt. But the Brazilian planter had not, like the colonists of Africa, the stimulus of a large subsidy from government; he could not, like the Viceroy of Egypt, seize 80,000 men in a single district and transport them to his plantations; neither did he, like the Egyptian fellah, abandon all other branches of agriculture in order to devote himself exclusively to that of cotton. In fact, the general interests of agriculture prospered in Brazil, in the midst of this new enterprise.

I have insisted on these facts, which I think are little known, because they seem to me to show a greater energy and vitality than is usually supposed to exist in the productive forces of Brazil. To stimulate this movement, the government has recently taken the initiatory steps in the organization of an Agricultural School in the vicinity of Bahia, in which all the modern improvements suggested by the progress of science and invention, are to be tested in their application to the natural products of the tropics.

The importance of the basin of the Amazons to Brazil, from an industrial point of view, can hardly be overestimated. Its woods alone have an almost priceless value. Nowhere in the world is there finer timber, either for solid construction or for works of ornament; and yet it is scarcely used even for the local buildings, and makes no part whatever of the exports. It is strange that the development of this branch of industry should not even have begun in Brazil, for the rivers which flow past these magnificent forests seem meant to serve, first as a water-power for the saw-mills which ought to be established along their borders, and then as a means of transportation for the material so provided. Setting aside the woods as timber, what shall I say of the mass of fruits, resins, oils, coloring matters textile fibres, which they yield? When I stopped at Parà. on my way home to the United States, an exhibition of Amazonian products, brought together in preparation for the World's Fair at Paris, was still open. Much as I had admired, during my journey, the richness and variety of the materials native to the soil, I was amazed when I saw them thus side by side. There I noticed, among others, a collection of no less than one hundred and seventeen different kinds of highly valuable woods, cut from a piece of land less than half a mile square. Of these many were dark-colored, veined woods susceptible of a high polish, — as beautiful as rosewood or ebony. There was a great variety of vegetable oils, all remarkable for their clearness and purity. There were a number of fabrics made from the fibres of the palm, and an endless variety of fruits. An empire might esteem itself rich in any one of the sources of industry which abound in this valley, and yet the greater part of its vast growth rots on the ground, and goes to form a little more river-mud or to stain the waters on the shores of which its manifold products die and decompose. But what surprised me most was to find that a great part of this region was favorable to the raising of cattle. Fine sheep are fed on the grassy plains and on the hills which stretch between Obydos and Almeyrim, and I have rarely eaten better mutton than at Ereré, in the midst of these serras. And yet the inhabitants of this fertile region suffer from hunger. The insufficiency of food is evident; but it arises solely from the inability of the people to avail themselves of the natural productions of the soil. As an instance of this, I may mention that, though living on the banks of rivers which abound in delicious fish, they make large use of salt cod, imported from other countries!

While travelling upon the Amazons, I have often asked myself what would be the best plan for developing the natural resources of that incomparable region. No doubt the opening of the great river to the commerce of all nations was a first step in the right direction; and this measure in itself shows what extraordinary progress Brazil is making, for it is hardly more than half a century, since, owing to the narrow policy and jealous disposition of the Portuguese government, the greatest traveller of modern times was forbidden to enter the valley of the Amazons; while to-day a scientific errand of a similar character is welcomed and fostered in every possible way by the government of a nation now independent of Europe. But a free competition is a necessary complement to the freedom already granted, and competition is scarcely possible where monopolies are kept up. I hold, therefore, that all the exceptional facilities granted by the Brazilian government to private companies are detrimental to its best interests. There is, however, another direct obstacle to progress which ought at once to be removed, since the change could in no way injure the general welfare. The present limitation of the provinces of Pará and of the Amazons is entirely unnatural. The whole valley is cut in two transversely, so that its lower half is of necessity a bar to the independent growth of the upper half. Pará, being made the centre of everything, drains the whole country without vitalizing the interior. The great river which should be an international highway has become an inland stream. But suppose for a moment that the Amazons, like our Mississippi, were made the boundary between a succession of independent provinces on either side of it; suppose that on the southern banks of the Amazons the province of Teffé should extend from the borders of Peru to the banks of the Madeira, the province of Santarem from the Madeira to the Xingu, and that of Pará be reduced to the country east of the Xingu, including the Island of Marajo; each of these separate provinces would then be at once bounded and traversed by great streams, securing the double activity of competition and the stimulus of internal conveniences. In like manner should the lands on the northern banks of the Amazons form several independent provinces; that of Monte Alégre, for instance, extending from the Rio Trombetas to the sea; that of Manaos, from the Rio Trombetas to the Rio Negro; and perhaps that of the Hyapura, enclosing the present wilderness between the Rio Negro and the Solimoens. It will, no doubt, be objected that such a change would involve an administrative staff quite disproportionate to the present population; but the government of such provinces, even with the few inhabitants they might number, if organized upon the plan of the territorial governments of our infant States, would only stimulate local energies, and develop local resources, without interfering in the least with the central government. Moreover, any one familiar with the working of the present system in the valley of the Amazons must be aware that all the cities started during the past century along the great river and its tributaries, far from progressing, are going to ruin and decay; and this is unquestionably owing to the centralization at Pará of all the real activity of the whole country.

Without a much denser population, the best efforts of

Brazil to increase its prosperity must be slow and ineffective. No wonder, then, that, immediately after the declaration of independence, Dom Pedro I. attempted to attract German emigrants to his new empire. From that period dates the Colony of San Leopoldo, near Porto Alégre, on the Rio Grande do Sul. It was not, however, till the year 1850, when the slave-trade was actually abolished, and it was no longer possible to import labor from Africa, that these colonization schemes assumed a more definite and settled character. In this attempt the planters and the government were agreed, but with a different object. The plan of the government, undertaken in perfect good faith, was to create a laboring population, and a class of small landed proprietors. The planters, on the contrary, accustomed to compulsory labor, thought only of recruiting their slave ranks by substituting Europeans for Africans. This led to terrible abuses; under pretence of advancing their passage-money, poor emigrants, and especially the ignorant Portuguese from the Azores, were virtually sold under a contract which they subsequently found it very difficult to break. These abuses have thrown discredit upon the attempts of the Brazilian government to colonize the interior, but the iniquities practised under the name of emigration are now corrected. In fact, the colonies established directly by the government, on public lands, have never suffered wrong; on the contrary, the German settlements in Sta Catherina, on the Rio Grande do Sul and on the San Francisco do Sul are very prosperous. The best evidence of the improvement in the condition of the colonists, and of the more liberal spirit of the nation towards them, is the spontaneous formation in Rio de Janeiro of an international society of emigration independent of all government influence, consisting of Brazilians, Portuguese, Germans, Swiss, Americans, French, &c. (The objects of this society, of which Mr. Tavares Bastos is one of the most influential members, are, first, to reform the constitution in all which may place the foreigner at a disadvantage; second, to redress the wrongs of the emigrants; third, to provide them with such assistance and information as they may need on arriving.) This society has been in existence only two years, but has already rendered valuable services. It is to be hoped that the government will persevere in the liberal course it has entered upon, and, above all, put an end to the unnecessary legal formalities by which the emigrant is prevented from taking immediate possession of his new home. This is especially important in the region of the Amazons, where the new-comer finds none of those facilities which welcome the emigrant in the United States. I cannot too often repeat, also, that all monopoly of transport in the Amazons should speedily be abolished. As soon as the wild products of its shores are subjected to a regular culture, even of a very imperfect kind, and are no longer gathered at random, — as soon as organized labor, directed by an intelligent activity, takes the place of the thoughtless and uncertain efforts of the Indians, the variety and excellence of its staples will be increased beyond all expectation. As it is, a little foresight would prevent an immense deal of suffering in this fertile region, where food abounds and people die of hunger. Accustomed to live upon fish, the natives make little use either of milk or meat, and the fine pasturage which might maintain herds of cattle is allowed to run to waste. Careless of the inclemency of the weather when gathering the harvest of the forest, they scarcely build a shelter against the heavy rains, allow their wet clothes to dry upon their skin, and expose themselves to constant alternations of heat and cold. Add to this, that they do not hesitate to drink stagnant water, if it be nearer at hand than spring water, and we have causes enough for the prevalence of intermittent fever and malarious diseases, without attributing them to a climate which is in the main salubrious, and far more moderate in temperature than is generally supposed. The false notions generally current, even in Brazil, in regard to the climate of the Amazons might have been removed long ago, were the public officers of the northern provinces of the Empire not interested in keeping up the delusion. The Amazonian provinces are made stepping-stones to higher employments. The young candidates who accept these posts claim a reward for the disinterestedness they have shown in exposing themselves to disease, and make the reputed fatality of the climate an excuse for leaving these remote stations after a few months' sojourn. The northern provinces of Brazil need an administration less liable to change, and based upon patient study of their local interests, and a faithful adherence to them. It is impossible that the president who comes for six months, and is daily longing for his return to the society and amusements of the larger cities, should even initiate, far less complete, any systematic improvements. Like every country struggling for recognition among the self-reliant nations of the world, Brazil has to contend with the prejudiced reports of a floating foreign population, indifferent to the welfare of the land they temporarily inhabit, and whose appreciations are mainly influenced by private interest. It is much to be regretted that the government has not thought it worth while to take decided measures to correct the erroneous impressions current abroad concerning its administration, and that its diplomatic agents do so little to circulate truthful and authoritative statements of their domestic concerns. As far as I know, the recent World's Fair at Paris was the first occasion when an attempt was made to present a comprehensive report of the resources of the Empire, and the prizes awarded to the Brazilians testify to their success.

Imperfect as is this sketch, I trust I have been able to show, what I deeply feel, that there are elements of a high progress in Brazil, that it has institutions which are shaping the country to worthy ends, that it has a nationality already active, showing its power at the present moment in carrying on one of the most important wars ever undertaken in South America. Neither is this struggle maintained by Brazil for selfish ends; in her conflict with Paraguay she may truly be counted among the standard-bearers of civilization. The facts which have come to my knowledge respecting this war have convinced me that it originated in honorable purposes, and, setting aside the selfish intrigues of individuals, inevitably connected with such movements, is carried on with disinterestedness. It deserves the sympathy of the civilized world, for it strikes at a tyrannical organization, half clerical, half military, which, calling itself a republic, disgraces the name it assumes.

Will my Brazilian friends who read this summary say that I have given but grudging praise to their public institutions, accompanied by an unkind criticism of their social condition? I hope not. I should do myself great wrong did I give the impression that I part from Brazil with any feeling but that of warm sympathy, a deep-rooted belief in her future progress and prosperity, and sincere personal gratitude toward her. I recognize in the Brazilians as a nation their susceptibility to lofty impulses and emotions, their love of theoretical liberty, their natural generosity, their aptness to learn, their ready eloquence; if also I miss among them something of the stronger and more persistent qualities of the Northern races, I do but recall a distinction which is as ancient as the tropical and temperate zones themselves.

APPENDIX.

I.—THE GULF STREAM.

As the results of the systematic investigation of the Gulf Stream upon a plan laid out by Dr. A. D. Bache, and executed, under his direction, by his most able assistants, have hardly yet been presented in a popular form, a sketch of the whole may not be out of place here. This investigation embraced not only surface-phenomena, but the whole internal structure and movement of this wonderful current. It is well known that the Gulf Stream has its origin in the equatorial current which, starting from the Gulf of Guinea, flows for a time in a westerly direction, till it approaches Cape St. Roque. This great projection of the eastern coast of South America interrupts its onward progress, and causes it to divide into two branches, one of which follows the coast of Brazil, in a southerly direction, while the other continues its course to the northwest, until it reaches the Caribbean Sea. After pouring into that basin, the great stream turns to the east to enter the Atlantic again off Cape Florida. The high temperature of the equatorial current is owing to its origin in the tropical zone, its westward course being determined by the rotation of the earth and by the trade-winds. On issuing from the Gulf of Mexico the stream is encased between the island of Cuba and the Bahamas on one side and the coast of Florida on the other. Here it meets the Atlantic in a latitude where the ocean-waters have no longer the high temperature of the tropics, whereas the stream itself has acquired an increased warmth on the shoals of the Gulf. This accounts for the great difference of temperature between the waters of the stream and those of the ocean to the east of it; while the still greater cold of the sea-water on its western side, between the Gulf Stream and the continental shore, is explained by the great Arctic current, pouring down from Baffin's Bay, and skirting the shore of North America as far as the Coast of Florida, until it is lost in that latitude under the Gulf Stream. The object of Dr. Bache's investigation was to trace the mutual relations of these two great currents of warm and cold water, flowing side by side in opposite directions, and to discover the conditions which regulate their movements and keep them within definite limits.

The investigation is even now by no means complete, though it has been going on for many years. It has, however, been ascertained that, while the ocean-bed deepens more or less rapidly as we recede from the shore, forming a trough in which the Gulf Stream flows, this trough is limited on its eastern side by a range of hills trending in the direction of the current, outside of which is another depression or valley. Indeed, the sea-bottom exhibits parallel ridges and depressions, running like the shore of the continent itself, in a northeasterly direction. The water presents differences of temperature, not only on the surface, but at various depths below. These inequalities have been determined by a succession of thermometric observations along several lines, crossing the Gulf Stream from the shore to the ocean water on its eastern side, at intervals of about a hundred miles. The observations have been made first at the surface, and then at successively greater depths, varying from ten to twenty, thirty, one hundred, two hundred, and even three and four hundred fathoms. This survey has shown that, while the Gulf Stream has a temperature higher than that of the waters on either side, it is also alternately warmer and colder within itself, being made up as it were of distinct streaks of water of different temperature. These alternations continue to as great a depth as the observations have been carried, and are found to extend even to the very bottom of the sea, where this has been reached. The most surprising part of this result is the abruptness of the change along the line where the two great currents touch each other. So sharp is this division that the boundary of the Arctic current is now technically designated as the "Cold wall" of the Gulf Stream. Of course as the latter flows northward and eastward it gradually widens, and its temperature is lowered; but even as far north as Sandy Hook the difference between its temperature at the surface and that of the surrounding waters is still marked.

Off Cape Florida the width of the Gulf Stream is not over forty miles; off Charleston it is one hundred and fifty miles; while at Sandy Hook it exceeds three hundred miles.

The inequality of the bottom may be appreciated by the soundings off Charleston, where, from the shore to a distance of two hundred miles, the following depth was successively measured: 10, 25, 100, 250, 300, 600, 350, 550, 450, 475, 450, and 400 fathoms.

The following table may give some idea of the temperature of the stream in connection with its depth: —

Off Sandy Hook, at successive distances from the coast, of

100,   150,   200,   250,   300,   350, and 400 miles,

the temperature near the surface to a depth of thirty fathoms averages:

65°,   66°,   64°,   81°,   80°, and 75° Fahr.;

at a depth of between forty and a hundred fathoms it averages:

50°,   52°,   50°,   47°,   72°,   68°, and 65° Fahr.;

at a depth below three hundred fathoms it averages:

37°,   39°,   40°,   37°,   55°,   57°, and 55° Fahr.

The rapid rise of the temperature after the fourth column of figures indicates the position of the Cold wall.

For further details see the United States Coast Survey Report for 1860, page 165, and the accompanying maps, — which should be copied into all our school atlases.

II. — FLYING-FISHES.

The motions of animals vary greatly with reference to the medium in which they live. Our present knowledge renders it, however, necessary that we should weigh these differences with reference to the structural character of the organs of locomotion themselves, as well as to that of the peculiar resistance of the element in which they move. When we speak of the flight of Birds, of Insects, of Fishes, of Bats, &c., and designate their locomotive organs indiscriminately as wings, it is evident that the character of the motion and not the special structure of the organs has determined our nomenclature. We are influenced by the same consideration when we give the name of fins to the organs of all animals which swim in the water, be they Whales, Turtles, Fishes, Crustacea, or Mollusks. It requires but a superficial acquaintance with the anatomy of the flying-fishes to perceive that their organs of flight are built upon exactly the same pattern as the pectoral fins of most fishes, and differ entirely from the wing of birds, as also from the wing of bats, the latter being in all essentials a paw, identical with the paw of ordinary quadrupeds, save the length of the fingers and the absence of nails on the longest of them. No wonder, then, that the flight of the flying-fishes should entirely differ from that of birds or bats.

I have had frequent occasions to observe the flying-fishes attentively. I am confident not only that they change the direction of their flight, but that they raise or lower their line of movement repeatedly, without returning to the water. I avoid the word falling designedly, for all the acts of these fishes during their flight seem to me completely voluntary. They raise themselves from the surface of the water by rapidly repeated blows with the tail, and more than once have I seen them descend again to the surface of the water in order to repeat this movement; thus renewing the impulse and enabling themselves to continue for a longer time their passage through the air. Their changes of direction, either to the right and left or in rising and descending, are not due to the beating of the wings, that is to say, of the great pectoral fins, but simply to an inflexion of the whole surface, in one or the other direction, by the contraction of the muscles controlling the action of the fin-rays, their pressure against the air determining the movement. The flying-fish is in fact a living shuttlecock, capable of directing its own course by the bending of its large fins. It probably maintains itself in the air until the necessity of breathing compels it to return to the water. The motive of its flight seems to me to be fear; for it is always in the immediate neighborhood and in front of the vessel that they are seen to rise; or perhaps at a distance when they are pursued by some large fish. Now that I have studied their movements, I am better able to appreciate the peculiarities of their structure, especially the inequality of the caudal fin. It is perfectly clear that the greater length of the lower lobe of the caudal is intended to facilitate the movements by which the whole body is thrown out of water and carried through the air; while the amplitude of the pectoral fins affords only a support during the passage through the lighter medium. Nothing shows more plainly the freedom of their movements than the fact that, when the surface of the sea is swelling into billows, the flying-fishes may hug its inequalities very closely and do not move in a regular curve, first ascending from and then descending again to the level of the water. Nor do they appear to fall into their natural element, as if the power that had impelled them was exhausted; they seem rather to dive voluntarily into the water, sometimes after a very short and sometimes after a rather protracted flight, during which they may change their direction, as well as the height at which they move.

The most common flying-fishes of the Atlantic belong to the genus Exocetus, and are closely allied to our Billfish (Belone).

J. Müller has shown that they differ greatly from the Herrings, with which they were formerly associated, and should form a distinct family, to which he has given the name of Scomberesoces. The other flying-fishes belong to the family of the Cottoids, of which our common Sculpins are the chief representatives.

III. — RESOLUTIONS PASSED ON BOARD THE COLORADO.

Resolved, That the cordial thanks of this meeting are due to Professor Agassiz for the highly interesting and instructive lectures which he has delivered daily during our voyage, and which, though intended more immediately to prepare his party for their proposed expedition, have furnished to all of us a rich repast.

Resolved, That the Professor and his companions will carry with them to their beneficent work the earnest prayers and good wishes of all with whom they have been associated on board this ship, that health and abundant success may be vouchsafed to them.

Resolved, That in this mission of science from one country convulsed by war to another not entirely at peace, we behold the humanizing and pacific influence of its aims and studies, and that we cannot but look forward to a day when nations engaged in the common pursuits of science and industry, and bound together by commerce and by enlightened views of interest and of Christian duty, will refer all questions in dispute to peaceful arbitrament rather than to one of violence and bloodshed.

Resolved, That in the facilities afforded by the government of the United States to this scientific expedition, in the munificent contribution of a single citizen of Boston towards its expenses, and in the generous manner in which the owners of this ship have placed its unsurpassed comforts and luxuries at the free use of Professor Agassiz and his party, this meeting beholds a pledge of the profound and growing interest of our entire people in the advancement of liberal and useful knowledge.

Resolved, That we cannot approach the capital of Brazil for the purpose of leaving this party, without expressing our admiration for the personal and political character of him who presides over this vast Empire, and who may well be held forth to all rulers as a model of intelligence, of virtue, and devotion to the public weal.

Resolved, That we cannot close this part of our voyage without tendering to Captain Bradbury, and his subordinate officers, our special thanks, not only for the masterly manner with which their vessel is handled, but for their unwearied devotion to the comfort of their guests.

IV.— DOM PEDRO SEGUNDO RAILROAD.

The part taken by American engineers in this great undertaking induces me to give here a short account of its history.

The decree conceding to one or more companies the entire or partial construction of a railway which, commencing in the municipality of Rio de Janeiro, should terminate in such points in the Provinces of Minas and St. Paulo as should be most advantageous, was promulgated in 1852. A company was organized with a capital of thirty-eight thousand Contos of reis, or nineteen millions of dollars; the general plan being to construct a trunk line from the city of Rio de Janeiro to the River Parahyba, a distance of about 67 miles from the coast. A contract was made with an English engineer, Mr. Edward Price, for the building of the first section of this road, extending a distance of 38½ miles, from Rio de Janeiro to Belem. For the construction of the second section, which embraced the mountain barrier separating the valley of Parahyba from the sea-coast, and in which the greatest difficulties were therefore to be encountered, it was proposed by Senhor Christiano B. Ottoni, President of the road, to employ American engineers, and if possible to engage the services of men who had actually constructed railways across mountain ranges in the United States. To this effect, Colonel C. F. M. Garnett was engaged as chief engineer, and came to Brazil in 1856, accompanied by Major A. Ellison, as his principal assistant. Colonel Garnett remained in the country somewhat more than two years, during which time the portion of the road known as the second section, and extending from Belem to Parahyba, was laid out and its construction commenced, surveys being also made of the branches up and down the river, constituting the third and fourth sections. On Colonel Garnett's departure, Major Ellison remained as chief engineer, having his brother, Mr. Wm. S. Ellison, associated with him in the direction of the road. In July, 1865, at which time the road was actually completed as far as Barro de Pirahy, the company being unable to raise funds for the continuation of the work, it was assumed by the government, as a national undertaking, and Major Ellison, resigning his position, was succeeded by Mr. Wm. S. Ellison as chief engineer.

The difficulties of construction throughout the second section were immense; indeed, there was an almost universal distrust of the practicability of the work. Even after it was considerably advanced, it would probably have been abandoned but for the energy of the President, who shared the confidence of the engineers, and pushed forward the enterprise almost single-handed, in spite of the incredulity of its friends and the objections of its opponents. The sharpness of the mountain spurs rendering it impossible in many cases to pass around them, tunnels became necessary, and fifteen were actually made, varying from 300 to more than 7,300 feet in length, forming, in the aggregate, three miles of subterraneous line. Of those tunnels, three pass through rock decomposed to such a degree that lining throughout was necessary, while the rest are pierced, for the greater part, through solid rock, though requiring the same precaution occasionally. The total length of lining with masonry is 5,700 feet. In the course of this operation constant danger and difficulty arose from the breaking in of the rock, and in one instance the whole mountain spur through which the tunnel had been driven parted from the main mass and, sliding down, obliterated the work, so that it was necessary to begin the perforation again, contending continually against the enormous pressure of the loose superincumbent *débris*. Were this the fitting place, it would be interesting to give the history of this enterprise more in detail; especially that of the work connected with building the great tunnel and the temporary track which was in use when I first passed over the road. Suffice it to say, that all that portion of the road which is included within the second section is a triumph of engineering, which excites the admiration of the most competent judges, and is in the highest degree creditable to those under whose direction it has been accomplished.

V. — PERMANENCE OF CHARACTERISTICS IN DIFFERENT HUMAN SPECIES.

As my special object of study in the Amazons had reference to the character and distribution of the fluviatile faunae, I could not undertake those more accurate investigations of the human races, based upon minute measurements repeated a thousand-fold, which characterize the latest researches of anthropologists. A thorough study of the different nations and cross-breeds inhabiting the Amazonian Valley would require years of observation and patient examination. I was forced to be satisfied with such data as I could gather aside from my other labors, and to limit myself in my study of the races to what I would call the natural history method; viz. the comparison of individuals of different kinds with one another, just as naturalists compare specimens of different species. This was less difficult in a hot country, where the uncultivated part of the population go half naked, and are frequently seen entirely undressed. During a protracted residence in Manaos, Mr. Hunnewell made a great many characteristic photographs of Indians and Negroes, and half-breeds between both these races and the Whites. All these portraits represent the individuals selected in three normal positions, in full face, in perfect profile, and from behind. I hope sooner or later to have an opportunity of publishing these illustrations, as well as those of pure negroes made for me in Rio by Messrs. Stahl and Wahnschaffe.

What struck me at first view, in seeing Indians and Negroes together, was the marked difference in the relative proportions of the different parts of the body. Like long-armed monkeys the Negroes are generally slender, with long legs, long arms, and a comparatively short body, while the Indians are short-legged, short-armed, and long-bodied, the trunk being also rather heavy in build. To continue the comparison, I may say that if the Negro by his bearing recalls the slender, active Hylobates, the Indian is more like the slow, inactive, stout Orang. Of course there are exceptions to this rule; short, thick-built Negroes are occasionally to be seen, as well as tall, lean Indians; but, so far as my observation goes, the essential difference between the Indian and Negro races, taken as a whole, consists in the length and square build of the trunk and the shortness of limbs in the Indian as compared with the lean frame, short trunk, deep-cleft legs, and long arms of the Negro.

Another feature not less striking, though it does not affect the whole figure so much, is the short neck and great width of the shoulders in the Indian. This peculiarity is quite as marked in the female as in the male, so that, when seen from behind, the Indian woman has a very masculine air, extending indeed more or less to her whole bearing; for even her features have rarely the feminine delicacy of higher womanhood. In the Negro, on the contrary, the narrowness of chest and shoulder characteristic of woman is almost as marked in the man; indeed, it may well be said, that, while the Indian female is remarkable for her masculine build, the Negro male is equally so for his feminine aspect. Nevertheless, the difference between the sexes in the two races is not equally marked. The female Indian resembles in every respect much more the male than is the case with the Negroes; the females among the latter having generally more delicate features than the males.

On following out the details concomitant with these general differences, we find that they agree most strikingly. In a front view of an Indian woman and a Negress the great difference is in the width between the breasts of the former as compared with their close approximation in the latter. In the Indian the interval between the two breasts is nearly equal to the diameter of one of them; while in the Negro they stand in almost immediate contact. But this is not all; the form of the breast itself is very different in the two. The Indian woman has a conical breast, firm and well supported, the point being turned so far sideways that the breast seems to arise under the arm-pit, the nipple being actually projected on the arm in a full-faced view of the chest. In the negress the breast is more cylindrical, looser, and more flaccid, the nipple being turned forward and downward, so that in a front view it is projected on the chest. In the Indian the inguinal region is broad and distinctly set off from the prominence of the abdomen, while in the Negro it is a mere fold. As to the limbs, they are not only much longer in proportion in the Negro than the Indian; their form and carriage differs also. The legs of the Indians are remarkably straight, in the Negro the knees are bent in, and the hip as well as knee-joint habitually flexed. Similar differences in other parts of the body are visible from behind; in the Indians the interval between the two shoulders, the shoulder-blades being comparatively short in themselves, is much greater than in any other race. In this respect the women do not differ from the men, but share in a feature characteristic of the whole race. This peculiarity is especially noticeable in a profile view of the figure, in which the broad rounded shoulder marks the outline in the upper part of the trunk and tapers gradually to a well-shaped arm, terminating usually in a rather small hand; the little finger is remarkably short. In the Negro, on the contrary, the shoulder-blades are long and placed more closely together, the shoulder being rather slim and narrow, and the hand disproportionately slender, though the fingers are more extensively webbed than in any other race. In this respect there is little difference between male and female, the build of the male being more muscular, but hardly stouter; in both, a profile view shows the back and breast projected forwards and backwards of the arm. The proportions between the length and width of the trunk, as compared with each other, and, measured from the shoulder to the base of the trunk, hardly differ in the Indian and Negro; this renders the difference in the relative length and strength of the arms and legs the more apparent.

I need not allude to the difference of the hair; everybody knows the heavy, straight black hair of the Indian, and the wrinkled, woolly hair of the Negro. Nor is it necessary for me to recall the characteristic features of the Whites in order to contrast them with what has been said above of the Indians and Negroes.

Only a few words more concerning half-breeds are needed to show how deeply seated are the primary differences between the pure races. Like distinct species among animals, different races of men, when crossing, bring forth half-breeds; and the half-breeds between these different races differ greatly. The hybrid between White and Negro, called Mulatto, is too well known to require further description. His features are handsome, his complexion clear, and his character confiding, but indolent. The hybrid between the Indian and Negro, known under the name of Cafuzo, is quite different. His features have nothing of the delicacy of the Mulatto; his complexion is dark; his hair long, wiry, and curly; and his character exhibits a happy combination between the jolly disposition of the Negro and the energetic, enduring powers of the Indian. The hybrid between White and Indian, called Mammeluco in Brazil, is pallid, effeminate, feeble, lazy, and rather obstinate; though it seems as if the Indian influence had only gone so far as to obliterate the higher characteristics of the White, without imparting its own energies to the offspring. It is very remarkable how, in both combinations, with Negroes as well as Whites, the Indian impresses his mark more deeply upon his progeny than the other races, and how readily, also, in further crossings, the pure Indian characteristics are reclaimed and those of the other races thrown off. I have known the offspring of an hybrid between Indian and Negro with an hybrid between Indian and White resume almost completely the characteristics of the pure Indian.

VI.— SKETCH OF SEPARATE JOURNEYS UNDERTAKEN BY DIFFERENT MEMBERS OF THE EXPEDITION.

IT is not possible for me to give here at length the narrative of the separate journeys undertaken by my young companions. To do them any justice, their reports should be illustrated by the accompanying maps, geological sections, &c., which are more appropriate in a special scientific account. I trust that I shall hereafter find resources for publishing all these materials in a fitting manner; but, in the mean while, I should do a wrong to my own feelings as well as to my assistants, did I not add to this volume such a sketch of their separate work as will show with how much energy, perseverance, and intelligence they carried out the instructions I had given them. It will be remembered by the reader that one object was kept constantly in view throughout this expedition,— namely, that of ascertaining how the fresh-water fishes are distributed throughout the great river-systems of Brazil. All the independent journeys, of which short sketches are given in this summary, were laid out with reference to this idea; the whole expedition being, in fact, a unit so far as its purpose and general plan were concerned. In this sense my own exploration, and those of all my assistants, belong together, as parts of one connected scheme.

That detachment of the party which was conducted by Mr. Orestes St. John left Rio de Janeiro on the 9th of June, 1865. This company consisted of Messrs. St. John, Allen, Ward, and Sceva. The first two were to reach the Atlantic coast by way of the Rio San Francisco and the Rio Paranahyba; while Mr. Ward was to descend the Tocantins to the Amazons, and Mr. Sceva to remain for some time in the fossiliferous region about Lagoa Sancta for the purpose of collecting. As far as Juiz de Fora they followed the road described in the foregoing narrative. Thence they crossed the Serra do Mantiqueira to Barbacena, and kept on from that place through Lagoa Dourada and Prados across the Rio Carandahy to the divide separating the head-waters of the Rio Grande on the south from those of the Rio Paraopeba on the north. They crossed the Paraopeba just above the water gap of the Serras of Piedade and Itatiaiassu, traversing the former Serra into the mountain valley in which the village of Morro Velho is situated. They thus found themselves successively in the basins of the Rio Parahyba, the Rio La Plata, and the Rio San Francisco; all these great streams being fed by rivulets which arise in this vicinity. On leaving the mountainous districts they continued their route through alternate campos and wooded tracts to Gequitibá, passing through Saburá, Santa Luzia, Lagoa Sancta, and Sette Lagoas.

At Lagoa Sancta, as had been previously agreed, Mr. Sceva left the party, with the purpose of exploring the caves of that region in search of fossil bones, and making skeletons of mammalia. He remained for some time in this neighborhood, and brought away a number of specimens, though he did not succeed in finding many fossils, the caves having been already despoiled of their fossil remains by Dr. Lund, whose indefatigable researches in this direction are so well known. Mr. Sceva, however, made very valuable collections of other kinds, and I am indebted to him for numerous carefully prepared specimens of Brazilian mammalia, which now await mounting in the Museum. On leaving Lagoa Sancta, Mr. Sceva returned to Rio de Janeiro, taking his collections with him. He passed some days there, in order to repack and put in safety his own specimens as well as those which had been sent back to Rio by other members of the party. He then proceeded to Canta-Gallo, and passed the remainder of the time in collecting and preparing specimens from that part of the country, until he joined me subsequently at Rio just before we returned to the United States. His contributions to our stores were exceedingly valuable, both on account of the localities from which they came and from the care with which they were put up.

Mr. Ward had already separated from his fellow-travellers at Barbacena, on his way to the Tocantins, taking the route by Ouro-Preto and Diamantina. And in order to keep together the adventures of the little band who left Rio in company, I may give here a short sketch of his journey, before completing the account of the route pursued by Messrs. St. John and Allen. After leaving the valley of the Rio Parahyba and crossing the Mantiqueira the party found itself in the water-basin of the Rio Grande, one of the principal tributaries of the Rio Parana, which, emptying into the Rio La Plata, reaches the ocean below Buenos Ayres. Eastward of this basin, on the ocean-side of the great ridge which bounds the valley of the Rio San Francisco, arise several large rivers, — the Rio Doce, the Rio Mucury, and the Rio Jequitinhonha. It was one of my most earnest desires to secure the means of comparing their inhabitants with each other and with those of the great rivers flowing north and east. As will be seen hereafter, Mr. Hartt, with the assistance of Mr. Copeland, had undertaken to explore the lower course of these rivers; but it was equally important that specimens should be obtained from their head-waters. While, therefore, Mr. St. John and his companion pursued their way across the region drained by the head-waters of the Rio San Francisco, Mr. Ward crossed the mountains, passing from one river-basin into another, in order to examine as many of the tributaries of the Rio Doce and the Rio Jequitinhonha as possible. To him I owe the materials necessary for a general comparison of the river faunæ in these different basins. His journey was a laborious and a lonely one. Separating from his companions at Barbacena he kept on by Ouro-Preto and Santa Barbara into the basin of the Rio Doce, which he followed nearly to the point where the Rio Antonio empties into it. This part of the journey gave him an opportunity of making a collection not only in the head-waters of the Rio Doce, but in one of its principal tributaries also. Thence crossing the Serra das Esmeraldas Mr. Ward entered the water-basin of the Rio Jequitinhonha, commonly called Rio Belmonte on the maps, and after passing Diamantina explored several arms of this great stream. The collections he made in this region are of special interest with reference to those gathered by Messrs. Hartt and Copeland on the lower course of the same rivers, and in many other streams along the Atlantic coast between Bahia and Rio de Janeiro. Having accomplished this part of his journey, Mr. Ward crossed the San Francisco at Januaria, making a number of excursions in that vicinity; then passing in a northwesterly direction over the ridges which separate the valley of the San Francisco from that of the Tocantins, he followed the whole course of this great stream to the Amazons. It was a daring and adventurous journey to be accomplished with no other companionship than that of the camarado who served him as guide, or the Indian boatmen who rowed his canoe, and it was a day of rejoicing for our whole party when we heard, in the month of January, 1866, of his safe arrival in Pará, whence he embarked a few weeks later for the United States.

From Lagoa Sancta, where they parted from Mr. Sceva, Messrs. St. John and Allen kept on to Januaria together, but at this point Mr. Allen, whose health had been failing from the time he left Rio de Janeiro, found himself unable to prosecute the journey farther, and he resolved to strike across the country to Bahia, taking in charge the collections they had brought together thus far. After a short rest at Januaria, he made his way to Chique-Chique on the Rio San Francisco; and his separate journal begins from the time he left this point, on his journey to Bahia. It gives a very full account of the physical features of the region through which he passed, of the geographical character of the soil, and of the distribution of plants and animals, including many original observations concerning the habits of birds, with a detailed itinerary of the route through Jacobina, Espelto, and Caxoeira. Prostrated by illness as he was, he has nevertheless furnished a report the character of which shows how completely his interest in the work overcame the lassitude of disease.

From Januaria Mr. St. John followed the San Francisco to the Villa do Barra, where he made a short stay, and then resumed his journey by land through the valley of the Rio Grande to the Villa da Santa Rita, thence to Mocambo and across the table-land separating the basin of the Rio San Francisco from that of the Rio Paranahyba. At Paranaguá he remained several days, and made a considerable collection from this vicinity. Thence he followed the valley of the Rio Gurugueia to Manga, one hundred and twenty leagues from Paranaguá. At Manga he embarked on one of the singular river-boats made of the leafstalks of the Buriti palm, and descended the Paranahyba to the villa of San Gonçallo. Here he stayed for some time to collect, and forwarded from this vicinity a considerable number of specimens, chiefly reptiles, birds, and insects. His next station was at Therezina, the capital of the province of Piauhy, where he made one of the most interesting collections of the whole journey from the waters of the Rio Poty. The Poty is a tributary of the Paranahyba, into which it empties below Therezina. In examining this collection, I was particularly struck with the general similarity of the fishes contained in it to those of the Amazons. They exhibit throughout the same kind of combination of genera and families, although the species are entirely distinct. Thus, from a zoölogical point of view, the basin of the Parahyba, though completely separated from it by the ocean, would seem to belong to the Amazonian basin, as it unquestionably does from a geological point of view. The character of the drift deposits along the Rio Gurugueia and the Rio Paranahyba shows this area to have been continuous with the basin in which the Amazonian drift was deposited; and the similarity of their zoölogical features is but another evidence, from an entirely different source, of the extensive denudations which have isolated these regions from one another by removing the tracts which formerly made them a unit.

From Therezina Mr. St. John proceeded to Caxias, and finally arrived in Maranham, by the way of the Rio Itapicurú, on the 8th January, 1866; having completed a journey of more than seven hundred leagues in seven months, over a route the greater part of which had never been examined from a zoölogical or geological point of view. His collections, though necessarily limited by the difficulty of transport and the insufficient provision of alcohol, were very valuable, and arrived at their destination in good condition. Of his geological observations I have said little; but it is from him I have obtained the data which have enabled me to compare the basin of Piauhy with that of the Amazons. He made careful geological surveys wherever he was able to do so, and has recorded the result of his observations in a manner which shows that he never lost sight of the general relations between the great structural features of the country through which he passed. At Maranham, the intermittent fever, under which Mr. St. John had been suffering during the latter part of his journey, culminated in a severe illness, from which he recovered under the care of Dr. Braga, who took him into his own house, and did not allow him to leave his roof until he was restored to health. From Maranham Mr. St. John joined me at Pará, where I had an opportunity of comparing notes with him on the spot.

During the first two months of his stay in Rio de Janeiro, Mr. Hartt was chiefly occupied with Mr. St. John in examining sections of the Dom Pedro Railroad, of which he prepared a very clear and careful geological survey, with ample illustrations. On the 19th of June, 1865, he left the city to explore the coast between the Rio Parahyba do Sul and Bahia; being accompanied by Mr. Edward Copeland, one of our volunteers, who gave him very efficient assistance in collecting, during the whole time they remained together. At Campos, on the Rio Parahyba, they obtained a large number of fishes, beside other specimens. From that point they went up the Rio Muriahy for some distance, and then, returning to Campos, ascended the Rio Parahyba to San Fidelis, where they again added largely to their collections. Taking mules at San Fidelis, they traversed the forest northward to Bom-Jesu, on the Rio Itabapuana, and then descended that river, stopping to collect at Porto da Limeira and at the Barra. Thence they followed the coast to Victoria; and it was their intention to have proceeded northward to the Rio Doce, but, for want of mules and money (their supplies having given out), they were obliged to make Nova Almeida, their farthest point. Thence they returned by way of Victoria to Rio de Janeiro in a sailing-vessel. In the course of this journey they obtained valuable collections both on the Rio Itapemérim and at Guarapary. Mr. Hartt also made a careful study of the geology of the coast, the result of which forms an interesting portion of his report.

On their return to Rio, Mr. Hartt and Mr. Copeland were detained for some time by the failure of a steamer. They occupied themselves in the mean while in various work for the expedition, making excursions in the vicinity, and collecting in the harbor of Rio. Disappointed in the steamer, they started on board a sailing-vessel, and had a slow and tedious voyage to San Matheos, collecting on their way wherever the stopping of the vessel enabled them to do so. Neither did Mr. Hartt neglect, on every such occasion, to examine the coast, and the phenomena connected with its general rise, of which he obtained unquestionable evidence. From San Matheos, where they made considerable collections, they took conveyance to the Rio Doce, and ascended this river for ninety miles to the first fall, Porto de Souza. Descending its course again to Linhares, they explored the river and lake of Juparanaã, and then returned to San Matheos; making large marine collections at Barra Secca, half-way between the Rio Doce and San Matheos. Thence they proceeded to the Rio Mucury, stopping a few days at its mouth to collect, and then ascending the river to Santa Clara. Here Mr. Copeland remained, and secured a fine collection of fishes; while Mr. Hartt crossed over the river Peruhype to the Colonia Leopoldina. On his return he was detained for some days by illness, but was soon able to resume his journey; and he and Mr. Copeland then went on with Mr. Schüeber* to Philadelphia, in the province of Minas

---

* This gentleman, who is thoroughly familiar with the whole country, was untiring in his attentions to Messrs. Hartt and Copeland, and gave them, so far as he could, every facility for their researches.

Geraes, collecting on the way at the Rio Urucu, and afterwards at Philadelphia. Along the coast, and indeed throughout his whole journey, Mr. Hartt continued his geological observations, which he carefully recorded. From Philadelphia he and his companion proceeded by land to Calháo, on the Rio Arassuahy; making a detour from Alahú to Alto dos Bois, in order to study the drift and the geological structure of the elevated Chapadas. At Calháo they also made good collections of fishes. Returning to Calháo from a visit to Minas Novas and a study of its gold-mines, Mr. Hartt descended the Rio Jequitinhonha three hundred and sixty miles to the sea. Mr. Copeland had preceded him in order to make an excursion to Caravellas; and they met again at Cannavieiras.

At Cannavieiras they made good collections, and then ascended the Rio Pardo to its first fall, fishing and geologizing along their route. They visited also Belmonte, and then went southward to Porto Seguro, where they stayed for several days, collecting corals and marine invertebrates. Here, as at several other points along the coast, Mr. Hartt made a careful examination of the stone-reefs. His researches on these "recifes," which constitute so remarkable a feature along the Atlantic coast of Brazil, are exceedingly interesting; and I do not know that any geologist has made a more careful and connected examination of them. He believes them to be formed by the solidification of beach ridges; the lower part of which being cemented by the lime dissolved from the shells contained in them remains intact, while the upper portion was carried off by storms; thus leaving a solid wall running along the coast, broken through here and there, and divided from the land by a narrow channel. He studied the coast reefs both at Santa Cruz and at Porto Seguro, and ascertained their southward extension to the Abrolhos. From Porto Seguro Messrs. Hartt and Copeland went northward to Bahia, touching at several points along the coast, and thence returned to Rio de Janeiro, whence we sailed together for the United States in the month of July, 1866.

Cambridge: Stereotyped and Printed by Welch, Bigelow, & Co.

www.ingramcontent.com/pod-product-compliance
Lightning Source LLC
Chambersburg PA
CBHW031936290426
44108CB00011B/581